"A rich resource covering one of the New Testament's most profound sections of Scripture, pastors and theologians of all persuasions will benefit from the thorough treatment Dr. Allen gives to these letters. This commentary, like John's letters, is brimming with gospel hope."

J. D. Greear, lead pastor, The Summit Church, Durham, North Carolina; author, *Stop Asking Jesus into Your Heart: How to Know for Sure You Are Saved*

"*1–3 John* is a welcomed addition to the Preaching the Word series. The 22 studies in this volume reveal careful research, theological insight, and exegetical integrity. Anyone preaching or teaching through the epistles of John will be greatly assisted by this volume. David Allen has rendered a valuable service to the church of the Lord Jesus that will bear fruit for years to come."

Daniel L. Akin, president, Southeastern Baptist Theological Seminary

"In an excellent follow-up to his edited volume *Text-Driven Preaching*, David Allen crafts 22 sermons on 1, 2, and 3 John that exemplify the qualities that should characterize excellent preaching. These sermons are thoroughly Biblical, hermeneutically sound, Christ-centered, eminently practical, passionate, challenging, clear, and interesting. And these qualities shine through even when he navigates complex semantic issues, deals with heresies like Gnosticism and Docetism, and tackles pressing theological topics like the extent of the atonement. Here is a fine resource for anyone preaching through these three important New Testament letters!"

Gregg R. Allison, professor of Christian theology, The Southern Baptist Theological Seminary

"Jesus spoke of the man who brought 'out of his treasure what is new and what is old.' David L. Allen does exactly that with these 22 well-researched expositions. Drawing on preachers and scholars from all ages of the church, he opens up John's epistles with admirable clarity and force. In every chapter, you will encounter the truth of the text, the heart of the preacher, and the direction of the Lord regarding how you should respond. Readable, illuminating, and convicting, this book deserves wide circulation among individuals and Bible study groups. Pastors will find here a refresher course in how to preach John's letters."

Robert W. Yarbrough, professor of New Testament, Covenant Theological Seminary

"The sermons in this book (Allen describes them as 'sermontaries—more than a sermon but less than a commentary') are undergirded by solid scholarship, supported by references to great preachers of the past, and enhanced by Allen's own wisdom and applications for today's believers. A fine resource that I am very pleased to commend to all serious preachers of Scripture."

Colin G. Kruse, senior lecturer in New Testament, Melbourne School of Theology

1–3 JOHN

PREACHING THE WORD
Edited by R. Kent Hughes

Genesis | R. Kent Hughes

Exodus | Philip Graham Ryken

Leviticus | Kenneth A. Mathews

Numbers | Iain M. Duguid

Deuteronomy | Ajith Fernando

Joshua | David Jackman

Judges and Ruth | Barry G. Webb

1 Samuel | John Woodhouse

2 Samuel | John Woodhouse

1 Kings | John Woodhouse

Job | Christopher Ash

Psalms, Vol. 1 | James Johnston

Proverbs | Raymond C. Ortlund Jr.

Ecclesiastes | Philip Graham Ryken

Song of Solomon | Douglas Sean O'Donnell

Isaiah | Raymond C. Ortlund Jr.

Jeremiah and Lamentations | R. Kent Hughes

Daniel | Rodney D. Stortz

Matthew | Douglas Sean O'Donnell

Mark | R. Kent Hughes

Luke | R. Kent Hughes

John | R. Kent Hughes

Acts | R. Kent Hughes

Romans | R. Kent Hughes

1 Corinthians | Stephen T. Um

2 Corinthians | R. Kent Hughes

Galatians | Todd Wilson

Ephesians | R. Kent Hughes

Philippians, Colossians, and Philemon | R. Kent Hughes

1–2 Thessalonians | James H. Grant Jr.

1–2 Timothy and Titus | R. Kent Hughes and Bryan Chapell

Hebrews | R. Kent Hughes

James | R. Kent Hughes

1–2 Peter and Jude | David R. Helm

1–3 John | David L. Allen

Revelation | James M. Hamilton Jr.

The Sermon on the Mount | R. Kent Hughes

(((PREACHING *the* WORD)))

1–3 JOHN

FELLOWSHIP *in* GOD'S FAMILY

DAVID L. ALLEN

R. Kent Hughes
Series Editor

WHEATON, ILLINOIS

1–3 John

Copyright © 2013 by David L. Allen

Published by Crossway
    1300 Crescent Street
    Wheaton, Illinois 60187

Cover design: Jon McGrath, Simplicated Studio

Cover image: Adam Green, illustrator

First printing 2013

Printed in the United States of America

ISBN-13: 978-1-4335-0285-9
ISBN-10: 1-4335-0285-2
PDF ISBN: 978-1-4335-3725-7
Mobipocket ISBN: 978-1-4335-3723-3
ePub ISBN: 978-1-4335-3724-0

Library of Congress Cataloging-in-Publication Data

Allen, David Lewis, 1957-
 1-3 John : fellowship in God's family / David L. Allen ; R. Kent Hughes, general editor.
   pages cm—(Preaching the Word)
  Includes bibliographical references and index.
  ISBN 978-1-4335-0285-9 (hc)
 1. Bible. N.T. Epistles of John—Commentaries. I. Hughes, R. Kent. II Title.
BS2805.53.A46   2013
227'.9407—dc23   2012017236

Crossway is a publishing ministry of Good News Publishers.

VP		29	28	27	26	25	24	23	22	21	20	19
15	14	13	12	11	10	9	8	7	6	5	4	3

For my pastor, mentor, and friend,
Dr. Jerry Vines
whose example week by week taught me
what expository preaching was all about
when I was a teenager and who through the years
has been a constant reminder to me that the sermon
is not an end in itself—it is a road map to Jesus.

*"Preacher? . . . what preacher?
. . . I saw no preacher. . . . I saw
only Jesus . . . only Jesus."*

FIRST-TIME VISITOR TO
CHARLES HADDON SPURGEON'S TABERNACLE,
UPON HEARING THE PRINCE OF PREACHERS

*In this is love, not that we have loved God
but that he loved us and sent his Son to be
the propitiation for our sins.
Beloved, if God so loved us,
we also ought to love one another.*

1 JOHN 4:10, 11

Contents

3 JOHN

A Word to Those Who Preach the Word

There are times when I am preaching that I have especially sensed the pleasure of God. I usually become aware of it through the unnatural silence. The ever-present coughing ceases, and the pews stop creaking, bringing an almost physical quiet to the sanctuary — through which my words sail like arrows. I experience a heightened eloquence, so that the cadence and volume of my voice intensify the truth I am preaching.

There is nothing quite like it — the Holy Spirit filling one's sails, the sense of his pleasure, and the awareness that something is happening among one's hearers. This experience is, of course, not unique, for thousands of preachers have similar experiences, even greater ones.

What has happened when this takes place? How do we account for this sense of his smile? The answer for me has come from the ancient rhetorical categories of *logos*, *ethos*, and *pathos*.

The first reason for his smile is the *logos* — in terms of preaching, God's Word. This means that as we stand before God's people to proclaim his Word, we have done our homework. We have exegeted the passage, mined the significance of its words in their context, and applied sound hermeneutical principles in interpreting the text so that we understand what its words meant to its hearers. And it means that we have labored long until we can express in a sentence what the theme of the text is — so that our outline springs from the text. Then our preparation will be such that as we preach, we will not be preaching our own thoughts about God's Word, but God's actual Word, his *logos*. This is fundamental to pleasing him in preaching.

The second element in knowing God's smile in preaching is *ethos* — what you are as a person. There is a danger endemic to preaching, which is having your hands and heart cauterized by holy things. Phillips Brooks illustrated it by the analogy of a train conductor who comes to believe that he has been to the places he announces because of his long and loud heralding of them. And that is why Brooks insisted that preaching must be "the bringing of truth through personality." Though we can never perfectly embody the truth we preach, we must be subject to it, long for it, and make it as much a part of our ethos as possible. As the Puritan William Ames said, "Next to the Scriptures, nothing makes a sermon more to pierce, than when it comes out of the inward affection of the heart without any affectation." When a preacher's *ethos* backs up his *logos*, there will be the pleasure of God.

Last, there is *pathos* — personal passion and conviction. David Hume, the Scottish philosopher and skeptic, was once challenged as he was seen going to hear George Whitefield preach: "I thought you do not believe in the gospel." Hume replied, "I don't, but he does." Just so! When a preacher believes what he preaches, there will be passion. And this belief and requisite passion will know the smile of God.

The pleasure of God is a matter of *logos* (the Word), *ethos* (what you are), and *pathos* (your passion). As you preach the Word may you experience his smile — the Holy Spirit in your sails!

R. Kent Hughes

Author's Preface

During the twenty-one years I served as a senior pastor of two churches, I preached through many books of the Bible. First John was the initial New Testament letter I worked through early in my first pastorate. It lays out for believers the foundational nature of truth and love within the context of the local church. Like all the letters of the New Testament, 1 John is theological and practical. In one sense all of the New Testament letters are essentially sermons to local congregations of believers. (Hebrews is, in fact, a written sermon!) What the New Testament authors wrote is what they would have preached had they been present in the churches to which they wrote.

I believe not only in the inerrancy of Scripture but also in the sufficiency of Scripture. When it comes to the spiritual needs of believers gathered together in the fellowship of local churches, God has designed that the preaching and teaching of his Word is the primary means of developing mature believers. The Scriptures are sufficient to accomplish this goal. I am committed to expositional preaching for theological reasons. I have nothing to say to God's people that is superior to what God himself has said to them in his Word. Since the Bible is not only the Word of God but is also the very words of God (verbal, plenary inspiration), then text-driven preaching becomes all the more vital, even mandated theologically as far as I'm concerned.

As one who has studied preaching now for many years, I have observed how often preachers take a very short text of only two or three verses from the New Testament letters that is usually only a part of a paragraph unit. When a verse or two is wrenched from its paragraph context (except when the paragraph consists of only a verse or two), meaning is misplaced, distorted, or lost. The superficial character of many modern sermons derives from the exclusive use of a short text. Additionally, when we preach only on short texts, we face the temptation of filling in the time with extra-Biblical material. I believe in preaching through paragraph units of meaning when preaching through the letters of the New Testament. The field of linguistics teaches us that meaning resides not only in the words, phrases, clauses, and sentences of discourse but in the paragraphs as well.[1] The whole is more than the sum of its parts.

In determining the paragraph and divisional structure of 1 John, I have relied heavily upon the work of Grace Sherman and John Tuggy, *A Semantic and Structural Analysis of the Johannine Epistles* (Dallas: Summer Institute of Linguistics, 1994). They justify their paragraph divisions linguistically. In accordance with their linguistic analysis, I have chosen to construct a sermon on each paragraph unit of 1 John. This means that on four occasions (2:1, 2; 2:26, 27; 2:28, 29; 5:21), I have written a sermon on paragraphs that are no more than two verses in length, and with respect to 5:21 only one verse. Sometimes there is a difference of opinion as to where paragraph breaks occur in 1 John. For example, In addition to being viewed as a paragraph itself, 2:1, 2 can be seen as the conclusion of the paragraph that begins at 1:5 or it can be viewed as the beginning of a new paragraph that concludes at 2:6. I have made the decision to write one sermon on 2:1, 2 because of the potent doctrinal word "propitiation," which needs careful explanation, and because verse 2 is one of the key verses in the New Testament dealing with the subject of the extent of the atonement, an important and often misunderstood doctrine today. Some interpreters consider 2:29 to begin a new paragraph that concludes with 3:10. Others think that verse 29 goes with verse 28 and that a new paragraph begins with 3:1. I have chosen the latter option for the same linguistic reasons given by Sherman and Tuggy. Second and 3 John, though composed of multiple paragraphs, are best treated as a whole for preaching purposes in my judgment since each of these letters is so short.

There are now countless sermon websites on the Internet available to preachers. Some of the sermons one finds on these sites are worthy of reading. Others, frankly, are a waste of time. In preparing the sermons in this volume, I have taken C. S. Lewis's advice to heart: "If [one] must read only the new or only the old, I would advise him to read only the old. . . . It is a good rule, after reading a new book, never to allow yourself another new one till you have read an old one in between."[2] The Scottish preacher Arthur Gossip's maxim from page 86 of his book *In His Stead* has stood me in good stead now for many years: "The greatest natural genius cannot subsist on its own stock: he who resolves never to ransack any brain but his own will soon be reduced, from mere barrenness, to the poorest of all imitations." For years I have collected sermon books and have been cataloguing the sermons by text in a database for my own research purposes. A computer printout of sermons catalogued on 1 John alone is dozens of pages in length. In scouring through these sermons, I have found golden nuggets in the form of exposition, illustrations, turns of phrase, doctrinal insight, application, etc, that are priceless. The reader will notice from the footnotes that I have consulted a number of sources on 1 John, old and new, including a number of published sermons from well-known preachers such as Augustine, Luther, Calvin, Wesley, Edwards, and Spurgeon, along with a host of lesser-known preachers from church history. Even when I have not quoted material directly from these sources, I have tried to footnote each time I have gleaned from them so the reader will have the opportunity to find and read some great sermons, and other works, that are sometimes off the beaten path. Thus the sermons in this volume are what you might call "sermontaries"—more than a sermon but less than a commentary. I hope the reader finds this helpful.

A good sermon should have several qualities. It should first and foremost be Biblical, both in truth and content. A good sermon should be hermeneutically sound. A good sermon should be Christ-centered. A good sermon should be practical, containing pertinent and textually warranted application. A good sermon should be delivered with passion, a missing ingredient in some preachers today. A good sermon should be motivational, challenging, and encouraging. A good sermon should be clear. Clarity must be crafted. Finally, a good sermon should be interesting. There should be nothing dull, boring, or pedestrian in good expository preaching. I have attempted to write these sermons as nearly as I would preach them. Written sermons simply cannot maintain the oral luster one experiences in listening to a sermon. I have used shorter sentences, contractions, and other modes of communication common to oral/aural discourse. There is certainly no contradiction between attention to style in sermons and attention to theology. In fact, theology usually impacts style.

I wish to express my deepest appreciation to Ted Griffin, editor for Crossway, whose keen eye and careful hand has made this volume much better than it would have been without his diligent attention.

Finally, I wish to thank my friend Kent Hughes for his kind invitation to participate in this series. I met Kent personally when I was teaching homiletics at the Criswell College in Dallas, Texas. I had been so impressed with his work in the Preaching the Word series that I invited him to be the speaker at one of our preaching workshops. He graciously consented, and I found my heart knit together with his on the subject of expository preaching. When I arrived at Southwestern Baptist Theological Seminary and became director of the Center for Expository Preaching, I immediately made plans to have Kent come and speak. Again he graciously consented and did a marvelous job. For years I have been recommending Kent's books to my students and fellow pastors, never dreaming that one day I would have the opportunity to write for this series. We preachers are always looking for word pictures to turn the ear into an eye. It is an honor to be a Chihuahua barking on the heels of a Great Dane like Kent Hughes!

David L. Allen
Dean, School of Theology
Southwestern Baptist Theological Seminary
Fort Worth, Texas

1 JOHN

That which was from the beginning, which we have heard, which we have seen with our eyes, which we looked upon and have touched with our hands, concerning the word of life—the life was made manifest, and we have seen it, and testify to it and proclaim to you the eternal life, which was with the Father and was made manifest to us—that which we have seen and heard we proclaim also to you, so that you too may have fellowship with us; and indeed our fellowship is with the Father and with his Son Jesus Christ. And we are writing these things so that our joy may be complete.

1 JOHN 1:1–4

1

Meet Jesus:
God in Human Flesh!

TUCKED AWAY AT THE BACK of your Bible is a little letter called 1 John. John
the Apostle, one of the original twelve disciples of Jesus, wrote it.[1] At the
time of writing, John was probably the only surviving member of the Twelve,
and the only one who did not die a martyr's death. He wrote five books in the
New Testament: the Gospel of John, which looks back to the past and presents the life, death, and resurrection of Jesus; 1, 2, 3 John, which concern the
present and teaches us how we should live now; and Revelation, which looks
to the future and shows us how God will consummate history in the return of
Jesus to this earth. Second and 3 John are very short letters, only one chapter
each. We know John spent his later years in and around Ephesus. He wrote
this letter to the churches of Asia Minor probably between A.D. 80 and 85.
The church was now composed of second- and third-generation Christians.
For some Christians this was a time of persecution. For others perhaps the
thrill was gone and the flame of devotion to Christ was flickering. False
teachers were infiltrating some of the churches, and some Christians were
becoming lax in their Christian standards. Into these circumstances steps
John with his letter.

John wrote with at least four purposes in mind. First, to combat false
teachers who were beginning to infiltrate the churches. He exposes false doctrine and promotes spiritual truth. John was not afraid to engage the culture
where first-century Christians lived. Second, John had an ethical purpose
in writing. Specifically, he deals with attitudes toward sin and the necessity
of love for other Christians. Third, John has a pastoral purpose in writing.
His pastoral heart beats for the health of the church, for the strengthening
of Christians in the faith, and for genuine fellowship among believers and

with Christ. His frequent references to his readers as "children" and "little children" reflect the pastoral tone of the letter. As one who was at least probably an octogenarian himself, John could tenderly refer to all in the churches, young and old, as "children." Fourth, John had a personal purpose for writing: "so that our joy may be complete" (1:4).[2]

Verses 1–4 of chapter 1 constitute the prologue to the letter. Its unusual structure can be confusing. What exactly is John trying to say here? The secret to understanding 1:1–4 lies somewhat behind the scenes, as we shall see. In these verses, "The greatest majesty is combined with the greatest simplicity."[3] John begins, "That which was from the beginning, which we have heard, which we have seen with our eyes, which we looked upon and touched with our hands, concerning the word of life." Notice after verse 1 there is a dash in the HVY translation, followed by another dash at the end of verse 2.[4] Verse 2 is a parenthetical statement: "the life was made manifest, and we have seen it, and testify to it, and proclaim to you the eternal life, which was with the Father and was made manifest to us." Verse 3 reverts back to the thought at the end of verse 1: "that which we have seen and heard." This is followed by the main verb in the paragraph: "we proclaim also to you." This is the most important semantic information John is conveying in verses 1–3.[5] Maybe it will be easier to understand what John is saying if you read it like this: "We proclaim to you that which was from the beginning, that which we have heard, that which we have seen, that which we have looked at, that which we have touched with our hands, concerning the Word of Life." Let's unpack these statements.

John's Declaration of Jesus the Word of Life (vv. 1–3a)

When John says "that which was from the beginning," the antecedent of "that" is "the word of life."[6] Although John does not name Jesus until the latter part of verse 3, "the word of life" clearly refers to Jesus. One of John's favorite descriptors for Jesus is "Word." John began his Gospel, "In the beginning was the Word, and the Word was with God, and the Word was God" (John 1:1). Here is an "unbeginning beginning."[7] When John says that Jesus was from the beginning, the question is, which beginning? Is this the beginning of Jesus' earthly life or perhaps the beginning of creation? Jesus' existence did not begin when he was born in Bethlehem. Likewise, Jesus was not a created being like angels before the creation of the heavens and the earth. Before history heard the starting gun,[8] Jesus was there. John's "beginning" goes all the way back to eternity past. This is a statement about the eternal preexistence and deity of Jesus. R. G. Lee, the great pastor of yesteryear at Bellevue Baptist Church in Memphis, Tennessee, often described it this way: "Jesus was the only man who had a heavenly Father, but no heavenly mother; who had an earthly mother but no earthly father; who was older than his mother and who was as old as his Father." Jesus is fully God and thus eternal.

It seems peculiar for John to tell us that he and the apostles heard, saw, touched, looked at, and handled Jesus. Why would John make such odd statements, employing so many verbs of perception? One answer to this question may have to do with a new philosophy beginning to gain ground at the end of the first century called Gnosticism.[9] The word *Gnosticism* comes from the Greek word *gnōsis*, which means "knowledge." It was a combination of pagan mysticism and Greek philosophy, predicated on two primary principles. First, Gnosticism taught that the way of salvation was through secret, superior knowledge granted to the initiated. Second, Gnostics considered all matter to be evil, but spirit to be good. Therefore the Gnostics taught that your physical body is evil, but your soul is good. Some of the false teachers John is combating in this letter had begun to infiltrate the church with incipient forms of this Gnostic teaching. The first error was a practical error, teaching Christians wrong ways to live. Imbibing this error, Christians went to one of two extremes. The first extreme we call asceticism, where you begin to punish your body. Why would anyone do this? To free the spirit. Remember, matter is evil, but spirit is good. The other extreme is licentiousness, a word that means to live any way you want. After all, if your body is evil and spirit is good, then it does not matter what you do with the body. Rules don't matter. You can get on drugs all you want, have all the sex outside of marriage you want. Why? Because the body is evil. It does not matter much what you do with your body. Do we have any Gnostics in our society today? Of course! Most of them just don't know that's what they are. Why is John harping on that? He is fighting the effects of incipient Gnosticism that had already begun to creep into the churches. First John was a general letter that was sent to all of the churches in Asia Minor to warn them of the practical dangers of Gnosticism.

Gnosticism also led to doctrinal error. Gnosticism generated two doctrinal errors concerning the person of Jesus Christ. The first one is called the docetic error. *Docetic* comes from a Greek word *dokeō*, which means "to seem" or "to appear." If the body is evil, then God, who is a Spirit being, cannot have any contact with the body. What would such a false belief do to the doctrine of the incarnation of Jesus? You can't have an incarnation if docetic Gnosticism is true. You could not have God becoming man. Thus the Docetic Gnostics taught that Jesus did not have a literal human body. They denied the real humanity of Jesus. They said Jesus was *from* God, but they denied he was God in human flesh. They said his spirit was *from* God, but when Jesus was on the earth that wasn't really Jesus in human form. That was just what he appeared to be. He did not have a literal physical body like you and I do. So when people saw Jesus they were seeing something like a ghost or a phantom. If you were to walk over and touch Jesus, he would have no physical body to touch. You couldn't shake hands with Jesus because he had no literal hand to shake. When Jesus walked on soft soil, he left no footprints. Docetic Gnosticism denied the incarnation of Jesus. Now we understand why, first rattle out of the box, John speaks about seeing, hearing, and touching Jesus. What John is saying is something like this: "Those Docetic Gnostics who slipped into your church are teaching you something that is entirely false. They deny the incarnation of Jesus. What they deny, I experienced personally. I was there with Jesus during his earthly ministry. I saw him with my own eyes, heard him speak with my own ears, and touched him with my own hands. I know beyond a shadow of a doubt that his body was real."

The second Gnostic error is called Cerinthian Gnosticism. Cerinthus was a contemporary of John and taught that because matter is evil, therefore the body is evil, but the spirit is good. Cerinthus taught that Jesus had a real human body (just the opposite of the Docetics), but he was just an ordinary man, and not God in human flesh. Joseph was his real father, Mary was his real mother, and he had a real human body. At Jesus' baptism the Holy Spirit came on him, and that's when the man Jesus became "the Christ." The Holy Spirit remained with Jesus for his three-year public ministry. However, when Jesus died on the cross, the Holy Spirit couldn't be associated with suffering and death according to Cerinthus, so the Spirit departed from him before he died. When the Spirit left him, that's why Jesus cried on the cross, "My God, my God, why have you forsaken me?" Thus Cerinthian Gnosticism taught that Jesus was born as an ordinary man, the Spirit came upon him for three years but then left him, and he died a mere man just like you and me. Imagine what such a teaching does to the doctrine of the atonement! If Jesus is a mere man just like you and me, how can he die for our sins? These two Gnostic errors lead to two serious doctrinal denials in the churches to which John is writing: the denial of the incarnation and the denial of the substitutionary atonement of Christ on the cross.

Gnosticism is not dead; it is only disguised today in new garb. There has been a rising interest in the Gnostic writings in recent years, brought on in part by the popularity of novels and movies such as *The DaVinci Code*. Teachings that deny the incarnation and substitutionary atonement of Jesus are very much alive and well today.

Look again at verse 1. John says: "we have heard . . . we have seen." Who does John intend to include in his use of "we"? He refers to himself and other eyewitnesses of Jesus' earthly ministry, which would include at least the other apostles. Notice also that the first two verbs are perfect tense verbs in Greek. The next two verbs in verse 1 ("looked upon" and "touched") are aorist tense verbs in Greek. Whether there is any semantic distinction intended by John here is difficult to say. The change may be purely stylistic. If John intends a distinction, it would be a change of focus from the continuing effect of what was heard and seen to a focus on the historical event in the verbs "which we looked upon and have touched." If this is the case, what John is saying is something like this: "What I heard from Jesus many years ago is still ringing in my ears as clear as a bell today as when I first heard it! What I saw many years ago when Jesus was on the earth is as clear and vivid to me today as it was then. We looked upon Jesus and touched him with our hands in specific times and specific incidents in the past." John is emphasizing the historical reality of what he is saying and maybe also the impact of it all that continues to inform his life. To add to all of this, John uses two different Greek words for "seeing" in verse 1. Though it is possible this is merely a stylistic difference, it seems more likely that John intends a distinction. The second verb, "we looked upon," may suggest seeing with careful attention and examination, implying something unusual in what is seen.[10] Finally, John stresses that he and other eyewitnesses had "touched [Jesus] with our hands." This is John's way of stressing the reality of the physical body of Jesus and may be another jab at false proto-Gnostic teaching. It is also John's way of stressing his authority as an eyewitness of the life and death of Jesus. John would swear in court that Jesus was the genuine article: God in human flesh.

Think back to seven days after the first Easter Sunday. In an upper room at night Jesus' disciples had gathered. Suddenly Jesus appeared in their midst! What did Jesus do and say? He showed them his hands, his side, and his feet. He told them to touch him and see (Luke 24:39).[11] Maybe John was thinking back to that night, now fifty or sixty years earlier, when he was there in that upper room and suddenly Jesus appeared. John saw him, hugged him, rejoiced with him, and talked to him. "We . . . touched with our hands, concerning the word of life," the word of resurrection life! John calls Jesus "the Word" in John 1:1 and again in Revelation 19:13. John calls Jesus "the life" in John 11:25 in the context of Jesus' raising Lazarus from the dead. Jesus is the Word of Life because he gives life. He alone can save us from our sins and give us eternal life.

John stresses the historical reality of the incarnation of Jesus in verse 1. All other issues that he will speak to in the letter hinge on this crucial truth:

God has become man in the person of Jesus Christ. This fact is the impregnable fortress from which John will defend the church against those false teachers who denied that "Jesus Christ has come in the flesh" (4:2).[12]

In verse 2 John makes an extended parenthetical comment about "the word of life." This life "was made manifest." The word "made manifest" means "made to be visible; made to be seen and understood." How was this "word of life" made visible and understandable? When the phrase is taken to refer to Jesus, this occurred in history at the incarnation and through his earthly life. If we understand John to refer to the spiritual life possessed by Jesus and imparted by him to others,[13] then the meaning is that this spiritual life became known, understandable, and available when Jesus appeared on the earth. God revealed his Son Jesus to the world.

As one of the apostles, John testifies to the reality and truth of Jesus and his gospel message of salvation and eternal life. He makes three statements in verse 2: "we have seen it [the word of life, Jesus], and testify to it and proclaim to you the eternal life." John does not use the name Jesus until verse 3 but describes Jesus with two further statements in verse 2: "[He] was with the Father and was made manifest to us." The little phrase "*with* the Father" is the same phrase John used in John 1:1, "In the beginning was the Word, and the Word was *with* God." That little preposition "with" in the Greek text of John 1:1 conveys the idea of being face-to-face with someone. John is emphasizing two things by that phrase there and here in 1 John 1:2. First, he is equating Jesus with God in terms of deity. As Luther said, "Where the Son of God is, there Christ is; where Christ is, there the Father is."[14] Second, he is not conflating them into one person but is emphasizing that though there is one divine nature, God and Jesus are distinct divine persons. To deny the distinct personhood of the Father and of the Son is to fall into the doctrinal error called modalism,[15] which teaches there is one God who appears in three different ways: Father, Son, and Spirit. That is heresy because it denies the three distinct persons of the Trinity.

The final statement in verse 2 is a repetition of the beginning statement in the verse: "made manifest to us." John is emphasizing the fact of the incarnation, which is how Jesus and his salvation was made known so people could understand that eternal life is wrapped up in the person and work of Christ. John is simply saying in verse 2 that Jesus was made clearly known.

Every discourse taught by Jesus, every miracle performed by Jesus, every act of grace, every tender touch, every word of wisdom, formed a part of God's gracious manifestation of Christ to us in words and actions we could all understand. John's shorthand reporting in verses 1, 2 is his way of saying to his readers and us, "Behind every one of these tactile statements are three plus years of personal experience with the God of this universe who became man in the person of Jesus Christ. I am an eyewitness. I listened to him, gazed on him, and touched him to such an extent that I virtually memorized him! I testify to the reality of Jesus. Through him I have found eternal life. I have been preaching this life now for more than fifty years, and in this letter I am preaching this good news of Jesus to you also." Just as John himself heard (overheard?) Jesus praying to the Father in heaven, "And this is eternal life, that they know you the only true God, and Jesus Christ whom you have sent" (John 17:3)," John now reexpresses the truth of that prayer as Jesus' messenger boy to the church.

John is now testifying and proclaiming that Jesus brings forgiveness of sins and eternal life. Eternal life is not just life in terms of length of life, but is also a Greek term that means quality of life. It is not just that you will live eternally when you die, but right now you have eternal life if you're a Christian. God's life dwells in you. Here in Jesus Christ is the solution to the problem of how sinful people can ever know God and be rightly related to him. The yawning chasm between God's holiness and my sinfulness is bridged by the incarnation, crucifixion, resurrection, and exaltation of Christ! John no doubt preached numerous sermons, but he is really only preaching one sermon: Salvation and eternal life are available through Christ! This is John's proclamation. Certain key words characterize the writings of the New Testament authors. For Paul, it is "faith"; for James, it is "works"; for Peter, it is "hope"; and for John it is "life." When I was a teenaged preacher back in the early seventies, I was part of a group of about thirty students from our church that would travel to other churches leading in youth revivals. We named our group Real Life from John's focus on Jesus as real life in the prologue of 1 John.

John's Purpose in Writing: Fellowship and Joy (vv. 3b, 4)

In verse 3 John writes, "that which we have seen and heard, we proclaim also to you." Here John returns to his thought from verse 1. John has been proclaiming Jesus through his preaching and now does so through his writing. John is simply saying, "The Jesus I saw and heard many years ago is the Jesus I have been proclaiming and continue to proclaim." John was both an eyewitness and an ear-witness.[16] Verse 3 provides the reason why John is proclaiming Jesus to his readers and to us: "so that you too may have fellowship with us." Several times in John's Gospel you read the word "fellowship."[17] This word, like an old coin, sometimes wears thin in our Christian vocabulary, especially when the word conjures up images of drinking coffee in paper cups while nibbling on a donut before or after the morning worship service. Fellowship means far more than that. The root meaning is a deep sharing of things in common. As used by the New Testament writers, "fellowship" means that which all Christians share and celebrate in common. What is it that believers share in common? Jesus Christ and salvation! Belief in Jesus brings about salvation that places us in fellowship with all other believers everywhere who also know Jesus Christ as their Lord and Savior. Only believers in Christ can have this kind of fellowship. We may have friendships in the world, but only Christians share and celebrate genuine fellowship with each other. Some of the New Testament things Christians are said to share together in are the fellowship of giving, loving, serving, and suffering.

The word "fellowship" has two foci—horizontal and vertical. John teaches us that our fellowship is not only with other believers (the horizontal aspect) but is also "with the Father and with his Son Jesus Christ" (the vertical aspect). From the beginning of history, humanity has pulled every trick out of the bag of philosophy and religion in an attempt to bridge the seemingly infinite chasm between man and God. Now that chasm has been bridged by Jesus Christ. John implies here in this statement, and will make clear later in the letter, that fellowship with God is not possible apart from fellowship with Jesus. You cannot be in fellowship with God but not in fellowship with his Son Jesus and vice versa. Think of fellowship as genuine spiritual connection with God and other believers.

The great preacher G. Campbell Morgan has an interesting sermon on 1 John 1:3 entitled "Fellowship with God." In it he suggests that the word "fellowship" is a "rich and spacious word, full of suggestiveness, almost impossible of full and final translation."[18] "Communion" and "partnership" are the two key concepts Morgan develops as he describes what it means for Christians to have fellowship with God. As to privilege, fellowship with God is communion with him. By this Morgan has in mind deep friendship. This is an appropriate picture, is it not, in light of what Jesus said in John 15:12–15: "This is my commandment, that you love one another as I have loved you. Greater love has no one than this, that someone lay down his life for his friends. You are my friends if you do what I command you. No longer do I call you servants, for the servant does not know what his master is doing; but I have called you friends, for all that I have heard from my Father I have made known to you." Here Jesus expresses his attitude toward the disciples in his final days before his crucifixion. Notice the conjunction here of commandment, love, friendship, and making known truth from the Father. All of these concepts are found in 1 John. The command to love one another will become a crucial focus of John in 1 John 2:7–11 and in other places in the letter. Knowledge of the truth will also be a key theme in the letter (2:20, 21, for example). As Jesus uses the word "friend" for the disciples, he is intimating a close relationship with them that the term "fellowship" also expresses. John has learned from Jesus that fellowship with God and Christ is a matter of a deep sharing of things in common, which is what friends do. As to privilege, fellowship with God is communion with God.

Morgan further develops the concept of fellowship with God as to responsibility. Here fellowship with God is partnership with him. ". . . fellowship with God means we have gone into business with God, that His enterprises are to be our enterprises."[19] Fellowship with God means we share mutual interests, devotion, and activity.[20] As Christians in close fellowship with God, his heartbeat becomes our heartbeat, his mission becomes our mission, his goals and plans become our goals and plans. We love what he loves, desire what he desires, hate what he hates, and will what he wills. The Christian life should be an ever-deepening fellowship with God that creates and reproduces within us the mind of Christ.

Think about it. Here is the answer to life's meaning and purpose. Only God through Christ can unlock the meaning and purpose of life. "Our heart is restless until it rests in you," said Augustine.[21] Here is the answer to life's peace. Jesus said: "my peace I give to you" (John 14:27). Here is the answer to life's loneliness. Fellowship with God and Jesus solves the problem of our spiritual loneliness. Even when you think you are alone, you are not alone. Jesus has said, "I will never leave you nor forsake you" (Hebrews 13:5). You may feel alone sometimes, but you are never alone. Fellowship with God and Christ takes care of life's spiritual loneliness. God's second answer to life's loneliness is fellowship with other Christians through a local church. Christians have more in common with other Christians than they do with unsaved members of their own family. That's why Jesus talked about leaving father and mother and following him. There is a fellowship among those who know Christ that is sweeter and closer than even that of blood relatives. That's the nature of Christian fellowship. One of the things that John is going to emphasize in this book is the nature of our fellowship with one another and with God. From several different angles in this letter, John will address the issue of our fellowship with God and other Christians, its conditions, practice, and results.

In 1 John 1:1–3 John has affirmed the reality of Christ eternally, historically, and experientially. All three are vital for Christianity and for all Christians. Jesus is more than a man; he is God in human flesh, the second member of the Trinity. As such, he is eternal. Were he less than God, he could never have been our Savior. Jesus is fully God, but he is also fully man by virtue of the incarnation. Jesus came to earth as one of us in history. As such, he is historically real. Because Jesus as the God-man is a real person, he can experience fellowship with other Christians and they with him, through the Holy Spirit. If Christianity is anything, it is a personal relationship with the God who made us through his Son who became one of us and paid the price for our sins on the cross.

Finally, John gives us another purpose for writing in verse 4: "so that our joy[22] may be complete." Who is included in "our?" This could be an exclusive "our," whereby John includes himself and perhaps other church leaders and believers but excludes his readers.[23] More likely this is an inclusive "our,"[24] referring to John's readers and probably beyond them to all believers everywhere. John's joy would be complete when he shares mutual fellowship with his readers/hearers. The phrase "may be complete" means "permanently full; permanently filled." John says in essence, "When we have fellowship with you, our joy is full." John speaks of joy in all three of his letters (1 John 1:4; 2 John 12; 3 John 4). Interestingly, Jesus speaks of joy in relationship to his disciples three times in his farewell discourse and prayer in John's Gospel (15:11; 16:24; 17:13). In all three examples, Jesus is concerned that the disciples' joy might be "full" or "fulfilled." In two of these three references, Jesus speaks of "my joy" remaining in the disciples and that "my joy" might be "fulfilled" in the disciples. John is concerned that his joy and that of his readers/hearers may not only be sustained but may increase to fullness, in fulfillment of Jesus' words. When Christ's joy is fulfilled in us, then will our joy be full!

Christian joy is far removed from what is commonly construed as happiness, which is dependent upon outward circumstances. It can certainly include such, but Christian joy is much deeper and richer in meaning. Joy is the presence of Jesus in our lives by means of the indwelling Holy Spirit. Joy describes a reality in life of genuine satisfaction intellectually, emotionally, and spiritually. Joy is a spirit of exultation regardless of circumstances. Joy is a sense of supernatural strength that can only come from the Lord: "the joy of the LORD is your strength" (Nehemiah 8:10). I have seen the joyless eyes of miserable people in many cities around the world. I have observed the joyless faces of people in Third World countries, clawing and scratching to eke out an existence for themselves and their families. Even those fortunate enough to be in decent economic shape along with those who have anything and everything money can buy might sometimes experience happiness, but without God through Christ they can never experience genuine joy. The wisest and richest man who ever lived found that out when he sailed the high seas of life in an effort to find fulfillment. The man on whom the world exhausted itself and for whom the world was not enough discovered the bitter truth that at the end of every paycheck, the bottom of every bottle, and the morning after every one-night stand there was no joy in Mudville. So he tells us in his personal memoirs known as Ecclesiastes. Mighty Solomon had struck out.[25] Only God can grant joy to the human soul. "You make known to me the path of life; in your presence is fullness of joy; at your right hand are pleasures forevermore" (Psalm 16:11). The crown of joy can only be worn by those who have been adopted into God's royal family through his Son, King Jesus. The banner of joy will only fly over the castle of your life when the King is in residence there.[26] Joy is the response of the soul that is rightly related to God through the knowledge of Christ as our Savior and Lord.

In one four-verse prologue the "Son of Thunder," as Jesus once called him, summarizes God's revelation of Christ and in so doing takes on the world of philosophy in his day and wrestles it to the mat. From the Platonic world comes the "Word," ideal and abstract; from John comes Jesus "the Word," divine and personal, the Word made flesh; from the Philonic world comes the "Word," the idea of God in creation; from John comes Jesus, who was from the beginning, the creative First Cause of all creation; from the Gnostic world comes the "Word," created and temporal; from John comes Jesus, uncreated and eternal. Philosophies had always dreamed of a Savior, but what philosophy could only dream about and aspire to, God has given to the world in the person of Christ Jesus. Joy to the world, the Lord has come!

This is the message we have heard from him and proclaim to you, that God is light, and in him is no darkness at all. If we say we have fellowship with him while we walk in darkness, we lie and do not practice the truth. But if we walk in the light, as he is in the light, we have fellowship with one another, and the blood of Jesus his Son cleanses us from all sin. If we say we have no sin, we deceive ourselves, and the truth is not in us. If we confess our sins, he is faithful and just to forgive us our sins and to cleanse us from all unrighteousness. If we say we have not sinned, we make him a liar, and his word is not in us.

1 JOHN 1:5–10

2

When Sin Meets Forgiveness

THE GREAT ACTOR and film director Woody Allen claims to be an atheist. On one occasion he was asked the question, "If there is a God, and if that God should speak to you, what would you most want to hear him say?" Woody Allen's answer speaks for all people. He said, "If there is a God who should speak to me, I would most want to hear him say three words, 'You are forgiven.'"[1] John says the only way you will ever hear from God the words "you are forgiven" is if you speak the words "I have sinned." J. B. Phillips said there are nearly as many wrong ideas about sin as there are false ideas about God.[2] As a Christian, what do you do when you sin? What should you do when you sin? Sometimes, even for Christians, sin is something we do and then deny. We love to rationalize it, and we love to refine it. Sometimes we just don't take seriously the reality and consequences of our sin.[3] We claim closeness with God but then defy his will and live contrary to his character! What scandal! Even for Christians, sometimes the three hardest words to say *when* they ought to be said and *like* they ought to be said are "I have sinned."[4] But when we utter those words in sincerity, God's response is always "You are forgiven."

Sin in our lives should be the aberration, not the norm. We should be sensitive to the Lord and his Word such that the moment we become aware of sin in our life, we immediately confess and forsake it. The more you grow in awareness of personal sin, you should become like Paul and shift from saying you are "the very least of all the saints" (Ephesians 3:8) to saying you are "the foremost" of sinners (1 Timothy 1:15). When you become mature spiritually, your sense of sin matures as well. You not only see it as the breaking God's of laws, which it surely is, but as wounding God's love.[5] If you keep God at arm's length, you will always have a hazy view of sin in your own life.

But when you do sin, you have one of two choices. You can choose to cover your sin. You can hide it, deny it, and lie to God, others, and yourself about it. Proverb 28:13 is a pungent verse to remember when you choose to cover your sin: "Whoever conceals his transgressions will not prosper, but he who confesses and forsakes them will obtain mercy." Your second option is to confess your sin. Admit it to God and come clean before him and with yourself. Confession is the order of the day for a believer who sins.

John talks about this very thing in 1 John 1:5–10.[6] For us as Christians, sin does indeed break our fellowship with God. Be very careful here. When a Christian sins, our sonship, the fact that we are in the family of God, is not changed. God does not take his sinning children out of his family when they sin any more than you disown your children when they disobey. Aren't you glad that the forgiveness of God given to us by grace through the atoning work of Christ is permanent? We need to understand the reality that sin doesn't break our sonship, but it does break our fellowship with God. Sin grieves God; it breaks his heart. It puts a barrier between us and God in terms of fellowship.

The structure of this paragraph is interesting. Verse 5 functions as the basis for two appeals that John makes in verses 6–10. The basis of the appeals is the character and nature of God as light, meaning God's complete purity and holiness. The two appeals are not made with direct commands but rather are mitigated by John. The first appeal is semantically expressed in verses 6, 7: Christians should live according to God's pure nature; that is, they should not sin. The second appeal is semantically expressed in verses 8–10: When we do not live according to God's pure nature, that is, when we do sin, we should confess our sin to God and experience his forgiveness.

God Is Light (v. 5)

In verse 5 John makes a statement about the origin of his message: "This is the message we have heard from him."[7] John's apostolic authority derives from what he learned from Jesus. There are no apostles today, but preachers who are called by God to preach the Word derive their authority not from themselves but from God, just like the apostles did. John says, "we . . . proclaim" this message to you. This is the only time in the letter that this specific Greek word translated "proclaim" occurs. It differs by only one letter in Greek from the word used in the previous paragraph translated in the HVY as "proclaim."[8] What is the significance of John's use of these two very similar words in Greek? The word used in verses 2, 3 stress the *source* of the message, while the word used in verse 5 stresses the *receptor* of the message. The word means "to herald important news" and was sometimes used for the declaration of a king. The king's herald would walk the streets of the city announcing the king's message. All the subjects of the kingdom were intently interested in the word of the king. When your television show is interrupted by the network with an important news bulletin, what do you do? Do you get up, go to the kitchen to get a snack, and leisurely return later? No, you intently listen to what is being said because the news might affect you personally. John says he has a message to announce to his readers, and it is a vital, crucially important, life-changing message.

Did you notice that before John ever talks about us, he talks about God? The Christian life begins with God, not us. The substance of the message is stated in the latter part of verse 5: "God is light." John makes a statement about the character of God three times in his writings. In John 4:24 God is a Spirit. In 1 John 4:7, 8 God is love. Here John tells us he is announcing what he heard from Jesus, namely, "God is light." This statement, "God is light," is not recorded in the Gospels, but John 3:19 does state concerning Jesus, "The light has come into the world, and people loved the darkness rather than the light." Two possibilities exist here. Jesus may have said it and it was not recorded. Many of the things Jesus did and taught during his public ministry are not recorded in the Gospels. John says in John 21:25, "Now there are also many other things that Jesus did. Were every one of them to be written, I suppose that the world itself could not contain the books that would be written." A second possibility may be that John is simply summing up Jesus' teaching about God with respect to his nature.

This statement, "God is light," has been interpreted in different ways. First, it could be a description of the visible manifestation of God's glory. Second, some have seen in this statement a reference to God's self-revelation to man. Light enables us to see. Though these first two options are true, contextually this does not seem to be what John has in mind. Most likely this is a phrase that refers to the moral perfection of God. There is not one blemish, stain, mark, or sin on the character of God. God is absolute perfection. Even the sun has its spots of darkness, but not God. He is absolute holiness and purity. This interpretation is further supported by two things. First, there is no article before "light" in the Greek text, which stresses character and nature. God is, as to his character and nature, morally pure and holy. Second, the following negative restatement, "in him is no darkness at all," supports this meaning.

An interesting feature of John's style of writing is to state something positively, then turn it around and put it in the negative. Notice that is exactly what he does here: "and in him is no darkness at all." Literally in Greek, this statement reads, "there is no darkness in him, none." John employs a double negative, poor grammar in English, but both good grammar and good theology in Greek. Grammatically this is the strongest way to express emphatic negation. Not only is God light, but there is absolutely no darkness, not one scintilla of darkness (moral imperfection) in him. In him is no shade, speck, or stain of moral imperfection. In him is no fault, failure, or falsehood. In him is no deceit, deviation, or dishonesty. Physical darkness is a terrible thing. "There is no distance in darkness. Darkness is limitation, darkness is imprisonment; there is no jail with walls so thick and impenetrable as darkness."[9] Darkness is an apt metaphor to describe sin. Unlike my heart and your heart where the light of the gospel shines, but where sometimes there may be pockets of sin that we allow to go unchecked, God in his character and nature possesses no moral imperfection whatsoever.

John's statement seems to us to be the plainest truth that hardly needs mentioning! But it was not so plain when John wrote it! His world was full of idols and gods who were sometimes no less evil than the men who worshipped them. The moral perfection of God was a new message in those days. It is a new message for many today still! Think of what kind of God most sinners desire: a God who is indulgent to his sin, who will shut his eyes to disobedience, who will always reward and never punish, who will always receive whether we come in truth or pretense, who is blind and willing to be taken in and imposed upon, who will put up with all excuses and bear all hypocrisy. But nonbelievers are not the only ones who need to be reminded that "God is light." How often do we as Christians sin, hoping that God will not think so severely of our sin as the Bible says he does? How often do we flatter ourselves with excuses for our sin such as "God is merciful, he won't be that hard on me! Surely he does not expect me to always be holy and self-denying"? I'm afraid we sometimes rationalize and delude ourselves into thinking that God can be bargained with, bribed, and otherwise bought off concerning our sin. John's forthright statement, "God is light" is a clear and needed reminder that God is who and what he is, however and whatever we may think or act.[10]

The basis of our fellowship with God is the character and nature of God. Sin radically affects our fellowship with God. In 1 John 1:1–4 our fellowship with God and other believers is a key theme. John continues this theme in verses 6–10. These verses contain a series of six conditional sentences in three pairs of negative falsehoods (1:6, 8, 10), each followed by positive truths (1:7, 9; 2:1). Three times John expresses a statement of what someone could say about their sin, expressed as "if we say."[11] When you look carefully at the three, you discover an unusual progression of thought. Each of these three statements is a shot across the bow of every Christian for whom the word "sin" was beginning to lose its meaning.[12] Have you met a Christian lately who does not take sin seriously enough, someone whose walk does not match his or her talk? Talk and walk go together in the Christian life, like the two wings of an airplane. If my life does not match my words, something is amiss in my Christian life. There is a huge gap between cheap talk and an authentic walk.

Walk in the Light (vv. 6, 7)

If someone claims to be in fellowship with God and yet the way he lives is characterized by sinful behavior, he is lying through his toothy grin and not practicing the truth (v. 6). It may be that some of the false teachers in John's day were claiming to have fellowship with God. It may be that some genuine believers in the church were under the delusion that their sinful lifestyle was somehow not incompatible with fellowship with God. More on this in a moment.

One of the common New Testament metaphors to describe conduct is the word "walk." The word "walk" expresses the notion of "behavior, conduct, and lifestyle." To "walk in darkness" is the opposite of walking in the light. The tense of the verb "walk" is present and conveys habitual lifestyle. You cannot "walk" in darkness and be practicing the truth at the same time. Notice here that the truth is not only something to be believed, but is something to be lived out. This is a vital concept that John will develop in the rest of the letter. Spurgeon was right when he said there may be all the difference in the world "between saying and being, between saying and doing."[13]

How does "we lie" differ from "not practic[ing] the truth?" Some identify the word "lie" with spoken falsehood and the phrase "not practic[ing] the truth" with actions contrary to what is spoken. Others say both refer to deliberate falseness in word and deed. Some interpret the word "lie" to mean "self-deceit." When our words don't match our life, we are not putting the truth of what we say we believe into action; hence, we in essence lie. What does John mean by "truth"?

When John speaks of truth in his letters, he uses the word in two primary senses: 1) true teaching, that is, the true message; and 2) actions consonant with the true message.[14] In this context, John is using "truth" to refer to the true message/doctrine.

A big question concerns whether John intends us to understand his statement to apply to Christians or unbelievers. The letter is written to believers. The issue is whether a true believer can "walk in darkness." Without going too far afield, we need to be reminded of two truths. First, if someone within the church lives contrary to the gospel on a regular basis, there is good reason to question the genuineness of his or her conversion. Second, it is possible for Christians to sin, live in periods of carnality, and yet be truly saved. The Bible affirms both of these realities. Though verse 6 could easily be referencing someone who is not a Christian, contextually it could also refer to someone who is a Christian. Notice that John says "we lie." About what? About being in fellowship with God while walking in darkness. Furthermore, we are not practicing the truth. He does not say we do not *know* the truth. Imagine someone who is a member of a health club and attends all the club nutrition meetings. But when he is not at the health club, he binges on the worst kind of foods you can imagine. He goes back to the health club meetings and says, "Today I ate three cranberries and half of a pear" when he actually consumed a Big Mac and a supersized order of fries! It is a sad spectacle when a Christian claims the moral high ground, but from God's perspective he actually languishes in the pit.[15] If we say we have fellowship with God, yet our life is lived in the darkness of sin and not in the light of truth, we are liars and are not "doing" the truth. It is interesting that in John 3:21 John records Jesus speaking of the one who "does what is true."[16] Jesus says such a person "comes to the light." John picks up on both concepts of "light" and "doing the truth" from Jesus and uses them here in his letter.

John speaks about a practical lie. The person who lies in this way is not only speaking a lie, but is acting a lie! His life is a practical falsehood! Walking in darkness is itself the lie, an acted untruth.[17] Light and darkness are mutually exclusive. They cannot coexist. At night when the lights go out, darkness comes. When the light comes on, the darkness is dispelled. Walking in darkness is the equivalent of walking in sin. You have to be careful about walking in the darkness because you can easily get hurt. One morning about 3:00 DIP 1, I awakened. Not wanting to wake my wife, I got up without turning on the light. I figured I knew my house pretty well and could maneuver without bumping into anything. But when I attempted to walk through a doorpost, I sustained quite a cut on my forehead. It does not pay to walk in darkness.

Walking in darkness can mean committing any sin great or small. Shrouding oneself with cover of night and wielding an assassin's knife, a would-be murderer stalks his victim. Or it might involve hatching a nefarious plot against the just to attempt to bring them down or tarnish their reputation, gloating over financial gains of avarice, nursing in your imagination an unchecked passion or lust, sitting in front of your computer under cover of late night to satisfy an addiction to Internet pornography, cheating on a test, lying to the IRS, hating your neighbor, defrauding your employer, wasting precious time given to you by God, neglecting spiritual disciplines such as Bible reading and prayer, or a thousand other sins of omission and commission, great and small, in thought, word, or deed. All of this is walking in darkness.[18] Walking in darkness can begin when we fall into the trap of renaming sins so they do not appear so bad. Political correctness abounds in our society. A person is not lazy, he is merely "motivationally dispossessed"; a shoplifter is not a thief, he is "a cost of living adjustment specialist"; a prostitute is not a prostitute, she is a "sex care provider."[19] Sin does not lose its sinfulness by giving it a less offensive name. A skunk by any other name still stinks.

In verse 7 John presents the opposite scenario. If we conduct our lives in the light, that is, if we live godly lives and behave as Christians should behave because that is how God conducts himself, then "we have fellowship with one another." We are to walk in the light as God is in the light. "Walking" and "light" are two metaphors that speak of living in the sphere of truth and holiness. Verse 5 says, "God is light"; now verse 7 says God is "in the light." Is there any difference between these two statements? It is difficult to say, but it seems likely that John intends to say that since God "is" the light in terms of nature and essence, everything he does is "in" the light in terms of total purity and holiness.[20] For us to walk in the light as God is in the light indicates likeness, but not degree. The light of God's nature is pristine holiness, untainted by sin. We can never walk in the light to that degree, but we can walk in the likeness of that light. Spurgeon mentions Trapp's memorable comment on this verse as to "how we are to be in the light as God is in the light for quality, but not for equality."[21] We can walk in the light in this sense, however limpingly, because Christ the Light is our Savior.

How do we "walk in the light"? The Scripture says, "Your word is a lamp to my feet and a light to my path" (Psalm 119:105). The Bible teaches us how to live day by day in a way that pleases God and avoids sin. When I read and study the Bible, I discover where my life contradicts Scripture, and I can make the proper spiritual adjustment. Furthermore, our ultimate reason for obeying the Word of God is love for Jesus. Jesus said, "if you love me, you will keep my commandments" (John 14:15).

If we walk in the light, two things result. First, "we have fellowship with one another." Stop right there and ask yourself, what is odd about that statement? The expected consequence is "we have fellowship with God," not "we have fellowship with one another." Why does John not say anything about fellowship with God here and yet speaks of fellowship with one another? The answer is that fellowship with God is already assumed to be true since John says "we walk in the light," and fellowship among Christians is a sign they have fellowship with God already.[22] Now let's unpack that word "fellowship" for a moment.[23] The word "fellowship" means more than just association. It means more than just friendship. It means more than just having a good conversation over a cup of coffee. "Fellowship" is a word that means a deep sharing of things in common via association and participation. To be in fellowship with God means more than just having an association or friendship with God. It means having a relationship with God. To have fellowship with one another is not just a matter of being in the same room at church, but it means having a relationship with each based on our relationship with Christ that causes us to participate together around a common bond. What is it that all Christians share in common? It is our common relationship with Jesus. What is it that binds all of us together? Ultimately what binds people together is the Lord Jesus Christ himself, through their mutual love for him and one another.

No one realizes his deepening need of heart-cleansing as much as the one who walks in the increasing light of fellowship with Jesus. When we walk in the light hidden, unsuspected sins are revealed. The terrible thing about sin is that it not only breaks fellowship with God but with other Christians as well. We cannot be in fellowship with one another when we have sin in our lives. Therefore, when I sin, it hurts you even if you don't know about it. When you sin, it hurts your fellow Christians even if they don't know about it. But when we "walk in the light . . . we have fellowship with one another."

The second thing we have when we walk in the light is cleansing from sin. Here is the first use of the word "sin" in the letter.[24] *Sin* is that ugly word that describes the condition of us all.

> Sin is the skull set amidst life's banquet, the desert breath that drinks every dew—a madness in the brain, a poison in the heart, an opiate in the will, a frenzy in the imagination. Sin, the disease of the soul, the instrument of everlasting ruin, the midnight blackness that invests man's whole moral being, subverted the constitutional order of man's nature. Sin, promising velvet and giving a shroud, promising liberty and giving slavery, promising nectar and giving gall . . . promising perfumed handkerchiefs and giving foul rags, promising silk and giving sackcloth.[25]

Today's culture has changed the label on the bottle called "sin" and falsely assumed that it has changed the contents of the bottle. A rose by any other name would smell as sweet. But sin by any other name still stinks to high heaven. We have banned sin from our vocabulary but not from our veins. Bulletproof windows, twelve-inch steel doors in banks, jails, police cars, and your key ring bear mute testimony to the fact that people are sinners. You lock your house, car, office, locker, and luggage because some people have forgotten the Eighth Commandment: "You shall not steal."[26] The criminal justice system is a harsh reminder that people are sinners. John assumes his readers know the concept of sin, but he will further describe its nature later on in the letter.

This cleansing in verse 7 is the daily cleansing from sin in the life of a believer. The ground of fellowship John spoke about is, "the blood of Jesus his Son cleanses us from all sin." Reference to "the blood of Jesus" is another way of speaking of the death of Christ on the cross as an atoning sacrifice. We tend to think about the death of Jesus on the cross as being what takes away our sin when we come to him for salvation initially. It is the death of Jesus on the cross that makes it possible for God to save us. That is certainly true. But many of us don't stop to reflect on the fact of the ongoing benefits of the death of Christ for us. The abiding effects of that work continue into our lives day by day. That's why John writes this in the present tense. The blood of Christ goes on cleansing us day by day from our sin. It is capable of cleansing us every time we sin as believers. But this does not refer just what he did on the cross in terms of justification; it is rather also what he does continually in our lives in what we call, in theological terms, progressive sanctification. Progressive sanctification simply means this—the process whereby every day God is working in our lives to make us more like Jesus. The root word in Hebrew and Greek for "sanctification" is the word "holy." God is light, God is holy, God wants you and me to be holy, and he works within us, forgiving us our sins on the basis of the cross. Further, the Holy Spirit applies the merits of salvation to forgive us and to cleanse us daily and to progressively work within our lives, so that we become what God wants us to be. When John says Jesus' blood purifies us from sin, he refers to both the forgiveness of sin and the removing of guilt that sin incurs.

The phrase "cleanses us from all sin" is a metaphor whose primary reference is to cleaning something that is dirty. Sin causes the Christian to be spiritually soiled, and cleansing is needed to rid him of the consequences of sin—namely, guilt. In Judaism the person who sinned became unfit for worship and service; hence the need for cleansing. The notion of cleansing indicates that John is not here viewing sin as a principle or as a power, but rather as an act that defiles and needs to be cleansed from the Christian life.[27] Notice it is not rites and rituals,[28] not sacraments or ceremonies, not knowledge or experience plus the blood of Jesus that cleanses us of sin. No! As the old hymn put it, "What can wash away my sin? Nothing but the blood of Jesus." The author of Hebrews made it clear: "It is impossible for the blood of bulls and goats to take away sins" (Hebrews 10:4). Only the blood of Jesus can do that. Such is the exclusivity of the cleansing; only the blood of Jesus can accomplish it! Such is the completeness of it. All our sins, sins in thought, word, and deed, are all gone. Sins where my heart has been cold toward him, sins against the Holy Spirit—all are gone! Sins of commission, sins of omission, big sins and little sins—they are all gone. Sins of breaking his law and despising his Word, profaning his name, failing to love him truly—all are gone! Sins of presumption, sins of ignorance, willful sins and unknown sins—all are cleansed by the blood of Jesus! Such is the certainty of it![29]

Verse 7 is the first mitigated command in the letter. Semantically, what John is really saying in this verse is: Christians should behave according to God's pure moral nature and not sin.[30] In verses 5–7 John lays down for us the basis of our fellowship with God. Now we turn our attention to verses 8–10, where he continues the subject of Christian fellowship and explains that our fellowship with God continues on the basis of our willingness to confess our sin. When John says in verse 8, "if we say we have no sin," he is referring to committing sinful acts. This is consistent with the plural "sins" in verse 9 and the equivalent concept in verse 10.

Don't Deny Sin, Confess It (vv. 8–10)

Verse 8 begins with another conditional statement: "If we say we have no sin . . ."[31] It seems impossible to us that anyone would make such a claim. Surely everyone admits to being a sinner!

Spurgeon said, "He who cannot find water in the sea is not more foolish than the man who cannot perceive sin in his members." Some people do indeed seem to think of sin as nonexistent, seeing sin as merely the dream of fusty theologians to keep everybody from having fun. Others are quick to rationalize or make excuses for their sin. The great Scottish preacher George Morrison said, "To wrap yourself up in excuses is to be naked before the great white throne."[32] Sometimes even Christians make excuses for their sins that they are quick to condemn in others.

Here it is helpful to consider briefly the Biblical doctrine of sin. Every human being enters this world at birth with a sin nature. What does it mean to have a sin nature? It means we have a bent, a propensity to sin. When you are old enough to discern right from wrong, you will choose to sin. You cannot stop yourself from sinning. You have a nature to sin. In one sense you are not a sinner because you sin; you sin because you are a sinner. You inherited your sin nature from your parents. Ultimately our sin nature goes back to the fall of Adam and Eve in Genesis 3.

I have four children and three grandchildren. When each of my children was born, I had such pride in them. They were, of course, beautiful. They were perfect. But it did not take me long to discover that babies grow into young children and begin to display their sin nature. Picture two children, around three years of age, playing in the same room. One child sees the other child playing with a toy. He toddles over and like lightning snatches the toy away from the child and says, "Mine." What does the robbed child do? He says to the little thief, "You go right ahead and play with my toy; that's fine with me. I'll wait until you're through with it and then I'll play with it again." Is that how it works? Not on your life! The robbed child will cry and at some point try to get the toy back. A tussle begins followed by weeping, wailing, and gnashing of teeth. If an adult does not step in, World War III might start. Suddenly it becomes apparent to all that these two precious children have a selfish nature. Where did those children acquire it? Do parents have to teach their children to be selfish? If you are a parent of a small child, do you have to teach your child how to get mad when another child takes your child's toy? "Now, darling, when someone takes your toy, you go and take that toy away from them and say 'my toy.'" You don't have to teach your children to be selfish, to lie, or to cheat. They do so naturally. In fact, you have to teach them *not* to do those things. Why? Because they have a sin nature.

People often ask, "Are some sins worse than other sins?" That is a good question. One of the best answers I've heard to that question is from Alvin Plantinga: "All sin is equally wrong, but not all sin is equally bad. Acts are either right or wrong, either consonant with God's will or not. But among good acts some are better than others, and among wrong acts some are worse than others."[33] This can be easily demonstrated. I would much prefer you hate me than to act out your hate and murder me. Even though hate is murder in the heart, the consequences of your heart hate alone are far less drastic for me personally than if you were to put your hate into action and take my life.

Satan is crafty when it comes to sin. Luther stated that when a Christian sins, the devil always alarms his heart and makes him tremble. "Look at you!" he scowls, "Now you've blown it!" Satan wants you to sink into the sin of despair. On the other hand, Luther said, Satan "lets some live smugly without temptation in order that they may think and believe that they are holy. And when somewhere he tears the Word out of one's heart, then he has conquered. This is his cunning. He wants to make saints sinners, and confident sinners saints."[34]

John teaches that if we say we have no sin, two things result. First, we are self-deceived. In what way? By choosing to ignore the evidence of sin in our life. Imagine a man whose doctor tells him he is terminally ill and has only a few weeks to live. But the man refuses to believe it. How foolish, even tragic, would that be. How much more foolish would it be for a man to deny the fact that he has cancer of the soul. The language John uses here implies our own responsibility for our deception. We ourselves become the deceivers, and we are responsible for leading ourselves astray.[35] You could translate this, "We lead ourselves astray." The ostrich, when pursued, thrusts its head in the sand and imagines because it has closed its eyes, it is safe from its predators. The only thing more humorously pitiful than this is the person who attempts to hide his sin from God.

The second result is, "the truth is not in us." This refers to the truth of the gospel. What does John mean? Is it an unsaved person or a Christian who is making this claim? If we take 1 John 5:13 seriously, John is writing to believers. It seems best to take this statement as coming from a Christian. In other words, if a Christian says he no longer has the capacity to sin, then he is self-deceived and the truth that he can indeed sin as a Christian is not in him. The truth is not controlling his thinking and living. Some in Christian history have taught a doctrine called sinless perfectionism. Sinless perfectionism is the supposed state a believer achieves in which he does not sin anymore. Verse 8 speaks against such an idea. Experience as a Christian makes it evident to each of us that somewhere along the line you are going to sin in word, thought, or deed. The possibility of sin in your life is a real danger. You are capable of sinning as a Christian. You should not sin, but you sometimes do. As John says in verse 8, "If we say we have no sin, we deceive ourselves." Notice how the word "sin" here is singular, not plural. The reference here may be to our sin nature. John is stating, "If we say we have no sin nature, then the truth is not in us." Christians still have a sin nature. It is not eradicated. It will be eradicated when we get to Heaven, but here on earth we are all capable of sin. A dog is not a dog because it barks; it barks because it's a dog. A sinner is not a sinner because he sins; he sins because he is a sinner. The bottom line of verse 8 is this: a Christian who thinks he is no longer capable of sinning is self-deceived and is not living according to the truth of the gospel. On rare occasions in my ministry I have run across people who have told me they have reached a state of sinless perfection. Whenever you encounter such people, mark it down in your little black book that you are dealing with someone who is spiritually a dozen fries short of a Happy Meal!

Now look at verse 9. Remember what you can do with your sin. You can either cover it up or confess it. First John 1:9 is a vital verse for every Christian to understand. Sin is a fact of life, but fortunately it does not prevent our fellowship with God if it is confessed. Confession should always be the natural response the moment we become cognizant of personal sin. But human nature being what it is, we often tend to minimize the seriousness of our own sin. I recently read about a newspaper that asked candidates running for office to write a short piece on the subject "something I did wrong in my life and what I learned from it." Nobody confessed anything of any significance. It was always minor things like "I got a ticket for speeding for going five miles over the speed limit." Each respondent minimized anything he did wrong and did not want to magnify it for fear that it might hurt him with voters. Sadly, we Christians often act the same way about our own sin. Some people live by the eleventh commandment they have added to the Lord's ten that reads, "Don't get caught." What if you can't think of any sins to confess? When a longtime church member came to her pastor after his sermon on 1 John 1:9 and said, "Preacher, I can't think of any sins to confess!," the pastor suggested to her, "Try guessing at it and you will hit on something!"

What does it mean to confess your sin? The word "confess" means "to say the same thing as." When you confess your sin, you are agreeing with God that what he says about your sin is true. It is an admission of guilt. To confess your sin is not just saying, "I got caught. I'm sorry, but if I can get away with it, I'll do it again." That's not confession of sin. Confession of sin is coming to the place where you honestly agree with God about your sin. Confession means genuine contrition for our sin and a genuine seeking of forgiveness. To whom do we confess? We confess our sin to God. Our sin is first and foremost against him, as David acknowledged in his prayer of confession in Psalm 51 when he said "against you, you only, have I sinned" (v. 4). Should we confess to the church as well in a public setting? The answer to that question depends on the nature of the sin and the extent to which it is known by other people. As a pastor, I always operated on the general principle that private sin should be confessed privately and public sin should be confessed publicly.

Verse 9 says, "if we confess our *sins*," plural. Why the change from the singular "sin" to the plural "sins"? John has in mind confession of our specific acts of sin. It's hard to confess sin in the abstract! A lady under conviction about the sin of gossip once responded to a public altar call to confess her sin. Bud Robinson, the preacher, received her at the front. "I want to lay my tongue on the altar," she said. Bud responded, "The altar is only sixteen feet long, but lay her on!"[36] I'm not too sure about the pastoral sensitivity in that situation, but the lady under conviction about the specific sin of gossip had the right idea: specific confession of her sin.

When you confess your sins, God acts. He forgives your sin, and he cleanses you from all unrighteousness. How can he be both "faithful and just" to forgive sin in the life of the Christian? The answer is in verse 7: "The blood of Jesus Christ continues to cleanse us from all sin" (literal translation). When John says in verse 9 that God is "faithful and just," he is presenting the grounds for why God will forgive our sin. This gets a little complicated, but stay with me for a moment. In the Greek text John uses a subordinating conjunction (*hina*) that functions to introduce the consequence (God forgives our sins) of the preceding conditional clause ("if we confess our sins"). John's meaning is this: "If we confess our sins, since God is faithful and just, he therefore will forgive our sins."

Think about those two words "faithful" and "just" for a moment. "[God] is faithful" means he is faithful to his promises concerning his willingness to forgive sin. For example, Jeremiah 31:34, the famous passage about the new covenant, is an important Old Testament promise concerning God's willingness to forgive sins: "For I will forgive their iniquity, and I will remember their sin no more." Micah 7:18–20 also speaks of God's willingness to pardon sin. But God is also "just" when he forgives our confessed sin. The word in Greek means "righteous." God as to his nature always does what is just and right. His righteousness requires that he keep his promise to forgive all who confess their sin. If he were to fail to do this, he would no longer be just and righteous. Since Christ's death has atoned for sin and made forgiveness possible, God can be just when he forgives confessed sin.

The death of Jesus on the cross actually covers all your sins—past, present, and future. When you sin as a Christian, you're not out of the family, but you do break fellowship. Sin breaks the heart of God. Sin takes you out of fellowship with God. It takes you out of fellowship with fellow believers. But when you come to the place where you confess that sin, when you admit it for what it is, then at that point you call it what God calls it, and God says, "My forgiveness is extended to you on the basis of what Christ did on the cross." You are restored to fellowship with God, and you are restored to fellowship with other people. He is faithful because he has made promises in both the Old Testament and New Testament that he will forgive our sin if we confess it and ask him to do so. He is righteous and just to do it because he has already punished sin when it was placed on Jesus at the cross. The bottom line is this: God will do what he said he would do (he is faithful) and what is perfectly right (he is just).

But notice that verse 9 does not end there. Sin brings guilt. If we can sin and not have the Holy Spirit convict us of that sin, then we are not God's children. If we are true believers, sooner or later that moral consciousness is going to catch up with us and we're going to sense what is called good guilt. The Holy Spirit in our own moral consciousness brings us to a place of guilt, and we sense that. And when we confess that sin, God says, "I have taken care of the sin; now I'm going to take care of your guilt. You are right with me again, and our relationship is restored." But God says something else: "Furthermore, I'm going to cleanse you from all unrighteousness. Not only am I going to take care of your guilt; I'm going to wash away the stain as well." That's what God does for us when we sin. He forgives our sin and purifies our character. Notice that John uses the word "sins" and "unrighteousness." The two words are basically synonymous, but John uses the second word for a reason. The Greek word translated "just" is *dikaios*, and the word translated "unrighteousness" is *adikaios*. The only difference is the addition of the Greek letter alpha. What John is saying with something of a play on words is, "God is 'righteous' to forgive and cleanse our 'unrighteousness.'"

In 1993 Alice Metzinger, wife, mother, and restaurant owner, could stand the guilt no longer. She turned herself in to authorities. Alice Metzinger was actually Katherine Power, who as a college student at Brandeis University in 1970 drove one of two getaway cars after a bank robbery went awry. Katherine disappeared. In the late 1970s she moved to Oregon and started a new life as Alice Metzinger. She was on the FBI's most-wanted list for years. Tormented by guilt, she did the only thing that could end her agony.[37] You cannot ultimately hide from guilt. When a believer sins, both the Holy Spirit and our conscience convicts us. Confession is the only way to forgiveness and cleansing.

Picture this Sunday morning scene. A mother says to her little boy, "We are getting ready to go to church, so do not go out and play because it rained last night and the ground is muddy." But the little boy slips outside when his mom's back is turned to get a little play time in before they go to church. He slips and falls in a mud puddle while wearing his Sunday best and gets mud all over him. He comes into the house crying and says, "Mom, I'm sorry. I fell, and I got mud all over my clothes. I'm sorry." At that point what does his mother say? She says, "I forgive you." That takes care of his guilt. Her child is still her son. But then what does his mother do? Does she send him to church wearing the stained clothes? No, she cleans him up and changes his clothes. That is what God is saying to you. God will take care of your guilt, and God will take care of your stain.

When we confess our sins, God is faithful: he will forgive; and he is just: he can forgive on the basis of Christ's shed blood. The penalty is paid, and the guilt is taken away. Restoration and renewal follow, since God also cleanses us from all unrighteousness. I have to have a shower every morning. I can't function during the day if I don't feel clean and fresh. Sin dirties our Christian life. We lose the joy and peace in our life. Confession is like a good shower.

We need to consider the fact that although our sin is forgiven and our guilt is removed, the consequences of our sinful choices are not necessarily taken away and in fact may be severe and permanent. The egg cannot be unscrambled. But verse 9 is a bright light at the end of sin's tunnel telling us that when we sin and then confess our sin, we need not despair because God is faithful to forgive us and to cleanse us from all unrighteousness. "Let neither a relapse into sin deter you from coming thus to Christ; nor the most spotless continuance in holiness render such a mode of coming to him unnecessary in your eyes. This is the way in which you *may* come, however aggravated may have been your guilt; and this is the way in which you *must* come, however eminent your attainments."[38]

Some Christians create their own unnecessary consequences once their sin is forgiven by either taking past sin too lightly[39] or going to the opposite extreme and doubting whether God has really forgiven them. They struggle with simply taking God at his word when he says what he says in 1 John 1:9. So they pull out their past sin, polish it up, and mumble something about whether God has really forgiven them or not. They live in constant defeat and discouragement. Such an attitude fails to take God at his word that he can and will forgive sin. Don't dredge up your forgiven past sins. If God has buried them in the deepest sea as the Scripture says, that means he has put up a no fishing sign over them. Live your life looking to the future, not the past.

First John 1:9 is the second mitigated exhortation in this paragraph (1:7 was the first). The conditional clause "if we confess our sins" carries the force of a mitigated command: "we should confess our sins." Instead of a direct imperative telling us to confess our sins, John chooses a less direct method of pressing on us the necessity of confession of sin to God when we as Christians sin.

In verse 10 we find the third "if we say" statement. Here John addresses the concept of committing individual acts of sin. John writes, "If we say we have not sinned . . ."[40] Notice that the word "sinned" is a verb whose tense (perfect)[41] expresses the notion "we do not commit acts of sin." It is human nature to deny our sin. We don't want to face the reality of our sin. We are quick to shift the blame on someone else. That's what Adam and Eve did back in Genesis 3. If we make this claim, two things result. First, "we make [God] a liar." How is that true? Romans 3:23 is the answer: "for all have sinned and come short of the glory of God." God's verdict upon humanity is that all have sinned. When a person denies he has committed acts of sin, he is in essence saying, "God, you are a liar."

What is sin? Sin is missing the mark. That is the root meaning for the word in the New Testament. I was never any good at archery. I was lucky if my arrow even hit the target, much less the bull's-eye. That is a description of what sin is: falling short of God's standard. Sin is also transgression and disobedience. It is stepping over the line. It is disobeying the Law. There is something of a progression in these verses. In verse 6 you become a liar; in verse 8 you deceive yourself; and in verse 10 you make God out to be a liar. Notice also how verse 10 functions as a summary to verses 6–10 and how John semantically parallels three concepts in verses 6 and 10: "If we say—If we say;" "We lie—we make him a liar;" "and do not practice the truth"—"and his word is not in us."

John concludes by saying, "his word is not in us." "His word" is a general reference that is inclusive of Scripture, the gospel, sound doctrine, etc. To say that his word is not "in us" means it has not affected our belief and conduct. Notice the similar statement at the conclusion of verse 8 where we read that the "truth is not in us." Though these statements are similar, there is a different focus to each one. The sense of the statement in verse 8 is refusing to behave according to God's true message. The sense of verse 10 is refusing to accept that God says we do commit acts of sin. The difference is in what is being refused—the message about the true way of living (v. 8) or the message that people do sin (v. 10).[42]

Persson provides a good paraphrase of what John is saying in verses 5–10.

But the message which Jesus told us and which we are proclaiming to you is this: God is light (sinless and pure), there is nothing at all darkness about him. If we were to claim to have fellowship with God, while living in the darkness of sin, what we are saying is untrue, and our behavior shows that we have rejected the truth God has revealed. But if we live in the light (do right things) just as God always acts rightly in accord with his pure nature, then we truly have fellowship with one another, and the atoning death of Christ makes us clean in God's sight and is removing all our sin from us. If we were to say that we never sin, then what we are saying is deceiving us, and we do not know the truth which God has revealed at all. But if instead we openly confess to God that we have sinned, then he will forgive us and remove all our wrong deeds from us and make us clean in his sight, because he has said he will forgive us and because he only does what is right. If we were to say that we had never sinned (done anything wrong), then by those words we are saying that God is a liar since he has said that all people have sinned, and that shows that we have not accepted his word so as to let what he says affect our lives.[43]

My little children, I am writing these things to you so that you may not sin. But if anyone does sin, we have an advocate with the Father, Jesus Christ the righteous. He is the propitiation for our sins, and not for ours only but also for the sins of the whole world.

1 JOHN 2:1, 2

3

Jesus Our Advocate at Heaven's Court

IF I WERE TO ADDRESS YOU AS "my little children," you would certainly wonder about me! It would not be appropriate for me to speak this way because at fifty-four years old at the time of writing this, I am older than some of you but younger than others of you. John, however, can use this term for two reasons. First, he was himself probably an octogenarian, at the very least. But John uses this word not only because of his age but as a term of endearment. It is characteristic of John to talk about the people to whom he is writing as "little children." Jesus referred to his disciples as "little children" in John 13:33. John came to be known for his great love for Jesus and for believers. Because of that love and because of his own advanced age at the time of writing, he refers to his readers as "my little children."

Jesus Our Advocate When We Sin (v. 1)

In verse 1 John indicates one of the purposes for his writing. What does the phrase "these things" refer to? This is probably a reference to 1:5–10. He reflects on what he has just written and perhaps worries that some will misunderstand what he is trying to say. There are two possible misapprehensions John may be concerned about. First, someone might be thinking, *If sin is a reality and it is impossible for me to live a sinless life, why bother? If I sin, big deal. God will forgive me.* John worries that some Christians will think sin is to be accepted as an inevitable part of the normal Christian life. I call this the "no big deal syndrome." Second, others might think, *As a Christian, I have liberty and am no longer under the Law, so I can do what I want to do. If I sin, God will forgive me.* I call this the "Rasputin syndrome," after the religious and political confidant of Empress Alexandra of the Romanov family in Russia at the beginning of the last century. Rasputin justified his own sinful lifestyle from a clever misuse of Romans 5:20, 21. There Paul says, "where sin increased, grace abounded all the more." Thus Rasputin said when we sin as Christians, we provide God an opportunity to exercise and magnify his grace, so sin away! Of course, both of these approaches are completely false. When large manufacturing companies provide on-site clinics for their employees, that does not mean these companies are encouraging accidents and illness! This passage might be considered something of a spiritual clinic with the caution, "Watch out that you don't sin! But if you do, you have an advocate with the Father, Jesus Christ the righteous one."[1]

What John means in verse 1 is: "I am writing these things so you won't regard sin as an inevitable part of the Christian life and so you won't presume on Christian liberty by thinking sin is no big deal." Christians are saved *from* sin, not *to* sin! If you think about it, Christians are caught between a rock and a hard place. We cannot reach sinless perfection in this life, yet we are commanded not to sin. The point is, our goal should be to live day by day without committing sin in thought, word, or deed. A tall order to be sure! Certainly Christians ought to be people who sin less after they are saved than they did before they were saved. The trajectory of our lives should be toward holiness and away from sin. Sin is a serious thing in your life. Don't take it lightly.

However, John is a realist about sin. He knows that Christians do occasionally sin. That is why he uses the word "if." "If anyone does sin" is a statement that is unqualified as to the person. Young, old, spiritually mature, spiritually immature, people or pastors—all are included. The ground is level at the foot of the cross. No one has privileged status as a Christian. But it is also a statement that is unqualified as to the sin. He does not divide up sins into categories such as big sins and little sins, mortal sins (which in Catholic theology would bring eternal damnation) and venial sins (which are forgivable). He does not speak about sins God will forgive and those he will not forgive. There is no statement about the multitude of sins or the magnitude of sins.[2] He just says, "If anyone does sin . . ." It is a statement unqualified as to the sin: any person, any sin. Think of it this way: our debt is paid, but we are ever incurring fresh debt, and we need fresh forgiveness.[3]

Why is it we can have our sins forgiven? John says it is because we have an advocate. That word "advocate" means "one who is called alongside to help in a time of need." John uses this word several times in John 14–16 concerning the Holy Spirit in the life of a Christian. The word there is translated "Helper." Here the word is rightly translated "advocate"[4] because it means not only one called alongside to help, but one who lends his voice in our defense, one who speaks up on our behalf. Jesus is our advocate. Therefore, as a believer you actually have two advocates. You have an advocate in your life indwelling you in the person of the Holy Spirit. He speaks on behalf of God to you and convicts you of sin. You also have an advocate in Heaven, Jesus Christ, who speaks to God on your behalf. As the author of Hebrews says in 7:25, as our High Priest and Advocate Jesus "always lives to make intercession for [us]."

Occasionally back in the 1970s I would watch reruns of the old *Perry Mason* television show. There is something about lawyers and courtroom dramas that fascinate us. That's why there are so many shows about lawyers on television. In all the years Perry Mason was on television, he never lost a case. Jesus, our advocate, is like that; he never lost a case . . . and he never will! William Barclay translates this statement, "we have one to plead our cause."[5] He is Jesus Christ, the righteous one. Because he is altogether righteous and paid my penalty on the cross when he died for my sins as my substitute, Jesus is my advocate. No other advocate do I possess. No pope or bishop or priest or the Virgin Mary is my advocate. No pastor or deacon or Bible study leader is my advocate. I have but one advocate, "Jesus Christ the righteous." The reason he alone is my advocate is because he alone paid the price for my sins.

In a courtroom scene at least four people are involved: the judge, the prosecutor, the defense attorney, and the defendant. Picture in your mind God as the judge. The prosecutor is Satan, and you are the accused. The attorney for your defense, Jesus, intercedes with the judge on your behalf. What a picture! Have you ever read Revelation 12:10? An interesting statement is made about Satan. He is called "the accuser" of Christians, and he accuses them before the throne of God "day and night." Apparently Satan has access to the very throne of God. He is called the accuser of the brethren, the prosecuting attorney. Then there is the defense attorney, Jesus Christ. When David Allen sins, I can imagine Satan rushing into the presence of God to accuse me. I can almost hear him as he quotes Scripture concerning the penalty for sin and how it is punishable by death. Then I can imagine my defense attorney, the Lord Jesus, saying, "Yes, Father, he is guilty of that sin. But, Father, I went to the cross and died for that sin. When he was a nine-year-old boy, through faith in me my atonement was applied to him and his sins were forgiven. I put my robe of righteousness on him. He is covered by my blood, and he is forgiven because he is my child." In the modern legal world, the defense attorney defends the defendant on the merits of the defendant's case. In John's thought, however, the merit on the part of the accused is entirely absent! All of the merit is on the part of the advocate![6]

In the legal world it is not permissible for an attorney who is involved in the case to be related to the judge. However, in Heaven's court it is perfectly legal! Jesus, the Son who loves the Father, and the Father, who loves the Son, serve as advocate and judge. Jesus our advocate can stand "face to face"[7] with God as Son in relationship and fellowship because he is divine.

In the legal world it is also impermissible for the defense attorney to be related to the defendant. But again in Heaven's court it is perfectly legal! Jesus can represent us as our advocate because he is fully human, calls us his brothers (Hebrews 2:12, 13), and, as Hebrews 4:15 says, "in every respect has been tempted as we are, yet without sin." Sometimes we may think that Jesus does not understand our predicament or what we are going through. But Jesus is fully qualified to serve as our advocate when we sin because he understands what it means to be tempted. As man he too was tempted; but he never sinned. Jesus' intercession for us is not temporary, and it is never interrupted. Though accomplished in time, it is eternally valid and continuous.

I'm afraid some of us feel like Robert Murray McCheyne when we sin. "I feel, when I have sinned, an immediate reluctance to go to Christ. I am ashamed to go. I feel as if it would do no good to go—as if it were making Christ a minister of sin, to go straight from the swine-trough to the best robe— and a thousand other excuses; but I am persuaded they are all lies, direct from hell."[8] They are indeed. The moment we are cognizant of our sin, may we flee to our Advocate, Jesus Christ. Speaking about Christians who sin, Luther sagaciously noted, "If someone errs and sins, he should not add the sin of despair. After sin the devil always alarms the heart and makes us tremble. For he hurls a person into sin in order that he may finally force him into despair. On the other hand, he lets some live smugly without temptation in order that they may think and believe that they are holy. . . . This is his cunning. He wants to make saints sinners, and confident sinners saints."[9]

Jesus Our Propitiation When We Sin (v. 2)

Now John explains in verse 2 why it is that Jesus can function as our advocate and forgive our sins. Verse 2 begins with an emphatic pronoun in the Greek text: "He himself and he alone is the propitiation, the atoning sacrifice, for our sins." No one in the universe except Jesus Christ can be the atoning sacrifice for our sins. Jesus is the one who through his death on the cross satisfies the honor and justice of God. Jesus' mercy and love extends to the one who sinned against God and violated that honor and justice. He not only was, but he is, present tense, "the atoning sacrifice for our sins."

It is vital that we understand what John means when he uses the term "propitiation." It is an uncommon word you don't hear every day. It is also uncommon in the Bible, used a total of four times in its noun form. It is a difficult word to translate because of the nuance of meaning it contains. One of the better translations is "atoning sacrifice." Jesus is able to be our advocate and to forgive sin because he himself became the sacrifice for sin.

To explain the meaning of propitiation, think with me about four words: wrath, justice, holiness, and love. Those words describe four characteristics of God. Have you ever wondered why God could not wave his magic wand and just say, "All your sins are forgiven"? God is a God of love, but he is also a God of holiness and justice. Because sin is an affront to God's holy nature as well as his sovereign rule of the universe, he has righteous anger toward sin. Paul summed it up in Romans 1:18: "For the wrath of God is revealed from heaven against all ungodliness and unrighteousness." Think about the sin problem for a moment. It is a universal problem. Paul says in Romans 3:23, "for all have sinned and fall short of the glory of God." You cannot atone for your sin or forgive yourself for your sins. If your sins are to be forgiven, someone who is without sin must pay the price for your sin. Our only hope of escape from the just penalty of our sin is if someone who is not himself under that penalty stands in our place as our substitute. There is only one in the entire universe who could do that and only one who did do that. No one other than Jesus Christ could provide the sacrifice. The reason God cannot wave his wand and forgive all our sins and allow everyone into Heaven is because sin is real, God is a holy God, his righteous anger stands against all sin, and justice must be served in such a way that sin is paid for. Jesus paid that price when he died on the cross to satisfy the penalty of the Law that condemned us. Why did Jesus die in our place as our substitute to deal with our sin penalty? "For God so loved the world, that he gave his only Son, that whoever believes in him should not perish but have eternal life" (John 3:16).

At the cross God's wrath, love, justice, and holiness met together. God's holiness makes sin an affront to his character and to his universal governance. God's justice demands payment for sin. God's love causes him to love sinners. Because of God's love, he sent his Son Jesus into the world to die on the cross for the world's sins. God's wrath was poured out in judgment upon Jesus, who bore our sin on the cross as our substitute. By his death on the cross for sin, Jesus satisfied the wrath and justice of God. Thus, when John says Jesus is "the propitiation" for our sins, he means that sin has been expiated (its penalty has been removed) and God's wrath is likewise propitiated, that is, turned away.

Jesus is the propitiation not only for our sins as believers, but also for those of the whole world (v. 2b). This verse raises the question of the extent of the atonement: for whose sins did Christ die?[10] There are two views on the subject of the extent of the atonement. Some believe that Jesus died only for the sins of those who believe in Christ. This view is traditionally called "limited atonement."[11] Others believe that Jesus died for the sins of all people.[12] These are the only two possible views on the question of the *extent* of the atonement.[13]

What does John means when he says that Jesus is the propitiation for the sins of "the whole world"? Those who believe Jesus died only for the sins of those who believe in him (the limited atonement position) suggest that when John uses the phrase "the whole world," he does not mean all people in the world. Rather, this phrase is given one of three different interpretations. First, some say John intends the phrase "not for our [sins] only" to refer to all Jewish believers, and the phrase "for the sins of the whole world" refers to all Gentile believers. Second, some say the phrase "for the sins of the whole world" refers to all kinds of people but not to all people individually. Third, some say "world" here means "the world of the elect." There are major problems with all three of these interpretations. It is impossible to determine that John's letter was addressed solely to Jewish believers. In fact, most scholars suggest that the readers were mainly Gentile or at the very least a mixture of Jewish and Gentile believers. The use of the adjective "whole" modifying "world" makes it difficult to interpret the phrase as referring to all kinds of people rather than all people individually. Also, as D. A. Carson noted, the word "world" is never used by John or anywhere else in the Bible to mean "the world of the elect."[14]

A face value reading of verse 2 would understand "the whole world" to be a reference to all humanity. This is based on two things. First, the use of the phrase "for the sins of the whole world" in this context indicates all the people in the world. "World" here is an example of metonymy, a figure of speech in which one term is used in place of another. John is using the word "world" to mean all the people who live in the world.[15] Notice John's use of "world" in 1 John 5:19 where it is clear that the word means "all unsaved humanity." This is important because contextually in 1 John the word "world" never means "the elect." Second, the use of the Greek adjective *holos*, "whole," further indicates that John intends to include all people in this designation. The death of Jesus on the cross was a death for the sins of all people. Jesus substituted himself for the sins of all humanity. That, of course, does not mean that everyone is going to be saved. This verse is not teaching universalism. This verse is simply teaching that Jesus is the propitiation for "our sins," meaning the sins of all John's intended readers, and by extension all believers. Jesus is also the propitiation for the sins of all humanity. This means that the sins of all people were imputed to Christ on the cross. Jesus satisfied the legal debt of sin for all, such that all humanity is savable should they meet God's condition for salvation, which is repentance of sin and faith in Jesus Christ. First John 2:2 makes an overt statement concerning the *extent* of the atonement: it is for the "whole world."[16]

What are the implications of these two verses for us today? If Jesus did not die for all humanity, what are we to make of passages such as John 17:21, 23, 1 Timothy 2:4, and 2 Peter 3:9? These verses all affirm that God desires the salvation of all people. Is our offer of the gospel a genuine offer to those for whom Christ did not die? Even more of an issue is the question, is God's offer of salvation through the preaching of the gospel a genuine offer from God himself? Second Corinthians 5:20 says that God is begging people through us, "be reconciled to God." Edward Polhill's point here is important for us to understand:

> Therefore, there cannot be a truer measure of the extent of Christ's death, than God's will of salvation, out of which the same did issue; so far forth as that will of salvation extends to all men, so far forth the death of Christ doth extend to all men.[17]

Without belief in the universal saving will of God and a universal extent in Christ's sin-bearing, there can be no well-meant offer of the salvation *from God* to all unbelievers who hear the gospel call.

I believe we can find at least five good reasons (motives) for evangelism and missions in the Bible: (1) our love for God, (2) our love for the unsaved, (3) obedience to Scripture, (4) Christ's death for the sins of all people, and (5) God's universal saving will. If 1 John 2:2 means that Christ died for the sins of all men, then when we preach and/or evangelize, we can look a congregation in the eyes or even a single unbelieving sinner in the eye and make the bold proclamation[18] of the gospel: "Christ died for your sins." Sometimes you will hear it argued that the offer of the gospel nowhere in Scripture requires telling people that Christ died for their sins. But in one of the central passages on the content of the gospel, 1 Corinthians 15:3, Paul tells the Corinthian congregation about the gospel that he received and that he preached to them *prior* to their conversion, and that gospel included the point that "Christ died for our sins." In Acts 3:26 Peter preaches to his Jewish audience, "God, having raised up his servant, sent him to you first, to bless you by turning every one of you from your wickedness."

Peter is telling his unbelieving audience that God sent Jesus to bless them and to turn away *"every one of you"* from their iniquities. The only way every one of them could be turned from their iniquity is if Christ had died for their sins. The free and well-meant offer of the gospel for all people necessarily presupposes that Christ died for the sins of all people, as John indicates in 1 John 2:2.[19]

One of my favorite writers of all time is J. C. Ryle. Listen to his convicting words:

> I will give place to no one in maintaining that Jesus loves all mankind, came into the world for all, died for all, provided redemption sufficient for all, calls on all, invites all, commands all to repent and believe, and ought to be offered to all—freely, fully, unreservedly, directly, unconditionally— without money and without price. If I did not hold this, I dare not get into a pulpit, and I should not understand how to preach the Gospel.
>
> But while I hold all this, I maintain firmly that Jesus does special work for those who believe, which He does not do for others. He quickens them by His Spirit, calls them by His grace, washes them in His blood—justifies them, sanctifies them, keeps them, leads them, and continually intercedes for them—that they may not fall. If I did not believe all this, I should be a very miserable, unhappy Christian.[20]

With respect to evangelism and missionary zeal, J. Stuart Holden's words concerning 1 John 2:2 are well worth hearing today:

> It would almost seem as though in every age Christian believers need to be convinced of the wideness of God's mercy and convicted of their own self-centered devotion. . . . Upon nothing less than the whole world, with all its sin and sorrow, does the eye of His pity rest and for nothing less than the redemption of every man did He give the Son of His love. . . . The entrance to the Kingdom may be "strait," and the pathway of Life "narrow"; but both entrance and pathway are wide enough to admit every creature on the terms of individual repentance and faith.
>
> It is failure to realize the breadth of God's love, while holding faithfully to the requirements of His righteousness, which explains the supineness of many Christians regarding the task of making Christ known to the nations. Did we but understand that it is their right to know of His death on their behalf we should feel the burden of guilt which unfaithfulness in this respect involves. The Gospel is not only our treasure but also our sacred trust. To divert to our own exclusive use, whether as individuals, as a Church, or as a nation, the blessings which we are commissioned to declare to the entire human family, is to discredit our own professions of faith. Saving apprehension of the benefits of Christ's death is proved by passionate self-sacrifice for its world-wide proclamation. "Not for ours only," is enshrined in every effective creed.[21]

Denney said, "Apart from a new interest in the Gospel, a revival of evangelical faith in Christ as the Redeemer, I believe we shall look in vain for a response to missionary appeals."[22] Denney went on to explain:

> But once He is seen in the character of propitiation, as a lamb bearing and bearing away sin, all limitations are removed. The only correlative of such a Christ is the whole world, and nothing vies us such a wonderful impression of what Christ was to His immediate followers as that they actually saw in Him as He died upon the cross a goodness that outweighed not only their sin but all sin, and could say God was in Christ reconciling the *world* to Himself. This is the consciousness out of which the missionary impulse springs.[23]

Our motives for preaching the gospel are not limited to the Biblical commands to do so. According to Denney, it is clear for some Christians, when it comes to the Great Commission in Matthew 28:18–20, "that for multitudes it does not constitute a motive at all. They are quite well aware of it, but they quite easily ignore it."[24] I have long been convicted that one of the greatest evangelistic and missionary motivations is the fact that God loves all and Christ has died for the sins of all humanity.

Luther expressed it in his own inimitable way: "Do not let your heart deceive you by saying: 'The Lord died for Peter and Paul; He rendered satisfaction for them, not for me.' Therefore let everyone who has sin be summoned here, for He was made the expiation for the sins of the whole world and bore the sins of the whole world. For all the godless have been put together and called, but they refuse to accept."[25] Leave it to John Newton to express it in his own poetic way:

I saw One hanging on a tree
In agony and blood,
Who fixed his languid eyes on me,
As near the Cross I stood.

Sure never, till my latest breath,
Can I forget that look;
It seemed to charge me with his death,
Tho not a word he spoke.

Alas! I knew not what I did,
But now my tears are vain;
Where shall my trembling soul be hid?
For I the Lord have slain!

A second look he gave that said,
"I freely all forgive;
This blood is for thy ransom paid;
I die that thou may'st live."

Thus while his death my sin displays
In all its blackest hue,
Such is the mystery of grace,
It seals my pardon, too.

"He is the propitiation for our sins, and not for ours only for also for the sins of the whole world" (1 John 2:2).

And by this we know that we have come to know him, if we keep his commandments. Whoever says "I know him" but does not keep his commandments is a liar, and the truth is not in him, but whoever keeps his word, in him truly the love of God is perfected. By this we may know that we are in him: whoever says he abides in him ought to walk in the same way in which he walked.

1 JOHN 2:3–6

4

The "Know So" Test

CONFIDENCE AND ASSURANCE are important human attributes. To lack either opens the door to trouble in life. The same is true in the Christian life. Trying to live the Christian life while lacking assurance that you are truly a Christian is like driving a car with the brakes on.[1] A common question Christians ask is, "Can I know that I really know God?" Or to put it in the common vernacular, "Can I know that I am saved?" Some people will tell you that you can never know. Many religious groups would tell you there is no way to know for sure whether you are going to Heaven or Hell (assuming they believe in Heaven or Hell). You just have to die and find out! Since Heaven or Hell awaits every human being when he or she dies, not to know where one will spend eternity is the worst form of ignorance and negligence! Your eternal destiny is not something about which you can afford to be ambivalent! There can be no more paramount issue in your life than the issue of whether or not your sins are forgiven and you are in a right relationship with God. If you don't know, you are in a precarious position. The religion of "I don't know" is the devil's religion. When you come to die, you will regret not making sure of this crucial matter earlier.

John provides us with a test of assurance that we are indeed in the family of God. Most of us don't like tests. Tests conjure up bad images in our minds: that horrible math final exam your senior year in high school, that stress test the doctor has ordered, or that dreaded driver's license test with a dour instructor in the car with you demanding that you display expertise in parallel parking. But some tests are actually fun. You can go on Internet sites and take an IQ test or a 1960s test, and you get to answer a lot of fun questions. But some tests are absolutely vital to take. John's test is that kind of test. John is going to give you an opportunity to test yourself as to whether you are truly a Christian.

Obedience to God's Commandments as a Test
for Genuine Salvation (vv. 3, 4)

John's test in 2:3–6 is the test of obedience to God's commandments. Notice how many times the word "know" occurs in this passage: four times in the ESV and in the Greek text. "By this we *know* that we have come to *know* him . . . Whoever who says 'I *know* him' . . . By this we may *know* that we are in him. . . . " God wants you to know something. Your salvation is not a matter of guesswork. You don't have to worry and wonder if you are truly a believer or not. God actually wants you to have assurance of your salvation. The first "know" in verse 3 is in the present tense in Greek. The idea is a progressive knowledge that is gained by experience. The sense is, "we are continually being able to know that we have come to know God." The second "know" is in the perfect tense, emphasizing that we have come to know him in a real, genuine, and complete way. Yarbrough captures the sense of the Greek verb tenses well: "This is how we maintain the awareness that we have come to know him fully."[2]

When any of the New Testament writers talk about knowing God, they are not referring merely to an intellectual apprehension of facts or truths. Knowledge of God is a robust concept that covers not only what you know about God, but also includes a personal relationship with God that begins with faith. It also includes an ever-deepening relationship and fellowship with God that is evidenced by love for him and obedience to him.

When John says, "by this we know that we have come to know him," what does he mean by the word "this?" He refers to the following statement: "if we keep his commandments." Notice that the word "keep" in verse 3 is also in the present tense and stresses continual, regular obedience to God's commandments. One of the ways you know you are a Christian is if you desire to obey God. If you have no interest in doing what God says, if God's principles and commandments are of little importance to you, that should be a red flag that you may not be a Christian. Assurance of your salvation is unattainable without obedience to God's commands.

One question we need to address is, what does John mean by the word "commandments"? He could be using the word in a more restrictive sense meaning a directive that would apply to a specific situation. Or he could be using the word in the sense of a directive that would be broad enough to have potential application for every situation. From examples of how John uses this word in his Gospel, most likely the latter meaning is in focus. Another question is, just exactly what commandments is John referring to in verse 3? From the immediate context of 1 John and the broader context of the Gospel of John, the answer is clear. John is referring to Jesus' command that Christians love one another (1 John 2:7–11; John 13:34; 15:12). But is this the extent of John's meaning?

Notice that John uses "commandments" in verse 3 synonymously with Jesus' "word" in verse 5. Furthermore, in verse 7, the beginning of the next paragraph specifically dealing with love for fellow believers, John uses "commandment" and "word" synonymously again. Basically anything that Jesus teaches (his "word") is his "commandment" for us to obey. When the young ruler asked Jesus, "Which commandments?" Jesus answered him that the Ten Commandments are summed up in two: love God and love your neighbor. Thinking that was easy enough, the rich young ruler informed Jesus that he had kept all these commandments from his youth. To him, it was a simple, ordinary matter of keeping the commandments. When Jesus told him to sell all he had, give the proceeds to the poor, and follow him, it became apparent that the young ruler lacked a deeper understanding of the commandments and what it meant to keep them. In fact, he was breaking the first commandment by putting his wealth above God. He was an idolater and did not know it!

In verse 3, there are three things we can know. First, we know that it is possible to know God. While some people don't believe it is possible to know God, the Bible is clear that God can be known because he has revealed himself to mankind in Jesus and in his written Word. Second, John says you can know that you know God. There is a difference between having salvation and being assured of the salvation you have. That's why sometimes Christians have difficulty in the area of having assurance that they are saved. Sometimes they have doubts. My eternal destiny is not something I want to leave hanging in the air. I don't want to guess about it; I want to know about it. That's true of a number of things in life, isn't it? I want to know whether I'm sick or well, whether the mortgage has been paid or not. If I want to know these kinds of things, how much more do I want to be certain about my eternal destiny! The third thing we can know is that obedience to the commandments of God becomes evidence that we know God. "Conduct is the best evidence of character. Conduct is to character what leaves and flowers and fruit are to a tree."[3]

John is fond of the word "know." He uses it thirty times in his letters. How many ways are there to know something? You can know by learning, and you can know by experience. Some of the greatest lessons of all in life are taught by experience. It is that second way of knowing that is the primary emphasis in this passage. It is a progressive knowing that only comes through experience, through the experience of being obedient through the commands of the Lord Jesus. The difference between a rookie and a veteran in sports is the difference between experience and lots of experience. The veteran who has played for many years has accumulated knowledge of the game by virtue of experience. Experience can only be learned by actually being in the game. The rookie may have more raw talent than the veteran. But because he is a rookie and doesn't have the kind of experience that the veteran has, he may not play as well. Why? Because he lacks the knowledge of the game that only comes by experience.

How is it we know that we know Christ? By keeping his commandments. The word "keep" literally means "to look upon something as your treasure and therefore to guard it as your treasure."[4] Your attitude toward God's commandments should be that they are your treasure. You carefully guard a treasure. That's the attitude we ought to have when it comes to obeying the Word of God. What does it mean to keep God's commandments? I think it means to keep them in two ways. First, the outward act is involved. Second, the inner attitude is involved. Those two things are always vital in the Christian life. When you live the Christian life, your outward conduct should flow from an attitude that characterizes your inner motivation. It is possible to obey and yet do it from an improper motivation in your heart. Jesus had a great deal to say about religious people who do outward acts with no inward reality to motivate those outward acts. Jesus called them hypocrites. "The heresy of all heresies of which teachers and Churches have been guilty, has been the thrusting of religious opinions and religious observances into greater prominence than moral purity. But beliefs unexceptionally orthodox are compatible with the life of devils, who believe and tremble."[5] B. H. Carroll was right on target when he said,

> A mere verbal orthodoxy is hypocrisy, and is more hateful to God and more hateful to man than avowed infidelity. I am quite sure that a strict application of this test would empty thousands of pulpits, hundreds of professors' chairs in Christian schools, and deplete thousands of church rolls. This emptying and depleting would not be deplorable but helpful. It would amount to a great revival.[6]

God puts the highest priority on obedience. This is clear throughout the Bible. Listen to Micah: "He has told you, O man, what is good; and what does the LORD require of you but to do justice, and to love kindness, and to walk humbly with your God?" (Micah 6:8). Listen to Samuel: "Behold, to obey is better than sacrifice" (1 Samuel 15:22). Listen to Hosea: "For I desire steadfast love and not sacrifice" (Hosea 6:6). Hear Jeremiah: "I did not speak to your fathers or command them concerning burnt offerings and sacrifices. But this command I gave them: 'Obey my voice. . . . '" (Jeremiah 7:22, 23).

Hear Amos . . . Isaiah . . . Micah . . . John the Baptist . . . and James ("Be doers of the word, and not hearers only"). John is simply repeating the echo that has come down through the canyons of Scripture: obedience to God is paramount.

Look at verse 4. Here is somebody who claims in summary "I have come to know Jesus." The one who says that and yet does not with some sense of regularity keep God's commandments John calls a liar! Some may read this and think, "I don't always keep the commandments of God. I wish I could, and I try, but sometimes I fail. In fact I failed just this week. Does that mean I'm not a Christian?" That's not what John is saying. We should not take John's statement and press it too far in either direction or we will get into something that is false that he is not trying to say. He doesn't say, "If you keep God's commandments perfectly and flawlessly, then you can know you're saved." Every Christian is going to fail to keep one of God's commandments in word, thought, or deed at various points. No one has reached sinless perfection. John has already made it clear that we will commit sin along the way. When we do, we have to apply 1 John 1:9 to our lives.

A little girl stole a doll from a store and hid it under her jacket. Immediately she became unhappy. She walked around for a moment, then returned to the shelf from which she had taken the doll and put it back in its place. But she still felt guilty. She had tried to undo her wrong, but her conscience continued to bother her. She told her mother about it and then said, "I don't think I broke one of the commandments, but I cracked one."[7] Christians are not immune from sometimes breaking God's commandments. We are not immune from "cracking" one on occasion either! When we do, we need to practice 1 John 1:9. What John is talking about in verse 4 is a consistency of life and a direction of life that is characterized by obedience. If I fail to love my fellow Christian while claiming to love God, I am a liar, because it is not possible to do both at the same time.[8]

The key to a proper understanding here is found in the verb tenses John uses. These present tense verbs describe habitual lifestyle. A Christian will have a trajectory of behavior that is characterized by obedience to God's commands. The word "walk" in verse 6 signifies a pattern of behavior. Although there will be times when you stumble, the basic trajectory of your life will be one of obedience to God if you are a Christian. On the other hand, if the trajectory of your life is away from God, you may still do some good things along the way. You may get a little prickly in your conscience and go to church one

Sunday. You may do a little good work here and there, but the problem is that the trajectory of your life is away from God. So the question is: what is the trajectory of your life? That is why John employs these present tense verbs. If the trajectory of your life is disobedience to God, yet you claim to know God, you are lying about it! You are self-deceived, and "the truth is not in [you]."

Some have winced at John's forthright, hard-hitting language. To call someone "a liar" is not politically correct these days. Maybe we should say about a liar that he is someone who has had an integrity operation![9] Such language is not exactly the way to win friends and influence people.[10] To this criticism I think I can hear John's response: "Well, Jesus said it! He called people 'liars,' and I recorded it in my Gospel! (John 8:55)." Actually, John is doing just what a pastor should do: "reprove, rebuke, and exhort" (2 Timothy 4:2). Remember also that John may have been writing to combat an incipient Gnosticism or some other false teaching that was evident in the church at the time he wrote. One of the things evidently being taught was "antinomianism," a fancy word that means "against law." The antinomians made light of sin in a believer's life. I am disturbed by the moral indifference of some professing Christians today. I'm not talking about the moral failures of Christians at certain points that are simply evidence of our sinful humanity. What I'm talking about is a mind-set and attitude in some people who seem to think that because they are eternally secure in their salvation, how they live does not matter much. This is the kind of thinking that John strongly refutes in verse 4.

Listen to F. W. Farrar practically apply verse 4 in his sermon on this passage:

> You know God if you are keeping His commandments; if not, you know Him in nowise. If you be wise you will give heed to these things. Have you an enemy? Then this very day forgive him. Have you wronged, or are you wronging, another? Then this very day make him restitution. Are you slanderer or a systematic depreciator of your brethren? Then cease to speak evil, and fling your unhallowed pen into the fire. Are you in debt? Live on bread and water rather than continue in that dishonesty. Are you idle? Go home and earn your own bread by the sweat of your brow. Are you a swearer? Conquer at all costs that profane and senseless habit. Are you a better or a gambler? Tear up your betting-book, and abandon that brainless and degrading excitement. Are you getting fond of drink? Then loose the grip upon you of that devil's hand of flame by taking the pledge. Are you living two lives, of which one is a mere self-deceiving hypocrisy? Then tear off your own mask, and in tears before Christ's throne entreat Him to make you true. Are you stained through and through with impurity? Then come with that leprosy to Him whose answer to the leper's cry, "Lord, if thou wilt, thou canst make me clean," came like an echo, "I will, be thou made clean."[11]

If we were to modernize somewhat Farrar's application, it might sound something like this:

> Keeping God's commandments is a key piece of evidence in the chain of proof of your love for God. If you have any spiritual smarts about you, you will pay attention. Do you have an enemy? Forgive him today! Have you wronged or are you wronging someone now? Make it right today! Are you a constantly bad-mouthing brothers in Christ? Then lay off your blog or Twitter account and turn off your computer and smart phone for a while. Are you maxed out with credit card debt? Then do some plastic surgery and live on soup and chicken pot pies for a while. (When I was in college in the 1970s, you could get chicken pot pies five for a dollar on sale.) Are you lazy? Quit lying around playing video games and look for a job. Do you struggle with cursing or crude language? Remember, we have to give an account for every idle word we speak, so clean out your mouth. Do you play the lottery or slink off to the casino? Quit trying to get something for nothing. For you to win, thousands of others have to lose. Are you a social drinker who thinks it's cool or even necessary to fit in with contemporary culture? Then try abstinence. Are you a two-faced hypocrite? Then get right with God and yourself and stop the Jekyll/Hyde charade. Bring all the junk and broken pieces of your life to Jesus. He will forgive you, heal you, restore you, and set you free when you walk in obedience to his will.

Obedience Illustrates Mature Love for God (vv. 5, 6)

In verse 5 John employs another one of his favorite terms: "love."[12] He turns from the negative expression of verse 4 to the positive of verse 5. "Whoever keeps his word" is a phrase that means "whoever is in the constant habit or lifestyle of keeping his word." That word "keep" is a military term that means "to guard." It means essentially to obey God's word. Notice how John talks about God's commandment and God's word. Is there any difference at all between God's commandments and his precepts, between his word and his promises? Not one iota. They are all from God. They are all the word of God. His positive commands, his negative commands, his precepts, anything that God teaches you from the Bible are all from God. Our responsibility is to obey.

John says, "whoever keeps his word, in him truly the love of God is perfected." What does the phrase "the love of God" mean? It can mean "God's love for me," or it can mean "my love for God." In this case context helps us. The context here is about our obeying God's commands because we love him. Therefore, the phrase "love of God" means our love for God. It is our love for God that is perfected.

The word "perfected" here in Greek means "brought to maturity."[13] It is important to notice that the phrase "is perfected" is in the passive voice and expresses the fact that it is God, not us, who perfects our love. Your love is a mature love when you love God, and your love for him is the ground for how you live. There are at least three possible reasons why people do what they do. Some people do things because they have to. Some people do things because they need to. Some people do things because they want to. A slave serves because he has to. A child at home obeys because he needs to—there are consequences if he does not obey. An adult goes to work on time because he needs to—he needs the paycheck. He may not particularly want to, but in order to get the paycheck he needs to. He has to follow the rules of the office, and he does that because he needs to. But neither of these is a mature reason for obedience. Mature obedience flows out of love.

For the Christian, it should not be "I need to," but "I want to." Listen to what Jesus says in John 14:15: "If you love me, you will keep my commandments." Do I keep God's commandments because I'm afraid of God—that he'll whack me if I don't? That's one reason to keep his commandments. Do students do what their parents tell them to do because they're afraid that they'll take away the keys to the car? If so, they don't obey them out of love for them but because they need to. Do you do the things you do because you love the authority who tells you what you should do? This is what John is saying. He is simply repeating what he had heard Jesus say fifty or more years earlier in that upper room before the Last Supper. John was there as a young man, and he heard Jesus say, "If you love me, you will keep my commandments." Obedience to the Lord's commands is the evidence of our love for him. External conformity to God's commandments should be predicated on our internal desire of conformity based on love for the one who gave the commandments.

Don't say that you love Jesus today if you are not obeying Jesus. If you do, John is going to look you square in the eye and say you are a liar. Don't say that you love Jesus if you are deliberately living contrary to his principles. If Jesus gave you some command, positive or negative, no matter what it is, if you love Jesus that is reason enough to obey it. You don't care who else does or doesn't do it. You don't care what other people think. Your number one goal is to please Jesus. You choose not to do something or you choose to do something based on what God says merely because God says it. That is the mature evidence of love in the life of a Christian. Some of us are obeying God's commandments because we have to or we are doing it because we need to, but we are not doing it because we want to. Love that bears the fruit of obedience is mature love. If you don't obey Jesus out of love, then whatever your love is, it is an immature kind of love. Most of the time when young people marry, their love is real, but it is not mature. Over time in the marriage, we learn how to mature in our love for our spouse. That is the way our relationship to Jesus should be. As we grow in our understanding of him and his love for us, and as we obey him, we grow in our own love for him. Our love for Jesus should be an ever-widening and ever-deepening love.

The principle of obedience can be used in the life of a Christian as evidence of genuine salvation. Obedience is not an *avenue* of salvation, for that would be a salvation by works, but obedience is certainly an *evidence* of genuine salvation, which is by grace. This does not mean that you can keep God's commandments in your own way and receive perfect love from God as a reward for your obedience. Rather John is saying that when God's love reaches you, it not only brings about your salvation, it enables your obedience. This love, as Leon Morris said, "does not leave people unchallenged or unchanged."[14]

Therefore John says in the latter part of verse 5, "by this we may know that we are in him"; that is, we know that we are related to Jesus. When John speaks of being "in him," he means to be in a state of salvation brought about by Christ coupled with being in a relationship with God (and Christ) that is based on faith and expresses itself in a right attitude toward sin and a right attitude toward other believers (love). What does the "this" refer to? It points to the rest of the statement in verse 6: "whoever says he [regularly] abides in him [Christ] ought to walk in the same way in which he walked." What you don't need to do is to put your religion on a bumper sticker or a wristband. Instead you need to put it in your life. John is saying that if you are a true believer, it ought to be reflected in how you live. Your life should be like Jesus'. You should pattern your life after him. Someone might say, "If I don't do some of the things they want me to do in my business, I may not be able to advance." Whom do you fear more—God, the supreme judge of the universe, or your boss? Who do you love more—your boss or God? You see, it all comes down to the issue of, is God real, is Jesus your Savior, and do you love him supremely? Ultimately everything comes down to that. It is not an issue of rules and regulations. It is an issue of love for Jesus.

In verse 6 John speaks about our pattern of obedience. Jesus, by his words and his life, teaches us how we should conduct ourselves as Christians in this world. When John uses the word "walked," he uses it as a metaphor for our conduct and lifestyle. How did Jesus walk? I think about the Savior's walk during childhood. He always obeyed his parents, the Bible says. As a man he always lived in obedience to his heavenly Father. His love for people, his unswerving faithfulness to Scripture, his moral purity, his selflessness, his servant heart—all this and much more illustrate for us how we should live. Jesus' obedience to the Father was voluntary, universal, complete, and based upon his love for the Father ("I do as the Father has commanded me, so that the world may know that I love the Father," John 14:31). Paul said in Romans 13:10, "love is the fulfilling of the law."

When John speaks of being "in him," he is using the language of union with Christ. The test of abiding union with Christ is imitation. In all conditions of life we are to conduct ourselves as Jesus lived: controlling our temper, curbing our caustic tongues, dealing with our corrupt desires, serving others, feeding and clothing the poor, standing up for the rights of the disenfranchised—humble, not domineering, a heart of sympathy for others, not one corroded with envies, monopolized by petty interests, or ruffled with small offenses, trustworthy in word, not one who stoops to professional tricks. To live as Jesus lived is to abide in him, keep his commandments, and thus walk as he walked.[15]

How do our lives measure up? Who is your pattern for Christian living? Some people want to pattern their lives after their favorite movie star or entertainer or musician or successful businessman or sports hero or parent, pastor, Bible study teacher, or other Christian. Certainly other Christians can furnish a good example for us, but ultimately our pattern for living must be Jesus. We should seek to imitate Jesus first and not other Christians for the simple reason that they are mere men themselves with frailties that may at any moment lead us astray. Where even the best of Christians "differ from Christ, it is our duty to differ from them. We may not pin our faith to any man's sleeve, for we know not where he will carry it."[16] As the author of Hebrews said, we must look to (keep our eyes fixed on) "Jesus, the founder and perfecter of our faith" (Hebrews 12:2).

To live as Jesus lived means to commit ourselves to follow him in full discipleship. Though we as Christians cannot duplicate the purity of the life of Christ, yet we can and should intentionally endeavor to imitate him in all walks of life. We don't have the option of choosing to act according to our own will. To do so "would be the highest invasion of the divine prerogative that could be imagined."[17] We lack the wisdom to live for Christ on our own strength. That is why we should abide in him and walk as he walked.

One of the popular Christian novels of yesteryear was Charles Sheldon's *In His Steps*.[18] It tells the story of the unusual event that occurred one Sunday morning in a traditional upscale downtown church. The morning service was abruptly interrupted by a shabbily dressed man who entered the door and made his way down the aisle. Eyes filled with disdain followed the unwelcome visitor. He got to the middle of the aisle, and the preacher stopped his sermon. The unknown visitor began to speak and said he needed someone to love him and take care of him. There was a moment of silence; then the man collapsed in the aisle and died. A few weeks elapsed when one Sunday the pastor got up and confessed he was ashamed by his own attitude toward the man who had so abruptly interrupted the service. One by one some of the members stood and said the same thing. After some discussion the people of the church covenanted together that before they did anything in their daily life, they would ask themselves the simple question, "What would Jesus do?" When they really began to take that question seriously, it changed their attitudes about life, others, and how they conducted themselves at their jobs and schools. The entire community was impacted by the transformation in the lives of these church people who simply began to ask in every situation, "What would Jesus do?" Wristbands and bumper stickers aside, in essence that is what John is telling us to do in verse 6.

Okay, now it's time to see how you did on John's test of right living based on obedience. Grade your own paper, that is, your own life. Did you pass? May God deliver us all from trafficking in unlived truth (as Howard Hendricks, distinguished professor at Dallas Theological Seminary, was fond of saying).

Beloved, I am writing you no new commandment, but an old commandment that you had from the beginning. The old commandment is the word that you have heard. At the same time, it is a new commandment that I am writing to you, which is true in him and in you, because the darkness is passing away and the true light is already shining. Whoever says he is in the light and hates his brother is still in darkness. Whoever loves his brother abides in the light, and in him there is no cause for stumbling. But whoever hates his brother is in the darkness and walks in the darkness, and does not know where he is going, because the darkness has blinded his eyes.

1 JOHN 2:7–11

5

All You Need Is Love

JUST WHEN WE THOUGHT we were through with John's test in 1 John 2:3–6, he whips out another one for us in verses 7–11. The first test was obedience. Test #2 is the test of love: do you love other Christians? If John were choosing hymns to entitle this paragraph, and his whole letter for that matter, he might have chosen "Love Is the Theme." The word "love" occurs no less than twenty-four times in these 105 verses of the letter. For John, as for all the New Testament writers, we might say love is the circulatory system of the church. The circulatory system in your body carries blood to every part of the body, nourishing every cell. If your circulatory system shuts down, you die. Just as this system is vital to your physical body, so the Church, the Body of Christ, has its own circulatory system: love. When Christians love one another, the body is healthy. When some Christians don't love as they should, spiritual arteries get clogged, and the Church is in danger of a spiritual coronary arrest.

Words are sometimes like coins. The more they are in circulation, the more they tend to wear out. The word *love* is like that. There is something odd about a word like *love* when it can be used for how you feel about your wife, your favorite sports team, a hobby, your enemy, and baked beans! In the Greek of the first century, four words could be translated by our English word *love*. Three of those four words occur in the New Testament. Occasionally the word *eros* is used, and it primarily means a physical kind of love. We get our word *erotic* from it. That Greek word did not always convey the notion of immoral sexual love, though sometimes it was used to refer to a lustful kind of love. Second, there is the word *phileō*. We see that word in our English word *Philadelphia*, the city of brotherly love. *Phileō* love can describe the kind of love that a friend has for a friend or a brother for a brother. The word that John uses for love throughout his letter is *agapē*, a word that the New Testament writers took from Greek vocabulary and invested with an elevated meaning.[1] This word was used to describe God's love for the church in Ephesians 5:22–33 and his love for the world in John 3:16. "God is love" according to 1 John 4:8, but his love is described in various ways in the Bible according to the diversity of relationships in which God himself is engaged.[2]

Love: The New Commandment (vv. 7, 8)

John writes about a new commandment, but then he says he is actually writing about an old commandment. John, please make up your mind! Is it a new commandment or is it an old one? I can hear John chuckle as he responds, "It is both!" Love is an old commandment because it was given in the Old Testament. It is a new commandment because Jesus gave it to the disciples when he said in John 13:34, "A new command I give to you, that you love one another." More than fifty years before John wrote his letter, Jesus gave that commandment. In one sense it is really an old commandment. But John says it is really not that old; it is actually new. It has a new emphasis, a new example (Jesus), and a new experience in our lives.

Sometimes people ask, "When the Bible tells me to love all people, does that mean I have to like them?" John does not say you have to like everybody. You're not going to like everybody, even in the church. I sometimes wonder if when I get to Heaven, God will put me next to the guy in my church that used to rub me the wrong way! I'm hoping he's not going to say, "David, for the first ten thousand years you get to live right here with that guy you found hard to love, the man whose personality clashed with yours and who bugged you all the time. When you learn to love him, then you can graduate to somebody else that you could not love as you should have." It is hard to love everybody, even in the church. But we are commanded to do so by him who loved us and gave himself for us in the greatest act of love: the cross. It has occurred to me that perhaps the Bible has so much to say about Christians loving other Christians because it is such a hard thing to do!

Agapē love is a love that is unselfish in nature, a love that gives and expects nothing in return. It is a love that says, "I love you in spite of yourself. I love you anyway, regardless of the circumstances." It is a love that puts the needs of the other person before your own. That is the kind of love God has for us and that we are to have for one another and for the world.

Notice in verses 3–6 that John uses the plural "commandments" twice. Now he uses the singular word "commandment" four times. Here John talks about "a new commandment."

On one occasion a young man came to Jesus and said, "Master, what must I do to inherit eternal life?" Do you remember what Jesus said? "Love God with all your heart and love your neighbor as yourself." Jesus was quoting the Old Testament at this point. He was referring to Deuteronomy 6:5 and Leviticus 19:18. So John says in effect, "I am writing an old commandment that is as old as the Old Testament. It is also a new commandment, new because Jesus invested it with new meaning by his life and death for us."

There are two different words for "new" in the Greek New Testament. One means new with respect to time.[3] The other word, the one John uses here, means new with respect to quality.[4] Sometimes something that is old and familiar can be given a freshness and newness like never before. Consider a piece of music. You've heard it for years and know the score well. Yet at the hands of a skilled conductor and a master symphony orchestra, that piece of music you have heard many times before becomes something new and fresh. Or consider a dish of food you've had many times before. But now in the hands of a culinary wizard that dish of food becomes a totally new experience. It's something old yet new. John says that is the way it is with love. It is something old and yet something new in terms of its quality and authority.[5]

In John 13:34 Jesus said, "A new commandment I give to you, that you love one another: just as I have loved you, you also are to love one another." John may be referring to this very statement from his Gospel. In John 13:35 Jesus continued, "By this all people will know that you are my disciples, if you have love for one another." Jesus did not say people will know that we are his followers by our doctrinal orthodoxy but by our love. The false teachers (Gnostics) John is combating said that knowledge was what was important. For them love was a secondary matter. Paul reminded the Corinthian Christians in 1 Corinthians 8:1, "This 'knowledge' puffs up, but love builds up." For Paul and John, knowledge of the truth is very important and is not to be discounted. But sometimes knowledge causes us to become proud and boastful. People will know that we are followers of Jesus not so much by what we know, but by what we do and how we love. So this new commandment he is talking about is both something old and something new. It is something old, having its roots in the command of God in Deuteronomy 6:5 and Leviticus 19:18. It is something new in terms of its quality and authority because with each day there opens up before our eyes new opportunities to practice this love that Jesus lavished on us and commanded us to show to others. This love is as old as the sun but as new as the dawn. Calvin cogently noted, "Every man's faith has its dawn before it gets to noonday."[6] We might say the same for love as well.

What is the connection between love and obedience to God's commands? If you love God, you should be able to love your neighbor. If you love your neighbor, you won't steal from your neighbor or covet his house or commit adultery with his wife or bear false witness against him. If you love your neighbor, all of the other commandments fall into place. If you really love your neighbor, then you're not going to violate any of the other commandments that have to do with your relationship with fellow human beings. That's why Jesus said these are the two greatest commandments and why all of the commandments hang on these two: love God and love your neighbor as yourself. *Agapē* love is not a syrupy sweet emotionalism. It is a disposition of the mind and will that loves unconditionally. It is easy to love those who love us. But John is talking about loving all people, whether they reciprocate our love or not.

This "old commandment" is one John's readers have had "from the beginning." There are three "beginnings" John may be referring to. First, it could be a specific reference to the beginning of their Christian experience. Second, it could be a reference to the beginning of the gospel as taught by Jesus himself and then his apostles. Third, it could be used by John as a general reference to what has been true for a long period of time.[7] Whatever meaning is intended, the command to love is foundational for Christianity.

In verse 8 the phrase "in him" means "in Jesus." The greatest definition of love is the person of Jesus Christ. If you want to see what love is all about, study the life of Jesus and you will discover that he is the supreme demonstration of love. Think about all the different kinds of people he loved. There was Mary Magdalene with her sordid past; there was the rich young ruler; there was Nicodemus, the religious Pharisee; there was Zacchaeus, the greedy tax collector. No group of people was more despised by the Jews than tax collectors. Nobody likes the IRS. Yet Jesus fastened his eyes of love on Zacchaeus up in that tree and called him by name. "Zacchaeus, today I will dine at your house!" Zacchaeus was shocked and thrilled at the same time. Here was Jesus, a religious man, willing to be seen in a tax collector's house! While Jesus was in his home, the icy heart of Zacchaeus began to melt by the warmth of Jesus' love for him. I think about Jesus' love and care for the woman at the well in John 4. Women were treated with little respect in Jesus' day. The social customs of the day prohibited Jesus from even speaking to that woman at the well. Yet Jesus' love for her brought her to himself, the water of life.

Think about those twelve disciples. If you were going to pick twelve to be disciples, you wouldn't pick them. There is impetuous Peter, sometimes speaking before he should, sometimes running ahead of the Lord, sometimes even contradicting Jesus. When Jesus needed him the most, Peter denied he ever knew him. Yet every time Jesus looked at Peter, it was with eyes of love. There was doubting Thomas. Thomas wanted empirical evidence for Jesus' resurrection. "If I can't see, I won't believe," he said. Yet Jesus loved Thomas. There is treacherous Judas, the one who betrayed Jesus. Yet Jesus loved Judas. If Judas had repented of his sin of betrayal, I have no doubt Jesus would have forgiven him. All of those twelve men, with all their weaknesses, internal disagreements, and failure to follow Jesus fully to the end, Jesus continued to love through it all.

We all know we should love our friends, but Jesus taught us we should love our enemies (Matthew 5:43–48) and then showed us how to do it. Jesus loved his enemies even when they were putting him to death. He prayed for his enemies, "Father, forgive them, for they know not what they do." He probably prayed this prayer not once but several times.[8] He prayed for the Jewish leaders who clamored for his death—"Father, forgive them." He prayed for the Roman soldiers who drove the spikes into his hands and feet—"Father, forgive them." He prayed for the Roman soldiers who gambled for his clothes at the foot of the cross—"Father, forgive them." Can you pray that today? If you walk up to a man on the street corner and tell him about Jesus and he spits on you, could you pray this prayer? Jesus loved even his enemies. God's love cannot be "hierarchialized," to use D. A. Carson's expression: ". . . if the different ways the Bible speaks about the love of God are not hierarchialized, why should the different ways the Bible speaks of Christian love be hierarchialized?"[9] When it comes to loving our enemies, it should not be! Listen again to Carson:

> . . . if Christians love Christians, it is not exactly the same thing as what Jesus has in mind when he speaks rather dismissively of tax collectors loving tax collectors and pagans loving pagans. What he means in these latter cases is that most people have their own little circle of "in" people, their own list of compatible people, their friends. Christian love, as we say . . . must go beyond that to include those outside this small group. The objects of our love must include those who are *not* "in": it must include enemies.[10]

Whether wealthy or poor, aristocratic or common, Jew or Gentile, Jesus loved people.

Everything about the life of Jesus exuded love. He lived love before the eyes of people, even in death. This world has never seen love like they saw in Jesus Christ. Jesus is the quintessential example of love.

The first church that was ever placed in western Pennsylvania was a little church built on the Beaver River by Moravian missionaries to the Delaware

Indians. The Moravians were among the most mission-minded people ever. Their founder, Count Ludwig von Zinzendorf, was converted to Jesus by standing in an art gallery gazing at a painting depicting the crucifixion of Jesus. He stood there and looked at the painting for many minutes weeping and finally came to understand that this was the Son of God dying for his sins. He was saved that day in that gallery. Years before Zinzendorf viewed that painting, the artist stepped into the gallery and drew a sketch of the face of the Lord that he wanted in the painting. Then he called in the girl of the landlady where he lived and asked whom that looked like. The girl said, "It looks like a good man to me." The artist recognized he had failed and tore the picture up. He drew another and brought the little girl back and asked the same question. She said, "He looks like a great sufferer." Again the author tore it up. He painted a third sketch and brought the girl in again. This time she responded, "The picture looks like Jesus." The artist knew he had found the face he wanted to paint, and he painted the picture of Jesus upon the cross. It was that painting that Zinzendorf wept over the day of his conversion in the art gallery. Our love for others, even our enemies, should look like Jesus!

But John says this new commandment of love is true not only in Jesus but "in you" (v. 8).

Jesus is our example, and we are the world's example. When Jesus entered the world, he became the light of the world. He is the true light that has appeared and is already shining. Spiritual darkness has been penetrated by Jesus, the light of the world. As Christians we are to let our light shine so that the world will see Christ through us. Today his light shines through all of his followers. In Luke 1:78 Jesus is described as "the sunrise" arising in our hearts. Have you ever gotten up before daybreak and watched the sun come up? Gradually, as the sun rises, the light begins to dispel the darkness. Jesus, the light of the world, has brought us the light of the gospel, and the darkness must retreat as his kingdom advances.

Loving Fellow Believers Is Walking in the Light (vv. 9–11)

In verses 9–11 John makes the point that our response toward other people is evidence of our Christian character. One of the evidences for knowing you're a genuine Christian is whether you have love for fellow Christians. You cannot say you are in the light and hate your brother. Notice that the tense of the verb "hates" is present and suggests habitual action. The tense of the verb is very important at this point. John is describing someone whose settled disposition and conduct is one of hatred toward his fellow believers. You can't have hate and love in your heart at the same time. It's impossible.

When we as Christians become angry with a brother or sister in Christ, if we are not careful, that anger over time can turn into resentment that, left unchecked, can give birth to hatred. It poisons our entire Christian life. I find it interesting in the Sermon on the Mount that Jesus equates killing with hating your brother. As a pastor I have heard Christian teenagers sometimes say, "I hate so and so." Adults say it sometimes, too. Those words should never pass across the lips of a Christian. They won't if they are never found in our heart in the first place.

John says if you say you are in the light but hate your brother, you are actually still in darkness. The moral and spiritual atmosphere in your life is darkness. It is difficult to determine exactly what John means by this statement. It could be that such a person has never truly been born again. Consistent hatred for people may evidence an unregenerate heart. In the subterranean streams of caves, there are fish that have lived in darkness so long that they have no eyes.[11] If you continually live in the darkness of hatred, your heart may be unregenerate. It is also possible John is referring to true believers who are failing in this area of love. You cannot say, "I know Jesus" and hate other Christians. If hatred characterizes your life, then you are in the dark spiritually and are not living according to the light of the gospel (1 John 2:3–6). John does not specify the reason or reasons for hating, but he certainly includes racial hatred in this passage. There is no place for racism in the church. There is no place for hatred of an individual because of his skin color.

I can hear some of you now. You are saying, "I don't hate any Christians in my church. I just don't like some of them!" There are two categories when it comes to disliking people: you can dislike them for a reason or you can dislike them for no reason. There are lots of reasons we may dislike others: they talk too much, they are too critical, they are know-it-alls, they have no personality, their personality differs from us, they are boring, they are physically displeasing, and a thousand other reasons. On the other hand, sometimes we just dislike someone for no particular reason at all!

I do not like thee, Dr. Fell,
The reason why I cannot tell;
But this I know, and know full well,
I do not like thee, Dr. Fell.[12]

George Bernard Shaw sent Winston Churchill two tickets to the opening night of one of his plays with a note: "Come and bring a friend, if you have one." Churchill wrote back that he could not come on opening night but would come on the second night, if there was a second night! Sometimes we

Christians fall into the trap of the Shaw-Churchill scenario. Even if we don't speak in such a way to one of our Christian brothers, we sometimes think like this! As William Barclay said, our brother cannot be disregarded; he is part of the landscape. The question is, how do we regard him? We may regard him as negligible, with contempt, as a nuisance, as an enemy, or as a brother. As a brother, his needs are our needs and his interests are our interests. He must be loved.[13]

In verse 10 John makes the first reference in this letter to one of the fundamental virtues of the Christian life: love. "Love" is the word that perfumes this entire letter.[14] John says two things about the one who loves. First, he "abides in the light." He is not only enlightened by the gospel and thus a true Christian, but he obeys the command of Jesus to love others and thus he abides continually in the light. Second, in such a Christian there is "no cause for stumbling." That could be understood in two ways. It can mean because we walk in the light we don't stumble ourselves. It is a dangerous thing to walk in the darkness. Have you ever gotten up in the night and did not turn on the light so as not to disturb your spouse? I walked around with a hole in my head for about two months from doing that once. I walked right into the doorpost. I thought I knew where I was in the dark. It is a dangerous thing to walk in the darkness! You will stumble! There could be a second meaning here. When you begin to hate others, you cause them to stumble. You become a stumbling block instead of a stepping stone. Psalm 119:165 says, "Great peace have those who love your law; nothing can make them stumble." Simply put, John says in verse 10 that living in the light means loving your brother.

In verse 11 John says three things are true concerning those who hate a brother. First, they are "in the darkness." Second, they "walk in the darkness." Character brings about conduct. People do what they do because they are what they are. Third, they are without direction in their life (v. 11). Hatred so zaps purpose and direction in life that you can't know God's direction for your life. Hatred takes you out of God's will. You cannot be in God's will and hate your brother. So John says he is writing a new commandment: love fellow believers. Jesus is our example. We are never more like Jesus than when we love like Jesus loved.

A young boy would get up on Sunday mornings and with Bible in hand walk several blocks to attend D. L. Moody's church in Chicago. The boy passed several churches on his way every Sunday. One Sunday a man who had observed the boy passing his own church that he attended week after week stopped him and asked, "Where do you go to church?" "I go to Mr.

Moody's church," the boy replied. "Well, son, that church is a long way from here. Why do you walk so far and pass so many churches on the way?" The boy's answer said it all: "Well, you see, sir, they just have a way of loving a fellow over there."

Do you love God's people? Do you love them enough to serve them? Do you love them enough to pray for them? Do you love them enough to worship with them? Do you love them enough to bear their burdens with them? Do you love them enough to forgive them? One of the finest sentences you will ever read on the subject of forgiveness is the one that Mark Twain said was given to him by an inmate of an insane asylum: "Forgiveness is the fragrance the violet sheds on the heel that crushes it."[15] "Greater love has no one than this, that someone lay down his life for his friends" (John 15:13). Jesus said that. Now that is love!

There is probably no better explanation of love given in the entire Bible than in 1 Corinthians 13:1–7. Here Paul explains in picturesque language the meaning of love.

> If I speak in the tongues of men and of angels, but have not love, I am a noisy gong or a clanging cymbal. And if I have prophetic powers, and understand all mysteries and all knowledge, and if I have all faith, so as to remove mountains, but have not love, I am nothing. If I give away all I have, and if I deliver up my body to be burned, but have not love, I gain nothing. Love is patient and kind; love does not envy or boast; it is not arrogant or rude. It does not insist on its own way; it is not irritable or resentful; it does not rejoice at wrongdoing, but rejoices with the truth. Love bears all things, believes all things, hopes all things, endures all things.

But there is no better *demonstration* of love given in the entire Bible than the love of God and Jesus demonstrated on the cross. John 3:16 makes this clear: "For God so loved the world, that he gave his only Son, that whoever believes in him should not perish but have eternal life."

There is a haunting photo in the October 1993 issue of *Life* magazine of a boy playing a flute. Ten-year-old Jeison lives in a charitable institution in Bogotá, Columbia. When you look at his eyes, that is, where his eyes should be beneath his long, dark bangs, you see only empty sockets. When he was ten months old, his mother took him to the hospital with acute diarrhea. Returning the next day, she was surprised to find that bandages covered Jeison's eyes and dried blood was spattered on his body. Horrified, she asked the doctor what had happened. He answered harshly, "Can't you see your child is dying?" and dismissed her. She rushed Jeison to another hospital in Bogotá. After examining him, the doctor gave the chilling news: "They've stolen his eyes." Jeison was the victim of "organ nappers." Eye thieves. Healthy eyes to be used for cornea transplants can bring a hefty price on the black market. Organ thieves in Bogota are not the only ones stealing eyes. There is someone who steals a person's ability to see in an even more tragic way: Satan.[16] He is the prince of darkness. But Jesus, the Light of the World, has dawned and shines in our hearts!

Hatred leads to spiritual blindness. No way can we walk in the light and hate someone else. If you want to punish an enemy, cause him to hate someone.[17] Although a Christian might temporarily succumb to the sin of hatred for someone, if he is a true Christian he cannot long live with such hatred. Those who exhibit ongoing hatred toward others simply make it clear by their habit of hatred that they have never truly come to know the Lord of love in saving faith.

I am writing to you, little children, because your sins are forgiven for his name's sake. I am writing to you, fathers, because you know him who is from the beginning. I am writing to you, young men, because you have overcome the evil one. I write to you, children, because you know the Father. I write to you, fathers, because you know him who is from the beginning. I write to you, young men, because you are strong, and the word of God abides in you, and you have overcome the evil one.

1 JOHN 2:12–14

6

Family Secrets

IN THE LATTER YEARS of his more than fifty years as pastor of First Baptist Church, Dallas, Texas, Dr. W. A. Criswell was fond of calling just about everyone, even men in their sixties, "lad." He could do that because of his extreme age. John did that as well. One of John's favorite designations for his recipients is "children." John uses this term of endearment in his epistles to describe all of the people under his leadership. For a period of time John was the pastor of the church at Ephesus. At the time of writing 1 John he was probably in his eighties, maybe older. By the time you get to that age, virtually everyone is younger than you are and can be referred to as "children." Whether you were a teenager, in your forties, or in your seventies, John could call you "little child." The term in Greek expresses the love John had for all to whom he wrote.

In fact, John uses three descriptive terms for the people to whom he writes: "children," "young men," and "fathers." Notice that he uses each of these terms twice. Your first thought when you read this is that John is dividing up the church into three groups of people according to their physical age. Thus children, youth, and adults are described.[1] However, upon further reflection another possibility comes to mind. John is dividing up the church according to their spiritual age. The new believers are the "little children," those who have been Christians for some time he calls "young men," and those who have been part of the church for a long time he calls "fathers."[2] But that does not appear to be what John is doing either. Several other times in this letter he addresses all the Christians with the title "little children."

Actually what John is doing is using a one-size-fits-all title, regardless of age, when he refers to the people to whom he writes as "little children." Then he is making a metaphorical twofold division of that group: those who have been Christians for a long time are the "fathers," and those who have been

Christians for a shorter length of time are the "young men." The inclusive group ("little children") is listed first and is used by John to refer to all believers. John then distributes this inclusive group into two constituent groups.[3] "Young men" refers to those who are younger in the faith; spiritual novices. "Fathers" refers to those who are more spiritually mature. Notice carefully that "young men" and "fathers" are never used by John for the entire audience. This does not mean that age plays no part, however. It would no doubt be true that there were people there, like John, who came to know the Lord during his earthly ministry or shortly thereafter and they would be well on up in years. Spiritually speaking, God's people are at different levels of spiritual maturity. Jesus referred to lambs and sheep when talking to Peter by the seashore in John 21. Paul talks about the "weaker" brother in his epistles. John's use of "young men" and "fathers" would seem to fit this paradigm. Spiritual maturity is a process that often has little to do with physical age.

Two kinds of spiritual infants are mentioned in the New Testament. First, there are Christians who are newly born again. Like newborn infants, new Christians need the same kind of things to grow. They need food. Peter tells how as "newborn infants" we need to "long for the pure spiritual milk, that by it you may grow up into salvation" (1 Peter 2:2). New Christians need love. They also need the atmosphere of a local church. Have you noticed how little children are ruled by their emotions, not their understanding? They get easily excited, are easily frightened, and are easily distracted. New Christians need the fellowship and care of more mature believers to help them grow spiritually. But there is another kind of spiritual infant mentioned in the New Testament. Paul refers to carnal believers, "people of the flesh" in 1 Corinthians 3:1. These are Christians who may have been believers for some period of time but who are stunted in their spiritual growth because of their carnality. The maternity wing is never intended to be a rest home. A nurse rocking a forty-year-old man with a bottle in his mouth is a pitiful picture that should never been seen in the local church.

Notice also that in the original Greek John shifts verb tenses the second time he addresses these groups. He shifts from the present tense "I am writing" to the perfect tense "I have written." Greek scholars have puzzled over this for a long time. One suggested that while John was writing, he got distracted, so he put down his pen and did not write for a while. Then he returned, picked up his pen, and said "Oh yes, I've already told you this; let me tell you again." I don't think that's the case. This tense shift is a stylistic device of a good writer who desires to emphasize something. The two tenses don't signal any significant change in meaning. On the other hand, the change is not merely stylistic either. The repetition highlights John's intensity of focus, which serves as an attention-getting device and an emphasis what he is saying.[4]

John Writes Because Our Sins Are Forgiven (v. 12)

John says in verse 12 that he is writing because[5] "your sins are forgiven." Literally in Greek John is saying, "your sins *have been forgiven*." This use of the perfect tense conveys the notion that "your sins have been once and for all forgiven and will never be brought up before God again." This is listed first by John because forgiveness[6] is the fundamental experience of the Christian life and the condition of fellowship with God. Forgiveness of our sins is the one thing we *all* have in common. Forgiveness of sins is at the very heart of the gospel and hence a centerpiece of apostolic preaching in the book of Acts (for example, Acts 2:38; 5:31; 10:43; 13:38: 26:18).

John wants to encourage his readers, so he adds a precious phrase: "for his name's sake." Their sins were forgiven because of what Jesus had done on the cross. God's "name" stands for his character. We are forgiven on the basis of who he is and what he has done. Our sins are forgiven, but not for our sake. They are forgiven for Jesus' sake. In other words, John is saying, "Your slate is clean, and it will always remain clean because Jesus died in your place." This is the concept of forensic forgiveness. Forensic forgiveness simply means that when you trust Christ as your Savior, God, through Christ, forgives you of your sin based on the atonement that Christ made on the cross. We need to make sure we understand the difference between forensic forgiveness and what's called filial forgiveness. When we sin as a Christian, we break fellowship with God, but we are still in the family. We do not lose our sonship, but we do lose our fellowship with God when we sin. When we practice 1 John 1:9 and confess our sins as Christians, the forgiveness we receive is a filial kind of forgiveness that restores fellowship, but our forensic forgiveness remains intact throughout. When John says, "your sins are forgiven," he is referring to forensic forgiveness.

God has forgiven our sins "for his name's sake." This is a familiar refrain in the book of Psalms. Psalm 23:3 says, "He leads me in the paths of righteousness for his name's sake." Asaph prayed in Psalm 79:9, "Help us, O God of our salvation, for the glory of your name; deliver us, and atone for our sins, for your name's sake!" My sins are not forgiven for my sake. They are not forgiven for anything I have done or deserved, but because of what Christ has done and earned for me! My contrition, my repentance, my faith could never earn God's forgiveness. They are the means for receiving that forgiveness, but the forgiveness itself is granted me "for his name's sake." God's forgiveness of our sin must be forever detached from our merit.

In the Bible the name of the Lord denotes generally God's nature and attributes. Many times in Scripture God's actions are said to be motivated "for his name's sake." For example, Ezekiel 20:8, 9 says,

> But they rebelled against me and were not willing to listen to me. None of them cast away the detestable things their eyes feasted on, nor did they forsake the idols of Egypt. Then I said I would pour out my wrath upon them and spend my anger against them in the midst of the land of Egypt. But I acted for the sake of my name, that it should not be profaned in the sight of the nations among whom they lived.

In Isaiah 43:25 God says, "I, I am he who blots out your transgressions for my own sake, and I will not remember your sins." God's divine honor itself is at stake if he were to refuse to forgive the sins of any repentant sinner who called upon the name of Jesus for salvation. We saved sinners are forgiven "for his name's sake." My sins, however massive, however filthy, were not too much for the great God of mercy to pardon! Because of the unsearchable riches of Christ's atonement, there is no single sin so great, no mass of sins so many that they are beyond the forgiveness of God! The disease appears fatal; I am a hopeless case. Yet the Great Physician heals on the basis of his shed blood on the cross and glorifies himself in the process![7]

It matters greatly in whose name I am forgiven if I am really forgiven! Public scandals of public figures have become almost commonplace. Wade Boggs was a five-time American League batting champion during his career, with a lifetime batting average of .356, and a 2005 Baseball Hall of Fame inductee. At the height of his career, for four years Boggs had a mistress traveling companion, Margo Adams. When news of the scandal broke, the affair had already ended. Boggs had already confessed to his wife. Shortly afterward, in a Barbara Walters interview with Boggs and his wife, Walters asked him, "What went wrong; was it the glitz and glitter of fame and fortune; was it the wicked other woman?" Boggs, sitting quietly before the camera and holding his wife's hand, said no to all of the above. In so many words he said he did what he did because he was a sinner. Walters seemed incredulous. She turned to Mrs. Boggs and asked, "And you actually forgave him?" Quietly Mrs. Boggs answered, "Yes." Barbara Walter's facial expression indicated that the clue phone was ringing, but no one was at home to answer. She simply didn't seem to get it.[8] "I forgive you" are three of the most powerful words in any language. When God himself speaks those words to you, they are based on the work of his dear Son, Jesus. It is for the sake of his name that we are forgiven.

A man was asked if he would like to make a donation to a particular charity fund in the name of his father who had died. The son at first contemplated giving a small amount, but then said, "No; if I give anything in my father's name, I must give as he would have given, I must give all I can."[9] We are forgiven today because of the great sacrificial gift Jesus made on our behalf. Our love, our service, and our devotion to Jesus should be in light of the great sacrifice he has made for us in bringing us forgiveness of our sins "for his name's sake." We might adapt a famous line in Luke 12:48 and say "to whom much is *forgiven*, much is required."

John Writes Because We Have Come to Know God (v. 13)

John continues in verse 13, "I am writing to you, fathers, because you know him who is from the beginning." Here he is speaking to the spiritually mature people of the church. John is referring to the fact that Jesus exists eternally; hence he "[has been] from the beginning." Though John is specifically referring to Jesus, it is not possible to separate God out of the picture here. Both context and John's theology indicate that to know the Son is to know the Father and vice versa. The key mark of maturity in this context is knowledge of God through Jesus Christ.

There is something about a mature Christian's walk with the Lord that comes from many years of trusting him. I see this in the lives of many senior adult Christians who have lived for Christ for many years. They just exude it. Charles Spurgeon wrote about an occasion when he was a young preacher and was talking about forgiveness in his sermon. His grandfather happened to be present. Spurgeon asked his grandfather to close the service in prayer. The elder Spurgeon came forward, put his hand on young Charles's shoulder, and said, "Charles can tell you about it, but I have lived it." Mature Christians tell me it really is true: "The longer I serve him, the sweeter he grows." Perhaps John is thinking about his own life now. He has walked with Jesus for over fifty years. When he was a young man, perhaps the youngest of the Twelve, he outran Peter to Jesus' tomb and found it empty. Now as a mature Christian who is also mature in years, John writes to the mature believers in the churches and says, "your sins are forgiven for his name's sake."

John now turns to address the "young men" in verse 13. Modern readers might be tempted to conclude that John was somehow sexist in that he does not refer to "mothers" and "young women." However, John's use of the masculine form here and throughout his letter in no way excludes women.[10]

He tells these "young men" they have "overcome the evil one." Christians are people who have overcome the devil through their victory in Christ. John does not want the younger believers to think that just because they do not have the mature years or maybe the spiritual maturity of some of the older saints they are of less importance or of less value. John tells them they know how to fight battles and win victories because they "have overcome" the devil. Here is that perfect tense verb again. "Young though you are, you have put Satan under your feet and have won the victory over him through Christ!"

Youth is typically a period of idealistic vision, high energy, strong passion, conflict, pride, and inexperience. The teenage years especially are like an emotional roller coaster. Inexperience is cured by living life. Pride is easy for young people because sometimes they think they already know everything! I remember my young adulthood when it began to dawn on me that the horizons of my knowledge were the frontiers of my ignorance! John appeals to the spiritual vitality of these younger believers in overcoming the temptations of Satan in their lives. So far they have fought a good fight. Fight on, John says, in the strength of the Lord and his Word.

Verse 13 concludes with an address to "children," this time with a different word in Greek than was translated "little children" in verse 12. This word is more common in the New Testament and generally connotes young age or the innocence that is associated with childhood.[11] John views all of his recipients as children who "know the Father." This is a hint at the theme he will develop in 1 John 3:1 and beyond when he speaks of our relationship with God as children to their father.

John Writes Because We Have Overcome Satan through the Word (v. 14)

John says in verse 14, "I write to you, fathers, because you know him who is from the beginning." Though it is true all Christians "know" God by virtue of the new birth, those who are spiritually mature have come into a deeper knowledge of the Father and know him with an intimacy that only comes with time. Notice here that when John mentions again the "young men," he does so with a slight nuance in what he says. In fact, he says three things about the "young men."[12]

First, he tells them they are "strong." What is one of the characteristics of youth? Strength. When my son Jeremy and I go play golf together, he can hit a golf ball farther than I can. The reason he can do so is he is stronger than I am. Youth is characterized by strength. John is saying, "Look, those of you who are younger in the faith, you are strong; and the reason you are strong is because the Word of God is in you." The second thing John says about the young men is they are strong spiritually because they know and use the Bible. Just as working out consistently with weights will give you strength, so working out spiritually with the weights of the Word will make you strong spiritually. Just as it takes discipline to work out regularly physically and thus enjoy the benefits, so too it takes discipline and study of the Word of God daily to be spiritually strong. As the psalmist says in Psalm 1:2, "his delight is in the law of the Lᴏʀᴅ, and on his law he meditates day and night." Do you delight in the Word of God? Do you relish in it? Do you desire to spend time in it? Does it permeate your life? Do you put it into regular practice? Is the Bible a high priority in your life? These are the kinds of things John is referring to when he makes the statement, "the word of God abides in you."

Third, as a result of their strength derived from their knowledge and practice of the Word of God in their lives, the young men "have overcome the evil one." "The evil one" here undoubtedly refers to Satan. Satan has no authority over your life unless you yield authority to him. You do not have to give ground to the devil. The authority you have in Christ as one who is united with Christ means Satan has no authority over you unless you give him authority and power over you. Notice John says that "the word of God abides" in these young men. This phrase "word of God" occurs numerous times in the New Testament and is ubiquitous in the Old Testament. It refers not only to the written Word of God, which we call the Bible, but to all of God's verbal self-expression including apostolic preaching and instruction.[13] The best way to defeat the devil in your life is to know and use the sword of the Spirit, the Bible, against him. That is exactly what Jesus did during his forty days of temptation in the wilderness. He used Scripture to defeat Satan. Jesus is our example of how we can go about defeating the devil as well. We must wield the sword of the Spirit, the Word of God, as Paul says in Ephesians 6:17. All believers should be characterized by spiritual strength. Don't be a pushover for the devil!

The secret of spiritual growth and strength is knowledge and practice of the Word of God. Knowledge of the Word takes the fangs out of the serpent, the devil; it takes the teeth out of the roaring lion, the devil, who walks about seeking to devour us (1 Peter 5:8). A fangless snake and a toothless lion cannot do much damage. Most people probably face no more than five major crises in all of life. But each day you experience a dozen trifling problems that must be defeated. Daily life is invaded with tiny warriors, the little things with which we do constant battle. You go to work and encounter a difficulty, a trivial annoyance, a lurking temptation. Yet if your mind is saturated with the Scriptures, the love of God, the daily presence of God in your life, you are equipped to win the victory over any temptation. You are not a soldier in enemy territory ill-equipped to handle the enemy; you are a soldier who daily can put on the whole armor of God (Ephesians 6:10–18) and who having done so can stand against all the schemes of the devil.

In these verses, John is preparing the church for what he wants to say in verses 15–17. Because of who and what they are, they must not yield to the temptation of loving the world, of putting anything in this world system ahead of God in his life. John has confidence in his readers, and he wants them to have confidence as well. These verses remind us of who we are as Christians. Short of carnality, regardless of our level of spiritual maturity, certain things are true about us. Our sins have been forgiven. We have come to know God through a saving relationship with Christ. But certain things ought to be consistently true about us as well. We should be strong spiritually. We should remain daily in the Word so we can be strong. We should overcome Satan's influence in our lives by means of our knowledge and practice of the Word. May God help us all to live up to who we are in the family!

Do not love the world or the things in the world. If anyone loves the world, the love of the Father is not in him. For all that is in the world—the desires of the flesh and the desires of the eyes and pride of life—is not from the Father but is from the world. And the world is passing away along with its desires, but whoever does the will of God abides forever.

1 JOHN 2:15–17

7

Don't Decorate Your Cell

A GROUP OF FIRST GRADERS had just completed their tour of a hospital. One of the children asked, "How come the people here are always washing their hands?" The nurse laughed and said, "For two reasons: they love health and they hate germs."[1] In more than one area of life love and hate go together. There is a right kind of love for Christians to have and a wrong kind of love—a love that God hates.

What exactly does John mean when he says, "Stop loving the world" (literal translation).[2] Does that mean I can't enjoy ice cream or popcorn? How about an afternoon at the ballpark? Should I prepare to move into a monastery or nunnery? Before you don your robe and head off to seclusion, hold on a minute. Charles Simeon wisely reminds us that in examining this passage, we need to be discriminatory and proceed with caution. On the one hand, we need to be careful we don't interpret John's prohibition more strictly than God intended; on the other hand we should not give it such a latitude that would in essence dilute its force. "A man who lives in monastic seclusion will be ready to say, that this passage forbids all intercourse with the world: whilst a person living in an unrestrained commerce with the world, will see in it nothing that condemns the most unrestrained compliance with the maxims and habits of the world, provided they be not palpably and grossly immoral."[3]

Do Not Love the World (v. 15a)

There are two key words in this passage: "love" and "world." Both of these words must be unpacked as to their meaning to understand John's point. "World" (*kosmos*) is used in three primary ways in the New Testament.[4] It is sometimes used to refer to Planet Earth. We sometimes talk about "the world" when we mean the earth. That is not the meaning here. It is often used to refer to people, as in John 3:16: "for God so loved the world." That is not the meaning here either. Sometimes the word "world" is used to refer to the organized evil system with its principles and its practices, all under the authority of Satan, which includes all teachings, ideas, culture, attitudes, activities, etc., that are opposed to God. A fixation on the material over the spiritual, promotion of self over others, pleasure over principle—these are just a few descriptors of the world system John is talking about. The word "world" here means everything that opposes Christ and his work on earth. Jesus called Satan "the ruler of this world" (John 14:30; 16:11), and Paul called him "the god of this world" (2 Corinthians 4:4). In Luke 16:8 Jesus referred to all unsaved people as "the sons of this world."

In 1961 ABC's *Wide World of Sports* aired for the first time and ran on television for the next thirty-seven years, the longest-running sports show ever. ABC continues to air sports events under this banner. The world of sports today is a multibillion dollar industry with teams, owners, players, coaches, games, rules, events, fans, stadiums, equipment, schedules, merchandise, memorabilia, and a host of other commodities. It is a huge conglomerate, a worldwide enterprise. Think about the world of fashion today. Designers, clothing, cosmetics, wholesale and retail outlets, advertising, thin but buxom models sporting wings and wearing Victoria's Secret underwear all contribute to the billion-dollar world of fashion. The world of sports and fashion are a small microcosm of the kind of thing John means when he talks about the world system that characterizes all cultures and includes everything that stands apart from God.

Let's also unpack that word "love." We use the word *love* in so many different contexts in the English language. We love pizza. We love football. We love our job. We love our spouse. We love fishing, hunting, food, art, or in my neck of the woods the Mavericks, the Rangers, and sometimes the Cowboys. With all this variety, what exactly does *love* mean? In its essence love is two things: a desire for something and a commitment to something. If you love pizza, you desire it. I love Schlotszky's sandwiches. Sometimes I just get a craving for one. I will sometimes drive out of my way just to get a Schlotszky's sandwich. If you don't like Schlotszky's, you may think that's nuts! But then you would drive out of *your* way for whatever you were craving, right? Whatever it is you desire and whatever you're committed to, that's where your time and resources will go. If you love football, that's where your time and resources will go. If you love hunting or fishing, that's where your time and resources will go. If you love your spouse, you desire to spend time with her and you are committed to her. Love is more than an emotional feeling. Love requires a commitment of time and resources. If you love the world's system that John is talking about, that's where your time and resources will go.

The word John uses is the verb form of *agapē*, and it is a word that the Christians took from common Greek vocabulary and invested with new meaning.[5]

John hits his readers right between the eyes in verse 15 with a knockout punch. It is significant that the exhortation to stop loving the world is the first overt imperative in the letter. John assumes that to some extent some of his readers were guilty of loving the world system. John also exhorts Christians not to love "the things in the world." Some Christians had become too cozy with the world system. They had begun to compromise with the world. They were giving too much ground to the world's way of thinking and acting. Things in the world began to look more and more glamorous. Some Christians had taken their eyes off Jesus and put them on the things of the world. In the next verse John will further explain just what kind of things he has in mind. At this point he tells us we should not love the world system, nor should we love anything associated with the world system. Doesn't Scripture teach that friendship with the world is hatred toward God (James 4:4)? Loving the world is the sin of allowing your appetites, ambitions, and conduct to be fashioned according to earthly values. "Lord, let me not think that the world is a *place*! That would lead me to underrate my difficulties. If the world were any particular place, I could easily get rid of it. The world is within me. I can carry it about to any place, and the place to which I carry it immediately *becomes* worldly."[6]

What are the telltale signs of loving the world? First, when the world, or any object in it, so engrosses our thoughts to such a degree that it excludes serious reflection on the things of God, we are guilty of loving the world. When the world is our constant associate, the last companion of our thoughts at night and the first when we awaken in the morning, we are loving the world. Second, when the things of the world engross most or all of our conversation, we are loving the world. Third, if we are unwilling to part with it when need be, or to give it or anything in it up to God's purposes, we are loving the world. Fourth, discontentment with our portion of the world's goods proclaims a criminal love for it. If we secretly grieve because we are not blessed with every earthly convenience or delight that others possess, we are loving the world. If we are not entirely willing that God should govern his own world and distribute his own gifts as he pleases and to whom he pleases, it proves that we pay homage to the world, which belongs only to God. Fifth, when we pursue it with greater zeal and enjoy it with higher relish than we do serving God and enjoying his favor, we are loving the world. Sixth, if we pride ourselves in earthly distinctions, if we expect great deference and resent the least contradiction or slight from others, we are loving the world. Seventh, when we seek to acquire or retain its objects in a wrong manner or by unwarrantable means, we are loving the world.[7]

If you are married, do you remember the day you proposed? You declared your love and asked her to be your wife. Suppose she responded like this: "Yes, I will marry you, live with you, work beside you, but you need to know from the outset that I love somebody else. You must allow me to continue my love for him." You would be speechless! You would also be the world's biggest moron if you married her! Imagine how Jesus feels when we say, "I will serve you, go to church, read the Bible, and pray daily. I will do my best, but you must remember, I love the world!" Ridiculous! You cannot be into the world's system and be into God at the same time.

The Impossibility of Loving God and the World Simultaneously (vv. 15b, 16)

John provides two reasons for his command in the rest of the passage. The first is found in verses 15, 16: it is impossible to love God and the world at the same time. Love for the world is not compatible with love for God. "If anyone loves the world, the love of the Father is not in him." Look at that phrase "the love of the Father." What John means is our love for the Father.[8] In verse 16 John explains why it is impossible to love God and the world system at the same time: everything in the world system is not from God; it does not have its source or origin in God. Because this is true, it is impossible for any Christian to love God and the world at the same time. That is John's point. Remember what Jesus said: "No one can serve two masters, for either he will hate the one and love the other, or he will be devoted to the one and despise the other. You cannot serve God and money" (Matthew 6:24). John may have been thinking about what Jesus said when he wrote this.

Some things are incompatible. Certain kinds of clothes are incompatible. I have a picture of myself when I preached back in 1978. I was wearing a pair of white patent shoes, a pair of brown and yellow checked pants, a dark brown shirt, a plaid jacket, and a tie with bright yellow on it, among other colors. I was twenty-one years old . . . and single. Some things just don't go together; they are not compatible. You can't take a shower and play baseball at the same time. You can't whistle and keep your lips closed at the same time. These things are simply incompatible. You can't love God and the world at the same time. As Augustine said, to love the world and not God would be like a maiden who loved the ring her lover had given her and cared nothing for him who gave it.[9]

It should be obvious to us just how inconsistent it would be to love God and the world at the same time. Human beings are simply not constituted in such a way as to love different, contrary entities supremely yet simultaneously. To obey one necessitates disobeying the other. Since we cannot love God when we love the world, we reveal ourselves to be idolaters. What is idolatry if it is not worshipping the creature and not the Creator? (Notice how John ends this letter with a reference to idolatry and a command to "keep yourselves from idols"!)

Verse 16 defines what the world system consists of with three parallel phrases: our fleshly desires, our desire for things we see, and the boastful pride of life. Let's unpack each of those phrases. When John talks about "the desires of the flesh,"[10] the word translated "desires" (ΩΙΥ, "lust") means "inordinate desire."[11] In our vocabulary "lust" is usually taken in reference to sexual desire and not chocolate cake. Here it includes but is not limited to sexual lust. The etymology of the word in Greek is "to be hot after something." In this context, lust is any sinful desire that is contrary to the will of God. It could be a woman, a car, a position, a dress, or any number of things. What does "flesh" mean in this statement? It is human nature corrupted by sin. Apart from the grace of God, the flesh offers a bridgehead to sin in our life. "Desires of the flesh" describes what it means to live life dominated by the senses. In the extreme, it would include "gluttonous in food, . . . slavish in pleasure, lustful and lax in morals, selfish in the use of possessions; regardless of all the spiritual values; extravagant in the gratification of material desires."[12] "The desires of the flesh" includes all desires centered in your nature without regard to the will of God. It is that which constantly fights against the things of God in your life. The lust of the flesh is contrary to the desire to do the will of God. In Galatians 5:19–24 we see probably the most familiar of all passages on the flesh versus the Spirit motif. Paul lists several examples of the deeds of the flesh followed by the familiar fruit of the Spirit. The contrast is stark!

Those who are "loving the world" and giving in to "the desires of the flesh" can expect to see these kinds of attitudes and actions characterizing their lives. On the other hand, those who are not loving the world system but rather are controlled by the Holy Spirit can expect to see the fruit of the Spirit in their lives. As difficult as it is, Paul instructs us in Romans 13:14 to "put on the Lord Jesus Christ, and make no provision for the flesh." Calvin used this Pauline passage to define the lust of the flesh: "When worldly men, desiring to live softly and delicately, are intent only on their own convenience."[13] Calvin is spot-on here because much of our flesh craves its own convenience. As the great Puritan Richard Sibbes said, "This flesh of mine is ready to betray me into the hands of the world and of the devil, therefore there must be a marvelous strong guard. I must not suffer my affections to rove."[14]

Flesh	Spirit
sexual immorality	love
impurity	joy
sensuality	peace
idolatry	patience
sorcery	kindness
enmity	goodness
strife	faithfulness
jealousy	gentleness
fits of anger	self-control
rivalries	
dissensions	
divisions	
envy	
drunkenness	
orgies	

The second phrase, "the desires of the eyes,"[15] means we desire what we see. In Scripture the eyes are the primary organ of perception and often the principal avenue of temptation. We see that in the case of David who saw Bathsheba, lusted after her, and later committed adultery with her. David should have read and practiced Job 31:1: "I have made a covenant with my eyes not to look lustfully at a young woman" (QLY). As in the former phrase "the desires of the flesh," so here again sexual lust is only a fraction of the meaning of the phrase. In Matthew 6:22 Jesus asserts that "the eye is the lamp of the body," adding, "If your eye is bad, your whole body will be full of darkness" (v. 23). Your eyes are closely related to your heart! Proverbs 17:24 says, "The discerning sets his face toward wisdom, but the eyes of a fool are on the ends of the earth." The psalmist says of the arrogant in Psalm 73:7, "Their eyes swell out through fatness; their hearts overflow with follies."

"The desires of the eyes" describes someone who is captivated by an outward show of materialism. See a new car, must have it. See a dress, must have it. See a position, must have it.

Cars, dresses, positions, etc., are not in and of themselves sinful. But the inordinate desire to have what we see is sinful. An inordinate desire to have anything contrary to God's will is sinful.

Since nature itself is a part of the created world, it is possible to have a love for it rather than love for God. C. S. Lewis wisely warned us about trying to find a direct path through nature to an increasing knowledge of God. The path peters out almost at once. We can't get through that way. We must make a detour from the hills and woods and go back to our Bible. Otherwise the love of nature will turn into some form of nature religion, which even if it does not lead to paganism leads to a great deal of nonsense. Nature "dies" on those who try to live for a love of nature.[16]

The third phrase, "pride of life,"[17] describes the arrogant spirit of self-sufficiency. It expresses the desire for recognition, applause, status, and advantage in life. The phrase describes the pride in what life can offer you. The Greek word translated "pride" describes the pretentious braggart. This is the guy who has zero in his bank account but tells you he has all the money in the world. This is the man who always wants to "one up" you. This is the person who, when you tell him about a trip you took across the state line, will tell you about his trip to Europe. If your house has 1,900 square feet, his has 2,900. The root of this word in Greek means "a wandering about" and was the word used in the first century to describe "wandering quacks who could be found shouting their wares in every market-place and in every fair-ground, and offering to sell men their patent cure-alls."[18]

Everything we desire to have, enjoy, or pride ourselves upon is the "pride of life." Everything from sensualism and self-indulgence to self-conceit, the ungodly gratification of fleshly appetites, mental self-satisfaction, egotistic arrogance—this is the "pride of life." All false views of pleasure, false views of possession, false views of superiority—this is the "pride of life."[19] Human egotism is like the mirror-lined walls in the old barber shops I went to when I was a kid. Sitting in the barber's chair, you see yourself reflected a seemingly infinite number of times. This is the pride of life—a millionfold reflection of self—I, I, I everywhere.

There is an interesting correlation between these three broad categories and Eve's temptation by Satan in the garden of Eden. Genesis 3:6 says: "So when the woman saw that the tree was good for food, and that it was a delight to the eyes, and that the tree was to be desired to make one wise . . ." Notice that the tree was "good for food" (lust of the flesh), "a delight to the eyes" (lust of the eyes), and "desired to make one wise" (pride of life). There is also something of a correlation between Matthew's account of Jesus' temptation by Satan in the wilderness for forty days and these three broad categories:

> Then Jesus was led up by the Spirit into the wilderness to be tempted by
> the devil. And after fasting forty days and forty nights, he was hungry. And
> the tempter came and said to him, "If you are the Son of God, command

these stones to become loaves of bread." But he answered, "It is written, 'Man shall not live by bread alone, but by every word that comes from the mouth of God.'"

Then the devil took him to the holy city and set him on the pinnacle of the temple and said to him, "If you are the Son of God, throw yourself down, for it is written, 'He will command his angels concerning you,' and 'On their hands they will bear you up, lest you strike your foot against a stone.'" Jesus said to him, "Again it is written, 'You shall not put the Lord your God to the test.'"

Again, the devil took him to a very high mountain and showed him all the kingdoms of the world and their glory. And he said to him, "All these I will give you, if you will fall down and worship me." Then Jesus said to him, "Be gone, Satan! For it is written, 'You shall worship the Lord your God and him only shall you serve.'" (Matthew 4:1–10)

The first temptation is an appeal to the lust of the flesh. The second temptation roughly corresponds to the lust of the eyes. The third temptation appeals to the pride of life. Phillips Brooks said it well in the last sentence of his sermon on this phrase "pride of life" in 1 John 2:16: "Outside of His gospel and His service there is the pride of life, and the pride of life is death."[20]

There is a time in your life, especially when you are younger, when the desires of the flesh exercise immense influence and subtle power over your imagination. They seem to promise illimitable delight and inexhaustible pleasure. Everywhere alluring forms appear enticing the flesh with potential intoxicating joys.[21] Every Christian has three great enemies: the world, the flesh, and the devil. Their combined power is impossible to overcome in our own strength. Loving God first and foremost, staying daily in his Word, and walking daily in the Spirit is the only way to win the victory over these three enemies. To ignore these three great enemies is like ignoring gravity and slipperiness while scaling the icy slopes of the Swiss Alps. You would before long find yourself at the bottom of a precipice.[22] Worldliness is what our culture does to make sin seem either less sinful or not sinful at all. Worldliness is what our culture does to make righteousness look odd, strange, or quirky.

It is evident from what John says in verse 16 that worldliness is more than a list of do's and don'ts. "I don't drink, I don't cuss, I don't chew, and I don't go with girls who do!" Many Christians fall into the trap of negative holiness. They think if they just refrain from certain activities, places, etc., they will not be worldly. But there is a problem! Different individuals' lists of do's and don'ts differ! Apparently it is considered worldly in Finland to whistle![23] Certainly there are some activities, places, etc., from which we Christians should refrain. That is not in question. But loving the world is not merely a matter of keeping somebody's rules. Loving the world begins in the heart before it is ever lived out in our lives.

John is teaching us that our relationship to this world system must be one of opposition. The world is ever opposed to the things of Christ. That means it will be opposed to you if you live for Christ! Our relationship to the world must be guided by Biblical principles that are inescapably unpopular with the world. The world ever loves its own and hates those who belong to Christ. This shouldn't surprise us in the least. It is exactly what Jesus said would happen in his final words to the disciples before his crucifixion (John 15:18–25). D. L. Moody shook North America for God during the nineteenth century. He was known for his down-home style and simple theology. When a man approached him and said, "Mr. Moody, now that I am converted do I have to give up the world?" Moody responded, "No, sir, you don't have to give up the world. If you give a good ringing testimony for the Son of God, the world will give you up pretty quick. They won't want you."[24]

The Impermanence of the World and the Permanence of Those Doing the Will of God (v. 17)

Verse 17 states the second reason why we are not to love the world system—it is impermanent: "And the world is passing away, along with its desires." The world system has a built-in design flaw—it is temporary. It is already on the way out. "Desires" here is used metonymically for all things in the world system that can be desired.[25] The tense and voice of this word in Greek is expressive of the fact that the world system is in the process right now of passing away in and of itself. One use of this word (*paragetai*) in the first century had to do with the theaters of the day. At the conclusion of a scene the curtain would come down, and the props would be picked up and moved offstage. In preparation for the next scene, new props would quickly be brought onstage. John's point is that the world system opposed to God is like a scene in a play. When the scene comes to an end, the curtain falls and the props are removed. The focus is on impermanence. The world system is passing away. All its desires directed to, stimulated by, and fed or starved on the fleeting things of this outward life are passing away.[26]

What if an investor came to you and said, "Have I got a deal for you! If you make an investment I will guarantee you a return for the first two or three years, but after that, you will lose your shirt and go bankrupt." No one in their right mind would invest in something that they knew would go belly-up. Loving the world is a bad investment. The world is passing away. Over everything in the world God has written, "Dust you are, and to dust you will return."

When you think about it, what really lasts forever? The knowledge of today will be the ignorance of tomorrow. If Aristotle, Galileo, or Isaac Newton were alive today, they would have to go to school again. Once it took a century to thrust the most brilliant discoveries into the dust heap of historical oblivion; now a single decade or even a year will do it. The powerful nations of yesteryear are now nothing more than a historian's or archaeologist's interest. Nothing lasts. What you know, what you acquire, and what you achieve will never last. Only God, his kingdom, and those who are rightly related to him will never fade throughout eternity. The world is passing away, but he who does the will of God abides forever.

Charles Dutton, the character actor, spent seven years in prison for manslaughter as a young man. While there, he developed an interest in acting and participated in some plays. Upon his release, he got small parts on Broadway and hit it big in the Broadway production *The Piano Player*. His career broadened to television and movies, where he became an excellent character actor. After his Broadway success, he was asked in an interview, "How did you make the remarkable transition through those prison years to Broadway?" "Unlike the other prisoners," he replied, "I never decorated my cell because I wanted to be reminded every day this place is temporary." Dutton never regarded his cell as his permanent home. This world system is not our home.[27] To love it is folly because it is passing away.

Be very careful about decorating your cell. One day God will ring the curtain down, the play will be over, and everything will be taken away. Imagine how foolish it would look for one of the actors in a play to chase the prop people as they remove "his" car, "his" furniture, "his" wardrobe, "his" bank account." "Wait, that's my car! Where are you going with my furniture? Hold it! That's my money!" What a pitiful sight! The wise person is the one who does the will of God. He is the one who "abides forever."[28] His life is on eternal standard time.

I was the Monopoly champion of Jefferson Drive in Rome, Georgia. My friends and I would play Monopoly, and I would amass houses and hotels. (We altered the rules a bit. If you had the money to buy them, you could place two or three hotels on a single piece of property). I discovered that if you could buy all the yellow pieces of property (Marvin Gardens, Ventnor, etc.) and all the green ones (North Carolina, Pacific, etc.), you could win the game virtually every time. You don't need to have Boardwalk and Park Place to win. After I won all of that money, hording a pile of $500 bills and more houses and hotels than you could shake a stick at, every single time the game ended, we folded up the board, took our houses, hotels, and money, and put them right back into the box. It was only a game. I really didn't own houses or hotels but pieces of plastic and paper that were of no value. Even my temporary wealth was an illusion.

In his famous book *Pilgrim's Progress*, John Bunyan describes Christian's visit to the town of Vanity Fair. In seventeenth-century England, much like today, towns and hamlets had fairs that people came from all over to attend. At the fair you could find all kinds of games and activities, as well as virtually any kind of merchandise for sale. Hawkers selling their wares constantly allured visitors. When Christian and Faithful were asked, "What will you buy?" Faithful responded, "We buy the truth, and we see none of it for sale here." This infuriated the shopkeepers, and they stirred up the people against Christian and Faithful. A mock trial followed, and a guilty verdict was swiftly returned. Faithful was martyred, but Christian barely escaped through the town gate to resume his journey toward the city of God.[29]

Too many Christians today are enamored with the world of "Vanity Fair." W. J. Dawson vividly describes the scene:

> It was the Vanity Fair, where the pilgrims of eternity forgot their noblest purposes and were allured from their Divine quest. Its gaiety and glory, its glittering baubles and visions of beauty, bewitched the sense and made man forget the greatness of his origin and the greatness of his destiny; in its booths of pleasure and chambers of delight, its novelty and fascination, and airy laughter, men were allured to destruction and forgot that they were pilgrims and sojourners as all their fathers were. And what, after all, was the world but a mere series of shows and vanities, like a village fair, all alive at night with light and music, and in the morning nothing left but the trodden grass and a broken pole or two to mark where it had been. It was passing away like a stage picture upon which the curtain would soon fall.[30]

What are you loving today? To all of us who are Christians God says, don't be in love with the world's system. Rather we need to remain in love with Jesus. The world will never satisfy. In fact, the more you are gratified, the less you are satisfied. Loving the world ultimately leaves a bad taste in your mouth, like a cold french fry, a mouthful of stale popcorn, or a tepid Coke. In this life the objects of worldly desire are all in the process of perishing. Reason, experience, and revelation all converge in an irrefutable threefold witness that everything "under the sun," as Solomon put it in Ecclesiastes, is vanity of vanity.[31]

There are only two ways to rid the human heart of its love for the world, and one of them won't work! You can demonstrate the world's utter and complete vanity, such that a person will have no logical choice but to give up love for the world. But human nature being as depraved as it is, that simply won't work. The other option is to set before the human heart God himself, who is so much more worthy of our love, so that our heart will resign, with the aid of regeneration and the daily help of the Holy Spirit, its old love affair with the world. Love may be thought of in two different conditions: 1) when its object remains unattained, it becomes a love of desire; or 2) when its object is possessed, it becomes a love of indulgence. The human heart will never relinquish its love affair with the world unless it finds something greater to love than the world. The only way to dispossess the heart of an old love is by the expulsive power of a new one.[32]

For those without a saving knowledge of Christ, their visit to Vanity Fair does not end with a cemetery plot. Hell awaits all who reject Christ, where not only do they perish eternally, but so too perishes the possibility of their desires ever being gratified. I wonder if in Hell people will still have their desires? Imagine, nothing to slake the thirsts of the body or the soul. No bank accounts or checkbooks for the materialist, no sexual fulfillment for the sensualist, no books or computers for the intellectual. The appetite remains, but the means of satisfying it are nonexistent.[33] Add to all this eternal torment.

According to the *Chicago Tribune*, on March 3, 1995, a thirty-eight-year-old man who was walking to his temporary job at a warehouse in Rosemont, Illinois tried to get there by cutting across eight lanes of the Tri-State Tollway. After he crossed the four northbound lanes, however, the wind blew his hat off. The hat flew back across the northbound lanes, and he chased it. A tractor-trailer truck struck and killed him. A person can lose everything by chasing after nothing.[34] A Christian stands to lose so much by chasing after the world.

"But whoever does the will of God abides forever," John says. I would have expected John to say, "but God abides forever." That is true, but it is not what he says! He says that people who do God's will abide forever! Wow! If I have God's eternal life in me via salvation from my sins through Jesus Christ, I am going to abide forever with God in Heaven! My life has meaning, value, and purpose through all eternity because I am connected with the God of all eternity! The world cannot give meaning, hope, or comfort. There is no worldly comfort in the long run. Only Heaven can give us heavenly comfort in the world in which we live.[35]

Heavenly Father, deliver me from ever loving this world or the things of this world, and keep my affections ever lashed to my Savior, who bled and died on the cross for my sins, that I might not perish with the world and its lusts.

Children, it is the last hour, and as you have heard that antichrist is coming, so now many antichrists have come. Therefore we know that it is the last hour. They went out from us, but they were not of us; for if they had been of us, they would have continued with us. But they went out, that it might become plain that they all are not of us. But you have been anointed by the Holy One, and you all have knowledge. I write to you, not because you do not know the truth, but because you know it, and because no lie is of the truth. Who is the liar but he who denies that Jesus is the Christ? This is the antichrist, he who denies the Father and the Son. No one who denies the Son has the Father. Whoever confesses the Son has the Father also. Let what you heard from the beginning abide in you. If what you heard from the beginning abides in you, then you too will abide in the Son and in the Father. And this is the promise that he made to us—eternal life.

1 JOHN 2:18–25

8

Liar! Liar!

HOW DO YOU DISCERN the presence of false teachers in the church? How do you distinguish false teachers from true teachers? From the very earliest days of the Christian church, there have always been false teachers. Whenever you find the genuine article, beware of Satan's counterfeits. In today's world, to listen to some people, you would get the idea that there is no such thing as a false teacher in the church. It seems today that almost anything can pass for Christian truth. Heresy is considered by many to be a dirty word. After all, who wants to be known as a heresy hunter? Who wants to be considered so narrow and bigoted as to say that his view of the truth is the only view of the truth? In fact, in some circles if you affirm evangelical Christianity, you are labeled a religious terrorist.

The Departure of False Teachers Confirms
Their Unsaved Status (vv. 18, 19)

John contrasts false teachers and true teachers in verses 18–21. The presence of false teachers is a sign of the end times (v. 18), and their defection is proof of their true nature (v. 19). In verse 18 John introduces another test of genuine Christian living: the test of right believing. It is very important that we believe rightly. If ever we live in a day when we are inundated with false doctrine, especially false doctrine about the person of Christ, it is today. John says his readers have heard that an antichrist (singular) is coming in the future. That is a reference to a final world ruler who will arise in the end times according to the book of Revelation. He will be Satan incarnate, and he will arise with such power and charisma that the world will follow him. Revelation says that the Antichrist will arise in the days of the return of Christ to the earth. No one knows when that will happen. It could be tomorrow, a hundred years from now, or a thousand years from now. We are not on the planning committee for the return of Christ; we are on the reception committee.

John says that many antichrists (plural) appeared in his own day. These are false prophets who pretend to be Christian but actually are not. They are precursors of the final antichrist who will appear in the end times. Their presence leads John to conclude that "it is the last hour." You might be wondering at this point, "If John thought the last hour was in his own day, and here we are more than 1,900 years down the road and Jesus has not yet returned to earth, that is one long hour!" I've been through what seemed like some interminably long hours in my life—in school, church, the hospital, and a host of other long hours. Of course, we have to understand that God does not operate on Eastern Standard Time, Central Time, or Mountain Time; rather, he operates on his time. Second Peter 3:8 says that a day with the Lord is like a thousand years and a thousand years is like a day. So when the Scripture writers talk about "the last hour," they are not speaking about duration of time, which is the way you and I calculate time. What John means is not time as it is reckoned sequentially, time as it tick-tocks off the clock second by second, but rather an epoch of time. Since the first coming of Jesus, we are literally in the days moving toward the end times when Jesus will return to the earth. By this understanding, since the death, resurrection, and ascension of Christ, in symbolic eschatological terms we have been in the last days or the last hour. Luther adds the interesting point that here John uses the phrase "the last hour" not because of the shortness of time but because of the nature of the teaching. The doctrine of the person and work of Christ is God's final word to us (Hebrews 1:1, 2). Thus this teaching is the last in the sense of ultimate, and another kind should not be expected.[1]

John's focus is not on the future figure called the Antichrist. Rather he says there are people like that figure who are already infiltrating the churches, and that is why John uses the word "antichrists" (plural). Many antichrists have appeared, which is why we know this is the last hour. Notice the prefix *anti* on the word "antichrists." This prefix can mean "against" or "instead of." There is a sense in which both are true in this context. False teachers in the church are like the final antichrist in the book of Revelation. He is literally "against Christ," and hence they are "false christs." However, these false teachers come talking about Jesus claiming to be his true teachers. Thus these false teachers are also substitute christs.

If you were Satan, how would you go about diluting and destroying the church of the Lord Jesus Christ? You might say, "I would bring foreign pagan armies in and try to kill all the Christians." But that has never worked.

If I were Satan, I would sow the seeds of false teachers within the church. I would not enter the church and say that Jesus is a liar and Jesus is not divine. I would come in like an angel of light, and with crafty cunning I would lead the sheep astray little by little through false teaching. That is what Satan does. He has his counterfeits in the churches and outside the churches. What does a counterfeit imply? A counterfeit implies the existence of the real thing. Why do people not counterfeit $3 bills? There is no such thing as a $3 bill. People don't counterfeit that which is not real. Satan counterfeits what is true. So he has his counterfeit preachers in churches. There are churches today with a false prophet, a counterfeiter, standing behind the pulpit teaching people. Jesus told us we should not be surprised about that. He said there will always be false prophets. Jesus said that when he went away (after his resurrection), many false prophets would arise to lead many astray (Matthew 24:11). They would claim to be the Messiah, and they would deceive many.

How can we tell the difference between a false teacher and a true Christian teacher? John says there are three marks. First, a false teacher departs from the fellowship of the church. Look at verse 19: "They went out from us, but they were not of us; for if they had been of us, they would have continued with us. But they went out, that it might become plain that they all are not of us." This is an important verse in 1 John. Something of a rift had occurred in the churches to whom John wrote. It is interesting that in Greek the phrase "from us"[2] appears first in the sentence and may be John's way of pointing out that those who are loyal to John and the other apostles' teaching were prior to the false teachers in the church. Yarbrough paraphrases it this way: "We were here first and doing fine; *they* were the ones who diverged and departed."[3] The reason they departed from the fellowship is stated by John: "they were not of us." The problem for us is that John does not state why they left. Given the context of the entire letter, it would seem clear that doctrinal issues concerning the person and work of Christ, along with ethical issues that flow from these doctrines, were part of the problem. Proto-gnosticism may have been the culprit here (see the earlier sermon on 1 John 1:1–4).[4]

Have you noticed that virtually every cult today was founded by someone who came out of the church? They became disgruntled with a church or denomination. They left the church to form what they called "the true church." There have always been those throughout church history who claimed that everybody else before them got it wrong, but then suddenly God spoke the truth to them personally. I remember shortly after Sherri and I married in 1978, Jim Jones and the Peoples Temple were in the news. Jim Jones started out in an evangelical church but somehow crossed over to the dark side. He persuaded some 800 people to move with him to Guyana to establish what he called a church. In the end 800 people plus their children died, committing suicide under his leadership. He was a false prophet. For a while he was a part of the church, but he departed from the faith, and as John says, he went out from the church. His exit and subsequent false teaching made it clear he was never genuinely a part of the church in the first place.

Joseph Smith said he was visited by an angel from Heaven named Moroni, who dropped down golden tablets of new scripture called the Book of Mormon. Joseph Smith had been a member of a local church but decided that the church was corrupt. He thought God wanted to begin a new church and had, of course, chosen him to begin it. Joseph Smith went out and founded a cult called Mormonism. Mormonism teaches false doctrine about the person of Jesus Christ. Most Mormons are morally responsible, good people. That is not in dispute. Right living is one thing. Right doctrine is altogether something else. You cannot combine right living with false doctrine and call yourself an orthodox Christian or an orthodox church.

These examples all illustrate 1 John 2:19: "They went out from us, but they were not of us; for if they had been of us, they would have continued with us. But they went out, that it might become plain that they all are not of us." The departure of false teachers serves an important purpose: to make clear to the true church that false teachers are not part of the true church. B. H. Carroll was a young man in the Civil War fighting for the Confederacy when he was wounded. He survived but then had an early marriage that failed. Carroll was a self-proclaimed atheist. When he was converted, God called him to preach. One of his greatest sermons is entitled "My Infidelity and What Became of It."[5] Carroll went on to Waco, Texas and founded the Religion Department at Baylor University and ultimately in 1908 was the founder and first president of Southwestern Baptist Theological Seminary in Fort Worth, Texas. He had a saying: "When you see a star fall you know it's not a star." Stars don't fall; stars shine. We call them shooting stars, but astronomically that is incorrect. When you see a star fall, what you are seeing is not actually a star. When you see a person who is a member of a church turn his back on Jesus and orthodox doctrine and depart into false doctrine, in the vast majority of cases you can be guaranteed that person was not a true Christian in the first place. Profession does not necessarily mean possession. Speaking of Jesus' parable in Matthew 13:2–30 and 1 John 2:19, James Boice is right on target: "The implication of Christ's parable and John's statement is that some Christians are so much like non-Christians and some non-Christians are so much like Christians that it is impossible to tell the difference between them in this life."[6] The first mark of false teachers is they depart from the fellowship of the church. The old saying is still true: "Faith that fizzles before the finish was faulty from the first."

The Holy Spirit Confirms Your Knowledge of the Truth (vv. 20, 21)

The second mark of false teachers is that they deny the faith. In verse 20 John places the pronoun "you" in emphatic position at the beginning of the clause. This creates a strong contrast between the false teachers and John's readers. False teachers deny the basic truths of Christianity as taught by Jesus and as revealed in the Bible, but true believers have an anointing from "the Holy One." This designation could refer to Jesus or to the Holy Spirit. Since Jesus is the one who promised the Holy Spirit to the disciples in John's Gospel, there is a sense in which both referents apply here. This is the first indirect reference to the Holy Spirit in the letter. John will refer to the Holy Spirit directly six times in the letter. Some of what John teaches here he has already taught in his Gospel. That word "anointing" is a Johannine metaphor from the Old Testament when kings (1 Samuel 9:16; 1 Kings 19:15, 16), priests (Exodus 29:7; Numbers 35:25), and prophets (1 Kings 19:16; Isaiah 61:1) were anointed for their ministries by the pouring of olive oil on their head,[7] thus setting them apart for special service. The Greek noun *chrisma*, translated "anointing," occurs only three times in the New Testament (1 John 2:20, 27a, 27b). The verbal form is used several times. This act as described by John signified Christians being endued with the Holy Spirit in order to succeed in their calling. Just before he went to the cross, Jesus promised the disciples that the Comforter would come and indwell them (John 14:16, 17). This anointing is the gift of the Holy Spirit who indwells all believers.[8] You don't have to seek an anointing; you already have it! You don't have to get some second portion of the Holy Spirit or second blessing from the Holy Spirit. If you are a Christian you have all the Holy Spirit that you are ever going to have in terms of his indwelling your life (1 Corinthians 12:13).

The problem for some of us is the Holy Spirit does not have all of us. He wants to fill us completely so that we might regularly bear fruit spiritually (Galatians 5:22, 23). This anointing is from "the Holy One." "The Holy One" could also refer to God the Father since according to Jesus in John 14:16, 26 it is the Father who will send the Holy Spirit at the request of Jesus the Son. More likely it refers directly to Jesus as the one who is the direct agent of sending the Holy Spirit to believers. There is an interesting play on words here in the Greek text. John speaks of "Christ" (v. 22), "antichrist" (vv. 18, 22), and "anointing" (v. 20). These words are cognates; they share the same root. "Christ" in Greek means "the anointed one." True Christians have an "anointing" in contrast to the false teachers who are "antichrist," that is, "against the true anointed one."

The result of this anointing is that all Christians have knowledge of the truth. You already have an anointing as a Christian, and thus John says, "you all have knowledge" (v. 20b). Some translations say, "you know all things." Once when I preached on this passage in 1 John, a teenager came up to me and said, "When John said 'you know all things,' I thought to myself 'not math!'" No one knows everything about Christian truth or anything else for that matter. Actually there is a variant reading at this point in the Greek New Testament. The two possible readings could be translated as "you all know" or "you know all things." Most commentators opt for the former, but the latter is also possible because of what John says in verse 27: "his anointing teaches you about everything."[9] What John means is, you know the truth because the Holy Spirit, who is truth, indwells you. In other words, you know the truth because you have been taught the truth. Christians need not feel deprived because the Gnostic false teachers appealed to "special knowledge." To know Christ is to know him who possesses "all the treasures of wisdom and knowledge" (Colossians 2:3). Christians know God, Christians know Jesus, Christians know the Word, Christians know the truth. We know how to distinguish truth from error and false teachers from true. This anointing teaches us everything that is necessary for spiritual life.

It is interesting that in 1 John we are said to "know" seven things:

1. "We know that we have come to know him, if we keep his commandments" (2:3).
2. "We know that when he appears we shall be like him" (3:2).
3. "We know we have passed out of death into life, because we love the brothers" (3:14).
4. "By this we shall know that we are of the truth and reassure our heart before him"(3:19).
5. "We know he abides in us" (3:24).
6. "And if we know that he hears us in whatever we ask, we know that we have the requests that we have asked of him" (5:15).
7. "We know that everyone who has been born of God does not keep on sinning, but he who was born of God protects him, and the evil one does not touch him" (5:18).[10]

There are three major ways to know if something is true. The first way is reason. You can use reason to understand and know things. For example, you can know and understand mathematically that 2+2 = 4. Reason is a gift of God. There is a second way you can know something is true: experience. The scientific method of experimentation is one way we learn truth from experience. For example, if I take 100 bars of Ivory soap and I put one at a time in a kitchen sink full of water and 100 times out of 100 times each bar of soap floats, then what might I conclude from that experiment? Ivory soap floats! How did I arrive at that conclusion? I came to such a conclusion from my experience via experimentation. There is a third way to know truth: divine revelation. If there is a God who knows all truth, and if that God chooses to come into history and tell us some of his truth, then we can know that something is true because God has revealed it as true. God has revealed himself through Jesus Christ and through his written Word, the Bible. But of course lots of religions claim to have a revelation from God that differs from the Bible. How do we know which one is the genuine article and which is the counterfeit? Test the product. This truth John speaks about can be known now, not later, and it can be known by believing it![11]

John continues in verse 21 to remind us that we do know the truth. He tells us he is not writing because we don't know the truth and so he wants to impart the truth to us. Rather, he is writing because we *do* know the truth. In fact in the previous verse as well as here he uses the perfect tense of the verb "know" to emphasize our reception and ongoing possession of this knowledge. John provides a second reason for why he is writing when he affirms, "no lie is of the truth." This statement implies two things. First, nothing untrue (a lie) comes from true Christian doctrine or teaching. Second, since God is the author of Christian truth and since God is truth and cannot lie, no lie comes from God. Both the content of the truth and the character of the God of truth appear to be in view here. Jesus said concerning God's word, "Your word is truth" (John 17:17). Notice he did not say, "your word is true." It certainly is, but Jesus says, "Your word is truth." God's truth is what makes everything else true.[12]

When John mentions a "lie" in verse 21, it leads him into a discussion of just what makes a person who is a false teacher a "liar" (v. 22). All lies are lies, but then again, there are lies and there are lies! In verse 22, in Greek, the definite article before the noun "liar" singles out the distinct characteristic of this class of liars: they are liars *par excellence*! These are not just liars, they are big fat liars! Their lie strikes at the very heart of the gospel in that it denies Jesus is the Christ, the "anointed one" of God, the second member of the Trinity, God in human flesh, whose purpose is to provide salvation through his death on the cross. Think through those people, movements, and religions that deny this truth. They are legion. John is an equal opportunity offender: he calls them all "liars."

Speaking of the devil who is behind these antichrists and their false doctrine, F. W. Farrar nailed it: "He is apt at quoting Scripture for his purpose, as he did thrice over the Lord of glory. He pares up the Bible into little snippings of verbal theology—'old odd ends stolen forth of Holy Writ'—and on the strength of these misinterpreted fragments makes men believe that God is not a loving Father, but a terrific Moloch. Through the wicket gate of a perverted text he lets in a flood of errors, in which he then glories as inspired and infallible truth, and anathematizes as 'heretics' the saints who reject his tyranny and his lies."[13]

Denial of the Son Is Denial of the Father as Well (vv. 22, 23)

A denial that Jesus is the Messiah is also a denial of God the Father! Many people say that we all worship the same God, we just disagree about Jesus. John speedily puts that error to rest. To deny the Son is *ipso facto* to deny the Father. No matter what your religion, if you deny the deity of Christ, don't tell me you worship the true God because John says you don't. You can't choose God and reject Jesus. Since God has revealed himself through his Son, Jesus, it is obvious that if you deny the Son, you are denying the Father as well.

John says that anybody who denies that Jesus is the Messiah, that is, that Jesus is God in human flesh, is "the antichrist." It doesn't matter whether he wears a religious robe or who he or she is or how much of the Bible he or she may believe or agree with or how he or she treats humanity. At that point of doctrinal truth they are of the spirit and mind-set of antichrist. You cannot believe in God and not believe in Jesus. The Scriptures do not give you that option. Jesus is God in human flesh, the second member of the Trinity. Scripture says that Jesus is the only way to the Father. There is only one God, and everybody who denies that Jesus is the Son of God, according to Scripture, is making it clear that they are not rightly related to God. They cannot be. I know this is not a popular view, but it is true. There is only one way to God, and that way is through Jesus Christ. "I am the way, and the truth, and the life. No one comes to the Father except through me" (John 14:6).

John's logic continues in verse 23: "No one who denies the Son has the Father." To deny the Son leads to a denial of the Father, which leads to the fact that the one who denies the Son does not have the Father either. To have the Father means to have a spiritual relationship with the Father. You see, this is more than just disagreeing over doctrinal statements. Relationships are involved. You cannot believe wrongly about Jesus and God and yet be in a right relationship with them. To know God and to have God are essentially ways of talking about relationship. If you don't know God, then you don't have God, and you are thus not in a genuine relationship with him. The only way we can have a spiritual relationship with God is through Jesus Christ. That is why John is so forceful when he says in essence, "To deny the Son is to deny the Father and to fail to be in a relationship with both." Nothing exhibits the antichristian spirit any more than when men identify their own fallible notions with the truths of God and all opposition to themselves as hostility to God.[14] John ends the verse by stating the opposite truth: to openly acknowledge Jesus is the Messiah, the Son of God, is to be in a right relationship with God the Father.

Abiding in the Father and the Son Is Eternal Life (vv. 24, 25)

In verses 24, 25 John now draws it all together with a challenge and a promise. The placement of "you" in the emphatic position in the clause in Greek strongly contrasts true believers with the false teachers of the previous verses. Some translations bring this out by translating this, "As for you . . ."[15] We are commanded to let the truth of the gospel that we have "heard from the beginning abide" in us. The phrase "from the beginning" refers to when John's readers first heard the gospel and believed. To let the truth of the gospel "abide" in you means two things: 1) to accept the truth, and 2) to interact with it and let it control your thinking and actions. In the next statement John reverses the order: what they had "heard from the beginning" precedes the word "abides." This is a stylistic difference that creates a chiasm, a parallel structure of inverse order. This kind of thing occurs frequently in both the Old and New Testaments and serves as a forceful rhetorical tool as well as a memory device. If we accept and adhere to the truth of the gospel, the result is we will continue in fellowship with Jesus and with God the Father.

Verse 25 closes the passage with a promise: those who know the Son and the Father in a saving way, those who obey his gospel and its precepts, have the "promise" of "eternal life." This promise is given by Jesus, who is the antecedent of "he." Being rightly related spiritually to Jesus and God is, in its essence, eternal life. Since the Biblical concept of eternal life includes both a quantity of time as well as a quality of time, Christians are people who have eternal life now in the sense that God's life is in them, but who will have eternal life in Heaven in the sense that this life will never end. Eternal life is a gift from God through Christ that every true believer shares.

I write these things to you about those who are trying to deceive you. But the anointing that you received from him abides in you, and you have no need that anyone should teach you. But as his anointing teaches you about everything, and is true, and is no lie—just as it has taught you, abide in him.

1 JOHN 2:26, 27

9

The Unction Function

DECEPTION COMES IN MANY FORMS. Sometimes our eyes are deceived by a sleight-of-hand trick. Hocus-pocus, now you see it, now you don't. Wow, where did that ace of spades come from? Wow, where did that ace of spades go? Sometimes people deceive us with lies. A salesperson promises that your furniture will be delivered in four weeks from the factory. Three months later, when the furniture still has not been delivered, you realize you were deceived, perhaps along with the salesperson! On occasion deception can occur unintentionally, but most deception is intentional. The absolute worst kind of deception is spiritual deception, since eternal souls hang in the balance.

Christ's Anointing Guards You Against Spiritual Deception (v. 26)

John has already written about false teachers and their characteristics. Because of this, it is difficult to discern whether verse 26 concludes the previous section or introduces a new section. Perhaps John intended both. Here he discusses another characteristic of false teachers: they seek to "deceive" the faithful (v. 26). Satan is a counterfeiter. He is a deceiver. Jesus said concerning Satan that he was a liar from the beginning: "You are of your father the devil, and your will is to do your father's desires. He was a murderer from the beginning, and does not stand in the truth, because there is no truth in him. When he lies, he speaks out of his own character, for he is a liar and the father of lies" (John 8:44). Notice here that Jesus says there is "no truth" in Satan! Satan lies because "he is a liar," and he is the source of lies. Historically Satan's first lie was to Eve in the Garden of Eden when he questioned what God had said. From then until now Satan is ultimately behind all false teaching and spiritual deception. In Matthew 24:24 Jesus said, "For false christs and false prophets will arise and perform great signs and wonders, so as to lead astray, if possible, even the elect." Paul said in 2 Timothy 3:13 that "evil people and impostors will go on from bad to worse, deceiving and being deceived." In Revelation 2:20 John wrote about "that woman Jezebel, who calls herself a prophetess and is teaching and seducing my servants to practice sexual immorality and to eat food sacrificed to idols." Here the word "misleading" is the same word in Greek (*planaō*) that John uses in verse 26 translated "deceive." This word in Greek means "wandering." We get our English word *planet* from this word. False prophets and false teachings are deceptive since they "wander" from the truth of God and his Word and cause others to wander as well.

The world today is filled with false doctrine. The personal nature of God is denied in many false religions. Even within Evangelicalism some question God's omniscience concerning all future events in what is known as the "openness of God" movement.[1]

Today it is common for so-called Christian theologians to question or outright deny the inerrancy of Scripture, again sometimes even in the evangelical camp. Many deny Adam was a special creation of God and affirm either evolution or theistic evolution. When it comes to the person and work of Christ, false doctrine abounds. His full deity is denied by some, while others deny his full humanity. His eternal nature is denied by some. His substitutionary atonement on the cross is denied by others. Some have overtly stated that to believe in the penal substitutionary atonement of Jesus is tantamount to divine child abuse![2] The exclusivity of Christ as the only way of salvation is routinely questioned and outrightly denied. For some, while Jesus may be the only way of salvation for us, he may not be the only way for all people.[3] Some deny the necessity of the church in God's program today. Many cults have the word "church" attached to their name, though in their doctrine they deny basic doctrines of the Christian faith. Errors concerning the person and work of the Holy Spirit abound. The doctrine of the personal return of Christ to the earth is also denied by many. Many other examples of false doctrine today could be listed.

How is it that John can say his readers are not already deceived? Because "the anointing . . . abides in you" (v. 27). What does that mean? Notice that John says "you received" (past tense) this anointing. As a result, this anointing currently "abides in you." This is a reference to the Holy Spirit who abides in (indwells) believers. At the moment of conversion the Holy Spirit comes to live in every believer. The indwelling Holy Spirit is a vital part of the Christian life. The coming of the Holy Spirit to indwell believers was foretold by Jesus, narrated by Luke in Acts, and theologically explained by Paul in his letters. But John likely means more than just a reference to the indwelling Holy Spirit in our lives. The Holy Spirit not only indwells all Christians, he is also among all believers, as evidenced when Christians gather together for worship and other corporate occasions.[4] It is likely that John views this anointing as the divine act that heightens horizontal ties among fellow believers no less than vertical relationships with God. The anointing and its effects abide among them, with them, in their midst corporately, and not merely *in* them as individuals.

Note that the word "anointing" occurs twice in these verses. This word was used back in verse 20 when John said, "but you have been anointed by the Holy One." Clearly John is referring to the Holy Spirit in the life of a believer. Even though the actual words "Holy Spirit" do not occur, "anointing" is the action of the Holy Spirit and is symbolic of the Holy Spirit.[5] In Old Testament times, prophets, priests, and kings were anointed with oil to symbolize their chosen status by God himself and to set them apart for the service to which God had called them. In the New Testament we read about Jesus being "anointed" with the Holy Spirit (Acts 10:38). In the final hours before the crucifixion, Jesus spoke to his disciples about the anointing of the Holy Spirit. John's point is that every Christian has this anointing from the Holy Spirit, not just a chosen few.[6]

Because of the presence and continual abiding of the Holy Spirit in the life of a believer, John says, "You have no need that anyone should teach you." That does not mean there is no need for teachers in the church. Other verses say that one of the groups of leaders given to the church is shepherd/teacher (Ephesians 4:11, 12). Nor does it mean you will suddenly make all A's in math or understand physics better. The difference is in the direction of your life and the quality of your living.[7] The fruit of the Spirit will be produced in you. You will still be you, but a better you! What John means is that Christians who are indwelt by the Holy Spirit do not need to have someone teach them the basic truths of Christianity because the Holy Spirit helps them to recognize basic spiritual truth.

He goes on to say that this anointing is "true." The mark of a false teacher is that he seeks to deceive the faithful with doctrine that is false. Again John's words cut across the grain of today's distorted view of truth. Many believe there is no such thing as absolute truth, and thus there can be no "false" doctrine. All viewpoints are equally true as far as many are concerned today. Sadly, statistics show that even among Christians a high percentage of people do not believe in absolute truth. According to the Barna Research Group, statistics (as of 2008) on the question of absolute truth are alarming, even shocking. From a random poll of just over 1,000 adults in the United States, only one-third of all adults (34 percent) believe that moral truth is absolute and unaffected by the circumstances. Slightly less than half of the born-again adults (46 percent) believe in absolute moral truth.[8]

The visible church always will have within it some who are not genuine Christians. Jesus confirmed this in his agricultural Parable of the Wheat and the Tares. Wheat and tares look so much alike that it is difficult to distinguish them. Jesus said the true sower sows the wheat. Satan comes in and sows the tares among the wheat, and they grow together. Some would say the tares need to be weeded out. Jesus said we should not do that. The wheat and tares look so much alike that if we were to go in and uproot all the tares, we might accidently weed out someone who is wheat! God will weed out the tares from the wheat at the end of time, at the last judgment. Therefore, there will always be people who are not true Christians in the local church. Some people depend on their baptism to make them a Christian. Some depend on their outward church membership. Others depend on their works. None of this will get you into Heaven. You can be a member of a church your entire life, die, and end up in Hell. What makes a person a Christian has nothing to do with his baptism, the church he attends, the denomination he belongs to, or the money he gives. What makes someone a Christian is the fact that he or she has repented of sin and put his or her faith in Jesus Christ.

These verses remind us that there is a difference between deception and ignorance. Some people are spiritually ignorant and just don't know any better. I suspect some false teachers do not have an evil agenda to deceive others; they are just being used by the devil. For whatever reason, they don't know the Scriptures. That's a case of spiritual ignorance. There is a difference between deliberate deception and spiritual ignorance, but both are bad. You don't want to be spiritually ignorant. You also don't want to be deceived spiritually. Paul warns that in the last times "evil people and imposters will go on from bad to worse, deceiving and being deceived (2 Timothy 3:13). Notice that Paul calls these people "evil" and "imposters." He says they will go from "bad to worse" in their activities. Their character determines their activity: "deceiving and being deceived." This last phrase is particularly interesting. These deceivers are themselves deceived! Satan has deceived them and then uses them to deceive others.

Abide in Christ to Tap into His Truth (v. 27)

How can we keep from being deceived by the deceivers? We must immerse ourselves in the Scriptures. Notice that John says in verse 27 this anointing "teaches you about everything." How does the Holy Spirit do this? Through the Scriptures. Remember what Paul said about young Timothy in 2 Timothy 3:15: ". . . from childhood you have been acquainted with the sacred writings, which are able to make you wise for salvation through faith in Christ Jesus." In 2 Timothy 3:16 Paul affirms, "All Scripture is breathed out by God and profitable for teaching, for reproof, for correction, and for training in righteousness." Notice that it is because the Bible is divinely inspired that it is valuable for teaching doctrine. In fact, the Bible is the *only* true source of sound doctrine. All teaching should be measured by whether it comports with Scripture or not. Furthermore, the Bible is profitable for "reproof," "correction," and "training in righteousness." We measure all teaching about spiritual things by the yardstick of the Bible. The Holy Spirit uses the Word of God to teach truth and refute error. This is what John is talking about when he says the Holy Spirit "teaches" us about everything of a spiritual nature. The presence of the Holy Spirit in our life coupled with knowledge of the Word of God is sufficient to guide us into truth so we will not be deceived by false teachers.

John says in verse 27 that this anointing, that is, the Holy Spirit, "is true, and is no lie." In John 14:17 and 16:13 Jesus referred to the Holy Spirit as "the Spirit of truth." "When the Spirit of truth comes, he will guide you into all the truth, for he will not speak on his own authority, but whatever he hears he will speak, and he will declare to you the things that are to come" (John 16:13). ". . . even the Spirit of truth, whom the world cannot receive, because it neither sees him nor knows him. You know him, for he dwells with you and will be in you" (John 14:17). Notice in John 16:13 that Jesus says the Holy Spirit will guide the disciples into "all the truth." In John 14:17 Jesus says that the Spirit of Truth "dwells with you and will be in you." This indwelling was fulfilled on the Day of Pentecost according to Acts 2. Elements of both of these verses from the Gospel of John now reappear in 1 John 2:26, 27.

The Holy Spirit up to this point in the lives of John's readers has been their teacher. Just as he has protected them from error in the past, so he will do in the present and into the future. As a result of the Holy Spirit of truth who teaches us and who indwells us, John exhorts his readers and us to "abide in him." What does this mean, and how can we go about accomplishing it? To "abide" in the Holy Spirit means to obey the Spirit's Word, the Scriptures. To obey is to abide. To know the truth and rest in the truth is to abide. In verse 27a the Holy Spirit abides in us. In verse 27b we are to abide in the Holy Spirit by obeying the Word of God.

Certain Christians today talk a great deal about being "Spirit-anointed." Many in the charismatic branch of Christianity believe the Holy Spirit is giving new revelation today that is on par with the Scriptures themselves.[9]

Notice that John does not say the Holy Spirit is teaching *new* truth today. The Holy Spirit is not revealing new truth but is rather teaching old truth. The old truth is the truth of the Scriptures. We should always distinguish the doctrine of revelation from the doctrine of illumination. Revelation is completed in Scripture and in the person of Jesus Christ. Illumination is an ongoing process whereby the Holy Spirit illumines this revealed truth to help us apprehend and comprehend it.[10] One of the most important roles the Holy Spirit plays in our lives is that of illumination, helping us to understand the Scripture and discern the will of God. In context John is probably combating the false teachers who were attempting to bring so-called "new knowledge" into the church. The old maxim "if it is new it isn't true" actually works pretty well when it comes to orthodox doctrine. We should always be wary of all who come in the name of Christ attempting to teach some new doctrine that they or their group have found in the Bible that everyone else has somehow missed over the past 2,000 years.

The point of these two verses is simple and clear. False teachers are counteracted by the true teacher, the Holy Spirit. In order to avoid being deceived, we must persevere in our relationship with Christ through the Holy Spirit. The ground for our abiding in the Holy Spirit is found in the fact that since the Holy Spirit's character is "true" and is "no lie," therefore his teaching is truth. Veteran pastor and preacher Jerry Vines is exactly right: "Unfortunately, some people who claim to be led by the Holy Spirit do things contrary to the example of Jesus. Jesus is the truth (John 14:6). The word of God is the truth (John 17:17). The Holy Spirit is the Spirit of Truth (John 16:13). Where the Holy Spirit is at work, there will be truth. The Holy Spirit will never lead anyone to do anything contrary to the Word of God or inconsistent with the Son of God."[11]

All teaching and religious experience that claims to be from God can be subjected to five tests that will help every Christian discern its true source. The first test is *the Bible test*. Since the Bible is the Word of God, inerrant and infallible, it is the benchmark for all religious truth. All religious teaching and experience must be measured by the yardstick of Scripture. If such teaching or experience does not measure up, it should be rejected. The second test is *the Jesus test*. Does this teaching or religious experience magnify Christ or in any way denigrate him? Remember, the Holy Spirit will testify about Jesus and point people to him. Bob Hunter made a study of three months of sermons at Toronto's Airport Vineyard Church several years ago. Using a computer database of the nightly sermons preached, he found 372 references to prophecy, 383 to the Holy Spirit, but only 143 to Jesus. He remarked, "This is no picky point about word games. It is about lost opportunity in the preaching to give clear focus on the Son of God."[12] The third test is *the character test*. Does this teaching or religious experience promote godly living? Are those who do the teaching living holy lives? The fourth test is the *decency and order test*. This test is set forth by Paul in 1 Corinthians 12–14 when he addressed the subject of tongues in the church. All things must be done "decently and in order" (1 Corinthians 14:40). The fifth test is *the evangelism test*. Does this teaching or experience promote winning people to Jesus? Does this doctrine or experience help or hinder people from coming to Christ?[13]

First John 2:26, 27 should be read in conjunction with John 15:1–10. Jesus taught us there that he is the vine and we are the branches. If we abide in him, we will bring forth fruit. Stay connected to Jesus. That's what John is saying to us. To "abide in him" means to stay connected to Jesus through the Holy Spirit and the Word of God. Jesus is our source. We must love him supremely and stay connected to him relationally. We must stay grounded in Christ, in the Holy Spirit, and in Scripture. Since each of these is the truth, each is the standard for measuring whatever claims to be true. For John, anointing is intertwined with instruction.[14] We are to adhere to sound doctrine, but that is not the end. We are to live out that doctrine ethically. This can only be done as we "abide in him."

And now, little children, abide in him, so that when he appears we may have confidence and not shrink from him in shame at his coming. If you know that he is righteous, you may be sure that everyone who practices righteousness has been born of him.

1 JOHN 2:28, 29

10

Ready or Not, Here I Come!

HAVE YOU EVER HAD A visitor appear at your door when you least expected it? Maybe you were wearing that old, worn-out, but comfortable shirt that hadn't been washed in a few days. Maybe you had been on vacation and hadn't shaved in a couple of days. When you opened the door, you felt a little bit self-conscious because you did not feel presentable. Now imagine if Jesus should suddenly arrive at your front door, would you be presentable to him or would you be ashamed? This is the question John asks in these verses.

First John 2:28, 29 is a hinge paragraph in the letter.[1] As a door swings on hinges, this passage serves as a transition to close out the previous paragraph with its focus on abiding (note that the word "abide" occurs ten times in 1 John 2) and to introduce a new section in the letter focusing on sonship via the new birth. The word "born" has not been used before this point in the letter but will now occur nine times from this point forward. The expression of salvation as the "new birth" is a prominent Johannine concept (John 1:12, 13; 3:1–16). Once again John speaks of his readers as "little children." This reference, coupled with the introductory conjunction "and" followed by "now," indicates the beginning of a new paragraph and section. Fellowship is a basic theme for John, as he indicated in his statement in 1:3. Abiding in Christ is also a basic theme for John. Now John introduces a new thought related to these themes: confidence before Christ at his coming. The word "confidence" is *parrēsia,* a word that can signify a bold freedom of speech.[2] John used it again in 3:21, 4:17, and 5:14. Twice John uses "confidence" in the context of the return of Christ and the final judgment (2:28; 4:17), and once it has to do with prayer (3:21, 22). Notice that in all these examples John's focus is on our confidence *before God.* Fellowship with God maintained by abiding in him allows us to enjoy a genuine confidence when we meet the Lord. How this can be so is the subject of 2:29—4:19. When our lives are properly related to God and revealed to others, then God himself is revealed in our lives to others, as John says in 4:12–16.

Confidence at Christ's Second Coming (v. 28)

John repeats the exhortation from the previous two verses to abide in Christ,[3] but this time he adds a new motivation for doing so: confidence when Jesus returns to the earth a second time. The second coming of Christ is one of the clear teachings of the Bible. Exactly when Jesus will return in relation to all of the prophesied end-time events is not as clear. What is clear is that not only is Jesus coming back to this earth, but that coming could occur at any time. Since we don't know when he will return, we should live every day prepared for his return. Remember, we're not on the planning committee; we're on the reception committee! When Jesus returns to this earth, every Christian alive at that time will greet him in confidence or shame. If we abide in Christ during his absence, we can be assured of confidence in his presence when he appears once again.

In this passage John gives us an incentive to abide in Christ. In the field of economics or sociology, there are at least four different classes of incentives. Financial incentive involves expectation of financial reward. Moral incentive involves the motivation to do the right thing resulting in personal or community approval. Coercive incentives are involved when failure to act in a certain way will result in physical force being used against one or one's family. Natural incentives are such things as fear, anger, pain, joy, etc. For example, if a car sales team is given a $500 bonus for every car sold, that is a financial incentive to sell cars! The incentive we are given for the command to "abide" in Christ is the second coming of Jesus (v. 28). John has spoken about the coming of antichrist, but now he speaks of the coming of Christ! In the New Testament three main words are used to describe the second coming of Jesus. The first is the Greek word *apokalupsis*, which means "unveiling" and is translated "revelation." The focus here is on disclosure of something previously hidden.

The next two words are both used by John in verse 28. The word "appears" (*epiphaneia*) emphasizes not only the fact of the return of Christ, but the suddenness and unexpectedness of his return as well.[4] We get our English word *epiphany* from this Greek word. John used a form of this word in Greek in 1 John to describe the first coming of Jesus (1:2; 3:5, 8, 11) and his second coming (2:28; 3:2). This word, "appearing," focuses on the visibility of the return of Christ. In other words, when he returns, as the Scripture says, "every eye will see him" (Revelation 1:7). This is John's way of expressing the literal reality and factuality of Christ's first and second coming to the earth. Interestingly, this word "appearing" is never used of God or the Holy Spirit, but only of Jesus. Jesus came the first time as a baby in a manger; he is coming the second time as King of kings and Lord of lords. His first coming was signaled by a star in the east; he will come the second time as the bright and morning star. He came the first time riding on a donkey into Jerusalem; he will come the second time riding on a white horse.

The word translated "coming" is the Greek *parousia*, meaning "coming" or "arrival." John uses this word only here in this letter. In common Greek usage in the first century, this word was used to refer to the arrival of a king, ruler, or dignitary. The word connotes pomp and circumstance, splendor, dignity, and the concomitant respect owed to the arriving monarch. This word occurs frequently in the New Testament epistles to refer to the second coming of Christ.

The source of the doctrine concerning the second coming of Jesus is the Old Testament prophesies that were not fulfilled the first time he came.[5] These prophecies will be fulfilled at his second coming. Jesus himself taught that he would return to the earth. In what is called the Olivet Discourse in Matthew 24, 25, Jesus spoke of his second coming several times.

> Therefore, stay awake, for you do not know on what day your Lord is coming. But know this, that if the master of the house had known in what part of the night the thief was coming, he would have stayed awake and would not have let his house be broken into. Therefore you also must be ready, for the Son of Man is coming at an hour you do not expect. (Matthew 24:42–44)

"When the Son of Man comes in his glory, and all the angels with him, then he will sit on his glorious throne" (Matthew 25:31). Luke records this as well in the conclusion of the Parable of the Watching Servants: "You also must be ready, for the Son of Man is coming at an hour you do not expect" (12:40). Jesus' emphasis in these passages is the necessity of believers being watchful and ready for him when he returns.

Two words in verse 28, antonyms in fact, describe possible attitudes we Christians may have at the second coming of Jesus: "confidence" and "shrink from him." The first is a word we have already seen in this letter. It is the Greek word *parrasia*, which literally means "all speech," and hence to have boldness or to be confident (2:28; 3:21, 22; 4:17). God's desire for all of us is that we be confident when Jesus returns. No second-guessing, no wondering about whether we are prepared to meet him or not, but a solid confidence based on preparedness when Christ returns. John even uses a play on words here that is impossible to render in our English translations. The Greek word for Christ's coming is *parousia*, and the Greek word for "confidence" is *parrasia*. Each word has three syllables, the first and the third exactly alike, with only the middle syllable (vowels) slightly different in sound. John is saying we should have *parrasia* at Jesus' *parousia*!

The opposite of confidence is to be ashamed. To "shrink from him" means "to be ashamed." The unsaved will be ashamed when Christ comes because for them his coming means their judgment. Zuck states the issue well:

> Jesus' return was not explained; it was assumed as common knowledge among the readers. The reference to shame may imply a negative judgment resulting in Christ's rejection of the individual involved. Again this is future. John was not suggesting that a believer in Christ could ultimately be rejected by Him at the final judgment. John was reminding his readers that (just as in his gospel) one's response to Jesus in the present determines one's future destiny. To accept the false teaching of the opponents would be to reject Jesus and incur condemnation at the future judgment, for it would show that the person had never really belonged to Christ at all. To remain faithful to the apostolic teaching about the person of Jesus, on the other hand, would assure confidence before Christ in the day of judgment.[6]

Why would Christians be ashamed to see Jesus when he returns? If we are caught up short, living in ways that are displeasing to the Lord at his coming, the natural reaction would be shame. This is what John wants Christians to avoid. I remember when I was a teenager on occasion being in a place or situation in which I would certainly not be very comfortable if my mother or father suddenly appeared! As a child probably the worst thing my parents could have ever said to me that would have cut to my heart would be the words "I am ashamed of you." Come to think of it, I can recall a few situations in more recent years when if the Lord had come and caught me at a particular moment with a particular attitude, conversation, or action I was engaged in at the time, I would have been ashamed to see him! I don't want my heavenly Father to be ashamed of my life when Jesus comes, nor do I want to be ashamed of my life when he comes! John tells us that the surefire way to have confidence when Jesus returns is to "abide" in Christ, which contextually means living rightly (righteously) day by day. That way, no matter when Jesus comes, we'll be ready!

Nothing unnerves most of us more than unexpected company at an inopportune time. The doorbell rings, and there they stand. You cannot leave them out in the cold. You must invite them in. But the house is a wreck, and the kids are half-dressed with food on their face and dirt on their clothes. You and your spouse are less than presentable yourselves. When we are in such a situation, it is normal to want to shrink back from answering the door! Why? We are unprepared for company. In a similar way, if the doorbell of the return of Christ should ring at an inopportune moment in our life, we would shrink back in shame because we would be unprepared to meet the King.

When Dwight Eisenhower was President, he vacationed in Denver. A six-year-old boy with cancer had expressed a desire to see the President. One Sunday morning the presidential limousine pulled up in front of this boy's house. His father came to the door in blue jeans, a T-shirt, and a day's growth of beard. Seeing the President of the United States on his front porch, he was speechless. After the surprise visit ended, the father exclaimed later, "What a way to meet the President!" Every Christian will meet Jesus at his second coming with either confidence or shame.

Right Living Evidences the New Birth (v. 29)

If John gives us the incentive for living rightly as Jesus' second coming in verse 28, then in verse 29 he gives us the grounds for living rightly: the new birth. When John uses the word "if" in verse 29, he does not mean to convey uncertainty. The word really means "since" in this context. Since we know that Jesus himself is righteous, that is, he is sinless and always does what is right, then we also know that all who have been born again through Christ should be righteous as well. Like father, like son. This divine birth is a birth that is accomplished by God alone. Notice that John says in the last part of verse 29, "has been born."[7] In other words, God is the source, the originator, the one who causes this new spiritual birth to take place. You had nothing to do with your physical birth; likewise, you did nothing to bring about your new birth spiritually. Faith in Jesus Christ is simply the condition that you fulfill in order for God to save you. Your salvation was initiated by God, not you. There is not a scintilla of a hint of anything that smacks of good works as bringing about salvation here or anywhere else in the New Testament.

Our practice of right living gives evidence that we have truly been born into the family of God. To whom does the "he" refer in the phrase "he is righteous" in verse 29? "He" can refer to God or Jesus. Since we know Jesus is righteous, therefore, John says, we know that all who practice righteousness give evidence of the fact that they have been born into the family of God. We behave like our Father. If you have children, you hope they will act like you, and in some cases you hope they will act better than you! Our children often imitate our actions. The world ought to know you're in the family of God by the way you act. All Christians should live in keeping with Jesus' own righteous character. His character governs his conduct. So should ours. We should live up to our name.

John uses two different Greek words for knowledge in verse 29. If this diversity is not merely stylistic, then John may be emphasizing absolute and intuitive knowledge in his use of "know" at the beginning of the verse when he says, "if you know that he is righteous . . ." Then he may be stressing knowledge learned by experience in the phrase translated "you may be sure."[8] "Righteousness" means essentially living rightly. It is a word that describes moral behavior acceptable to God. This is one of the distinct characteristics of one who has been born of God. But notice carefully that this righteousness is *evidence* of the new birth, not the *cause* of it. The metaphor of the new birth is common in John's Gospel and letter. When you see real righteousness exhibited, righteousness defined by God in his Word and not mere human morality, you can rest assured that the person who exhibits it is a child of God.

These verses teach us the reality of the return of Jesus to this earth and the importance of our watchfulness for his return. The second coming of Jesus is our incentive to practice righteousness, to live rightly. Think of how practical this doctrine of the second coming of Christ is to our daily behavior. If I know Jesus' coming is imminent, how should I transact my business today? If I know his coming could occur at any moment, what kind of husband and father should I be? How will I conduct myself in my leisure time, at the ball game, at the office, in church, and a hundred other places if any moment the trumpet may sound announcing his appearing? It is impossible to stuff your sins in a dusty attic somewhere in a desperate attempt to hide them from the all-seeing eyes of Jesus at his second coming. The Biblical promise of the return of Christ is one of the best motives for holy living.

If I love Jesus, and if I am looking forward to his return, I can have confidence now and when I see him face-to-face. Remember Paul's words in 2 Timothy 4:8: the crown of righteousness is laid up for all those who love Jesus' appearing. Let's live every day loving Jesus and looking for Jesus! Even if Jesus tarries in his return, we should live loving him and looking for him until our dying day. Don't put thorns in your dying pillow by the lethargy of your Christian life.[9]

See what kind of love the Father has given to us, that we should be called children of God; and so we are. The reason why the world does not know us is that it did not know him. Beloved, we are God's children now, and what we will be has not yet appeared; but we know that when he appears we shall be like him, because we shall see him as he is. And everyone who thus hopes in him purifies himself as he is pure. Everyone who makes a practice of sinning also practices lawlessness; sin is lawlessness. You know that he appeared in order to take away sins, and in him there is no sin. No one who abides in him keeps on sinning; no one who keeps on sinning has either seen him or known him. Little children, let no one deceive you. Whoever practices righteousness is righteous, as he is righteous. Whoever makes a practice of sinning is of the devil, for the devil has been sinning from the beginning. The reason the Son of God appeared was to destroy the works of the devil. No one born of God makes a practice of sinning, for God's seed abides in him, and he cannot keep on sinning because he has been born of God. By this it is evident who are the children of God, and who are the children of the devil: whoever does not practice righteousness is not of God, nor is the one who does not love his brother.

1 JOHN 3:1–10

11

Who's Your Daddy?

EVERY CHRISTIAN should always live in three arenas: 1) what we are, 2) what we shall be, and 3) what we should be. What we are is God's children (v. 1); what we shall be is conformed to the image of Christ when we get to Heaven (v. 2); what we should be on the basis of these two are people who live pure lives (v. 3). John is fond of using family terms to talk about the Christian life. He records how Nicodemus came to Jesus and Jesus said, "Nicodemus, unless you are born again you cannot see the kingdom of God." All through John's Gospel and his letters, salvation is a "new birth," being "born into the family of God," and becoming "children of God." The family is an apt metaphor for salvation since Christians have God as their Father.

First John 2:29 is a transitional verse in the letter. Notice the use of the word "born" or "begotten." Prior to verse 29, that word does not occur at all in the first two chapters, but it occurs eight times from this point forward. John's focus from this point on will be what it means to be in the family of God.

Children of God Now and Forever (vv. 1–3)

In 3:1 John writes, "See what kind of love the Father has given to us, that we should be called children of God." When John uses the word "see" or "behold," he intends for us to direct our attention and reflect on the greatness of the Father's love for us. The word indicates "to ponder, to study." It invites us to, as Spurgeon said, "Pry into this secret!"[1] In his letters John frequently refers to Christians as "children" of God. On the other hand, Paul characteristically refers to Christians as "sons" of God. Both are true, of course. What is the difference? "Son" is something of a legal term describing our relationship with God through Christ. Christians have been declared to be "sons" of God; they have been adopted into the family legally. John does not use the term "sons"; rather he uses here the word "children." This is a term that describes origin, birth, family relationship, family likeness, and family characteristics. We are the children of God.

If children have been born into your family, you well remember the day they were born. All the family came to the hospital and gathered around the new baby. Grandparents, aunts, uncles, brothers, sisters were present, along with other family members. What was the topic of conversation? Of course, it was the baby and his or her family likeness. "Look, he has Grandpa's eyes!" "She has a full head of black hair like Grandma!" "Did you notice how he has Uncle Joe's ears?" That is something of the idea John is conveying here. As Christians, we are part of the family of God, and we should have something of the family likeness.

How did it come about that we gained entrance into God's family? John tells us in verse 1 it is because of God's love for us: "See what kind of love the Father has given to us." John places the word "Father" in a key position to emphasize the family relationship. God himself is the source of this love to us, and what a marvelous love it is! Had you lived in the first century in a Greek seaport town, you might one day be about your business, and suddenly there would be a rustle among the people down on the docks, and word would spread through the town that a ship was coming. People would move down toward the docks and look out on the horizon at the approaching ship. By the sail configuration they could tell whether the ship was from their own country or a foreign nation. You would hear people asking in Greek, "*Potapēn?*" which literally means, "Of what country?" "What new people are coming to visit us? What new things are we going to learn?" This is the word translated "what kind of" in 3:1. This is a very unusual word that only occurs six times in the whole New Testament, and it bristles with surprise, astonishment, urgency, and excitement. ". . . what kind of love the Father has given to us . . ." This is the word the astonished disciples uttered when Jesus calmed the sea: "What manner of man is this? Where is he from that even the wind and the sea obey him?"

Notice that this love of God is wonderful and unique because it actually does come from another country: in fact it comes from Heaven! The love of God is broad, deep, marvelous, unimaginable, incomprehensible, boundless, endless, measureless. When Paul tried to measure it, language forced him to resort to the only standard phrases available to him: ". . . the breadth and length and height and depth . . . the love of Christ that surpasses knowledge" (Ephesians 3:18, 19). It is like measuring the content of the ocean with a teacup or making a personal inspection of the known universe. It is like setting up a yardstick to see how tall God is or using a tape measure to determine the breadth of his reach.[2] When I look at the cross, I see there a love that shrinks from no sacrifice, is evoked by no lovableness on my part, but comes from the depth of God's own infinite being. God is a God who loves because he must and who must because he is God. I see on the cross a love that will not be extinguished by sinfulness but pours its treasures on the unworthy, like sunshine on a dunghill.[3] This love of God is one of the main themes of Christian hymnody. Contemporary Christian songs often focus on the love of God. Christians should never cease to be amazed and to marvel at God's love for us. It's a love that comes from another country. It far exceeds all other loves.

This love, John says, "has [been] given to us, that we should be called children of God." The meaning of this verb coupled with the tense[4] John uses suggests that this gift cannot be earned, bought, or withdrawn. This is not a love that you and I deserve. This love is a gift. God reaches down to us, unlovely though we are in the midst of our sins. Jesus died for our sins on the cross. God has "given" this love to us and has "called" each of us his child. These words describe titles of honor. God has given us the honor of bearing his name! Perhaps you bear a family name given to you in honor of a father or grandfather or other family member. God bestows an undeserved honor on us when his love for us causes him to adopt us into his family.

Lest one of us be so overwhelmed with this unbelievable fact that we are children of God, John says, "and so we are." The missionary Ziegenbalg tells how, in translating this text with the aid of a Hindu youth, the youth rendered it "that we should be allowed to kiss His feet." When asked why he thus diverged from the text he said, "'Children of God!' that is too much— too high!"[5] But it is not too high! It is what God himself declares us to be! In C. S. Lewis's famous book *Screwtape Letters*, Screwtape, the senior demon who is instructing his younger, inexperienced understudy, Wormwood, in the art of guiding a human being into Hell warns his pupil that his task is all the more difficult because the "Enemy" (God) "has a curious fantasy of making all these disgusting little human vermin into sons."[6]

To function well as a Christian, you have to know who you are in Christ. No matter what problems you may be facing at the moment, you *are* his child. You are in his family now. But the news gets even better! Just as we are born only once into our family, so the new birth, which places us in the family of God, is a once-for-all event as well. We can never be disowned by God as a member of his family. You may bring dishonor to your earthly family name; you may do things the family frowns on; but you cannot get out of the family even if your family in an official capacity disowns you. You will always be a part of your earthly family biologically. The same is true of your spiritual family. You did nothing to cause yourself to be born into your earthly family. Likewise, you had nothing to do with your spiritual birth (John 1:12, 13). Adoption gives us the name of God's children, the new birth gives us the nature of God's children, and in both senses such we are! Adoption is the legal act by which our Father places us in his family; regeneration is the spiritual birth by which we receive the nature of our Father.[7]

By means of God's forgiveness of our sins and the new birth, we are in the family of God. Unable to deal with sin, Buddhism despairs of the present life and longs for release in Nirvana, which is "nothingness." Hinduism seeks to solve the sin problem through escape from the wheel of karma via reincarnation (rebirth). Christianity solves the sin problem not by escape into nothingness or by rebirth but rather by the new birth! "We are God's children now."

People who are not God's children do not know God or recognize him as Father. They don't recognize us as children of God either. Most of the world rejected Jesus the first time he came. The world does not know the Father; so it should not be any surprise to us that the world does not recognize us as children of God. The reason the world does not "know us" is because it did not "know him." By "him" John could be referring to God or Christ or, most likely, God in Christ (cf. John 15:18—16:4). Remember what John said in his Gospel: Jesus was in the world, but the world did not know him. He came to his own, and they did not receive him (John 1:10, 11). Don't you find that amazing? The majority of people missed who Jesus is when he came to this earth! Because the world does not know Jesus, they will not know us. When we enter into the family of God, our old family doesn't know us anymore. Don't be surprised when the world doesn't know us.

In verse 2 John refers to his readers who are God's children as "beloved." Though we are currently children of God, all of the implications of what that will mean for us when we get to Heaven are not realized in this life. This is what John means when he says, "What we will be has not yet appeared." Now we are children of God, but it has not appeared as yet what we will be. The present is the prophet of the future.[8] Now we are limited to speak in the language of earth; on that day we will learn the vocabulary of Heaven.[9] With respect to our future state, John affirms both our ignorance and our knowledge. He affirms our ignorance inasmuch as "what we will be has not yet appeared"; he affirms our knowledge since we have the assurance that "when [Christ] appears we shall be like him."[10] All our heart's questions are answered in the statement "we shall be like him, because we shall see him as he is." Richard Baxter said it well:

My knowledge of that life is small,
The eye of faith is dim;
But 'tis enough that Christ knows all,
And I shall be like Him![11]

At this point John shifts to talk about what we will be. In order to understand what we will be we have to start with who we are: children of God. But God is not only interested in making us his children; he desires for all his children to bear the family likeness. God is about the business of making us more like Jesus. Did you know that every day of your life as a Christian God is silently at work to create in you the mind of Christ? He is at work to help us learn to think like Jesus, talk like Jesus, and act like Jesus. God is about making all of his children conform to the image of our Lord Jesus Christ. Our full and final spiritual inheritance is in Heaven and awaits the return of Christ. But that inheritance is ours now, even though we have not yet come into possession of it.

E. V. Hill, the great African-American preacher, once hired a young girl to be his secretary. He did not know who she was other than her name. One day one of his friends came by and said, "Do you know who your secretary is?" Hill responded, "Of course. That's Natalie Cole." He said, "But do you know who Natalie Cole is?" Hill said, "Of course. She's a very nice young lady who works very well, and I pay her $2 an hour." The friend said, "That's Nat King Cole's daughter." Hill was stunned. He asked Natalie to come into his office and asked her if she was indeed Nat King Cole's daughter. "Yes," she said. "Why didn't you tell me?" asked Hill. She said, "I didn't know it was required. I just wanted a job. My daddy left me something, but I haven't come into it yet. It won't be mine until I am twenty-one."[12] That is the way it is with all of us who are Christians. We are children of King Jesus, but we have not yet come into our full inheritance. It is ours now, but we don't come into it until we get to Heaven! To the world we Christians are an odd lot of people from many different walks of life. Our earthly vocations may be humble, but we are children of the King! Harriett Buell wrote the words for "I'm A Child of the King" as she walked home from church one Sunday:

My Father is rich in houses and lands;
He holdeth the wealth of the world in His hands!
Of rubies and diamonds, of silver and gold,
His coffers are full—He has riches untold.

My Father's own Son, the Savior of men,
Once wandered o'er earth as the poorest of them;

But now He is reigning forever on high,
And will give me a home in heav'n by and by.

I once was an outcast stranger on earth,
A sinner by choice and an alien by birth;
But I've been adopted; my name's written down—
An heir to a mansion, a robe, and a crown.

A tent or a cottage, why should I care?
They're building a palace for me over there!
Though exiled from home, yet still I may sing:
All glory to God, I'm a child of the King.

Chorus:
I'm a child of the King, a child of the King!
With Jesus my Savior, I'm a child of the King!

Some of us live and work in very modest circumstances. The world would never guess that even now are we sons of God! It doesn't look like it—we haven't come into our inheritance yet!

"When he [Jesus] appears we shall be like him because we shall see him as he is." When Jesus returns again to this earth, we shall be "like him." Greek has two primary words to describe likeness. One word describes equality in number, size, and weight; the other word means similarity in characteristic. It is this second word that John uses here. There is one sense in which we can never be like Jesus because Jesus is divine, God in human flesh, the second person of the Trinity. We will never be "like him" in the sense of equality with his divine nature.[13] We do not become little gods! But we will be like him in spiritual unity and righteousness. Did you know that God saved us for more reasons than just to keep us out of Hell? The Bible says that God saved us to conform us to the image of his Son and make us like Jesus. God will fulfill that purpose, and there will come a day when we will be just like Jesus in that we will be perfectly righteous. Think of it—redesigned as the spitting image of Jesus in terms of righteousness![14] I scarcely can imagine it. Until then we are utter strangers to our future selves. Out of prison we come to reign.[15]

What does it mean for John to say, "we shall be like him"? First, we will have glorified resurrected bodies in Heaven. John offers no outward evidence for the resurrection of Jesus or for our resurrected bodies. This is the case not because he thinks that evidences are unimportant, but because he is sure they are not enough. Evidences alone don't satisfy. The human heart can no more be satisfied by evidences of the resurrection than hungry people can be satisfied by evidences of bread or thirsty people by evidences of water. For John, there is no point in marshaling arguments for our resurrected body. Verbal proof is unnecessary. You don't need proof of the reality of water when your parched lips meet a gushing spring.

Paul says in Philippians 3:21 that Jesus will "transform our lowly body to be like his glorious body." Personally I would like to be taller and thinner. I'm glad I will be able to spend Heaven in a body that I will enjoy. When you live in Heaven eternally you don't want to be shackled by the difficulties that plague your physical body now. Your heavenly body will be something like Jesus' resurrection body—not bound by the space/time/matter continuum. I'm looking forward to that (whether I'm taller and thinner or not!). Second, we will have purified character. We don't want to go to Heaven as we are now because there is no sin in Heaven. If we went like we are now, we wouldn't fit in. We would be like an Oklahoma University fan at a University of Texas alumni meeting. (Feel free to reverse the analogy if you are an OU fan!) When we go to Heaven, God will cleanse us once and for all from sin. He will eliminate once and for all that sin nature in our heart. Third, we will have a satisfied heart. Listen to Psalm 17:15: "As for me, I shall behold your face in righteousness; when I awake, I shall be satisfied with your likeness." When we awake in Heaven after the sleep of death, we will awake in Jesus' likeness and will be eternally satisfied! I'm not satisfied today with my life spiritually, are you? I want to do more and be more for my Savior.

By virtue of the incarnation, Jesus retains his humanity now in his glorified exalted state. Think of it, perfect humanity, the God-man, on the throne in Heaven! One day we are going to be like him, sinless in every way. One day we will see Jesus "as he is." We will see him in all of his glory, his majesty, his perfection. I've seen some beautiful sights in my lifetime. The faces of my wife, children, and grandchildren are beautiful sights to me. I have seen a beautiful bride adorned in her wedding white walk down an aisle. I've stood atop the Rockies and looked down at the majesty of God's creation. I've stood on the shoreline in California at Carmel-by-the-Sea and on the beautiful white sands of Destin, Florida and watched the sea as it rolls in. I've seen the sunset paint its spangled colors on an Arizona mountain. I have flown parallel to the Andes Mountains on my way to and from Peru, and what an incredible sight! But each of those beautiful sights simply cannot hold a candle to the face of Jesus in all his glory and splendor. Peter got it right when he said about Jesus, "Though you have not seen him, you love him" (1 Peter 1:8).

When I look in the mirror each morning, sometimes I don't particularly like what I see. A shower and shave always help, but even then sometimes I don't like what I see! In 1993 the rock group Pearl Jam released their second album entitled "P.S." In five days they sold a record 950,000 copies. *TIME* magazine put the face of lead singer Eddie Vedder on the front cover. I was intrigued by what Eddie Vedder said: "I'm being honest, when I say some- times when I see a picture of the band or a picture of my face taking up a whole page of a magazine, I hate that guy."[16] When I think about my spiritual face, reflected in the life I live, what I really want to see and what I really want other people to see when they look at me is Jesus. I want them to see a man who thinks, talks, and acts like Jesus. All the fame and fortune bestowed on you by the world means nothing unless you have God's saving love bestowed upon you as one of his children, and you thus bear the family likeness.

Brian Kelley of Detroit underwent intestinal surgery in July 1994, and something went wrong. The doctors told him he was not going to live. Brian Kelley gathered his family around him and gave specific instructions for his body after his death. He worked at a fireworks company. He instructed his family to have his body cremated, and then his ashes were to be rolled into a twelve-inch fireworks shell. On August 12, 1994 at a pyrotechnic conven- tion, a cannon report was heard launching that shell into the air. It had two silver streaming comet tails that followed in its ascent; then it burst, and for four seconds there were green and red stars everywhere intermingled with his ashes. Four seconds of glory and the show was over.[17] Without Christ, no matter how long or short a life we live, and no matter whether we make it in this life or not, that is about all of life there is. A few seconds of glory, and then everything flickers and fades into darkness. But those who know Christ will one day be with Jesus and will become like Jesus and, as the Bible says, will shine as the stars forever with him. That is what God does for those who are his children.

What do you think makes Heaven Heaven? Not that your grandmother or grandfather are there; not that your mother or father or other family members are there; not that the angels, other Christian friends, or the street of gold are there. (Revelation never mentions "streets" of gold; only a "street" of gold!) All of that contributes to the joy of Heaven, but those are side benefits. What makes Heaven Heaven is the fact that Jesus is going to be there! A true child of God wants to be with Jesus. You want to walk with him, love him more, and just be in his presence. There is nothing more desolate than a beautiful home when somebody who was its light is gone. It may be adorned with every treasure that wealth can purchase, and yet the heart may be very lonely there. What would Heaven be without Jesus? When Paul thinks of Heaven, he always seems to think of Jesus. He never says, when life is hard and difficult,

"I have a desire to depart and go to Heaven"; he says, "My desire is to depart and be *with Christ*" (Philippians 1:23).[18]

When it comes to the afterlife in Heaven, the Bible is consistently reticent. It does not undertake to tell us all that we would like to know. It makes no effort to satisfy our curiosity. Christians should be very wary of the spate of recent books purporting to tell us how someone went to Heaven when he or she died and then came back to life. I personally doubt that Jesus helped little Colton with his homework while he was supposedly in Heaven for a time during his near-death experience, as he claims in the New York Times bestseller *Heaven Is for Real*.[19]

I think about our men and women in uniform who have served in Iraq and Afghanistan over the past several years. Many of them have been deployed for a year or longer, and some have seen multiple deployments. Some military fathers in Iraq and Afghanistan have had a child born back home, and they have only seen pictures or videos or live video on Skype of their child. They have not yet had the joy of looking into the face of their own child. Imagine that daddy when he finally gets to come home and for the first time see and hold his own child. The face of his own child moves him to tears of joy. The songwriter had it right when he said, "It will be worth it all when we see Jesus; life's trials will seem so small when we see Christ. One glimpse of His dear face all sorrows will erase, so bravely run the race till we see Christ." What a glorious day it will be when 1 Corinthians 13:12 is fulfilled: "now we see in a mirror dimly, but then face to face."

When I was in London a few years back, I toured the famous St. Paul's Cathedral. One of the monuments was a white marble statue of John Donne, famous poet, preacher, and Dean of St. Paul's Church from 1621 until his death in 1631. During the last few weeks of his life, Donne lay on his bed in pain as his life ebbed away. The church employed a carver to design a monument for their Dean. Donne posed for him in the posture of death as a living cadaver, hands folded, eyes closed, and a winding sheet wrapped around him. After his death it was mounted over his funeral urn. His face wears a serene expression that ironically contrasts with the suffering he endured in later life. Donne wrote and preached as much or more about pain and death than any of his contemporaries. But in spite of all he suffered, he was well acquainted with 1 John 3:1, 2, as is evidenced by the following words from one of his later sermons:

> Our last day is our first day; our Saturday is our Sunday; our eve is our holy day; our sunsetting is our morning; the day of our death is the first

day of our eternal life. The next day after that . . . comes that day that shall show me to myself. Here I never saw God too. . . . Here I have one faculty enlightened, and another left in darkness; mine understanding sometimes cleared, my will at the same time perverted. There I shall be all light, no shadow upon me; my soul invested in the light of joy, and my body in the light of glory.[20]

In verses 1, 2 John has told us what we are: "children of God." He has told us what we will be: like Jesus when we see his face someday. Now John tells us in verse 3 what we should be: "And everyone who has thus hopes in him [Jesus] purifies himself as he is pure." To keep us from floating away on a cloud of mysticism, John reminds us that our future destiny helps us to know our present duty. If we are to be like Christ in Heaven, then we must act like Christ now![21] What are we to be doing now before we come to the time of "what we will be"? John says what we should be is holy and how we should live is a pure life. The reason we can and should do this is because we have hope. *Hope* is a very important word. In English *hope* conveys a wishful optimism with no guarantee that the thing hoped for will ever materialize. "I hope it doesn't rain today." "I hope we have fried chicken for lunch today." Earthly hope is often satiating but never satisfying. But in the New Testament "hope" means a settled certainty and confident expectation based on the promises of God. Notice carefully the object of our hope: "hopes in him." That is, our hope is fixed on Jesus. Hope is a settled fact for Christians provided for us by Jesus who is himself our hope (Hebrews 6:19).

Hope is future-oriented. John's "hope" is the second coming of Jesus and the fact that Christians will be conformed to his image. What should we be when Jesus returns? Holy in character and conduct. We know what we are, the "children of God"; we know what we shall be, conformed to his image. But now he says in light of all of those things what we should be today is holy in character and holy in conduct. We'll never be holy in conduct until our character is right. Holiness begins internally and then works itself out in terms of our actions. We Christians are responsible to see to it that we are walking in holiness. Is that true for you? Think about your life. Are you walking in holiness and godliness? Are you purifying yourself day by day, hour by hour, moment by moment? Notice the pattern: we are to purify ourselves "as he is pure." The pattern for our purity today is not our spouse or another Christian but Jesus Christ. He alone is our pattern.

"Everyone who thus hopes in him purifies himself as he [Jesus] is pure." Notice that our incentive for living a holy life is not rules but a relationship with Jesus. My incentive for right living is based on a higher love, a greater devotion to Jesus. When you love Jesus, you desire to be like Jesus. He is pure and holy, and his children should desire the same thing. The practical implication of living the life of hope is self-purification. There is a sense in which we partly can and a sense in which we absolutely cannot purify ourselves. We cannot do it, yet it cannot be done without us. It can only be done by our uniting our own will to the will of God.[22]

As Calvin said, "Our desire for holiness should not grow cold because our happiness has not yet appeared, for the hope is sufficient."[23] Our righteousness is not the ground of our hope, nor is it our warrant to hope in Christ. The only ground of our hope is Christ himself.[24]

A Christian teenage girl was out with friends when the decision was made by the group to go to a particular place and do things there that she was uncomfortable with. She had just a few seconds of hesitation and then spoke out and asked to be taken home. People began to snicker. One of the boys said to her, "Why don't you want to go with us? Are you afraid your dad will hurt you if he finds out?" "No," she said. "I'm afraid if I go there I will hurt my father." That should be the attitude and action of Christians today. It's not that you are afraid God will hurt you if you sin, but you love him so much that you don't want to hurt him.

Verse 2 is a strong incentive to fulfill verse 3. "We are God's children now." It does not yet appear what we shall be when we see Jesus. But until then this hope motivates us to live pure lives. Satan's deception tries to convince us that we cannot help but yield to sin. Satan is like crafty Cortes, who when the Spaniards invaded Mexico sought to make the Mexicans believe that a Spaniard cannot die, a deception that utterly unnerved them in battle. Think of it this way. When a baseball player hits a home run, he cannot be put out. But he also has to run the bases and make sure he touches all the bases. Though he is in no danger of being thrown or tagged or called out, he still has to run the bases. No one, on the field or in the bleachers, can throw him out! When Jesus died on the cross, he put it over the fence! As a Christian, I am a son of God, but I still have to run the bases of the Christian life. I'm not in any danger of losing my salvation. He who began a good work in me will bring it to completion at the day of Jesus Christ (Philippians 1:6). I'm saved, sanctified, and safe . . . for all eternity![25]

True Children of God Do Not Exhibit a Sinful Lifestyle (vv. 4–6)

John further develops his point from verse 3 in verses 4–10. This passage has caused confusion because it seems that verses 6 and 9 imply that a Christian cannot sin. At first blush it might appear John has contradicted himself based on what he has already said in 1:8–10 and 2:1. However, a closer inspection reveals that is not what John means. Both grammar and context provide the interpretive key to solve the problem.[26] Notice how many times phrases such as "practice of sinning," "keep on sinning," and "practice righteousness" occur here. The use of "practice" and "keep on" in the HVY translators clearly renders the present tense aspect in these verbs. This is the key to a proper understanding of what John is saying. Our attitude to sin as Christians is of vital importance to John. Apparently the false teachers John is combating were indifferent to sin. This is something that should never be true of a Christian. You can be no more indifferent to sin than you could be indifferent to a rattlesnake in your house.

There is an important distinction to be made between a state of purity and a maintained condition of purity. Suppose you walked through a dark room with a lighted candle, and upon exiting the room, the room remained lighted because the candle had passed through it. Such a condition is impossible! If this were possible, the room would no longer be dependent upon the candle for its light. It would only be indebted to the candle for its introduction of light into the room. Sin is darkness, and Christ is the light. What the candle is to the dark room, Christ is to our hearts. By the light of his indwelling presence he keeps sin away. The cleansing we experience is not a state but a maintained condition; a condition that can only exist because of Christ's presence in our life. Light dispels darkness, but the tendency to darkness remains. A room can only be maintained in a condition of illumination by the continual counteraction of that tendency. When we are saved, we do not possess a *state* of purity. We are constantly dependent upon Christ's presence in our lives to counteract the constant tendency to sin.[27]

In verses 4–8 John states or imply several things about sin. He tells us what sin is, what sin does, why sin is, from where sin comes, and how sin is conquered.[28] Verse 4 makes the point that "sin is lawlessness." Lawlessness is willful rejection and active disobedience to the will of God. Hence anyone who practices sin practices lawlessness.[29] "Lawlessness is a self-chosen disobedience that subverts man's true relation to the will of God. The objective habit is coextensive with the subjective condition."[30] Spurgeon noted how sometimes we mistakenly judge the gravity of sin merely by its consequences. But it is not the amount of damage that results from it that makes the sin; it is the thing itself.[31]

John makes the point in verse 5 that Jesus' purpose for coming into the world was "to take away sins." John the Baptist stated in John 1:29, "Behold, the Lamb of God, who takes away the sin of the world!" This statement focuses on the expiatory nature of Christ's atonement on the cross. The finality of his sacrifice is emphasized.[32] Furthermore, Jesus is himself sinless, a necessary condition for him to be qualified to atone for sin. The author of Hebrews clearly affirms the sinlessness of Christ in Hebrews 4:15: Jesus "in every respect has been tempted as we are, yet without sin." Some have questioned whether his temptations could have been real if he could not have sinned as the Son of God.[33] However, this misses the point. Think of unbreakable dishware. You go to the store and ask the salesperson how he knows this dishware is unbreakable. The salesperson pulls out a plate, throws it on the ground, and it does not break. He takes it and hits it against the table and the wall, yet it does not break. He beats it with a hammer. Still the plate does not break. Were the tests the plate underwent any less real just because it was unbreakable? Not at all. The trials and temptations Jesus experienced in his earthly ministry were just as real as the same kind of trials and temptations we face today. Yet Jesus did not sin.

In verse 6 John affirms that no one who "abides in [Christ]," meaning no one who is genuinely a Christian, "keeps on sinning." The key here is the present tense verb expressing an ongoing sinful lifestyle. John has already affirmed the possibility that a Christian can sin. That is not his point here. He does not refer to an occasional specific act of sin but rather a lifestyle of sin. Such a lifestyle indicates someone who has neither "seen" nor "known" Jesus.[34] The use of the word "know" here suggests knowledge based on experience. Not to "know" Christ here describes someone who is not genuinely saved.

Those Who Do Exhibit a Sinful Lifestyle Are from Their Father, the Devil (vv. 7–10)

Verse 7 provides the obverse scenario: the one who practices righteousness is righteous, just as Jesus is righteous. John couches this assertion in a tender pastoral tone: "Little children, let no one deceive you." False teachers are behind the notion that one can be born again and yet practice a sinful lifestyle. John refutes such attempted deception. "We do not attach ourselves to Christ by our own righteous acts; but because we are attached to Christ we are able to perform righteous acts. We do not make ourselves God's children because we are good; but being the children of a good God, we can live as His children."[35] Imagine a professional football player who is an all-pro and master of his position. He knows what his responsibilities are and how to carry out his assignments. Normally he performs his tasks as he should. But occasionally he misses an assignment. He may miss a block or a tackle. But that is not the norm for him. Rather it is the exception.[36] That is the way it is in our Christian life. Sin is the exception, not the rule. If sin is the rule rather than the exception, you have not been born of God.

In verse 8 John carries the trajectory of his argument even further. He tracks the source of habitual sin to Satan himself. Jesus made the same connection in John 8:44: "You are of your father the devil, and your will is to do your father's desires. He was a murderer from the beginning, and does not stand in the truth, because there is no truth in him. When he lies, he speaks out of his own character, for he is a liar and the father of lies." The name "devil" means "slanderer; accuser." The devil's lifestyle of sin has been so "from the beginning." This probably refers to the beginning of Satan's rebellion against God.[37] John then states why Jesus "appeared" with respect to the devil: that he might destroy his works. This sounds very much like the author of Hebrews in Hebrews 2:14 where the word "destroy" is also used. John's use of the word "appeared" emphasizes the preexistence of Christ and the historical reality of his incarnation. For the first of seven times in the letter, John refers to Jesus as the "Son of God." This title emphasizes his deity. All the works of the devil, including atheism, ignorance, unbelief, indifference, doubting, idolatry, blasphemy, pride, deceit, hypocrisy, hate, and a hundred other sins, will one day be completely eradicated by the power of "the Son of God."

John now begins to draw his argument to a close by stating in verse 9 that no one who has been born of God practices sin. His use of the perfect tense again stresses the complete and final nature of the new birth. The reason why the Christian cannot practice sin is because he has been given new birth by God himself. The crucial question is, what does John mean by the phrase "God's seed"? There are four possibilities. The "seed' could be the Word of God itself (James 1:18). A second option is the Holy Spirit. The third view is that "seed" refers to both the Word of God and the Holy Spirit. The final interpretation is the best option given the context. John is referring to the fact of the divine nature in us by virtue of the new birth. This new birth prohibits a lifestyle of sin in one who is truly born again. Christians may sin as John has already confirmed in his letter (1:5–10). But genuine Christians don't want to sin. Sometimes people assume that the doctrine of the eternal security of the believer becomes a license for Christians to sin with impunity. Have you ever heard someone say something like, "If I believe such a doctrine, I would do as I want to since I would be saved regardless." W. T. Conner, professor of theology at Southwestern Baptist Theological Seminary in a bygone era, had a good answer to such an egregious slur on God's saving grace: "That's right. I do what I want to do, but in regeneration Christ did something to my 'wanter.' I just don't want to do the things that you are talking about."[38]

John Wesley has an interesting sermon on 1 John 3:9. He attempts to describe how it is that "no one born of God makes a practice of sinning." If a believer is walking by faith and love, watching in prayer, then sin is excluded from his life, though even then we are liable to temptation. But if we cease to walk by faith, love, and prayer, we easily fall into the snare of the devil and commit sin. He notes that great men who clearly were children of God like David and Peter did indeed sin, and the reason for their sin is that they failed to walk by faith, love, and prayer. The Holy Spirit continually acts on our soul, and as long as this is followed by a reciprocal action of faith and love offered back to the Holy Spirit, we are able to walk in holiness. But if we turn a deaf ear to the constant work of the Holy Spirit in our lives, we open ourselves up to the possibility, even the inevitability, of sin.[39]

John's final point is found in verse 10. Every person is a member of one of two families: God's family or the devil's family. The distinguishing mark is what one practices: righteousness or sin. One who does not practice righteousness is not "of God," meaning God is not his spiritual Father. The foolproof test in this paternity dispute is to take swabs of lifestyle, and the one that shows no evidence of someone doing the right thing can't be God's child.[40] John then adds a final comment specifying one act of righteousness that he has already addressed and will address again: loving Christian brothers and sisters in the church. In essence God and Satan are the heads of two families. You are either a child of God or of Satan. Every person who has not been born into the family of God is a member of the family of Satan. The new birth determines what family you are in today. If you have not repented of your sin and believed on Jesus Christ as your Savior, you are still in the family of Satan. At the risk of being too culturally colloquial, in essence John is asking us a crucial question: "Who's your daddy?"

For this is the message that you have heard from the beginning, that we should love one another. We should not be like Cain, who was of the evil one and murdered his brother. And why did he murder him? Because his own deeds were evil and his brother's righteous. Do not be surprised, brothers, that the world hates you. We know that we have passed out of death into life, because we love the brothers. Whoever does not love abides in death. Everyone who hates his brother is a murderer, and you know that no murderer has eternal life abiding in him. By this we know love, that he laid down his life for us, and we ought to lay down our lives for the brothers. But if anyone has the world's goods and sees his brother in need, yet closes his heart against him, how does God's love abide in him? Little children, let us not love in word or talk but in deed and in truth.

1 JOHN 3:11–18

12

Love:
The Church's Circulatory System

LOVE IS THE circulatory system of the church. If the arteries of love get
clogged, the church is in danger of spiritual cardiac arrest. One key evidence of spiritual maturity in our lives is the depth of our love for one
another. John returns to this theme of Christian love for a second time.
Interestingly, when it comes to love, John speaks of four different levels
of relationships in which we can choose to live: murder (vv. 11, 12),
hatred (vv. 13–15), indifference (vv. 16, 17), and Christian love in action (v. 18).[1] John develops each of these in order. He reminds us of what
Christians have "heard from the beginning, that we should love one another." This is illustrated by Cain's murder of Abel as an example of the
difference between righteousness and evil. John then tells us we should
not be surprised when the world hates us rather than loves us. Love for
other believers evidences the fact that Christians have passed out of spiritual death into spiritual life. Hatred is a form of murder, according to
John, and by his logic, no murderer has eternal life dwelling in him. On
the other hand, mature love is willing to die for those loved, as Jesus did
for us. Since we ought to be willing to die for fellow believers, how much
more incongruous is it for Christians to be indifferent to the needs of others by refusing to sacrifice to provide them with what they need from their
own storehouse. Finally John draws it all to a close by telling us we are
not to love in word only, for such is not love at all. Rather, we must love
in genuine action. Loving one another for John is both a duty and a test.
It is a duty in that we are commanded as Christians to practice love. It is
a test in that our practice of love for others demonstrates the reality of our
Christian faith.

Love and Hate Are Mutually Exclusive in the Christian Life (vv. 11–15)

Verse 11 introduces a paragraph providing the grounds for John's concluding statement in verse 10. In the previous paragraph John reminds us of who we are: "children of God." Children of God are to behave like children of God. It is not enough to believe rightly. We must behave rightly. Being precedes doing, but all Christian doing must be based on being, that is, on who we are in Christ. Our practice proclaims who and what we are. "Message" is another word for the gospel, which includes the specific command to love. This message is one that John's readers have heard "from the beginning," meaning from the first time they heard the gospel.[2] John gives an illustrative example of the brothers Cain and Abel in verse 12 that is related to verse 11 as positive to negative. Hatred is the opposite of love. Cain's underlying attitude of jealousy and hatred for his brother led to his murder of Abel. This account is related in Genesis 4:1–16.[3]

Several important points need to be noted about the situation of Cain and Abel. Both were brothers with the same parents. Both brought sacrifices to God. Both sought to worship God. The problem was that Cain's sacrifice was apparently contrary to God's specified rules for the kind of sacrifice he should have brought. When Cain saw that God accepted his brother's sacrifice but rejected his own, he became angry. Cain demonstrated his spiritual and ethical relationship to Satan when he acted as he did. John had referred to "the devil" in verse 8, and now he refers to him as "the evil one," which connects Cain's evil heart and deed with its ultimate source, Satan. Cain's spiritual father, if you will, was Satan. Cain murdered Abel because "his own deeds were evil and his brother's righteous." John uses a word for "murder" in the Greek New Testament that means "to butcher or slaughter." Rendered literally, it would be translated "to cut the throat." Abel died a violent death at the hands of his own brother. This illustrates the fact that it is often the nature of the wicked to hate the righteous.

John answers three questions about Cain in these verses. First, where did Cain come from? Answer: "the evil one." What did Cain do? Answer: he "murdered his brother." Third, why did Cain do it? Answer: "his own deeds were evil." Cain failed the test of love for his brother.

John draws a conclusion in verse 13: "Stop being surprised[4] that the world (people like Cain) hates you." The world hates Christians for the same reason Cain hated Abel. Abel's righteousness was the fruit of his obedience to the Lord, and all this revealed Cain's disobedience and unrighteousness for what it was in reality. The present tense verb "hates" in verse 13 indicates a state of hostility. Few men are as qualified as Martin Niemoller to speak about the world's hatred of Christians:

> The fellowship of Jesus has no promise that it will ever be in the majority; we must indeed guard against thinking that there can ever be any kind of human security or assurance against the world's hatred. All parleys, all truces, all peace treaties are unreal, for the world must hate the Christian fellowship; and because of the fellowship, so long as it is a Christian fellowship, cannot hate, it must suffer at the hands of the world. . . . The motto of the community of Jesus is: "We are troubled on every side, yet not distressed; we are perplexed, but not in despair; persecuted, but not forsaken; cast down, but not destroyed." It is indeed a conquered world which seeks to terrify us; it is indeed a condemned and dying hatred which attacks us.[5]

Note the shift from "children" to "brothers" in verse 14 since John is dealing with the topic of brotherly love and Cain and Abel were brothers. John says we have come to know through experience that we have permanently passed from spiritual death to spiritual life (v. 14). The experience he refers to is our love for fellow believers. John views life and death as opposite spiritual domains that we more commonly refer to as "saved" and "unsaved." To "pass" from death to life is to experience the permanent change from a state of lostness to a state of being saved. Spiritually dead, though respectable; dead, though honored of men; dead, though positioned in places of political power. Spiritually dead, though educated and cultured; dead, though decent and satisfied with an outward form of godliness; dead, because of rejecting God's Son as Savior.[6] Nothing is more striking than the contrasts used in the Bible to illustrate the complete change the gospel brings. The difference between the saved and the unsaved is variously depicted as that between people who are lost and found, blind and seeing, bound and free, sick and whole, in darkness and enlightened. But probably the starkest and startling contrast of all is "out of death into life." We know that we are saved because we habitually practice love for our fellow believers. Whoever does not love continues to remain in a state of being unsaved, according to John. The now famous line from the French existentialist Jean-Paul Sartre's play *No Exit* is, "Hell is other people." Each character needs the other even when each hates the other.[7] Those who don't love abide in death, John says. They have the smell of the grave about them.

> The apostle talked of death. We try not to mention the word, but here our sophistication stops. For death is the leveler. We know infinitely more about the human body and the human mind than the apostle John; but we

die just as he did. We talk of our plans to fertilize the earth and colonize
the moon, but we die just like our ancestors. We are the generation "come
of age" who are reckoned to take charge of events, to decide our future,
and to need no God; yet we are as vulnerable as the most superstitious
savage. A stray germ, a gangster's knife, a drunken driver—and the most
brilliant modern mind is as dead as the caveman. All we have done is
to prolong life expectation by a few decades. The punctuation mark remains. Full stop.[8]

We might ask the question, how is it that one who hates his brother is
a murderer? Jesus answers the question in Matthew 5:21, 22. Hatred is an
intense emotional feeling, the desire to get rid of a person, even hoping he
will die. Hate is the first step toward murder. A person who hates is no different from a murderer in his attitude. The person who hates is potentially a
murderer as illustrated by Cain. John continues his logic: hate is attitudinally
no different than murder, and no murderer possesses eternal life. The question
is not so much, what did you do but what did you want to do? The English
Romantic poet and philosopher Samuel Taylor Coleridge said, "I have several
times seen the stiletto and the rosary come out of the same pocket."[9]

Recall that our Lord taught that what makes an act sinful is not only the
act itself but also the motive behind it. In fact, oftentimes what makes an act
good or bad, sinful or not sinful, is not the act itself, nor its consequences, but
its motive.[10] When Jesus passes judgment on our actions, he looks first at the
motive behind the act. If our heart is right, he is long-suffering with us even
when our deeds are incomplete or flawed in some way. If our heart is wrong,
none of our spiritual acts can ever be pleasing to him. Our love should not
be limited only to believers, according to John. Notice he tells us not to be
surprised if the world hates us, and immediately proceeds, "We know that we
have passed out of death into life, because we love the brothers" (v. 14). The
emphatic use of "we" in the Greek text contrasts the way Christians love and
the way the non-Christian world loves. But there is no emphatic contrast if
Christians love their own little group in the same way that the world loves its
own. When John goes on to say, "Whoever does not love . . ." notice that no
overt object is stated. In fact, some manuscripts add "the brothers," but the
best textual reading leaves it out. As Brooke says, to add the object "the brothers" "narrows down the writer's meaning unnecessarily. In his more absolute
statements he shows himself fully aware that the duty of love is absolute, and
has a wider application than the Christian society, even as the Christ is the
propitiation for the whole world."[11] This passage actually demands that our
love be more inclusive than the love of the world, which loves only its own.

Our love should include everybody, whether Christians or not, just as God's love includes everybody.[12]

Love Must Be Demonstrated in the Christian Life (vv. 16–18)

Everybody knows John 3:16. But do you know 1 John 3:16? Like John 3:16, 1 John 3:16 talks about the love of Christ for us as evidenced in his death on the cross. We have known (perfect tense) this love in its essence and meaning because we are the direct recipients of it. This knowledge is based on the historical event of the crucifixion where Jesus "laid down his life for us." What a simple yet sublime statement! Here is a direct statement that Jesus' death on the cross was voluntary. In John 10:17, 18 Jesus said that he lays down his life and no one takes it from him, but he gives it of his own will. Jesus' death on the cross was also a substitutionary death.[13] Most people consider the first law of life to be self-preservation. Jesus teaches us that the first law of spiritual life is self-sacrifice. He not only teaches us this truth, but he demonstrated it on our behalf. Who can fathom the love that drew salvation's plan?

> When Jesus came to die for our sins, there was nothing lovely about us. It was like the sunshine shining upon the garbage dump. The pristine son of God stepped into this kind of world and let his love shine. The epitome of love is seen at the cross. Jesus is the walking definition of love. Only in the cross can we understand the love of God.[14]

As if speaking directly to the Savior himself, Spurgeon said in his sermon on this passage, "Ah, Lord Jesus! I never knew Thy love till I understood the meaning of Thy death."[15] The most astounding thing in all the world is the fact that Jesus was willing, out of love for us, to die in our place as our substitute.

There is a famous picture by a great artist of an angel standing by the cross of Christ. With his fingers he is feeling the sharp points of the thorns that had pierced the Savior's brow, and on his face is a great look of wonder and astonishment. The angel cannot understand the marvel of that love.[16] In fact, no one can fully fathom such love. During his only visit to the United States, the eminent Swiss theologian Karl Barth lectured at Union Seminary in Richmond, Virginia. After his formal address he engaged in some informal conversation with the students. One young man asked Barth if he could state the core of what he believed. Barth took a moment to light his pipe, and then, as the smoke drifted away, he replied, "Yes, I think I can summarize my theology in these words: 'Jesus loves me, this I know, for the Bible tells me so.'"[17]

John essentially says three things about Jesus' death on the cross: it was voluntary, it was vicarious, and it was victorious. Jesus laid down his life for us once for all. His work on the cross is done and cannot be undone or redone. On the basis of Christ's death for us, John states emphatically[18] that we are under moral obligation to love, if necessary, by laying down our lives for others. I remember when I first read about Boris Kornfeld. I have never forgotten his story. I was in my second year as pastor of my first church in 1983. Chuck Colson's book *Loving God* had just been published the previous year. Colson told the riveting story of the Jewish doctor in a Russian concentration camp known as a gulag. What crime against the state he had committed no one knows. Kornfeld met a fellow prisoner, a committed Christian whose name we don't know, who engaged him in conversation about Jesus. He often heard the prisoner recite the Lord's Prayer and found himself strangely drawn to the words. While carrying on his medical duties amidst filth and squalor day after day, Kornfeld began to see the parallels in the Jewish people who had suffered so much as a nation and the suffering of Jesus. He became a Christian. When Kornfeld discovered an orderly stealing food from his patients, he reported him to the commandant. Though there had been a rash of murders in the camp, with each victim being a stoolie who had ratted someone else out and then paid for it with his life, Kornfeld didn't care. He knew his life would be in danger as soon as the orderly was released from his cellblock. Kornfeld felt a sense of newfound freedom in Christ. He wanted to tell someone about it, but the prisoner who had spoken to him about Christ had been transferred to another camp. One gray afternoon he examined a patient who had just been operated on for intestinal cancer. The man's eyes were sorrowful and suspicious, thought Kornfeld, and his face reflected the depth of his spiritual and physical misery. So the doctor began to talk to the patient, describing what had happened to him to change his life. Drifting in and out of the anesthesia's influence and shaking with fever, the patient heard the doctor's testimony about Christ and how all of our suffering is in one sense deserved on this earth for our sins. He hung on the doctor's words until he finally fell asleep. The next morning he was awakened by a commotion in the area. He wondered where his doctor friend was. Then a fellow patient told him of Kornfeld's fate. During the night, as Kornfeld slept in the infirmary, someone dealt him fatal blows to his skull with a mallet. Kornfeld died, but his testimony did not. The patient pondered the doctor's last, impassioned words about Christ, suffering, and salvation. He too became a Christian. He survived the prison camp and went on to tell the world what he had learned there. His name was Alexander Solzhenitsyn, winner of the Nobel Prize in literature in 1970 for his major work *The Gulag Archipelago*, which brought international exposure to the Soviet Union's labor camp system. He was expelled from the Soviet Union in 1974.[19]

Although it is possible that Christians would be called upon to give their lives for others as did Boris Kornfeld, more often we are called upon to show love in less drastic ways. John moves to practicalities and details of loving in verse 17. Notice he shifts from the plural "brothers" to the singular "brother" to individualize our duty to love in specific circumstances. Saying we love everybody in general may become an excuse for loving nobody in particular! Like the little boy on the crowded elevator who was overheard to say, "Mommy, I love mankind; it's people I can't stand," many of us find clever ways to disguise our dislike or hatred of someone. "How often does polite civility disguise undisclosed feelings of antipathy and aversion?" is a question well asked by Gary Burge.[20]

If we are to love everybody, does that mean we have to like everybody? How do I go about loving people I don't like, even in the church? I'm just asking the question I know you are asking right now in your mind! It seems to me there is a very clear, practical distinction between liking and loving. Common sense coupled with life experience makes it evident that we simply cannot and will not like everybody we meet, even in the church. Personalities being what they are, not to mention temperament, appearance, behavior, and mannerisms, make it inevitable that in life's journey you are going to like some people more than others. Remember, not everybody likes you either! Liking is a matter of personal preference. Loving is a matter of obedience to Christ and the Word of God. Love penetrates beyond the superficial and moves to the essence of the person. It overcomes obstacles and excuses. Love sees beyond what it does not like in a person and minimizes it in order to see the person as Christ sees him. Then seeing the person in that way opens the door to acting toward that person in a Christlike way. Loving people you don't like means treating them as if you did like them! You choose to act toward them in a way that is pleasing to Christ and that exhibits how Christ would act toward them. The nature of Christian love is that it acts, it gives, it expresses itself toward others.[21]

John paints a vivid picture in verse 17. First, he speaks of having "the world's goods." The word in Greek is *bios* and conveys the meaning of "livelihood." John does not describe someone here who is rich in this world's goods, but the average, ordinary person who has the basics of livelihood at his disposal and could help someone in need. John speaks of "seeing" a brother in need, using a word here meaning much more than a casual glance but rather a careful awareness of the situation where you understand the need.[22] When he speaks of someone who would "close his heart" to a brother in need, the word "close" conveys the notion of slamming the door,[23] locking it, and throwing away the key! The word "heart" in Greek is the word that includes not only the heart but the lungs, lower intestines, and liver. The Greeks regarded the "heart" as the seat of the emotions. The word connotes compassion and pity. Fellow Christians in need should arouse our compassion and pity to the point that we act to help. If we don't do so, John asks a pertinent rhetorical question: "how does God's love abide in him?"

What does the phrase "God's love" (or in some translations, "the love of God") mean here? There are several options: 1) God's love for us; 2) our love for God; 3) the kind of love God gives believers; and 4) the divine quality of love. John clearly does not mean to say that if we don't love, God does not love us. However, the other three options convey some truth. Our love for God is certainly inhibited if we don't love by our actions. Furthermore, the kind of love God gives us as believers is not being exhibited to others when we don't love as we ought. Finally, the divine quality of love that is evidenced in the life of a genuine believer is absent when we don't love, which then calls into question whether we are truly born again. When John asks, "How does God's love abide in him?" if we don't love fellow Christians, the answer, of course, is that it does not.

One question concerning verses 16, 17 is the extent of the meaning of "brothers." Does John refer *only* to fellow Christians, or is the word, and the command to love, to be extended to anyone in need, Christians and others? The term *brother* cannot be limited to Christians since the term is being used in the general sense of "fellowman."[24] Our love for the world is to be translated into helping those in need: "But if anyone has the world's goods and sees his brother in need, yet closes his heart against him, how does God's love abide in him?" (v. 17). Leon Morris is right: this cannot refer only to believers.[25] You do not have to murder in order to sin; hatred is murder in the heart. You do not have to hate in order to sin; all you have to do is be indifferent. Sometimes the greatest sin we can commit is the sin of indifference. Everyone has to learn to get over the stupor of self.

By returning to his address form ("little children") in verse 18, John introduces a final exhortation based on his preceding argument. We should not merely love in "word" and "talk." The two words are essentially synonymous. People in need don't just need to hear a word of encouragement such as James speaks of when he talks about the person who says to the one in need, "be warmed and filled," but then sends him on his way without any tangible assistance (James 2:15, 16). Rather, we are to love "in deed and in truth." The word for "deed" in the Greek New Testament is the noun *ergon*, which means "work" or "action." In our culture we use a word the first part of which comes from this Greek word *ergon—ergonomics*. Ergonomics is the study of how the workplace and the equipment used in the workplace can best be designed for efficiency, productivity, comfort, and safety. It also is used to describe the qualities in the design of equipment used at work that contributes to efficiency and productivity. Our love for others should be ergonomically effective in the sense that its distinctive quality should be that it is Christlike in every way. Our love should be productive; it should accomplish the meeting of needs in a tangible way. In one of his sermons, George Whitfield told the story of the poor beggar who asked a pastor for alms. When the pastor refused, the beggar asked the pastor for a blessing. "God bless you," answered the pastor. "Oh," replied the beggar, "you would not give me that if it was worth anything."[26]

John further describes how we should love: "in truth." His use of "truth" here is probably an idiom that means "actually" or "really."[27] Our love should be genuinely demonstrated in action. A modern version of the Parable of the Good Samaritan would have the priest and the Levite saying to the beaten-up traveler, "Man, you need help, but I don't need you."[28] I sometimes think fundamentally some of us really would like nothing better in this world than to purchase a life membership in the "Association of Bystanders."[29] We can't just give lip service to love; we must do something about it. When it comes to putting love into action, some Christians are like the occasional lazy student I have had in my class: they want to get a passing grade but do as little work as possible.

If our view of God is skewed, our actions will also be skewed. Many view God as the cosmic policeman, brandishing his Ten Commandments at everything that moves. Others see God as a cosmic bellhop, ready to do anything to make life pleasant and safe without asking for anything more than a reasonable tip. But the true God is neither. He demonstrated his love on the cross. He deserves our love and expects us to love others as he has loved us. But we will never do so as long as we are so focused on Number One. A certain book is called *I Prayed Myself Slim*. The author, with God on her side and the help of a crash diet, lost eighty-two pounds and for the first time in her life had dates, dates, dates! She was even invited to the Governor's Inaugural Ball, where praise be to God, she was no longer a waddling wallflower! This book and a hundred like it may have their dietary benefits for those of us who cast inelegant shadows, but I mention it for another reason. It contains fifty-eight prayers by the author, but only four acknowledge the existence of other people.[30]

By some accounts William Booth, founder of the Salvation Army, once sent a one-word telegraph message: "Others!" to encourage his officers around the world. Whether the story is true or not, one thing is for sure: Salvation Army workers were known for their unselfish commitment to others. On May 29, 1914 the *Empress of Ireland* sank with 130 Salvation Army officers on board. One hundred and nine of those officers were drowned, and not one body that was picked up had on a life belt. The few survivors told how the Salvationists, finding there were not enough life preservers for all, took off their own belts and strapped them upon even strong men, saying, "I can die better than you can." From the deck of that sinking ship they heralded their battle-cry around the world: "Others!"[31]

May we all pray this prayer by William Sloane Coffin: "We have taken advantage of Thy great and unqualified love. We have presumed upon Thy patience to do less than we might have done, to have been timid where we should have shown courage, to have been careful where we should have been reckless, not counting the cost. We pray now, O Father, to be used roughly. Stamp on our selfishness."[32]

By this we shall know that we are of the truth and reassure our heart before him; for whenever our heart condemns us, God is greater than our heart, and he knows everything. Beloved, if our heart does not condemn us, we have confidence before God; and whatever we ask we receive from him, because we keep his commandments and do what pleases him. And this is his commandment, that we believe in the name of his Son Jesus Christ and love one another, just as he has commanded us. Whoever keeps his commandments abides in God, and God in him. And by this we know that he abides in us, by the Spirit whom he has given us.

1 JOHN 3:19–24

13

How to Send Your Guilt Trip Packing

HAVE YOU EVER BEEN PRAYING and suddenly your conscience says something like this to you: "Look at you! Who do you think you are to come before God and ask anything from him! Why just this week you did things and said things that would disqualify you from ever receiving anything from God. Don't you remember that attitude you had yesterday? Don't you remember how you got angry with your wife for no reason last week? What about that unclean thought that passed through your mind three days ago? You passed someone broken down on the road and could have stopped to help, but you didn't. You're sure not much of a Christian, are you? What right do you have now to come to God and ask him for anything?" Thoughts such as these can shut down your prayer time in a New York minute. It's hard to pray when you don't have assurance and confidence that God welcomes you and is willing to hear your prayers.

John has something vital to say about this situation in 3:19–24. The center of this passage is John's appeal in verse 23: we should believe in Jesus and love one another. This appeal is flanked on both sides with a motivational basis. Verses 19–22 provide the first motivation: when our conscience condemns us, God is greater than our conscience, giving us assurance that we will receive what we ask from him in prayer. Verse 24 constitutes the second motivation: we can be assured that God lives in us and we abide in him. The topic of this paragraph is confidence. Notice John's use of words like "know," "reassure," and "confidence." Confidence is based on the fact that we have believed in Jesus and are thus in the family of God and that, as obedient children in the family, we love others in the family. Since we are in the family and since we love others in the family, we can come to our Father with our prayer requests with confident assurance that he will hear us.

Assurance for an Unsure Heart (vv. 19–22)

When John says "by this" at the beginning of verse 19, he refers back to the previous paragraph where the topic is love for fellow believers. By means of our truly loving our Christian brothers we know that "we are of the truth"; that is, that we are truly Christians and are behaving according to the truth of the gospel and thus the will of God. Notice that the phrase "by this we know" occurs again at the end of verse 24, bracketing the paragraph. John places the phrase "we are of the truth" at the beginning of the clause in Greek to give it prominence and focus. As a result, this knowledge allows us to "reassure our heart." Here the word "heart" actually refers to the conscience. A clear conscience provides us confidence to approach God at any time in prayer and worship. Wesley said the conscience functions in three ways: "First. It is a witness, testifying to what we have done in thought, or word, or action. Secondly. It is a judge, passing sentence on what we have done, that it is good or evil. And, thirdly, it, in some sort, executes the sentence, by occasioning a degree of complacency in him that does well, and a degree of uneasiness in him that does evil."[1]

Cars have a number of digital warning lights. One warns that the emergency brake has been left on. Another reminds the driver that the engine is running hot. Another warns that the alternator is not charging the battery properly. God has given us a built-in warning signal called conscience. Just as the warning lights in your car have to be properly wired, so to speak, in order to function properly, so your conscience must be properly schooled in the truth of God's Word in order to function as God intended. But this is not at all. Even your conscience in good working order cannot force obedience! The driver may disregard the red lights of warning. If he does so, he may burn out the brakes, ruin the battery, or crack the motor block. Christians who disregard their conscience are headed for trouble.

As a Christian, your conscience now functions according to a new standard. You now have a sharper sense of sin, and you now see wrong in what did not seem wrong before. This produces in us a great sense of responsibility. There is some question as to whether "reassure" means "to be persuaded" or "to be certain." The latter is contextually best.[2] The word means "to exhibit confidence and assurance in a situation that might otherwise cause dismay or fear." The tense of the verb is future and applies to any future prayer situation.

To stand "before him" refers to our position of living under God's continual observation, including when we address him in prayer.

Conscience, left to itself, is not an adequate guide. John continues to say in verse 20 that our conscience might condemn us when we are praying. Verses 20, 21 remind me of a courtroom scene. There is to be a trial within the jurisdiction of my conscience. Oddly enough, in this courtroom my conscience is going to act as prosecutor, defense attorney, witness, judge, and jury! Furthermore, it seems court is in session at some point every day of my life! My conscience is subpoenaed by my actions. If we think about it, normally we could not wish to be tried by a more favorable judge than our own conscience! We usually have no reason to decline our conscience's jurisdiction under any pretense of prejudice against us! Nevertheless, our conscience is far from being an infallible judge since the judge can be blinded or bribed! After hearing all of the evidence in my case, sometimes the judge (my conscience) condemns me for what I've done, said, or thought. If I am indeed guilty of the infractions my conscience condemns me for, I can expect that if I were to appeal my case to the Supreme Court Judge of the universe, God would more than confirm the sentence!

But sometimes our conscience may condemn us when we are not guilty of overt sin. We sometimes become keenly aware of our unworthiness before God, especially at times of prayer. Sometimes this unworthiness is satanic in nature. As Luther said, "Sometimes the devil interprets the best things badly and the bad things well, weakens the good things and makes much of the things that are bad. From a little laughter he can make eternal damnation."[3] Yet God is greater than our conscience and knows everything concerning us, including our deepest motives. God is omniscient. He never has to subpoena any witnesses to find out about our public or private life. No one can teach God anything; he already knows it all. In fact, God has never learned anything! If God had to learn something, he would not have been God before he had to learn it! God has never forgotten anything either. If he had, he would cease to be God![4]

Because God knows everything about us, God is sometimes more merciful with us than we are with ourselves. Since God is greater than our accusing conscience in the sense that he has greater knowledge of it than we do, we can be confident he understands our weaknesses and loves us in spite of them.[5] Though we desire to meet the standards of conscience, sometimes we fall short. When we are living and loving as we ought, even if our oversensitive conscience condemns us, we take comfort in knowing that God is greater than our conscience. Our conscience is not the Supreme Court! There is a higher court: God! Peter took his case to the highest court when Jesus asked him a third time, "Do you love me?" in John 21. Peter responded, "Lord, you know everything; you know that I love you." We rest in his forgiveness. Our conscience is at ease. We have "confidence"[6] that we can speak freely with God and ask him for whatever we need (v. 21). Luther's descriptive picture is worth a thousand words: "Conscience is one drop; the reconciled God is a sea of comfort."[7]

When the commanding officer enters the barracks, everyone snaps to attention. When the commanding officer says, "At ease!" everyone breathes a little easier. God, who knows our hearts, says to our conscience, "At ease!"

Not only that, John continues, but we have confidence that we will receive from God what we request because we do what he commands and because we "do what pleases him" (v. 22). What is the relationship between the phrases "we keep his commandments" and "do what pleases him"? This may simply be two ways of expressing the same thing. On the other hand, John could be laying out two conditions for receiving answers to our prayers: 1) obedience to his commands, and 2) spontaneous obedience to God's will whenever that is discerned in our lives. Our keeping God's commands is not merely out of duty. The higher motivation of love causes us to desire to obey God's commands.

This passage should not be taken to mean that we have carte blanche to get anything we ask for in prayer from God. God is a wise and loving father, not an indulgent father. No father gives his children everything they ask for. The result would be spoiled and self-centered children. As Christians we are sometimes like children who ask for things that would harm us in the long run. Our loving heavenly Father knows when to say no. But John's point is that as we live in obedience to the Word and will of God, our prayers will be reflections of his will and thus will be readily answered.

Childlike confidence makes you pray as nothing else can. It makes you pray for big things that you would never have asked for if you did not have this confidence. It makes you pray for small things because you know nothing is too small in your life to occupy God's attention. Some might imagine that our little prayer requests are so trifling that it would be almost an insult to bring them to God. What is sometimes a big matter to a little child is a small matter to parents; yet the parents do not measure the request only from their own point of view, but from the point of view of the child as well.[8] Our heavenly Father is pleased when we come before him in prayer to ask for things big and small. We can do so because we have confidence just like a child with his or her parent. If it is big enough to concern you, it is big enough to concern God! But unlike a child, we need to be spiritually mature enough to understand what John is saying. ". . . everything has been heard, even though one does not know what has been heard. . . . Therefore every prayer is heard, and whatever we ask for happens, even though we do not recognize in what way it happens."[9]

First John 3:19, 20 functions as the reason for verses 21, 22. There are two reasons that assure us we are truly believers. The first is our awareness of the love God has placed in us (v. 19a). The second is our awareness of the grace of God that accepts our humanness because Christ knows our motives (v. 20b). On this basis, God is greater than our conscience, and there is no need for fear and trepidation when we approach God.

When I was a child, my favorite movie was *The Wizard of Oz*. My favorite part was when Dorothy and her three friends, the Scarecrow, the Tin Man, and the Cowardly Lion, all are walking down that long corridor leading to the huge doors behind which lies the great and powerful Wizard of Oz. As the doors slowly open, the music reaches crescendo volume, and fire and smoke surround the throne. A booming voice bellows forth from the throne. Dorothy and her three friends are quaking with fear. Suddenly the Wizard says, "Step forward, Tin Man!" The Tin Man steps forward, and he is shaking and rattling all over. The Wizard says to him, "Do you dare to come to me to ask for a heart? You clinking, clanking, clattering collection of caliginous junk!" Is that how Christians are to come into the presence of God in prayer—with quaking fear? Of course not! We have confidence! The author of Hebrews put it like this in 4:16: "Let us then with confidence draw near to the throne of grace, that we may receive mercy and find grace to help in time of need." Again in Hebrews 10:19 we read, "We have confidence to enter the holy places by the blood of Jesus." Fear and timidity before God melts away in the face of such confidence. This is the confidence our Lord desires each of us to have as we approach him.

Apart from the work of the Holy Spirit in me, I cannot hate sin and love God. I know in my conscience that God cannot and will not lower his standard one hundredth of an inch. I also know it is absolutely impossible for me to comply with his commands in my own strength. Yet because of the Holy Spirit, I can both hate sin and love God!

In verse 22 John gives two reasons for why we have confidence in prayer and thus receive what we ask of God. First, we have confidence because we obey God's commands. John has already talked about the importance of obedience in the Christian life as an evidence of genuine conversion. Now he speaks about obedience as a prerequisite for answered prayer. Second, we have this confidence in prayer because we "do what pleases him." This may be simply another way of expressing obedience. God is pleased when we obey him. The implication is that the converse is also true: God is displeased when we disobey him. John does not mean that confidence in prayer is founded on our works. Rather, godliness and sincere worship cannot be separated from faith.[10] Too many spiritual forgers sign Jesus' name to their prayer checks.[11] Only those who are true believers "in the name" of Jesus (v. 23) have the right to claim the promise of verse 22. And don't forget: God's promises are not mottos to hang on the wall, they are checks to take to the bank!

Faith and Obedience Are the Grounds of Our Assurance (vv. 23, 24)

The heart of Paul's appeal is seen in verse 23. We are given a twofold command: "believe in the name of his Son Jesus Christ," and "love" fellow believers. Here is the first use of "believe" in the letter. When John says we are to believe in the "name" of God's Son, the use of "name" for Jesus is a literary device called metonymy, which means using the part as a reference for the whole. Here Jesus' "name" is a reference to his whole person. Trusting in the name of Jesus suggests trusting in all that name implies. Calvin's point is well taken when he says that John's reference to "the name" refers to preaching. The only right faith is that which embraces Christ as he is preached in the gospel.[12] "This" refers to "commandment" and is placed first in the clause for emphasis. When John speaks about "his commandments" in verses 22c and 24a, in both places the phrase is placed in the forefront in the clause for emphasis. The content of the command contains the full name "Son" and "Jesus Christ." Since the word "commandment" is singular, a shift from the plural "commandments" in the previous verse, John is combining both the concept of believing in Jesus and loving the brothers into a single action. What we have is one command with two parts: believe and love.

When John says we are to do these two things "just as he commanded us," he is referring to Jesus' command to do these things, reiterated several times in John's Gospel. Isn't it interesting that John tells us it is a command to believe in the name of Jesus? The gospel is not only something to be believed but something to be obeyed, and all people are commanded to repent and believe the gospel. This concept is not unique to John but is found as well in Paul. In his Areopagus sermon he said to the Athenians, "The times of ignorance God overlooked, but now he commands all people everywhere to repent, because he has fixed a day on which he will judge the world in righteousness by a man whom he has appointed; and of this he has given assurance to all by raising him from the dead" (Acts 17:30, 31). Likewise in Romans 1:5 Paul speaks of the gospel as something to be obeyed when he says the reason he was given grace and apostleship was to "bring about the obedience of faith for the sake of his name." John himself tells us that he wrote his own Gospel so that people would believe on the Lord Jesus Christ and be saved: "But these are written so that you may believe that Jesus is the Christ, the Son of God, and that by believing you may have life in his name" (John 20:31). Notice how in this key verse in John's Gospel there are five words that occur in 1 John 3:23: believe, name, Son, Jesus, and Christ.

But John is also deeply concerned in his gospel to teach us the importance of loving one another. It is Jesus who has given us the new commandment to love one another (John 13:34). Much of the final teaching Jesus gave his disciples before his crucifixion as recorded in John's Gospel has to do with the importance of their loving one another.

John closes his trajectory of thought with verse 24: "Whoever keeps his commandments abides in God, and God in him. And by this we know that he abides in us, by the Spirit whom he has given us." If anyone does what God commands him to do, that person lives united with God in the sense that he or she maintains close fellowship (abides) with God and God lives (abides) in him. In this situation God's fellowship with us remains uninterrupted. Of course, it is true that all who are genuine believers are constantly united with God and God is constantly united with them. The assurance of this abiding is the presence of the Holy Spirit in our lives, whom Jesus has given us. The Holy Spirit is the believer's assurance of salvation. John 14:17 speaks of the Spirit as abiding "with you" and "in you." This promise finds its fulfillment in the abiding presence of the Holy Spirit (1 Corinthians 3:16, 17; 6:19).

When John uses the verb "has given" in verse 24, the implied subject is Jesus. The means of our assuring knowledge is the presence of the Holy Spirit. This is the first direct mention of the Holy Spirit in the letter.[13] It is difficult to know whether John intends to convey the fact of the presence of the Holy Spirit as proof we abide in Christ or whether the Holy Spirit causes us to know with assurance that we abide in him and he in us. Both are certainly true. Either way verse 24 serves as John's second motivation for his appeal in verse 23. The Holy Spirit is God's gift to his children, a divine bestowal. In this gift of the Holy Spirit, God gives himself to us. This is that precious truth of our union with Christ.

Sometimes we Christians underestimate the importance of the role of the Holy Spirit in our lives. The Holy Spirit receives scant attention compared to God the Father and God the Son. But the Holy Spirit is, after all, the third member of the Trinity. His presence in our lives is the guarantee of our salvation (Ephesians 1:13, 14). The Holy Spirit indwells every believer at the moment of conversion (1 Corinthians 12:13). We are commanded to be filled with the Holy Spirit continually (Ephesians 5:18). We are to take up and wield "the sword of the Spirit, which is the word of God" in our spiritual warfare against Satan (Ephesians 6:17).

It is interesting to me that John says in verse 24 that it is the indwelling Holy Spirit who serves as the means of our knowing that God abides in us; yet John does not say that the presence of the Holy Spirit is the means of our knowing that we abide in God. Our keeping God's commandments is the evidence that we are abiding in him. Obedience is the key here. In one sense we genuine believers are always abiding in Christ by virtue of our eternal salvation, which is God's gift. In another sense we are only abiding in Christ when we are walking in obedience to his will. Our fellowship with him is contingent on our obedience. When we choose to commit an act of sin and thus disobey God, we break that fellowship temporarily. However, our sonship, the fact that we are saved, remains unaffected. As John has already taught in 1 John 1:9, when we sin, we are to confess that sin and receive cleansing, which brings renewed fellowship with the Father, Son, and Holy Spirit.

A Christian knows he or she is a Christian because of the presence of the abiding Holy Spirit. John Flavel expressed it this way: "Interest in Christ may be certainly gathered and concluded from the gift of the Spirit to us."[14] John Wesley agreed: "By the testimony of the Spirit, I mean, an inward impression on the soul, whereby the Spirit of God immediately and directly witnesses to my spirit, that I am a child of God . . . and I, even I, am reconciled to God."[15] The New Testament writers speak of the presence of the Holy Spirit in both positive and negative terms. John speaks positively here of the presence of the Spirit as the ground of Christian assurance. We see the negative side from the absence of the Holy Spirit, as in Romans 8:9: "Anyone who does not have the Spirit of Christ does not belong to him."

Wesley spoke to the question of how we know the Holy Spirit witnesses to our salvation experience.

> And how am I assured . . . that I do not mistake the voice of the Spirit? Even by the testimony of your own spirit: by "the answer of a good conscience toward God." By the fruits which He hath wrought in your spirit, you shall know the testimony of the Spirit of God. Hereby you shall know that you are in no delusion . . . the immediate fruits of the Spirit, ruling in the heart . . . And the outward fruits are, the doing good to all men; the doing no evil to any; and the walking in the light a zealous, uniform obedience to all the commandments of God.[16]

What about the question of sanctification? Listen to Wesley again as he tells us we know of our sanctification in the same way we know of our justification:

> Q. But how do you know, that you are sanctified . . . ?
>   A. I can know it no otherwise than I know that I am justified. "Hereby know we that we are of God," in either sense, "by the Spirit that he hath given us."[17]

Sanctification is a twofold work. First, it is a work of God. The indwelling of the Holy Spirit at regeneration is wholly the work of God. Without the Holy Spirit in our lives as believers, we would be doomed to spiritual defeat. He is the source of divine power to win victory over sin. Second, it is the work of the believer. It is the work of the believer in the sense that we must cooperate with the Holy Spirit at work within us to live holy lives. This is how we make progress spiritually.[18]

In 1 John 3:19–24 John teaches us several vital truths. First, Christians should not treat sin lightly. This is a reiteration of what he taught in 1:5–10. But on the other hand, neither should we be harder on ourselves than God is. A constant morbid introspection leads to a defeated Christian life. Our thoughts, words, and deeds will always be tinged with imperfection. As David Jackman well said, "It is easy to become so tense about our failures, to be so hard on ourselves for not doing better, and so miserable about our state, that we lose the sunshine of God's love."[19] Second, John is not teaching that we somehow earn the right to have our prayers answered by means of loving fellow believers. On the contrary, loving fellow believers, in obedience to God's command, shows we are in the will of God and thus in a place where God can and will answer our prayers. Warren Wiersbe got it right: "When our *delight* is in the love of God, our *desires* will be in the will of God."[20] Third, we learn that our prayer life cannot be divorced from our relationship to fellow Christians. Peter made this point even more specifically in 1 Peter 3:7 when he spoke about how our relationship with our spouse can hinder our prayer life. Fourth, although our conscience is a God-given faculty to help us determine right from wrong, it is not infallible. If our conscience condemns us, the probability is that God, the all-knowing Judge, will confirm the sentence! But your conscience can also put you on a guilt trip. If the trial in the court of conscience leads to an acquittal, that acquittal brings confidence before God, especially in our prayer life. Sometimes we need the Lord to say to our conscience, "At ease!" Whenever your conscience puts you on trial, remember, God is in your corner! He knows you better than you know yourself. Your case goes to his Supreme Court for his final ruling.

A French proverb says, "There is no pillow so soft as a clear conscience." The benefits of a clear conscience are confidence before God and confidence that our prayers will be answered. We all face the challenge of a condemning conscience on occasion along with the challenge of an imperfect obedience. We are keenly aware that our love for fellow Christians sometimes falls short of what it ought to be. We are also keenly aware that, try as we may, we cannot live the Christian life in our own strength. The presence of the Holy Spirit turns the Christian life from an impossible dream into a dream come true![21] Our consciences know things unknown to others, but not unknown to God. God knows exactly where we are spiritually. He never minimizes our failures, but it is comforting to know that God knows the sincerity of the love we do have, for him and for others, even if such love is imperfect. Even this becomes welcome evidence we have been born again.[22]

Beloved, do not believe every spirit, but test the spirits to see whether they are from God, for many false prophets have gone out into the world. By this you know the Spirit of God: every spirit that confesses that Jesus Christ has come in the flesh is from God, and every spirit that does not confess Jesus is not from God. This is the spirit of the antichrist, which you heard was coming and now is in the world already. Little children, you are from God and have overcome them, for he who is in you is greater than he who is in the world. They are from the world; therefore they speak from the world, and the world listens to them. We are from God. Whoever knows God listens to us; whoever is not from God does not listen to us. By this we know the Spirit of truth and the spirit of error.

1 JOHN 4:1–6

14

Discerning Truth and Error

IT IS EASY TO DETERMINE intellectually that the equation $2 + 2 = 5$ is mathematically incorrect: $2 + 2$ does not equal 5 (in a base ten mathematical system). It is easy to verify intellectually that the earth is not flat but round. It is easy to verify intellectually that Abraham Lincoln actually lived and served as President of the United States. However, spiritual truth and error are not identified by reasoning alone. Satan desires spiritual truth's destruction, and failing that, he desires its corruption. In John 7:17 Jesus says, "If anyone's will is to do God's will, he will know whether the teaching is from God or whether I am speaking on my own authority." We learn here that the gateway to spiritual truth is not so much the intellect but the will. Because there is spiritual truth, there is also spiritual error and falsehood. Spiritual truth and error are not discerned by logical or intellectual reasoning alone. Intellectual reasoning is a part of the truth discernment process, but truth is not discerned that way *alone*. Some of the brightest people on the face on the earth are dead wrong about some things they believe and teach. Spiritual truth is not discerned, known, or identified by reasoning alone. Spiritual discernment plays a crucial role as well. To know God you must come to him in faith and love. Intellectuals who are intoxicated with their own wisdom and knowledge can't quite seem to figure out that their own investigative methodologies are flawed to the core when it comes to discerning spiritual truth.

The context of 4:1–6 concerns the source of true and false teaching. Note that the phrase "from God" occurs six times in these six verses (in every verse except verse 5 and twice in verse 6). The Book of Acts confirms that in the early church the Holy Spirit was particularly associated with the function of preaching and teaching. The source of true Christian teaching is God through the Holy Spirit. In this paragraph John uses the word "Spirit," which in English translation is capitalized to indicate John is referring to the Holy

Spirit. He uses the word "spirit" with a lowercase *s* when referring to demonic spirits and as a metonymy (a literary device meaning using the part for the whole) for the person who speaks about God and what he teaches about God.[1] The supernatural is real, but it is not always from God!

Test the Teaching (v. 1)

John begins this passage by telling us not to believe every spirit but to test the spirits to see if they are from God.[2] Christians are not to "believe" every teaching that comes down the pike. Only teaching that comes from God is to be believed. Rather, we are to "test" teaching to determine its source and quality. The Greek word translated "test" here was commonly used in the first century for the testing of metals to see if they were unalloyed and genuine. What does it mean "to test the spirits"?

Anytime we hear a sermon, read a book, hear a speaker, or go to a seminar, we must not just automatically believe everything that person tells us because we assume him to be an authority. What he is telling us may be wrong. John is using the word "spirit" in verse 1 in the sense of the spirit that is behind the person who is doing the preaching and teaching.[3] There are two possibilities here. Either a preacher or teacher is operating from the Holy Spirit of God or from some demonic spirit. "Testing" is how we go about determining if something is genuine. Is God the source of this teaching, or is a demonic spirit behind it? The reason we are told to test the spirits is because many false prophets have gone out into the world.

The multiplicity of "spirits" activating the many false prophets can refer either to the large number of false prophets or to the large number of evil spirits that activate them. Actually both meanings are true. In contrast to the many false "spirits," there is only one "Spirit of God" (v. 2a).

These false prophets "have gone out into the world." Some take this statement to mean that Christian prophets once in the church have gone out of the church into the world to teach false doctrine. This is impossible to know for sure, unless perhaps this is a reference to the false teachers whom John mentioned in 2:19. Others take the phrase to indicate that the false teachers went into the world empowered by satanic teaching. This is certainly true on the basis of what John has already said in his letter. But most likely John is just employing the verb to indicate that these false teachers appeared teaching among people, regardless of where they came from.

Throughout the Bible and church history there have always been false prophets. God gave very specific and strict regulations for dealing with false prophets in the Old Testament era. In fact, they were to be stoned. Taking his cue from the severity of punishment in the Old Testament, albeit it with a tinge of exaggeration (but only a tinge!), Luther said, "But you will test them in the following way: He who wants to teach things that are new or different must have been called by God and must confirm his calling with true miracles. If he does not do this, let him depart from this place and be hanged!"[4]

Today false prophets are to be discerned, their teaching condemned, and then avoided. The purpose of testing is not to discern whether their motivation is from God, but rather whether the message they speak is true or false. This is what enables us to know whether the message comes from God. If the message is true, it comes from God. If it is false, it does not. "Eyes wide open" should be the watchword for every Christian. Unfortunately, for some, when it comes to discerning false teaching, the watchword seems to be, "eyes wide shut."

First Timothy 4:1 makes an important statement about the source of false doctrine: "In later times some will depart from the faith by devoting themselves to deceitful spirits and teachings of demons." The source of false doctrine is Satan and his demons. Satan's plan is to distort true doctrine by means of false prophets who teach something less than sound doctrine. We should consider not only the source of false doctrine but the danger of false doctrine. False doctrine denies true doctrine. False doctrine distorts truth. False doctrine deceives. Consider how cults operate. They come to you masquerading as a valid Christian group. Sometimes they present themselves as "just another denomination." Jesus said in Matthew 24:5 that many false christs would come in his name claiming to be the Messiah, and they will deceive many. Jesus said in Mark 13:22, 23 that false messiahs and false prophets will rise up and perform signs and wonders. The result is deception, sometimes of God's own people. Paul in his address to the Ephesian elders in Acts 20:29, 30 identifies two places from which false teacher will try to come and disrupt the church. One is from the outside; the other is from the inside. Peter also warns of the danger of false teachers in 2 Peter 2:1.

I never cease to be amazed at the gullibility of some people. When I turn on my television and see some of those so-called faith healers plying their trade, I marvel at how many people are following them. There is a sucker born every minute![5] Even when documentaries expose some of these people as the hucksters they are, large crowds still follow them, looking for a miracle. We cannot afford spiritual naiveté about spiritual teaching. All teaching must be tested.

Nobody wants to be known for being a heresy hunter. In our day of watered-down doctrine, some believe we should not get hung up on doctrine.

"Doctrine divides," they say. *We just all need to love everybody and get along. Let's have an Oprah group hug and all sing "Kumbaya" around the ecumenical campfire. Why, you don't want to be intolerant and judgmental of people who don't agree with you, do you?* That sounds altruistic and appealing, does it not? The fact of the matter is, true Christianity is doctrinally intolerant. Jesus said, "I am the way." There is no other way. Either he is right or wrong. Either John 14:6 is true or false. Christianity is by definition a God-revealed religion whereby God says this is truth and this is error. God gets to make the rules. It is his world. We need to remember that Satan is out for the destruction of truth, and where he cannot succeed in that, he is interested in truth corruption. Satan knows that if he comes directly to you and says that Jesus isn't really God in human flesh, most Christians will see through the lie. So what does he do? He sends someone into the church who is wishy-washy on some doctrines, someone who is willing to compromise on some truths. Satan can sound so educated and so reasonable. He dilutes and distorts until finally he destroys truth.

In his famous sermon *The Distinguishing Marks of a Work of the Spirit of God* preached at Yale's commencement on September 10, 1741, Jonathan Edwards takes as his text 1 John 4:1. In Section One he discusses nine "negative signs" that cannot be deemed as showing that a work is not from God. For example, Edwards points out, "If some who were thought to be wrought upon fall away into gross errors or scandalous practices, it is no argument that the work in general is not the work of the Spirit of God. That there are some counterfeits is no argument that nothing is true; such things are always expected in a time of reformation."[6] Wise words. In Section Two Edwards identifies the distinguishing Scriptural evidences of a genuine work of God. Here he confines himself to principles laid out mostly in 1 John 4:1–6.

In 1 John 4:1–6 John gives us three tests to determine truth and error. The first is found in verses 2, 3. Placed in the form of a question posed to suspected false teachers, test number 1 is, do they confess Jesus as the divine Lord? Test number 2 is, do they possess divine life? Test number 3 is, do they profess the divine truth?

Do They Confess the Divine Lord? (vv. 2, 3)

Here John tells us how we can know[7] the presence of the Spirit of God as the source of teaching. Here the word "know" indicates "come to know, ascertain." Genuine knowledge of Christian experience does not arise from within but has a supernatural origin. It is God's gift to the believer. This is a blow to the proto-Gnostics and their false teaching of secret, superior knowledge as a way of salvation. There is no salvation by knowledge but only a salvation by grace through Christ.

When John says that every "spirit" that confesses Jesus has come in the flesh is "from God," he is emphasizing the issue of source and origin. When John says those that do not so confess Jesus are "not from God," again he is emphasizing source or origin, but with the added thought of opposition to the true teaching that is from God. John is not just speaking casually when he says "Jesus Christ has come." Rather he is emphasizing that Jesus came from another realm entirely. He has entered into our world by erupting into history. In the face of all those in John's day who were denying his unique deity and eternal sonship, John emphasizes both.[8]

I recommend that you read Walter Martin's classic book *The Kingdom of the Cults*, an excellent work on the subject of the cults. Chapter 17 is entitled "The Jesus of the Cults." Martin surveys what the various cults teach about the person of Christ. For example, the Jesus of the Jehovah Witnesses, according to their publication *Watchtower*, is *a* god, not *the* God. Official doctrine of the Jehovah Witnesses teaches that Jesus was the first creation of God. Charles Russell, the founder, described this Jesus as having been Michael the Archangel prior to his divesting himself of his angelic nature and appearing in the world as a man. Jesus is thus an angel who became a man. He is a godlike figure, but he is not God the Son, the second member of the Trinity, as the Bible teaches. Jehovah's Witnesses are explicit in their denial of the deity of Jesus, both in their writings and at your doorstep!

Consider the Jesus of the Mormons. Mormonism teaches, ". . . each of these gods, including Jesus and his Father, being in possession of not merely a spirit but a body of flesh and bones."[9] According to Mormonism, there is a pantheon of gods, and God was once a man. Furthermore, Jesus, before his incarnation, was a created being and the brother of Lucifer. Jesus was born of Mary his mother, but he was not conceived by either Joseph or the Holy Spirit. A heavenly father, a god of flesh and bones, had sexual relations with Mary, and Jesus was conceived. Not only that, Jesus was the husband of both Mary and Martha (and perhaps Mary Magdalene as well) and had children by all of his wives. He was rewarded for his faithfulness by becoming the ruler of this earth. This is official Mormon doctrine.[10]

One branch of Gnosticism in the late first century and second century sought to deny the reality of the body and in fact of all physical matter. The modern-day heir of this error is the Christian Science cult. How can you be sure you are following the true Spirit of God? The Spirit who represents the incarnate Jesus is the true Spirit of God. Any spirit denying the incarnate Jesus is a spirit of antichrist.

At this point let me remind you of the difference between criticizing someone individually and criticizing the doctrinal position of a false religion. We live in a world that doesn't want to criticize anyone. We are perceived as being bigoted and intolerant if we do. Yet both John and Jude remind us and command us to earnestly "contend for the faith that was once for all delivered to the saints" (Jude 3).

The first test John gives to determine whether teachers are true or false is, do they confess the truth about Jesus? All of the major world religions and cults don't do that. Consider Islam. No Muslim considers Jesus to be divine or the Son of God. In Timothy George's book *Is the Father of Jesus the God of Mohammad?* Chapter 4 is entitled "Why the Trinity Matters." George states: "Christians predicate something essential and irreducible about God that no Muslim can accept. We call Him our heavenly Father."[11] Bilquis Sheikh was a Pakistani woman of noble birth who had been a Muslim her entire life. Through a series of strange encounters, she came to know and believe in Jesus Christ as her Savior and Lord. She titled the book narrating the story of her conversion *I Dared to Call Him Father.*[12] On the side of the Dome of the Rock, the mosque on the temple mount in Jerusalem, are written in Arabic these words: "God has no son." Ironically, this mosque faces the Church of the Holy Sepulcher in Jerusalem. In stark contrast, the fundamental difference between Christianity, Judaism, and Islam are visually illustrated in the heart of the holy city, Jerusalem. The words of God himself spoken of Jesus at his baptism declare, "This is my beloved Son, with whom I am well pleased" (Matthew 3:17). What you believe about Jesus and the Trinity is absolutely essential. Every world religion and cult without exception denies that Jesus is the Son of God who "has come in the flesh."[13]

We should also be aware of the fact that mere acceptance of the teaching of Jesus does not make you a Christian. Mahatma Gandhi did that. He was not a Christian, but he praised the teaching of Christ and told people they ought to try to practice it. Likewise, antichristian teaching is not necessarily an open denial of Christ. Sometimes it is a misrepresentation of Christ, adding something to him or detracting something from him. False teachers either deny or distort apostolic teaching. The apostles and prophets, according to Ephesians 2:20, are the foundation of the church. Any teaching that contradicts them is the spirit of antichrist and is false.

John goes out of his way in this letter to emphasize that Jesus has come "in the flesh." As Martyn Lloyd-Jones rightly noted, "If the Incarnation is not an actual fact, if He really has not been made flesh and dwelt among us, then there was no real humiliation involved in His coming into this world. He really did not limit Himself, as it were, to the position of a man dependent upon God; there is no real meaning in the laying aside of the insignia of the eternal glory; there is no true humiliation."[14] In 4:2, 3 we have three emphases: 1) certain knowledge, 2) divine identification, and 3) demonic differentiation.

Do They Possess the Divine Life? (v. 4)

The second test to determine false teachers and false doctrine is found in verse 4: do they possess the divine life? As Christians, our life comes from God. John places the "you" first in the clause for emphasis and to contrast with the false teachers of the previous verse. We are "from God"; hence, we are his children, a point already established from 1 John 3. Our motivating source, life, and teaching have their origin in God. For this reason we "have overcome" false teachers. John uses the word *nikaō*, which means "to conquer; to overcome." It is the word for victory. If you have any article of clothing with the Nike logo on it, that word comes from this Greek word meaning "victory." Furthermore, John uses the perfect tense here to indicate complete and abiding victory. This is the same word Jesus used in John 16:33 when he taught the disciples on the eve of his own crucifixion, "I have overcome the world." The manner in which we have overcome is not overtly stated, but the implication is that this occurs by means of our relying on true teaching and rejecting false teaching.

John informs his readers that they have "overcome" false teachers because "he who is in you is greater than he who is in the world." "Greater" here means "stronger." All false teachers claim to be from God. However, John says God is not their source. False teachers do not possess the Holy Spirit as do believers. The one who is in the world is, of course, Satan. The Holy Spirit who is in you is greater than Satan. Thus you are able to overcome false teachers and false doctrine, because the Holy Spirit in you is greater than the spirit of antichrist in those who are false teachers. Union General George McClellan always seemed fearful that the enemy had superior forces; so he never attacked Robert E. Lee in the early days of the Civil War. At Richmond he sent a spy, Allan Pinkerton, to assess the Confederate forces. Pinkerton assumed there were more Confederates than he could see, so he inflated the numbers. As a result McClellan did not attack.[15] That is often the way we Christians are. We overestimate the power of the enemy, and we underestimate the power of our God.

But there is another nuance in John's language here. John's use of "in you" has a corporate, distributive sense as well. As Yarbrough put it, "Christ is not present in the individual to any greater extent than the individual participates in the presence of Christ amid the apostolic fellowship as a whole."[16] God himself strengthens us as believers and our belief system.

Though John does not specifically state it, we learn to discern false teachers from true teachers as we become students of the Word of God. There is no substitute for a knowledge of Biblical teaching in combating falsehood. Remember Paul said we are to take up "the sword of the Spirit, which is the word of God" to do battle against Satan and his emissaries (Ephesians 6:17). Bank tellers do not have to go through training to spot a counterfeit dollar bill. They handle the real thing so much, they can tell a counterfeit when they see it and touch it. If we will become familiar with the truth of God's Word, we won't have too much trouble spotting counterfeit doctrine and their peddlers when they come along. Calvin insightfully noted,

> Those who say the Word of God is the rule by which everything should be tested, say something but not everything. I grant that doctrines should be tested by God's Word. But there is little or no profit in having God's Word in our hands, for its meaning will not be certain to us. . . . But the Spirit will only guide us to a true discrimination if we subject all our thoughts to the Word.[17]

Jonathan Edwards rightly noted, "When the spirit that is at work operates against the interests of Satan's kingdom, which lies in encouraging and establishing sin and cherishing men's worldly lusts, this is a sure sign that it is a true and not a false spirit."[18]

Do They Profess the Divine Truth? (vv. 5, 6)

The third test to determine false teachers and false doctrine is found in verses 5, 6: do they possess the divine law? The word "they" contrasts strongly with "you" in verse 4. False teachers are not from God but from the world. Their source and motivation is from godless humanity, the world system that is opposed to God. Therefore they speak as those who are from the world. Furthermore the world listens to them. We should always scrutinize the message of all who claim to speak for God. Are they declaring the Bible and the Bible alone as the Word of God? Are they interpreting it within the framework of orthodox Christianity, or are they twisting or distorting its message? John says that those who know God will hear—that is, listen to—those who are true gospel preachers. But those who do not know God will not listen to true gospel preaching. This is the measuring stick we use to discern false teaching from that which is true. John concludes verse 6 with the summary statement, "By this we know the Spirit of truth and the spirit of error."[19] The phrase "by this" refers to verses 5, 6a. Those following the spirit of truth listen to the apostles; those following the spirit of error do not.[20] "When we speak from the Spirit of God, the majority snore," said Luther.[21]

Here is a summary of what John is saying: You must test the teaching you hear as to whether it comes from God or not, whether it acknowledges that Jesus Christ came to earth in human form, and whether the world of unsaved people listen to it. You have prevailed over false teachers.

The New Testament clearly emphasizes the sufficiency of Christ and the Bible as the Word of God. The veneration of the Virgin Mary in Roman Catholicism is an example of how false doctrine detracts from the all-sufficiency of Jesus. In 1990 I went on a mission trip to Mexico City with about thirty members of our church. After a week of evangelistic work we had a day of sightseeing. One of the places we visited was the famous Catholic cathedral in the heart of Mexico City, the Basilica de Guadalupe. Considered by many Catholics to be the holiest place in the Americas, it is probably the second most visited shrine in the entire Catholic world, second only to Saint Peter's in The Vatican. Paintings and statuary of Mary permeate the building. Many of these depictions included Mary holding the dead body of Jesus. While we were inside, one of my deacons in our group engaged one of the Catholic priests available to answer questions from tourists. Walking up I could just make out the end of their conversation. My deacon was saying, "The difference between me and you is you believe in a living Mary and a dead Jesus; I believe in a dead Mary and a living Jesus!"[22] All false teaching ultimately detracts from Jesus and the sufficiency of his work on the cross for salvation.

Beloved, let us love one another, for love is from God, and whoever loves has been born of God and knows God. Anyone who does not love does not know God, because God is love. In this the love of God was made manifest among us, that God sent his only Son into the world, so that we might live through him. In this is love, not that we have loved God but that he loved us and sent his Son to be the propitiation for our sins. Beloved, if God so loved us, we also ought to love one another.

1 JOHN 4:7–11

15

Want to Play Catch?

WHEN MY OLDEST SON JEREMY was about five years old, we played catch for the first time. I came home one spring day and presented Jeremy with a new baseball glove. After showing him how to use it, I pulled out my old baseball glove and a baseball from the deep recesses of the closet and asked him, "Want to play catch?" His eyes lit up! I backed up about ten feet and gently threw the ball to him. The first few times he dropped the ball. When he returned the throw, it was usually errant to the left or right or too high or too low. Gradually over the next few weeks and months as we played catch in the front yard, his ability in throwing and catching improved. I initiated the game of catch by buying him a glove, showing him how to use it, and pitching the ball to him for the first time. From then on he could hardly wait for me to get home from work to play catch with him outside. I don't know how many times we played catch together over the next thirteen years. It seemed like a million. Watching him play in tee ball and all the way up through high school baseball, I often pictured that first time as a five-year-old when he donned a glove and we played catch. For a five-year-old, playing catch was one way of showing my son I loved him and wanted to spend time with him.

Dozens of times in this letter alone John uses the word "love." Primarily he speaks about three kinds of love: God's love for us, our love for God, and our love for one another. The concept of love is so important to John that three times he discusses it in this letter. This is the third passage. The first time was in chapter 2, he talked about love as evidence for our fellowship with God. In chapter 3 it was an evidence of our sonship with God. Now in chapter 4 John comes to the apex of what love is. He traces the stream of love to its source: "God is love." There are three spiritual truths we learn from this passage. The first is found in verses 7, 8.

Love Personified (vv. 7, 8)

Love is not like other subjects. It cannot be understood and then practiced. It can only be understood *by* practice. It is more like measles than math.[1] John affirms that the essence and evidence of Christian living is love. We are commanded to love one another, and John gives two reasons for doing so. The first reason is, love has its source in God. Just as light radiates from the sun, love radiates from God's very nature. We have already seen in our previous studies what John means by the term "love." Love is not a sentimental, squidgy, emotional word. It is not an Oprah group hug word. It is more than a description of how you feel. "Love" is a word that involves your emotions, but more than that the Biblical concept of *agapē* is a love that is unconditional, a love that seeks the highest good for the one who is loved, a love of total commitment. When God loves in the Bible, he does not say: "I love you if . . ." or "I love you because . . ." There is nothing in us that would cause God to love us. We are sinners. God's love for us does not have anything to do with something in us that caused God to love us. God's love for us is motivated by who he is, not by who we are. Later in this passage we see that we did not first love God; rather he first loved us. There is nothing lovely about us. There is nothing within us that would cause a perfect and holy God to express his love to us. Why on earth would he do that? Geddes MacGregor said this news "may well be deemed astonishing, since there is no reason why a being who is able to do anything he pleases should also be a loving being. Indeed, it seems *prima facie* unlikely."[2] From our perspective, of course that would seem true. But God loves because it is his nature to love. He desires that we know him.

We who are exhorted to love are already loved by God. This is the ground for the command to love others. John is not speaking of our love as only an imitation of what we see in God, though that is true. Our love is not an imitation from a distance but participation from within. Nor is he speaking of our love as only gratitude or mere emotion. His concept of love goes much deeper than that. God's love is creative! It actually produces its like in us! We love *from* God's fullness and not *for* it as some ideal to achieve to quench the thirst of our own emptiness. Feelings come to us. *Agapē* comes from us. Feelings are passive and receptive. *Agapē* is active and creative. Feelings are instinctive. *Agapē* is chosen. We fall in love, but we do not fall into *agapē*. Our choice to love comes not from weather, digestion, good vibrations, heredity, or environment but from our own heart, the center of our being.[3]

The second reason we are commanded to love one another is that "whoever loves has been born of God and knows God." Two things are said to be true about Christians who practice love: 1) they have been "born of God," and 2) they know God. The presence of love in your life is an evidence of your Christian experience. Of course, John does not mean that anybody in the world who has a feeling of love for somebody else is therefore a Christian. John is talking about the relationship between God and believers. If you have children, they possess your DNA. Your children have your nature, which has been genetically passed on to them. John is saying that a similar thing is true of those who have been born of God. If God as to his nature is love, then everyone who has truly been born of God partakes of his nature of love. Not only have we been born of God, but a second thing is true about us: we know God. The word "knows" here conveys the meaning of having an intimate relationship with God. It is more than knowing facts about God or understanding perceived truths about God. To know God really means to be rightly related to him.

God's love produces genuine change in us. When we respond to God's love, we are able to become loving people. This is why John speaks more than once in his letter about love being "perfected" in us (2:5; 4:12, 17). By "perfected" John means that love has reached its aim, purpose, and goal for our lives. You cannot command unsaved people to love others. They may or may not do it. But you can command Christian love. As one who has been born again, I now have the capacity to love. Though I am tempted to act like my old unsaved self, as a Christian I recognize I have no right to live like an unsaved person. I must live like the Christian I am.[4]

In verse 8 John states the same thing he said in verse 7 but now from a negative perspective. What he said in verse 7 is now emphasized by stating the reverse in verse 8. Those who do not love in the way described by John in verse 7 give evidence that they do not know God. If you score minus points in the love league, you don't have a clue who God is![5] The reason for this is then given: "God is love." Three times in John's writings we read statements about God's nature: John 4:24: "God is spirit," 1 John 1:5: "God is light," and now in this verse and later in verse 16 John says, "God is love." What a powerful statement that is.[6] We need to unpack its meaning and implications. First, we cannot reverse this statement and say "love is God."[7] All love is not Godlike love. In logic, "A is B" does not mean the same thing as "A equals B." If A = B then B = A. But if A is B that does not mean that B is A. God is love, but love is not God. Love doesn't define God. God defines love. God cannot fall in love; he *is* love. God cannot fall in love for the same reason water can't get wet: it *is* wet. God is love-in-eternal-action.[8]

By means of his revelation of himself through Jesus and the Scriptures,

God teaches us what love is all about. Love is a part of God's very nature and can never be absent from God. Love is not just an attribute of God; it is a part of his nature. Second, God's love is more than mere emotion or good will. It is his settled disposition toward us that flows from his being, nature, and divine attributes. Human love comes second in the sense that it is usually defined and described in terms of response to something desirable in the situation, object, or person. "I love her because she is beautiful." "I love him because he is handsome." "I love her because she is smart." "I love him because he is rich!" Human love is usually response love. *Agapē* love comes first. It creates value in its object whether there is any intrinsic value there or not. The sun shines on the earth not because the earth is the earth but because the sun is the sun.[9] God loves me because he is he, not because I am I.

When John says "God is love," he means to say more than just "God loves us," as marvelous as that truth is in and of itself. As C. H. Dodd rightly pointed out, this statement

> might stand alongside other statements, such as "God creates," "God rules," "God judges"; that is to say, it means that love is *one* of His activities. But to say "God is love" implies that *all* His activity is loving activity, even his judgment. If He creates, He creates in love; if He rules, He rules in love; if He judges, He judges in love. All that He does is to the expression of His nature, which is to love.[10]

God's love is, according to C. S. Lewis, "Gift-love. In God there is no hunger that needs to be filled, only plenteousness that desires to give. This kind of love in us enables us to love those who to us are naturally unloveable."[11]

That our God, who is by his very nature perfect, sovereign over all, needing nothing, with no ambitions to fulfill or goals to attain, chose to create is a marvel! Yet he not only created the universe, but he chose to create human beings and love them! Further, even when they rebelled against him and deserved eternal death, he chose to love them still and provide a way for their salvation. God became man in the person of Jesus Christ and by self-limitation and self-abnegation paid for the sins of the world! What love!

Love Proven (vv. 9, 10)

Verse 9 gives us the grounds of God's love: "In this the love of God was made manifest among us, that God sent his only Son into the world, so that we might live through him." What a statement about the greatness of God's love! To "manifest" something means to make it visible and known. The love of God was made known "among us." It is also possible that the Greek construction means "God's love in us," as in the QDVE. God's love is seen in the sending of his Son so that we might have eternal life through him.

The greatness of God's love is shown in five ways. First, notice it was God's love that caused the mission of sending his Son. Notice the words "God sent . . ." Stop right there! If there is going to be reconciliation between God and man, you would think the offender should be the one to initiate it. After all, he is the one who caused the problem in the first place. Suppose you and I are sitting next to each other in church on a Sunday morning. After the service concludes, in my haste to exit and beat everybody to the restaurant, I bump into you abruptly and step on your toes. Do you turn to me and say, "Oh, excuse me, I'm sorry"? No! I am the one pauses and apologizes to you for my behavior and seeks your forgiveness. I am the offending party. In social etiquette, the offender seeks forgiveness from the offended. But God did not wait for rebellious humanity to send word to his throne for terms of reconciliation. God himself commenced negotiations![12]

Second, notice whom God sent: his only Son. God did not send Abraham, Moses, or one of the prophets. He did not send an angel. He sent Jesus who is his only Son. The word order in Greek puts emphasis on "his Son": "that his son, his only Son, has God sent. . . . " Furthermore, the verb translated "sent" is in the perfect tense in Greek, conveying the connotation, "God has sent Jesus, and we now enjoy the blessings of his mission!"[13] In Greek the word translated "only" is *monogenēs*. It is made up of two words that we have borrowed from Greek and brought into English. *Mono* means "one," and *genēs* is the word from which we get our word gene. Jesus as Son is "one of a kind," unique, sharing in the very nature of the Godhead in a way that no other created being shares. Jesus is the Son of God who is divine. Our sin caused such a mess that only the Son of God himself could extricate us from it! The greatness of God's love for you and me is of such a nature that his love is expressed in the fact that he sent his only Son. God could not have given us a greater gift.

Third, the greatness of God's love is revealed in the purpose of his sending the Son: "so that we might live through him." As Paul says in Ephesians 2:1, we were "dead in [our] trespasses and sins." Our only hope of eternal life is forgiveness of sins and a relationship with God through his Son, Jesus. Fourth, the greatness of God's love is that it originates with God and not with us. God first bestowed his love on us, and only after regeneration could we even begin to love God.

Fifth, the greatness of God's love is demonstrated by its cost: God sent his Son Jesus to be "the propitiation for our sins" (v. 10)."Propitiation"—now there is a five-dollar stained-glass word we don't use every day. I'll bet when you and your friend were running late to math class in school you did not say to your friend, "We are going to be late, and the teacher is going to be mad; so we'd better find a way to make propitiation." We don't talk that way. But this word is a very important word in the Bible; so let's camp out on it for a moment. *Propitiation* is a word that means "to appease someone's wrath." In ancient Greek mythology, the gods were capricious and easily angered by humans. Humans sought to appease that anger by offering sacrifices to the gods.

Why is it necessary that there be "propitiation" for our sins? Why doesn't God just wave his magic wand and forgive everyone's sin? Let me answer this question with another question. Why doesn't the state of Colorado just wave its magic wand and forgive James Holmes for murdering twelve people and wounding fifty-eight others in a theater in Aurora in the summer of 2012? To ask the question is to answer it. To do so would be an egregious violation of justice. If God were to do the same for our sins, it would be a denial of the seriousness of sin and a gross violation of his justice. Sin is so bad that it leads to a state of affairs where the Son of God himself ends up being crucified.

Propitiation is a word that includes six things in its definition: God's holiness, wrath, justice, mercy, love, and grace. Why does there need to be a propitiation in the first place? All sin is an affront to God's holiness. God's wrath is his settled disposition against all sin (Romans 1:18). God is angry with sin and sinners. You say, "Wait a minute, you just got through telling me about God's love for us." Yes, I did. "Now you are telling me God is angry with us." Yes, I am. God can be angry with sinners and love them at the same time. Sin violates God's law, and his law demands that justice be done. God is just. He must punish sin. But God is also merciful. He is willing that sinners not receive all they deserve for their sin. Even more, God is love. His love extends to all people. God desires the salvation of all people. But there is nothing sinners can do to earn God's forgiveness for their sins. This is where God's grace comes into the picture. God does something for us that we could never do for ourselves. He pays the price for our sin. When Jesus died on the cross, he became our substitute and took the wrath of God against our sin upon himself, thus satisfying God's justice in a payment for sin. In Jesus' death on the cross, God's holiness, justice, wrath, mercy, love, and grace all converge.

That is the "why" of it. Now let's talk about the "who" of it. In Greek mythology humans always sought to propitiate the capricious wrath of the gods. But there is nothing we can do to turn away God's righteous anger against us and our sin. So God himself takes the initiative to propitiate his own wrath. God's love through Jesus on the cross provides the atoning sacrifice for our sins. Anselm rightly said only man *should* make the sacrifice for his sins because he is the offender. But only God *could* make the sacrifice for our sins since he has demanded it. Jesus, as God and man, is the only Savior in whom the "should" and the "could" are united. The Father gave the Son; the Son gave himself. The Father sent the Son; the Son came. The Father did not lay on the Son a cross he was reluctant to bear. The Son did not extract from the Father a salvation he was reluctant to bestow.

So, what is propitiation all about? God giving himself in his Son for our sins. God himself in his holy wrath needs to be propitiated. God himself in holy love undertook propitiation. God himself in the person of Jesus died to make propitiation for our sins, and not for ours only, but for the entire world (1 John 2:2). The initiative is from God; the response must be from us. God first moves toward us so that we can move toward him. God first loved us so that we might be able to love him.

Ty Cobb was one of the all-time greats in the game of baseball. He had a .367 lifetime batting average, with 4,191 hits and 892 stolen bases. He won nine straight batting titles. But Ty Cobb was also the meanest man in baseball. Known for stopping at nothing to win, he would insult, humiliate, and even injure other players in his quest for victory. Even his own teammates once rooted against him when he was in a tight race one season for the batting title. He was known to make unprovoked racial slurs. He had three wives, all of whom he verbally and physically abused. He was constantly involved in fistfights, arguments, and tirades against fans and players. He once pistol-whipped a would-be mugger so badly that the face of the corpse could not be identified. Some players, like the famous Ted Williams, tried to help Cobb, but to no avail. Cobb was worth millions because of his early investment in Coca-Cola. When he died, he had in his possession millions in stocks, bonds, and cash because he was an early investor in Coca-Cola. And yet it would be hard to find a more apt specimen of total depravity. But the story does not end there.

Not long before he died, Cobb was visited by a Presbyterian minister named John Richardson. Cobb curtly told the preacher to leave. Two days later he returned. This time Cobb listened as Richardson explained to him the plan of salvation. Hearing of Christ's love for sinners and how he had come to die for the likes of Ty Cobb, "the Georgia Peach" was overcome with emotion. Richardson continued to explain the necessity of repentance toward sin and faith in Jesus as the only way of salvation. Cobb told the preacher he was ready to put his complete trust in Jesus Christ as his Savior. Two days before he died, Ty Cobb told Richardson, "I feel the strong arms of God underneath me."[14] "In this is love, not that we have loved God but that he loved us and sent his Son to be the propitiation for our sins." No one has ever sinned himself or herself beyond the love of God. There is nothing you can do to make God love you any *more* than he loves you right now. There is nothing you can do to make God love you any *less* than he loves you right now.

Love Practiced (v. 11)

When we truly understand what God has done for us and how much he loves us, we must love one another. That's why John defines love for us before he exhorts us to love. You can't love as you ought until you understand how God has loved you! Focus on that little word "ought" in verse 11. It means obligation. Some Christians view loving others all the time as optional. Love is not optional; it's obligatory. We are under moral obligation to love one another. The expression of our divine duty is, "we also ought to love one another." If the greatest commandment is to love God with all our heart and to love our neighbor as ourselves, then the greatest sin is not to do it![15] Godlike living demands Godlike loving. This is the divine imperative based on divine logic.

"Beloved, if God so loved us, we also ought to love one another" (v. 11). Once again it is Christ's propitiatory death that is the standard of our own love: we are to love sinners with a sacrificial love because Jesus did. God "so loved." The little word "so" translates a Greek adverb meaning "so intensely."[16] It is not easy to understand "one another" here as meaning "Christians only," because the model is Christ, who died for sinners, and we are to love as he did. This is the way we should understand verse 12: "No one has ever seen God; if we love one another, God abides in us and his love is perfected [or has reached its purpose, aim, goal] in us." As John will say in 4:14, "We have seen and testify that the Father has sent his Son to be the Savior of the world." God's love extends beyond those who believe and includes the world. Our love should go and do likewise. Leon Morris said, "Passages like these make it clear that this epistle pictures God as loving sinful people outside the Christian brotherhood."[17]

John draws a practical conclusion from the love of God expressed in the death of Christ on the cross: we ought to love one another. Godlike living demands love. Look at the word "ought." The word in Greek means we are bound to love. It is our responsibility to love one another. We are bound to love one another in response to God's love for us. We have an obligation to love one another. The false gospel that is preached by those in the so-called faith movement (health and wealth gospel) says that the abundant life is yours for the taking—God wants you healthy and wealthy—get your best life now!

This is totally contrary to the New Testament writers. They say to believers, "You have no right to live like you once did before you were saved. To do so is to deny the gospel you believe." John says, "We also ought to love one another." This is the divine imperative based on divine logic. If we have really come to know God in salvation, our Christian life will be the outworking of the truth that we claim to believe.[18]

But there is a problem. Some Christians are difficult to love. "To dwell above with saints I love, that will be glory. But to dwell below with saints I know, now that is a different story." Our love for others should grow out of our love for God and his own love for us. Love is not predicated on like. Love is not predicated on agreement, though it helps. Through Jesus you can love people with whom you don't agree. I can just picture the scene in the Upper Room with Jesus in John 13 when he gives them the new commandment. Peter looks over at John and thinks, *You mean I have to love that dreamer, that guy who has his head in the clouds?* John looks at Peter and thinks, *You mean I have to love that loudmouth?* Matthew looks at Thomas and thinks, *You mean I have to love that skeptic?* Thomas looks at Matthew and reflects, *I have to love that tax collector?* Can you imagine what went through the minds of those men when Jesus gave them the new commandment to love one another?

How did they do it? How do we do it? We remind ourselves of the words, "if God so loved us . . ." Those words are a game-changer. They keep me from thinking or feeling that I'm the one being wronged, that I'm the one being shortchanged. Not so fast! says the gospel. Remember who you are; remember who you were before you came to Christ. It used to be all about me. Self on the throne. Self-centeredness, self-assertion, self-conceit, self-indulgence, self-pleasing, self-seeking, self-sensitiveness, self-defensiveness, self-sufficiency.[19] Now, because of Christ in my life, it is all about him and others. When I see myself as I really am, when I have died to self, it is impossible for someone to insult me or offend me. Whatever the world may say about me, the truth is probably worse![20] "If God so loved us . . ." "There is something in each of us that cannot be naturally loved. It is no one's fault if they do not so love it. Only lovable can be naturally loved. You might as well ask people to like the taste of rotten bread or the sound of a mechanical drill."[21] How can you love someone if you don't like them? Easy! We do it to ourselves continually. Sometimes we feel foolish, stupid, asinine, or wicked. But we can still love ourselves.[22]

The early church father Tertullian tells us that he was brought to Christ not because he had studied the Scriptures but because he had seen Christians' lives and coveted what they possessed that caused them to live the way they lived. Would to God that could be said of me . . . and you!

The love of God is the answer to the quest for life's supreme value and reality but also to life's deepest meaning and purpose. Since God is love, we must love God and love whatever God loves. He is the divine conductor. If we follow his baton, the music of our life will be a symphony.[23]

God sent us a love letter in the person of his Son Jesus. "For God so loved the world, that he gave his only Son, that whoever believes in him should not perish but have eternal life" (John 3:16). God's love for us is so great that he overcomes all the many reasons he could give for not loving the sinful people we are. The question for us is this: if God has bestowed such love on us, will we overcome all our petty reasons for not loving one another? I find it interesting that the word *amateur* means literally "a lover." Amateur athletes do what they do for love of the game. They are not professionals. When it comes to loving, we should be amateurs, not professionals. Professionals don't do much screaming, hugging, or crying. Amateurs do. It's the cost of loving those you really care about.[24]

The greatest love you can show to those who don't know Christ is to tell them about Jesus. John's point is to ground our love for others in the love that God has for us and for the world in Christ. As Spurgeon in his sermon on this passage said:

> Go forth at once, and try and make reconciliation, not only between your-self and your friend, but between every man and God. Let that be your object. Christ has become man's reconciliation, and we are to try and bring this reconciliation near to every poor sinner that comes in our way. We are to tell him that God in Christ is reconciled. . . . God is now able to deal on gospel terms with the whole race. We need never think that we shall meet with men to whom God will not consent to be reconciled.[25]

Ask men you know to list their top five baseball movies. Most men will place *Field of Dreams* on their list. Ray Kinsella, played by Kevin Costner, lives in rural Iowa with his wife Annie and his young daughter Karin. While walking through the cornfield, Ray hears a voice whisper, "If you build it, he will come." Ray concludes that the voice is telling him to build a baseball field. So he plows under his corn and does just that. He waits and watches, but nothing happens. Suddenly one summer night the ghosts of several deceased baseball players appear out of nowhere and are practicing on Ray's field. It's unbelievable! Why, there is Shoeless Joe Jackson and other players from the 1919 Chicago White Sox! The plot of the movie twists and turns to the final scene. The sun is westering in the sky, and the ballplayers leave the field and disappear in the corn. Shoeless Shoe Jackson, played by Ray Liotta, looks at Ray and tells him, "If you build it, he will come." Then he glances toward the catcher near home plate who is removing his chest protector and mask.

Ray suddenly recognizes that the player is his father, John Kinsella, as a young man, before Ray was even born. When Ray was seventeen, he had a big fight with his father. He packed his things, said something awful to his father, and left. He never spoke to his father again. Ray had regretted this all his life, but his father had died, and Ray had lost his chance to make things right. Now he and his father converse for a moment, both understanding, but neither saying anything more. Ray's father turns and begins to walk toward the cornfield to leave. With deep emotion, choking back the tears, Ray calls out to this father, "Dad . . . wanna play catch?" His father turns, pauses, and responds, "Yes, I'd like that very much." Ray dons a glove, and he and his father play catch as the movie draws to a close.

But *Field of Dreams* got it exactly backwards. In the movie the wayward son asks the father, "Wanna play catch?" But in the Bible it is God the Father who asks his rebellious son, "Wanna play catch?" Because of his great love for us, God initiated our salvation. Think of your life and your love like a baseball, and throw the ball back to the divine pitcher who threw it to you first, and the game continues. Do you hear that heavenly voice? "Wanna play catch?"

No one has ever seen God; if we love one another, God abides in us and his love is perfected in us. By this we know that we abide in him and he in us, because he has given us of his Spirit. And we have seen and testify that the Father has sent his Son to be the Savior of the world. Whoever confesses that Jesus is the Son of God, God abides in him, and he in God. So we have come to know and to believe the love that God has for us. God is love, and whoever abides in love abides in God, and God abides in him. By this is love perfected with us, so that we may have confidence for the day of judgment, because as he is so also are we in this world. There is no fear in love, but perfect love casts out fear. For fear has to do with punishment, and whoever fears has not been perfected in love. We love because he first loved us. If anyone says, "I love God," and hates his brother, he is a liar; for he who does not love his brother whom he has seen cannot love God whom he has not seen. And this commandment we have from him: whoever loves God must also love his brother.

1 JOHN 4:12–21

16

"Be My Valentine"—God

FOR SOME REASON when I read this text in preparation for this sermon, my mind went back to 1966, when I was in the third grade. It was the week before Valentine's Day. Everybody in our class received a white paper sack, slightly larger than a lunch sack but smaller than a grocery sack. We were informed that this was our "mailbox" for the valentines that other classmates would be giving us on Valentine's Day. We all wrote our names on our sack. It was easy to distinguish the girls' sacks from the boys' sacks. The girls would have perfectly printed names adorned with butterflies and flowers on their sacks. The boys' sacks would have names indecipherably scribbled without even a stickman for adornment. Across the chalk tray underneath the blackboard at the front of the room all those sacks would be hung alphabetically. Mother bought my valentines, and two days before Valentine's Day I made up my valentines for every person in my class. I brought them to school and delivered each one to the appropriate "mailbox." Then on Valentine's Day there was a little party during the class, and we could get our mail sacks and see all of the valentines that we'd received. It was always interesting to see if anybody would go beyond the traditional valentine signed by Judy, Bill, Karen, etc., and add some extra greeting. Some of the girls would make their own valentines rather than settle for bland store-bought ones. This I never understood. Who in their right mind would go to that much trouble? Rummaging through my sack, I had hoped to find an extra-special valentine from one of the girls, but sadly it was business as usual. I even got a couple of valentines that were unsigned and a couple that did not have my name on them. What a downer.

Valentine's Day is a special day. It is a day when we tell special people that we love them. Did you know that God has expressed himself in such a way that he invites people to be his valentine? In saying this I am not being trite or flippant. In one sense Jesus is God's valentine to us. Through Jesus God says, "I love you." Because of what Jesus has done for us, we should love one another as well. When we love as we ought, John says we will have confidence before God and genuine concern for other people.

God's Love Is Completed in Us When We Abide in Him (v. 12)

In verse 12 John makes a statement about how our love fulfills two important functions. First, our love for others is evidence that God is real and dwells in us. The first part of verse 12 at first seems to be out-of-place. What does God's invisibility have to do with love? But when we read the entire verse, the statement makes sense. John is saying that others' seeing you loving others is evidence to other people that God is real and that God lives in you. You can sit down with someone and for twenty-four hours you can talk about theology and God's attributes, you can lecture on systematic theology, and your listener may still not know God. But when that same person sees God's love lived out in your life toward him and others, then he begins to see God. The invisible God becomes visible to him through you. That's what John is saying. You're able to teach others about God because of your love for others.

As a Spirit (John 4:24), God cannot be seen with our physical eyes. Since no one has seen God, how are we supposed to get people who don't know God to believe that he exists? When the world observes Christians loving unconditionally as Jesus loved, they will be open to the gospel. The only God and Jesus that most people will ever see is the one they see in you. They're not going to read about him in a book or go to the church, but they will see him in your life. Edgar Guest has a poem entitled "Sermons We See." It begins like this:

> I'd rather see a sermon
> than hear one any day;
> I'd rather one should walk with me
> than merely tell the way.
> The eye's a better pupil
> and more willing than the ear,
> Fine counsel is confusing,
> but example's always clear;
> And the best of all preachers
> are the men who live their creeds,
> For to see good put in action
> is what everybody needs.[1]

The best way people will see Christ is by means of your love for them and others. John says your love is evidence that God dwells in you.

Second, this lifestyle of love is the evidence that the goal of God's love has been "perfected in us."[2] Once again John returns to this concept of perfection. God desires that we become like him. We are never more like him than when we love others. One of the evidences of spiritual maturity is love. The evidence of the genuine Christian life is love. Your spiritual maturity is not measured by your age, how long you have been a Christian, how long you have been a church member, how much Bible knowledge you have, or your level of service in the church. It is measured by your love. "By this all people will know that you are my disciples, if you have love for one another," said Jesus (John 13:35). When John speaks of God's love being "perfected" in us, he may be saying that God's love reaches its intended goal when those whom God loves practice love toward others. On the other hand, John may be saying that our love for God is complete only when we love other people. Both concepts are true, but it is difficult to determine which meaning John intends to convey here. Interestingly, four times in this passage John juxtaposes the word "perfect(ed)" with "love." As John uses the word "perfection," he is not speaking about moral perfection or a perfection in the sense of "without flaw." Rather, the word means "mature, complete, full-orbed." God's love for us, which is indeed a perfect love, finds its most complete expression when we respond to that love and then practice that love in our relationships with others.

Loving one another evidences two realities in our lives according to verse 12: God abides in us, and his love is brought to completion in us. John is very fond of using this word "abide." It is common in his Gospel as well as in this letter. In verses 12–16 alone, John uses this word six times. To abide in God (or Christ) not only is a statement of fact concerning our relationship to God and his relationship to us, but it is also a statement concerning our conduct. When we abide in Christ, we are behaving according to his character. This is why John links the concept of abiding with that of loving in these verses.

The Spirit's Testimony to Christ Is Our Testimony (vv. 13–15)

In verse 13 John makes the important point that we have assurance we are truly saved because God has given us his Holy Spirit to indwell our lives. The presence of the Holy Spirit in our lives is the means of assurance that we are truly united to Christ. This is what John means when he speaks of our "abiding" in God or Christ and "he in us." If we "abide" in him, we are going to reflect his character in our lives. Our conduct toward others will be commensurate with God's character.

When does the Holy Spirit come to dwell in the life of a believer? The Scripture says it happens at the moment of our conversion. Some teach that you can believe in Jesus and then sometime later in your Christian life receive the Holy Spirit. This is, as Martyn Lloyd-Jones put it, "an utter impossibility"[3] and is "utterly unscriptural."[4] The Holy Spirit comes to indwell the believer at the moment of conversion. At that moment we are baptized by the Holy Spirit into the Body of Christ, the Church universal (1 Corinthians 12:13). Notice here that the Holy Spirit is the agent of baptism, not the one into whom we are immersed. There is one baptism of the Holy Spirit, but there are many fillings of the Holy Spirit. This is the clear teaching of the book of Acts as well as the Pauline epistles.

John makes the point in verse 14 that "*we* have seen and testify that the Father has sent the Son [Jesus] to be the Savior of the world." Here, according to John Stott, "is the essence of the gospel." "The world" means all sinful people, estranged from God and under the dominion of the evil one.[5] What John saw of the life, ministry, and death of Jesus was not a passing glimpse of curiosity but a steady gaze of contemplation. Regardless of race, regardless of face, regardless of place, Jesus came to save sinners. Whether big sinners or little sinners, rich sinners or poor sinners, open sinners or secret sinners, it matters not. Jesus came to save just plain sinners. In preaching on this passage Spurgeon said when we preach Christ, we should do so after the apostolic manner: their message, their simplicity, their power (the Holy Spirit), and their fervency. "Those first preachers of the gospel never preached cold sermons. Why, some sermons hang like icicles upon the lips of the speaker; but the apostles preached as if they were all on fire."[6]

In verse 15, to "confess" is the idea of saying a hearty "amen!" to what God has said and done. Confession of Jesus as Son of God means confession of the full deity of Christ. This is something the false teachers were not willing to confess. Right belief about who Jesus is and what he has done on the cross is essential to salvation. The phrase "God abides in him, and he in God" is John's way of speaking about someone's genuine salvation.

Love Brings Confidence in the Day of Judgment (vv. 16–19)

In verse 16 John says we have come to know and believe God's love for us. This means we have come to know by believing, as Calvin rightly noted.[7] God is faithful to his promises. All that he has given us through his love is ours now and will always be ours. His past faithfulness and his present faithfulness guarantee his future faithfulness to us. Though the promise is past tense and the fulfillment is future tense, God is with us moment by moment in the present. Christ saves us from the penalty of sin, the power of sin, the pollution of sin, and ultimately in Heaven from the very presence of sin. All this being true, John says, "We have come to know and to believe the love that God has for us." The fact that "God is love" (vv. 8, 16) is demonstrated by what he did on the cross for sinners.

I'm not a big fan of art galleries. I appreciate art, at least most of it, but my eyes begin to glaze over, and my adult ADD kicks in pretty fast when I move slowly through room after room of pictures. I have noticed, however, that I much prefer looking at pictures that convey some kind of action as opposed to an endless array of portraits. Portraits have their place, but give me the large scenes of conflict involving two or more people. Looking at Washington cross the Delaware is much more interesting to me than looking at a portrait of Washington himself. Why is that? We are stirred by action.[8] So it is with love. People are stirred not by a static depiction of our still-life portraits of love. They are drawn into large action renditions where love is being demonstrated. John can tell us in this letter that "God is love" because God demonstrated that love for us when Jesus died on the cross for our sins. People are little moved by our static affirmation, "we love you." Rather, they are moved when they see us go to work on their behalf and put our love into action. That's when we are most like our heavenly Father. John says we are to "abide" in love. This is the foundation for our loving action that John commands all of us to engage in (vv. 20, 21).

"Whoever abides in love abides in God, and God abides in him." This is John's way of speaking about our salvation. To abide in God is to be saved; to be saved is to abide in God. Jonathan Edwards has an expanded sermon on verse 16 entitled "The Spirit of the True Saints Is a Spirit of Divine Love."[9] The best part of the sermon is the lengthy application section that constitutes three-fourths of the sermon. Edwards notes: "Hence we learn the distinguishing nature of true spiritual light, that it brings divine love into the heart with it."[10] Edwards invites his hearers to self-examination: "Don't only enquire whether you ever have felt any affection to God or Christ but whether a high and exalting esteem of God and the Redeemer and a thirsting appetite after God and a complacence and delight in him be the spirit that dwells in you. Do you esteem Christ precious? Do you esteem him above all? Does your heart go after him more than all? Do you choose him before all?"[11] He proceeds to discuss six distinguishing marks of true divine love against what he calls "hypocritical love":

1. True divine love is not so much because of the kindness that we have received of him as for himself, not so much for our sakes as for his own sake.

2. Do you love God for his holiness? Holiness is the beauty of the divine nature, and none but those who are holy truly love God for his holiness.
3. Can you take complacency in the awful attributes of God as well as those that [are] especially winning and drawing?
4. True divine love is distinguished from the seeming love of hypocrites in that it makes choice of its object for its portion. The heart of a true saint doth choose God and Jesus Christ and so does not the hypocrite.
5. Another thing wherein true divine love is distinguished from the seeming love of hypocrites is that it is accompanied with a denying of ourselves.
6. And lastly, a true divine love is an effectual, fruitful love. A barren love is a false, hypocritical love.[12]

Edwards's final application is an exhortation, first to believers. All Christians must actively exercise this love in daily life, as John says. We should live a life of love toward God and men. "Love should return back to the fountain as God is infinite love. . . . He is the author of love, and he should be the object of it."[13]

"By this is love perfected with us, so that we may have confidence for the day of judgment, because as he is so also are we in this world" (v. 17). Once again we are likened to Christ in his death for the world. This being the case, our love cannot be limited to the saved but must include all people, believers or not.[14]

God wants you to have a loving confidence (v. 17) toward God that causes you to look forward to the future meeting with God without fear of punishment. This verse is a reminder that every person, Christian or not, will one day give an account of his or her life in the day of judgment. A person who is not a Christian ought to be afraid of future judgment. But we Christians have no fear of future judgment because our judgment is already past. It occurred on the cross. For this reason we can have confidence in the day of judgment. In Greek the word translated "confidence" is a word that etymologically means "all speech." Imagine you are speeding down the road. A police officer pulls you over, and you give him your driver's license. "Mr. Allen, were you aware that you were speeding?" "Yes, sir." "Do you know what the speed limit is?" "Yes, sir." The conversation concludes with the reception of a ticket, and you say very little during the whole episode. Why? When you know you are guilty, you have nothing to say. You say as little as you can say.

Now picture a high school baseball game. I stole second base. I slid in underneath the tag, and everybody in the whole place knew I was safe—except the second base umpire, who happened to be a member of my church. We knew each other well. He knew I had been called to preach and was the young preacher boy. I knew I was safe, so I began to argue with him like my life depended on it, and words like a torrent were flowing. I argued until the coach finally came out to get me off the field. I had to see that umpire in church the next day and still argued about it with him. (In hindsight my Christian testimony would have been better served if I had just accepted being called out.) I had confidence, boldness, all speech about the situation. That is the word John uses here in the Greek New Testament—*parrasia*, literally "all speech." Because I had confidence about it, I defended my case with no fear. A day of judgment is coming when those who are believers will not be as if they have just been stopped for speeding by a celestial, eternal police officer and have nothing to say because they are guilty. In that day Christians will have confidence. Why? Because God looks at us in the same way he looks at his Son, Jesus. I am in Christ, and my sins are covered. As Jesus is loved by the Father, so I am loved by the Father. I will have confidence in the day that I leave this world and enter that world to stand before a holy God. I will have no fear because as Jesus is loved, so God loves me now in the world. As Jesus is treated there now, so I will be treated there then, because of the love of God for me. We have a loving confidence because "as he is so also are we in this world."

Three things are inevitable consequences of dwelling in love. First, to dwell in love is proof of the fact that God dwells in us and that we are in God (v. 16). Second, this is the demonstration of the fact that love has been perfected in us (v. 17). This is the issue of our sanctification. Sanctification is a five-dollar word that simply means we are day by day being made into the image of Jesus by the Holy Spirit at work in our lives. Sanctification is both positive and negative. Sanctification is not merely the absence of certain sins, it is the presence of the Holy Spirit and the right thinking, speaking, and living that the Spirit motivates. Third, we have boldness before God in the day of judgment (v. 17). The day of judgment will be formal, public, and final. Christ himself will be the Judge (Matthew 25:31; John 5:27; Acts 10:42; 17:31).

Who will be judged? Believers will be judged at what the Bible calls the Judgment Seat of Christ (2 Corinthians 5:10; cf. Romans 14:10). This judgment will involve only believers. The issue at this judgment is not one's eternal destiny. The issue here has to do with how believers have lived while on this earth. In Greek "judgment seat" is *bema*, a word in the Greek and Roman world describing the place where the judge would sit. It can refer to a legal setting or to an athletic setting. All of us as Christians are accountable to God. In Matthew 12:36 Jesus says that "every careless word they speak" will be called into account. This refers both to the saved and the unsaved no doubt. In

Colossians 3:24, 25 Paul addresses Christians when he speaks about receiving "the inheritance as your reward," but those believers who do wrong will likewise receive according to the wrong they have done. Romans 14:10–12 is specific in its statement that "each of us [all Christians] will give account of himself to God." The same is taught in 2 Corinthians 5:10: "We must all appear before the judgment seat of Christ, so that each one may receive what is due for what he has done in the body, whether good or evil." The results of this judgment are clear. Those who are approved will receive a reward; those whose works are not approved will "suffer loss" (1 Corinthians 3:15). The text is clear, however, that this loss is not eternal loss. They are said to be saved "but only as through fire." The nature of the rewards mentioned in these passages is not specifically described, but it is clear that something other than eternal life is involved.[15] The impetus for us as believers is to serve the Lord now with all our heart. None of us serves perfectly, but we don't want to stand before the Judgment Seat of Christ and see much of our works on this earth burned up as it were under the fiery gaze of the Lord Jesus Christ. The image of someone standing before Jesus and pressing into his nail-scarred hands the charred embers of a wasted life should haunt each of us and stir us to godly living.

Unbelievers will be judged at the Great White Throne Judgment (Revelation 20:11–15). What is the standard of judgment? It is the revealed will of God through the Word of God. Unsaved people will be judged according to their works and the fact that their name is not written in the Lamb's book of life (Revelation 20:11–15). The unsaved will experience eternal separation from God in a literal place called Hell.

John continues to develop this thought in verse 18: "There is no fear in love, but perfect love casts out fear. For fear has to do with punishment." Christians have no need to fear at the final judgment because their eternal destiny is not at stake. The word translated "fear" is *phobia*. Do you have a phobia? What are you afraid of? If you have arachnophobia you are afraid of spiders. If you have hydrophobia you are afraid of water. If you have acrophobia you are afraid of heights. Remember that scene in *A Charlie Brown Christmas* when Charlie Brown consults with Counselor Lucy about his fears? After rattling off a number of phobias to each of which Charlie Brown said, "I don't think that's quite it," Lucy says, "Maybe you have pantophobia!" Charlie Brown asked, "What is pantophobia?" "Fear of everything!" Lucy yells. There is one fear that all who are without Christ should have and all who know Christ should never have: fear of judgment. We who are Christians have no fear of judgment because when you love God and know you are loved by God, you are not afraid of the future. God's perfect love for you serves to cast out your fear. We don't need to have any spiritual phobias today. Some people have fear because of their past. For others the present worries them. For still others the future threatens them. If you fear having dental work and you know you have to go to the dentist tomorrow, you are a nervous wreck between now and then because you are tormented by that fear. The fear of the future torments you now.

Love for God and others frees people from fear. "There is no fear in love," John writes, "but perfect love casts out fear. For fear has to do with punishment, and whoever fears has not been perfected in love" (4:18). Christians in John's day as well as in our own have many reasons to be fearful. It really does not matter whether John is thinking primarily about God's love for us or our love for God and others. John's point covers all situations. When we live within the security of God's love for us and practice love for others, we will experience freedom from all fear. As Jonathan Edwards said in his sermon on this passage:

> Fear hath torment, intimating that divine love tends to banish and drive away from the mind whatsoever is tormenting and afflictive and to give ease and rest and it will do so when it is perfect, when it is strong and in lively exercises. By perfect love here we need not understand absolutely perfect but only strong love, love in its ardent exercises. Such love tends to cast out fear. Fear is the legal principle, love is the evangelical. Servile fear is the spirit of bondage, but love is the spirit of adoption. The evangelical principle gives boldness and confidence. . . . Fear keeps at a distance and prevents boldness of access.[16]

In John 5:24 Jesus said, "Whoever hears my word and believes him who sent me has eternal life. He does not come into judgment." If you are a Christian, rejoice because you know that you will never have to come under the judgment of God in the future. Your judgment has already occurred at the cross. God poured out your judgment on Jesus. Hebrews 9:27 states, "It is appointed for man to die once, and after that comes judgment." Some believe you should never scare people into Heaven, but Jesus was not afraid to do so. It was he who said in essence, "Don't fear what somebody can do on this earth, but you'd better fear him who is able to cast your soul and body into Hell" (see Matthew 10:28). Fear can be a very good motivation. I'm not going to drive 100 miles per hour around a hairpin curve because I'm afraid I might kill myself and others with me. Fear is sometimes a good thing. But as Christians we don't have to fear the future because of God's love for us and our love for him. The one who fears has not been made mature in love.

A loving confidence becomes a loving concern for others according to verse 19: "We love because he first loved us." In his pithy way Luther got it right: "God does not love because of our works; He loves because of His love."[17] Your love for Jesus did not originate with you. It is a response to Bethlehem and Calvary. The only reason you have the capacity to love is because you have been a recipient of God's love and have been born again. His love teaches you and triggers your love for him. You could never love God apart from God's loving you first. Ted Peters expressed it well when he said, "The promise of eternal life has the power to disarm anxiety for those who believe, for those who trust God to deliver on the promise. God's eternal being sustains our threatened being. God's faithfulness makes our faith possible, and our faith makes it possible to love others with abandon."[18] "We love because he first loved us."

Spurgeon captures something of what it is like for God's amazing love to sink in for us as believers.

> What is it we have been talking about? It is God's love to us. Get the thought into your head a minute: "God loves me"—not merely bears with me, thinks of me, feeds me, but loves me. Oh, it is a very sweet thing to feel that we have the love of a dear wife, or a kind husband; and there is much sweetness in the love of a fond child, or a tender mother; but to think that God loves me, this is infinitely better! Who is it that loves you? God, the Maker of heaven and earth, the Almighty, All in all, does He love me? Even He? If all men, and all angels, and all the living creatures that are before the throne loved me, it were nothing to this—the Infinite loves me! And who is it that He loves? *Me*. The text saith, "us." "We love Him because He first loved us." But this is the personal point—He loves me, an insignificant nobody, full of sin—who deserved to be in hell; who loves Him so little in return—God loves ME.[19]

First John 4:19 was William Tyndale's favorite text. At the age of thirty, Tyndale was the private tutor of a six-year-old named Harry Walsh, son of a knight of Gloucestershire, in Little Sodbury. Later in life Harry Walsh recounted with vivid memory the evening Tyndale informed him that he was leaving Little Sodbury. Turning in his Greek New Testament to 1 John 4, Tyndale began to read, translating into English, for young Harry. When he came to 1 John 4:19, Tyndale reminded Harry that these words were the pearly gates through which he would enter the Kingdom. "Why must you go?" queried Harry sadly. "Because it is time the people have the Bible in their own language," Tyndale responded. Tyndale was about to embark on the work for which he is justly famous: the translation of the New Testament into English, along with the Pentateuch and Jonah. Years later, on an October morning in 1536, Harry Walsh sat by the dining room fire with a faraway look in his eyes. He had just heard the news that his dear childhood tutor, William Tyndale, had been strangled and burned for his faith. Taking his wife by her arm, he led her across the room where they both stood in reverent silence before the text upon the wall: "We love him because he first loved us."[20]

It Is Impossible to Love God and Hate Your Brother (vv. 20, 21)

Verse 20 is terse and hard-hitting. "If anyone says, 'I love God,' and hates his brother, he is a liar." What you are lying about is your claim to love God. John's logic is impeccable: the one who cannot love his brother whom he has seen cannot love God whom he has not seen. Which is easier, to love God or to love people? If we put that to a vote, the majority would say that it is easier to love God and harder to love people. The reason is simple: God is perfect, and he loves me; people are imperfect and don't always love us. On top of that, some of them have rotten personalities. You would think John would agree, but he does not. For John it is harder to love God than people. People are visible, but God is not. If you don't love people whom you see, how can you claim to love God whom you have never seen? Furthermore, if you don't love people, then you are not loving God because God has declared that one of the ways you show your love for him is by visibly showing your love for others.

Not only should we love other believers, but we should love even our enemies, as Jesus taught us to do. If we Christians love only Christians, it is not exactly the same thing as what Jesus has in mind when he speaks rather dismissively of tax collectors loving tax collectors and pagans loving pagans. Like tax collectors, most people have their own little circle of "in" people.[21] The weekly message on a church sign read "Jesus only." A gust of wind blew off the first three letters, leaving the words "us only." That is an apt description of all too many Christians and churches. Christian love goes beyond just the "in" group and includes all those outside as well, including enemies. Edwards hits the nail on the head: "Love all men. . . . Love wicked men with a love of pity, weep and pray for them and seek the good of their souls and also the good of their bodies. Be ready at all times to do or to suffer for their welfare, wishing and praying that they may have the same mercy that God has given you."[22]

Verse 21 closes the passage with a command: "Whoever loves God must also love his brother." So the question is, do we love our brother? A loving

confidence toward God and the future and a loving concern toward the brothers and sisters in Christ is our mandate. When we respond to God's overture of
love and express love for him, he will create a desire in us to say to everybody
in the church, "Be my valentine."

Max Lucado introduced us all to Chad, a shy, quiet little boy. One day
he came home and told his mother he'd like to make a valentine for everyone
in his class. Her heart sank. "I wish he wouldn't do that!" she thought. She
had watched the children when they walked home from school. Her Chad
was always behind them. They laughed and hung on to each other and talked
to each other, but Chad was never included. Nevertheless, she decided she
would go along with her son. She purchased the paper, glue, and crayons and
for three whole weeks, night after night, Chad painstakingly made thirty-five
valentines. Valentine's Day dawned, and Chad was frantic with excitement!
He carefully placed the valentines in a bag and bolted out the door. His mom
decided to bake his favorite cookies because she knew he would be disap-
pointed when he came home from school. It hurt her to think that he wouldn't
get many valentines, maybe none at all. That afternoon she had the cookies
and milk on the table. Finally, when she heard their voices, she looked out
the window to see the children laughing and having the best time. As usual
there was Chad in the rear, but walking a little faster than usual. She fully
expected him to burst into tears as soon as he got inside. His arms were empty,
she noticed, and when the door opened, she choked back the tears. "Honey,
I have some warm cookies and milk for you," she said, but he hardly heard
her words. He just marched right on by, his face glowing, and all he could
say was, "Not a one—not a one." The mother's heart sank. Then he added, "I
didn't forget a one, not a single one!"[23] And Jesus didn't forget a single one
of us when he died on the cross.

There is an old hymn called "The Love of God." I was surprised to
discover that two verses in that hymn were found written on the walls of an
insane asylum. Those two verses scribbled on the wall, evidently beside the
bed of a man who found the love of God before he died, shared these words:

> The love of God is greater far
> Than tongue or pen can ever tell;
> It goes beyond the highest star,
> And reaches to the lowest hell;
> The guilty pair, bowed down with care,
> God gave His Son to win;
> His erring child He reconciled,
> And pardoned from his sin.

Could we with ink the ocean fill,
And were the skies of parchment made,
Were every stalk on earth a quill,
And every man a scribe by trade,
To write the love of God above,
Would drain the ocean dry.
Nor could the scroll contain the whole,
Though stretched from sky to sky.

"Be my valentine" — God.

Everyone who believes that Jesus is the Christ has been born of God, and everyone who loves the Father loves whoever has been born of him. By this we know that we love the children of God, when we love God and obey his commandments. For this is the love of God, that we keep his commandments. And his commandments are not burdensome. For everyone who has been born of God overcomes the world. And this is the victory that has overcome the world—our faith. Who is it that over-comes the world except the one who believes that Jesus is the Son of God?

1 JOHN 5:1–5

17

Faith Is the Victory!

AT SOUTHWESTERN BAPTIST THEOLOGICAL SEMINARY, we have an evangelistic program called "Taking the Hill." Students and faculty periodically team up in groups of two or three to do door-to-door evangelism. On one occasion a lovely young lady from China and a young Hispanic man were on my team. One of the people we talked to was an elderly gentleman of ninety-two who lived alone and who said he was a Christian. His wife of sixty-seven years had recently passed away, and his son had died of kidney failure. We spent some time encouraging him. One of the comments he made to us was, "You have to do the best you can in life, because even though you are a Christian, you just don't know for sure you are saved until you get to Heaven and find out." The three of us tried in the best way we knew how to say to him that you don't have to wait until you get there to know. You can know now that you have eternal life. We talked to him about the assurance we can have from what John says about this in the letter of 1 John. Can you really know that you are a Christian and going to Heaven when you die? John says absolutely you can know!

John has already spoken of our entrance into the kingdom of God as a spiritual birth. There is a physical birth and a spiritual birth. A physical birth brings one into this world, a human family, and a particular family. Many times family members are known by certain characteristics or certain birthmarks that go along with being in the family. Some members are identified because of the size of their frame, others because of the curvature of their nose or their hair color. Family members sometimes exhibit certain physical characteristics, and we use those characteristics to identify people with certain families. The same is true in the family of God. John talks about three spiritual birthmarks that identify people who are in the family of God. One of those birthmarks is love, another is obedience, and the third is faith. These three birthmarks recur in the letter, and we find them again here in our passage.

Love and Obedience to God Insure Our Love for Christians (vv. 1–3)

The first birthmark John employs is love. John says in 5:1, "Everyone who believes that Jesus is the Christ has been born of God, and everyone who loves the Father loves whoever has been born of him." John uses the example of birth again here to illustrate becoming a Christian. The birth of a baby is a common event. Two things are always are true when babies are born. First, every baby is born into some family. It may not be a functional family, but that child is born into a family. Second, the baby has certain physical characteristics of his or her parents. He may have the eyes of his mother or a nose like his father. Newborns have characteristics of their family that in time become even more pronounced and recognizable. The Christian life is like that. A Christian is someone who has experienced the new birth. This birth is a spiritual birth, and it is one of John's favorite terms to describe what it means to become a Christian. "Everyone who believes that Jesus is the Christ has been born of God." Notice the tense of the verb "has been born." Physical birth cannot be undone or redone. Once you're born, you're born. The same is true with the spiritual birth. The key to the new birth is faith in Jesus Christ. John is assuming this faith is genuine and more than mere mental assent. That is the only kind of faith that results in the new birth. Belief is a sign of the new birth, not a consequence of the new birth. John 1:12, 13 makes it clear that faith is the condition of the new birth.

It is a natural thing for a child to love his parents. When we understand all that God has done for us in bringing about our redemption, our love for him just flows out. Loving God is an easy thing to do for those of us who know Jesus as Lord and Savior. Paul said in Romans 8:14, 15 that all who are the sons of God have been given the Spirit of God in their heart and cry "Abba! Father!" The word "Abba" is an Aramaic word that approximates our word "daddy." Because we are in the family, we can come to the God of this universe not as a God out there somewhere but as our heavenly Father.

So John says that whoever loves the Father loves the child born of the Father. When you are born into a family, you love your father. But John is saying there are also children in the family, and if you love the father, it is a foregone conclusion that you are not only going to love the father who birthed you, but you are going to love everybody else in the family as well. Many of us have siblings in our family. In the process of growing up in our physical family we had to learn to love our siblings. Sometimes it didn't come easy for us, or for them to love us! I remember reading about a little boy who was hugging his father's neck. His other sibling was standing behind the father, so the back of the father was to him. His brother who was hugging his father was at the same time sticking out his tongue at his brother. Growing up, you have to learn to love everyone in the family. So it is in the family of God. Love for other believers is one of the key birthmarks of those in the family.

In 1 Corinthians 13 Paul describes love. Among the things he says about it is that it does not keep books on evil and hardly even notices when others do wrong. Sometimes we tend to keep books on evil. Sometimes when couples argue, one will bring up something that the other did over a year ago. But true love does not do that. True love does not keep records on evil. If someone wronged you last year and received your forgiveness, you should never bring the incident up again. Imagine if God treated us the way some of us treat one another. Suppose God said to you when you sin today, "You know, I seem to recall that you did something like that last month. I forgave you, but let's bring that back out on the table and talk about it." As Corrie ten Boom said, when God forgives us, our sins "are now cast in the deepest sea and a sign is then put up that says NO FISHING ALLOWED."[1]

John's second birthmark is closely related to the birthmark of love. The second birthmark is obedience. "By this we know that we love the children of God, when we love God and obey his commandments" (v. 2). When you are in the military you receive orders. What would you think about a soldier who understood verbatim the orders of his superior and yet never carried them out? What would happen to such a soldier? His commanding officer would not care that he could repeat those orders. The key issue is whether the soldier carried out his commander's orders. As Christians we should not just talk about God's commandments, memorize them, and understand them. We should carry out God's commandments. We must do more than just know the commandments. God is interested to see if we carry them out.

How do you show your love for God? Do what he says! Look at verse 3: "For this is the love of [for] God, that we keep his commandments." The highest credentials of love are to be found in obedience.[2] Obedience is the proof of your love. God himself says in the Old Testament, "To obey is better than sacrifice" (1 Samuel 15:22). Let me put that in our contemporary church context. To obey God is better than preaching about obeying God. To obey God is better than singing about obeying God. To obey God is better than having a Bible study lesson taught about obeying God. To obey God is better than bringing a tithe to church. To obey God is to do what God says. Ask yourself a simple question: Am I doing what God says? Are his commands really too hard to keep? Sometimes Christians may find the commands of the Bible difficult and burdensome. Ask yourself another simple question: Why do I keep the commandments, anyway? The answer to that question is vital because it reveals your spiritual maturity or lack thereof. Is your Christian life more of a duty you have to force yourself to fulfill? Do you feel that if you don't keep God's commandments you are afraid of what he might do if you don't? Or do you genuinely desire to obey God's commandments? When John says God's "commandments are not burdensome," he indicates that the world considers them onerous. But real Christians don't think that way. The primary motivation for keeping God's commandments should be our love for Jesus, the one who gave them in the first place!

Think about the Ten Commandments. "You shall have no other gods before me." I suspect when you got up today you did not bow down before a golden idol in your home. But do we have other kinds of idols that we do worship? "Remember the Sabbath day, to keep it holy." Sunday is our Sabbath now. The day of resurrection is the Lord's Day, and because of this we worship on the Lord's Day. Are we keeping the Lord's Day holy? "Honor your father and your mother." How are we going about obeying this commandment? "You shall not murder." This commandment about murder doesn't seem too hard to keep. But in Matthew 5 Jesus said we can break this commandment in our heart by hating a brother or wishing that somebody were dead (Matthew 5:21, 22). What about "you shall not commit adultery"? This one is not hard either, right? But Jesus said if we look on a woman lustfully, we have already committed adultery in our heart (Matthew 5:27, 28). "You shall not steal" sounds easy enough to keep. All I need to do is make sure I don't rob a bank or take anything from anybody that is not mine. Have we ever plagiarized, cheated on a test, or misinformed the IRS on our taxes? We could go through each of the Ten Commandments, but you get the point. If we love God, we will do as he says, and if we love our neighbor as ourselves we will not murder him, commit adultery with his wife, steal from him, lie to him, or covet anything he possesses. We can measure our love for God by how well our lifestyle matches our Maker's instructions![3]

That is also why he says at the end of verse 3 that God's commandments are not "burdensome." The word in Greek means "heavy, hard to bear." God's commandments are not burdensome when we love God and we have been born of God. When we submit our will to the Spirit of God, his commands are not burdensome. God's commandments are given for our spiritual good, and to disobey them could bring disaster. Some people view Christianity as a religion of rules, and keeping those rules is, for them, burdensome. To listen to those who don't know Christ talk about God's commands as "burdensome" is like listening to a madman bound in chains in a dungeon talk about how much he enjoys his freedom! Such people fail to realize that Christianity is a family relationship. The Christian life should be lived out of love for our heavenly Father. That's what makes our obedience to God's commands a matter of desire and delight. The reason God gives us his commands in the first place is because he loves us. Children sometimes think their parents are mean when they tell them not to do something. "There must obviously be some pleasure in touching that hot stove or my parents would not tell me not to do it!" Only maturity brings the knowledge that our parents prohibit certain things and tell us to do certain things because they love us and want the very best for us. Obedience brings freedom!

Think about it. When John says God's "commandments are not burdensome," he doesn't mean it is easy to keep the Law, especially the Old Testament Law. Luther thinks John is here referring to the commandments of the gospel in the New Testament. He references Matthew 11:28–30: "Come to me, all who labor and are heavy laden, and I will give you rest. . . . For my yoke is easy, and my burden is light."[4] Make no mistake, it's not easy to follow Jesus today and live a life obedient to the commands of God. It will take every ounce of your spiritual strength and all that God can give through you to live for God successfully. It's not easy to live for God. But that's not what John means. He means that God will never command without giving the strength to fulfill it. The wonderful thing about the Christian life is that God's commands can be carried out because he places the Holy Spirit within us who gives us the motivation and power to live out the commands of God. That's important for us to understand. No duty is too difficult when performed out of a heart of love.

General Charles Duke was one of those who walked on the moon during the Apollo 16 mission. He was asked at a dinner engagement if he wished, when he was on the moon, he could stay out a little longer or go a little further. Duke said he thought a lot about that and would have done so if he did not want to get back to earth. He said everything about being on the moon and getting back to earth safely totally depended on his implicit and complete obedience to NASA. When he and the crew landed on the moon, they had sixty seconds worth of fuel left for takeoff![5] Sometimes Christians whine about having to obey God's commandments like children complaining to their parents about having to obey. Our love for God is evidenced when we are willing to do what he says. "This is the love of God, that we keep his commandments. And his commandments are not burdensome."

John will have nothing to do with the notion that you can love God but not do what he says. You may say you love God all day long, but John says the proof of your love is the obedience of your life. The Bible makes it clear that where there is no obedience to God there is no true love for God. Have you ever stopped to think how everything in nature obeys the will of God? The wind, sea, moon and stars, plants, and animals obey the will of God. Man is the only member of God's creation who does not obey him. Read the book of Jonah and see how all of the elements obeyed God—the sea, the great fish, the plant that came up and shielded Jonah from the heat, and the worm that destroyed the plant. They all obeyed God, except for Jonah. People disobey God. James Boice summed up verse 3 well: "The life of God within makes obedience to the commands possible, and the love which the Christian has for God and for other Christians makes this obedience desirable."[6]

Faith Is the Victory That Conquers the World (vv. 4, 5)

Faith is John's third birthmark of the Christian. In verse 4 we read, "everyone who has been born of God overcomes the world. And this is the victory that has overcome the world—our faith." I love war movies. I don't know why, I just do. I love watching the depiction on the screen of some titanic struggle with empires in the balance. I have visited some of the sites of these great battles. The mountains, hills, valleys, plains, seas, and seashores of earth stand as mute testimony to great conflicts of days gone by. Regional wars continue to this very moment. But an even greater conflict rages daily over all the earth. It is an unseen battle but no less real. It is a spiritual battle between the forces of God and the forces of Satan. We Christians are soldiers in the army of the Captain of our Salvation, marching as to war. John tells us that faith is the victory!

Ron Dunn once queried, "Have you ever noticed the disturbing difference between what the Bible says we are and what we really are? It would be difficult to recognize most Christians from the description given of them in the Bible."[7] Let's take a look out our photograph in verse 4. Faith in Jesus and the new birth are inseparable. Faith in Christ is necessary for the new birth. John indicates that only the one who has been born of God can overcome the world. Faith is the victory that overcomes the world. Real faith, saving faith, is faith in Jesus the Christ. Notice how John repeats the phrase "believes that Jesus is the Christ" and "believes that Jesus is the Son of God" in verses 1 and 5. The Christian life begins with faith in Jesus as the Son of God. But faith is also a necessary component of the Christian life every single day. Every day of our lives we face three great enemies: the world, our own flesh, and the devil. Life is a struggle. The world, dressed as the prostitute Infidelity, comes near me and alluringly offers me her hand. She whispers seductively in my ear. She promises me worldly pleasure. She flirtingly lies to me by telling me that real joy comes from loving her and not from loving my Savior, Jesus. The world is a powerful seductress. How can I win the victory over her temptations? John says that daily victory comes from recognizing that faith teaches me how to overcome the world. Read Hebrews 11 and be reminded seventeen times that the great men and women of the Old Testament won the victory "by faith." Not by intellect, not by power, but by faith. Faith is the victory that overcomes the world.

When the Civil War broke out in 1861, Lincoln's Secretary of State, William Seward, predicted the war would be over in ninety days. Young men by the thousands came forward to volunteer to whip the South. Four long years later, half a million lives had been lost. The North underestimated the strength of the South. Christians should never overestimate the power of Satan, but we should not underestimate his power either. Conversion is like enlisting in the army. The newborn Christian is a member the moment he enlists. But he has yet to see combat.[8]

How do we conquer the world? Throughout the history of the church some have sought to answer this question with monasticism: overcoming the world by escaping the world. There are several problems with this attempted solution. First, only a few elite could ever do it! Ordinary Christians don't have the luxury of donning a cowl and stealing off to the monastery.

Second, this view tragically forgets that the world is not only outside me but is also inside me. Withdrawal from the world does not get rid of the world. Furthermore, the Bible teaches clearly that Christians are to be in the world but not of the world.

In verse 4 John says the believer "overcomes" and "has overcome" the world. In one sense the victory has already happened. Yet there is a sense in which we are still overcoming it. We are already victorious, but we still have to fight. At the Battle of Quebec, General Wolfe conquered the French soldier General Montcalm on the Heights of Abraham, and as a result Canada was conquered. Yet history books say that the fight for possessing Canada went on for many more years. The country was captured and then was captured in detail over the next seventy or eighty years. That is something of the situation in the Christian life. We are no longer under the dominion of Satan. He is a defeated foe. But that does not mean we have finished our fight with him.[9] If I am to overcome the world, I need a force and power beyond my own strength. I am given the weapon of faith. I see things that the world cannot see or understand. Like Elijah's servant whose eyes were opened and he saw the army of angels surrounding the army of Sennacherib, by faith I have the means of victory over the world. The world is strong, but Christ is stronger. I have a power within me and available to me that the world does not possess.[10]

Listen to John in verse 5: "Who is it that overcomes the world except the one who believes that Jesus is the Son of God?" My relationship to Christ, my union with Christ in salvation, enables me to overcome the world. It is not a matter of keeping the right rules or having enough willpower. By faith in Christ I see myself belonging to Christ. I am in Christ permanently. I can draw strength and power from him and from his fullness. A cartoon in *The New Yorker* once showed a psychologist reporting on some tests to a counselee. He said, "Our findings show that your problem is not an inferiority complex. You simply *are* inferior." Faith enables me to see that in Christ I am not inferior. I am an overcomer!

In a crisis moment the day before General Eisenhower was to lead the Allied Forces in one of the most decisive battles of World War II along the Rhine River, he was approached by a panicked young soldier. The lad pled to be sent back because he was sick. His appeal was denied by the field general. He then begged to be sent home to help his mother in her time of need. Again the request was turned down. As the general was about to leave he turned to the youth and said, "Would it make you feel better if we met here tomorrow morning and went down to the river together?" Biographers tell of the young man bravely walking down to the river by the general's side with great courage. The victory was theirs. Together they overcame.[11]

Do you own any clothing item with the Nike logo on it? Nike borrowed their logo and company name from the Greek goddess of victory, whose name was Nike. At the top of the Acropolis there was a small temple named Athena Nike, "to the victor." When you find the noun "victory" in the New Testament, it is the word *nikē*. John uses the noun or verb form of *nikē* four times in this passage. To give some idea of the use of this word, we might render the verse like this: "Whatever is born of God victories the world, and this is the victory that has victoried the world, even our faith." John Yates expressed it well in the old hymn "Faith Is the Victory:"

> Encamped along the hills of light, ye Christian soldiers, rise,
> And press the battle ere the night shall veil the glowing skies.
> Against the foe in veils below let all our strength be hurled;
> Faith is the victory, we know, that overcomes the world.

G. Campbell Morgan pointed out that key differences in the three statements of John in verses 4, 5 are worthy of notice.

> The subject of the first is neuter: "Whatsoever is begotten of God"; and the tense is present: "overcometh the world." This fastens attention upon a power. The subject of the second is again neuter: "This is the victory"; and the tense is past: "Which hath overcome the world." That fastens attention upon a principle. The subject of the third declaration is masculine "he," and attention is directed to a man; and its tense is present: "overcometh." The third declaration thus fastens attention upon a person.[12]

The power, the principle, the person. Understanding all three and being connected to all three brings victory over the world.

> What man can be the instrument of the power? What man can be the agent of the principle? The man who conforms to the principle; the man who believes that Jesus is the Son of God; the man who believes in the sovereignty and Saviourhood of Christ; and believes in it, not merely as an intellectual conviction, a philosophic assertion, but believes in the New Testament sense, by abandoning himself to the great conception of truth, by risking his own soul upon it, his own fortune upon it, his very lifeblood in the business. By that man God is moving toward the recapture of His lost world.[13]

Satan is a bully. He and his sidekick, the world, like to bully Christians. Have you ever had to put up with a bully in school? In the seventh grade I'll never forget I did. In those days elementary school concluded with the sixth grade, and seventh grade was the beginning of junior high. When you entered junior high school, you went from being top dog to being a low dog, from top to flop. I was a short, scrawny seventh grader; even the girls were taller than me. The bully in our class was a kid who had failed about three years straight and should have been in the tenth grade. He was nearly six feet tall and still in the seventh grade. One day at PE I don't know what came over me, but it was something akin to the Scut Farkas affair in the movie *A Christmas Story*, when Ralphie just goes haywire. This big guy was bullying somebody else, and suddenly I just shouted out, "Why don't you just bully somebody else, you fink!" He turned slowly around, glared at me, and slowly muttered, "Today when school lets out, you will die." I want you to know I believed him. The rest of the day I was miserable, trying to think how I could get my affairs in order. In those days you couldn't call your parents unless a nuclear bomb had been dropped on your school, and this situation was nowhere near DefCon One. I was dreading the final bell.

My dad worked third shift and usually picked me up from school on days I did not walk or ride my bike. My plan was to hang out in the hallways until I thought for sure Dad's car would be waiting outside in the back parking lot. After waiting what I thought was long enough, I exited the building and turned the corner at the parking lot. Dad was late that day, but the bully was waiting right around the corner with two of his cronies. With one hand he picked me up and held me upside down by my ankles. "I'm going to kill you today. You are dead." About that time one of the coaches came around the corner and saw and heard the whole thing. He walked right up behind the bully, tapped him on the shoulder, and said three words to him: "*You* are dead." He escorted the bully into the building, and I never saw him again. There is always a bully out there. Aren't we always grateful for somebody who comes along who is bigger than the bully?

Three young men hopped on a bus in Detroit in the 1930s and tried to pick a fight with a man sitting in the back. They insulted him. He didn't respond. They insulted him more. He said nothing. Eventually the stranger stood up. He was bigger than the three would-be assailants had estimated from his seated position—much bigger. He reached into his pocket, handed them his business card, and exited the bus. As the bus drove off, the young men gathered around the card to read the words: "Joe Louis. Boxer." They had just tried to pick a fight with the man who would be Heavyweight Boxing Champion of the World from 1937–1949 and the number one boxer of all time according to the International Boxing Research Organization.[14] What is the victory that overcomes the bully of the world? It is our faith. We have a big brother named Jesus who can defeat the bully and give us the victory.

That's why John says in verse 5 that the key to victory is believing in Jesus, the Son of God. When John uses the indefinite pronoun in the form of a question ("Who is it that overcomes the world . . . ?") he is basically saying, "If Christians aren't victorious, then no one is!"[15] Victory comes by faith not in yourself, your church, or your denomination but only in the Son of God, Jesus. In 1 John 5:1–5, as in all of 1 John, it is not *what* we Christians do (for example, when we love our neighbor) that stands in the foreground but rather *why* we do it. We do what we do because we have been "born of God." Our origin is in him. So the emphasis lies as much or more on the motive of what we do as on what we actually do.[16] I love my fellow believers, I keep God's commandments, and I have victory over the world by faith because of *who* I am and because of *whose* I am. Do you want to live the Christian life of victory? If so, John says in these verses that the Victory Express runs on two tracks: trust and obey.[17] Christians don't fight *for* victory; we fight *from* victory. Christ has already won the victory for us at Calvary. When a battle is fought, everybody wants to know who wins!

> Let every day my question be,
> Who rules this heart of mine?
> Do I stand in grace,
> Head toward that place
> Where I am ever thine?

Friedrich August Tholuck[18]

This is he who came by water and blood—Jesus Christ; not by the water only but by the water and the blood. And the Spirit is the one who testifies, because the Spirit is the truth. For there are three that testify: the Spirit and the water and the blood; and these three agree. If we receive the testimony of men, the testimony of God is greater, for this is the testimony of God that he has borne concerning his Son. Whoever believes in the Son of God has the testimony in himself. Whoever does not believe God has made him a liar, because he has not believed in the testimony that God has borne concerning his Son. And this is the testimony, that God gave us eternal life, and this life is in his Son. Whoever has the Son has life; whoever does not have the Son of God does not have life.

1 JOHN 5:6–12

18

A Tale of Three Witnesses

A KEY WORD recurs in these verses eight times. It is the word "testify" or "testimony."[1] We are entering in these verses into the courtroom. In this passage court is in session as John summons witnesses to the witness box to testify to the truth that Jesus is the Son of God and the only way of salvation.[2] Through the magic of time travel, you and I are members of the jury. "Hear ye, hear ye, court is now in session!"

As the courtroom comes to order, our eyes are riveted on an aged man who stands and approaches the front of the court. A former fisherman, he is now famous worldwide as the only surviving member of the original twelve disciples who followed Jesus. His name is John. Some of us are amazed that he can even stand up, much less walk, since he seems so old! Though he appears to be at least an octogenarian, there is still something of a twinkle in his eye and a spring in his step.

Testimony of the Water and the Blood (v. 6)

With a firm voice he speaks: "I call the water to the witness stand." Never in the history of the court has there been such an unusual witness! The "water" John is calling to testify is the water that was used by John the Baptist to baptize Jesus at the initiation of his earthly ministry as recorded in the Gospels. "Water of Jordan, do you swear to tell the truth, the whole truth, and nothing but the truth, so help you God?" "I do," replies the water. "You were there that day Jesus was baptized; please tell us what you saw." "Yes," answers the water. "I was there. Jesus walked down until he was about waist-deep in my waters where John the Baptist was standing. John immersed him and raised him up. I saw something very unusual occur after that. At first there was Jesus standing in me, but I also saw the heavens open, and there was a visual sign of a dove that descended on him. I heard a voice speak from Heaven, and it said,

'This is my beloved Son, with whom I am well pleased.' As clear as a bell I remember that voice as it called Jesus 'my beloved Son' and told him, 'with you I am well pleased.'" "Thank you, water. I have no further questions. You may be dismissed from the witness stand," John says.

John continues, "I call the blood to the witness stand." Eyes widen in the courtroom. Just when we thought we had heard from the strangest witness ever, John calls another witness even more peculiar than the water! He has called the blood of Jesus shed on the cross of Calvary to the stand to bear testimony. "Do you swear to tell the truth, the whole truth, and nothing but the truth, so help you God?" "I do," responds the blood. "Blood, you were there that day Jesus was crucified. You were in his body." "Yes, I can testify that at his trial before Pilate, Jesus was scourged with a cat of nine tails. The punishment left his back a bloody mess. The crown of thorns caused me to stream down his face. The nails were driven into his hands and feet. And then when he was placed on the cross I ran down from his head, hands, and feet. 'See from his head, his hands, his feet, sorrow and love flow mingled down! Did e'er such love and sorrow meet, or thorns compose so rich a crown?'" For a brief moment there is a hushed silence in the courtroom. Then John continues, "Can you tell us if Jesus actually died on that cross?" "Yes," said the blood. "I can verify that he actually died. As the blood of Jesus, I bear testimony that Jesus is the Son of the living God." John replies, "Thank you, blood of Jesus, you may step down from the witness box."[3]

The Testimony of the Holy Spirit (vv. 7, 8)

John turns to the jury and says, "Before I call my third witness to the stand, I wish to point out to the jury that in verse 5 of chapter 5 in my letter called 1 John, I refer to Jesus as 'the Son of God.' And in verse 6, I speak of Jesus as 'Christ.' This subtle shift is significant. Jesus, the Son of God, is no less than God's 'Anointed One,' the Messiah. This Messiah is the one who 'came' to the earth to be the Messiah not only for the Jewish people but for all people. He is the 'Christ,' the 'Anointed One' who fulfilled God's purpose by dying on the cross for the sins of the world."

Following a brief pause, John says, "To verify this claim, I call a third witness to the stand: the Holy Spirit."[4] A holy hush falls over the courtroom as the Holy Spirit moves to the witness stand. "Do you swear to tell the truth, the whole truth, and nothing but the truth?" John queries. "Yes, I am the Spirit of truth," replies the Holy Spirit. "Before I question this witness," John continued, "I would like to remind the jury that I have spoken about this witness, the Holy Spirit, in my Gospel. Just before his crucifixion Jesus taught us about the Holy Spirit, telling us that when the Holy Spirit comes upon us, he will testify concerning Jesus. Jesus said that one of the primary purposes of the Holy Spirit is to point people to Jesus as Savior. Jesus further taught us that the Holy Spirit will not magnify himself but rather will magnify the Lord Jesus."

John continues, "God the Holy Spirit reveals the significance of the coming of Jesus into this world. It's God the Holy Spirit who first dealt with your heart when you were lost in your sin. You cannot be saved unless God the Holy Spirit draws you to salvation. The work of the Holy Spirit in your salvation is so important that you can't be saved apart from him. God the Holy Spirit draws you to Jesus and teaches you the spiritual truth of the life, death, and resurrection of Jesus. It's his job to press to your heart the truth of these things."

"The witness of the Holy Spirit reveals the significance of Jesus' coming,"[5] John continues. "He testifies in our hearts and minds the truth of these things, drawing men and women to salvation. He enables men to preach the gospel and empowers people to live out the gospel. In this sense the Holy Spirit is the first witness to testify to Jesus and his salvation."

Then John turns to the Holy Spirit and begins his questioning. "Holy Spirit, were you present at the earthly ministry of Jesus?" "Yes. I was present at his birth, I was present at his baptism, I was present during his earthly life, and I was present at his crucifixion, his resurrection, and his ascension. I was present with him in Heaven in eternity past before the incarnation, and I will be present with him as the third member of the Trinity for all eternity." "Holy Spirit, is it your testimony that Jesus Christ is the Son of the living God?" John asks. "I bear witness that Jesus Christ is the Son of the living God," replies the Holy Spirit. "Thank you, Holy Spirit; you may step down," says John.

The Testimony of God the Father (v. 9)

After such powerful testimony, I fully expected John to move to his closing argument, but he surprises us all by calling a fourth witness to the stand. "I call God the Father to testify." Another holy hush falls over the courtroom. Heads are bowed as God the Father enters the witness box. With all the reverence one can imagine, yet with all the confidence of one who knows the Father in an intimate fashion, John proceeds to swear in the witness. "Heavenly Father, do you swear to tell the truth, the whole truth, and nothing but the truth, so help you you?" "I do," says the Father with a voice that rings like a bell. John begins the questioning. "Heavenly Father, do you recognize this man Jesus? Is he indeed your Son whom you sent to this earth?" "Yes," replies the Father. "He is my beloved Son in whom I am well pleased." With a firm voice John queries, "Do you testify that he and he alone is your Son and the only way of salvation?" "Yes. From the very beginning, even before I created Adam and Eve and before they sinned causing all of humanity to be plunged into sin, I had a plan of salvation. My plan was for Jesus my Son, my only-begotten, to come to earth and pay the penalty of humanity's sin through his death on the cross. I foretold his coming through my prophets. I sent John the Baptist as his forerunner. I sent an angel to Mary to announce to her that she was my choice to be the human mother of my Son Jesus. Though Jesus existed one with me throughout eternity as the third person of the Trinity, yet he became man. The night of his birth my angels sang about it. I sent shepherds to witness it. Wise men came to observe it and pay homage to him. As a man Jesus entered his ministry and was baptized, as has already been testified. The heavens opened, and I spoke and said, 'This is my beloved Son, with whom I am well pleased.' The night before his crucifixion, he called out to me, 'Father, if it can be your will let this cup pass.' But it was not my will. And I turned over my only Son to evil men to crucify. But I did it for a purpose, and he did it willingly. This purpose was to make an atonement for your sins. My Son Jesus was crucified and buried, but three days later I raised him from the dead. Forty days later he ascended to Heaven where today he sits at my right hand. One day I will determine the time has come, and my Son will come again to this earth. I give eternal life as a gift, and this eternal life is in my Son, Jesus. So say I, God the Father." After a pause that seems to last an eternity, John speaks with reverent softness. "Thank you, Father. You may step down from the witness box."

The Testimony of "Whoever" (v. 10)

My heart was in my throat. I thought for sure John would now turn to us, the jury, and initiate his closing argument. Instead to my amazement he declared he had two final witnesses to summon to the stand, two witnesses found in verse 10. They are twins who bear the same name: "Whoever." Never before in the history of the court have two witnesses taken the stand at the same time. In a strange way everyone in the courtroom, whether believers in Jesus or not, are represented now on the witness stand. "I call Whoever to the stand," John intones. "Do you both swear to tell the truth, the whole truth, and nothing but the truth, so help you God?" "We do." The first Whoever is one who has believed the testimony of God and these other witnesses concerning Jesus. John begins his questioning. "Have you come to Jesus Christ and found him to be the Savior from your sins?" "I have," responds Whoever. "Do you then testify concerning the truth of what I myself have said about Jesus in my writings?" asks John. "I do indeed," responds Whoever. Turning to the other

Whoever, John asks, "Have you come to Jesus Christ and found him to be the Savior of your sins?" "I have not," responds the other Whoever. John looks at him and in a stern voice says, "Do you refuse to believe the testimony that God the Father himself has borne in this very courtroom?" "I do indeed," says Whoever without blinking an eye. "I believe God is a liar about what he has said concerning his Son Jesus. He has perjured himself under oath." Stunned silence fills the courtroom. Mouths are *agapē*. Finally John speaks. "Thank you, Whoever. You may both step down from the witness box."

Closing Argument: Eternal Life in the Son Alone (vv. 11, 12)

John turns to the jury and now begins his closing argument (vv. 11, 12). "The testimony of the witnesses is clear and irrefutable. God has given us eternal life, and this life is in his Son, Jesus. He who has the Son possesses this eternal life. He who does not have the Son of God does not have eternal life. As an old man, let me cut through the fog and speak with clear simplicity. Argue all you want, talk about all the gray areas you want, but the issue is clear-cut. I was there when Jesus died for our sins on that cross. I am a personal eyewitness, as I have already reminded you in 1:1–4. I was the first to see the empty tomb. I was there in the Upper Room a week after Jesus' resurrection when he appeared to his twelve disciples. I was there when Jesus ascended to Heaven. From that day until this I have been telling others about this Jesus. I wrote five books about it in your Bibles telling you that Jesus is the Son of God. Whoever has the Son as his Savior possesses this eternal life. Whoever does not have this Son as his Savior does not have eternal life. If you don't have Jesus, you don't have life, but only death. If you die apart from Jesus you will spend an eternity apart from Jesus in a place called Hell."

John continues, "God has given us eternal life as I state in verse 11. Eternal life is a gift. It cannot be merited or earned. You cannot work for it. When someone gives you a gift, you don't pay him for it, do you? If you do, that's an insult! A gift by definition is something you don't merit or earn. That's the way salvation is. You couldn't pay for it anyway. How would we pay for salvation? All the money in the world could not purchase it. Our salvation is the costliest gift ever. The price was the death of God's Son for our sins. God himself paid the price through the death of Jesus on the cross. He did not make a down payment on our salvation and then we take up the payments. No, Jesus paid the price in full."

John resumes, "How do you get this eternal life? The same way you get any gift: by receiving it. Remember what I wrote in John 1:12: 'But to all who did receive him, who believed in his name, he gave the right to become children of God.' To believe on Jesus is to receive this gift of salvation through Jesus. Only in Jesus is salvation possible. I recorded what Jesus told the disciples just before his crucifixion in John 14:6: 'I am the way, and the truth, and the life. No one comes to the Father except through me.' The only way you get eternal life from God is through his Son Jesus. To have the Son is just another way of saying that you have believed on the Son and God has given you eternal life. To not have the Son is another way of saying that you have not believed in Jesus for salvation and thus you do not possess eternal life. If you have the Son you have that life; if you do not have the Son you don't have life. Faith in Jesus, who completed the work of atonement on the cross, is the only way to receive God's gift of eternal life. What is the nature of this eternal life? Eternal life is not just a quantity of life; it is also a quality of life. It's not just living forever. Eternal life is God's life in us.

"So why should you believe on Jesus Christ? Well, if you have no other answer, God himself has told you that this Jesus is the Messiah! His testimony is not merely the testimony of man but the testimony of God himself! Above all other testimony the case rests on this fact—God has revealed Christ Jesus to us, and Jesus is God's final word! To refuse this testimony is to call God a liar! We must believe this testimony or suffer the consequences: loss of eternal life."

As I listened to John, my mind went back to that Sunday in 1966 when as a nine-year-old boy the Holy Spirit worked in my life, drawing me to Jesus the Savior. I didn't have many emotional feelings about it. I didn't cry or laugh as I recall. Though I knew what I was doing when I trusted Christ as my Savior, at the time there was so much I did not understand. Later, as I grew in my Christian life, I had a deeper sense of emotion about my salvation, more than I did when I was younger. Sometimes people want a certain feeling in their spine or a vision along the way, but that's seldom how it works. One thing is for sure: the Holy Spirit who indwells me bears witness with my spirit that I am a child of God!

John's concluding argument ends with a stark, terse point: "'Whoever has the Son has life; whoever does not have the Son of God does not have life" (v. 12). "All people on Planet Earth are headed to only one of two destinies: eternal life or eternal death," John intones with heightened pitch. "Notice I use the word 'have,' present tense. Are you in possession of the Son, Jesus? Of course, the real question is whether Jesus has possession of you! The fundamental truth lies in the words of Jesus: 'As the living Father sent me, and I live because of the Father, so whoever feeds on me, he also will live because of me' (from my Gospel, 6:57), That is to say, life resides in God, 'the living Father'; it is shared by the Son, who 'lives because of the Father'; through him it is mediated to everyone who will make it his own by laying hold directly and deliberately upon the Son through repentance of sin and faith in Christ. If you want this life-imparting gospel to be yours, you must receive Jesus as the Word of life. Life flows from the Father to the Son and through the Son into us when we believe the gospel. Eternal life is not about our being good but about Christ being God!" John's eyes are fixed on us, the jury. Time seems frozen for a moment. "I rest my case," John says, his voice trailing off as he speaks.

In the ensuing silence I cannot help but be struck by the note of certainty in every witness who has testified in court. I have heard John use the words "we know" like a refrain throughout his letter and in these proceedings. No presumption; no guesswork. The basis of the truth of Jesus Christ is the testimony of God himself! We Christians partake of this certainty as well. I bear this testimony in myself, validated by God's Holy Spirit who indwells me. Now I begin to see why this knowledge is essential if I am to experience a victorious life. I know now that my own feelings can never serve as the ground of my assurance. I need something far more permanent than my fluctuating feelings. God's character of unchanging love and faithfulness, coupled with the permanent work of Jesus that he accomplished on the cross for my salvation, remains unaffected by my shifting feelings and grounds my Christian life. What confidence! I recall the words of the great preacher Spurgeon who drove the point home: "Many go to heaven with very little comfort on the road. I do not commend them for their want [lack] of comfort; but I do advise you, instead of looking to singular experiences as a ground of confidence, look to the bleeding Saviour, and rest alone in Him, for if you have Him you have eternal life."[6] The eternal Holy Spirit testifies continually in my heart and gives me such assurance.[7] May God's name be praised! As Adrian Rogers said, "It is much better to be a shouting Christian than a doubting Christian. We ought not walk around like a question mark with our heads bent over but like an exclamation mark."[8]

> Until the purposes of God are thwarted and He skulks away in chagrin; until the control of the universe is wrested from His hands; until the creature like a Frankenstein conquers the Creator; until God violates His own nature and becomes a sufferer in hell; until Satan is big enough to defeat the Father, Son, and Holy Spirit; until the sacrifice of Jesus is no better than the death of a dog; until the Spirit goes on a vacation or proves inadequate to finish what He started; until God becomes unmitigated a liar, I am safe.[9]

The gavel falls in the courtroom, and we, the jury, retreat to make a decision. What is your decision about Jesus? In Deuteronomy 17:6 we read, "On the evidence of two witness or of three witnesses" there is truth. In the words of C. S. Lewis, your choices as to who Jesus is are limited. In light of what Jesus has said about himself, in light of what God has said about him, in light of what the water and blood and the Holy Spirit have said about him, Jesus is either a liar, a lunatic, or Lord. You have no other options. If he is a liar, then dismiss him. If he is a lunatic, then dismiss him. But if he is Lord, repent of your sin, believe in him for salvation, and fall at his feet and worship him because he is worthy of the devotion of your life.

I write these things to you who believe in the name of the Son of God that you may know that you have eternal life. And this is the confidence that we have toward him, that if we ask anything according to his will he hears us. And if we know that he hears us in whatever we ask, we know that we have the requests that we have asked of him. If anyone sees his brother committing a sin not leading to death, he shall ask, and God will give him life—to those who commit sins that do not lead to death. There is sin that leads to death; I do not say that one should pray for that. All wrongdoing is sin, but there is sin that does not lead to death. We know that everyone who has been born of God does not keep on sinning, but he who was born of God protects him, and the evil one does not touch him. We know that we are from God, and the whole world lies in the power of the evil one. And we know that the Son of God has come and has given us understanding, so that we may know him who is true; and we are in him who is true, in his Son Jesus Christ. He is the true God and eternal life.

1 JOHN 5:13–20

19

The Haves and the Have-Nots

DO YOU REMEMBER the television game show *The $10,000 Pyramid*? Contestants would play in pairs, and one partner would give the other a list of specific items, and the clue recipient had to guess what they all had in common. For example, the clues might be "a boat, a buoy, an empty plastic bottle, etc.," and the answer would be "things that float." In these verses John gives us a specific list of six items that he discusses, three in verses 13–15 and three in verses 18–21: eternal life, confidence, answered prayer (vv. 13–15); right attitude toward sin, divine spiritual origin, and Jesus the true God (vv. 18–21). What do all these items have in common? What if I were to say, "You have eternal life, God hears your prayers always, and God answers your prayers even before you know the answer." What category would fit that list? The answer is "things every Christian knows and possesses."

Notice that the word "have" occurs in each verse in verses 13–15. In each case it is associated with one of these three things: "you *have* eternal life," "this is the confidence that we *have*," and "we know that we *have* the requests . . ." Notice again how in verses 13–15 the word "know" is associated with each of these three things: "that you may *know* that you have eternal life," "if we *know* that he hears us in whatever we ask," and "we *know* that we have the request that we have asked of him." Verses 13–15 speak of three things we "have" and three things we "know."

Assurance of Eternal Life (v. 13)

The first thing John desires that we "know" is that we "have eternal life" (v. 13). Did you know that you can know that you have eternal life? You can know that you are saved. You don't have to doubt it, guess about it, or wonder about it. I'm glad I don't have to live in the fog on this one! Verse 13 is a strategic verse in this entire letter because it gives us the purpose for John's writing. When we receive a letter, we want to know who wrote it and why he or she wrote it. Some people today believe that you cannot know with certainty that you are a Christian. According to them, you just have to wait until you die to find out if you get into Heaven or not. Muslims believe they cannot know in this life whether they are acceptable to Allah or not. John explodes all this doubt into the limbo of nonsense.[1] But God does not want his children to worry, doubt, or lack assurance about whether they are Christians or not. In this letter John provides some tests to determine if you are a believer or not. We have already seen some of those tests in earlier chapters. There is the test of love for the brethren. Do you love other Christians? There is the test of righteousness. Do you desire to live correctly and in a way that pleases God? There is the test of right believing. Have you believed that Jesus is the Son of God? If you pass those three tests, mark it down, you are a Christian.

Verse 13 implies that it is possible to be truly saved and yet not have assurance of your salvation. I have met many people like that and have counseled many people about this issue throughout my ministry. People often have doubts about their salvation. There are many reasons why Christians doubt. Sometimes it is because they are not living in a right way before the Lord. Another reason why Christians doubt is that God is calling them to a higher plane of Christian service, but they are not responding. Still another reason why Christians doubt is that the devil knows that he cannot get at some Christians unless he gets them in this way. If he can keep them in a state of doubt, they will not be able to serve God because they are always introspective. Such lack of assurance robs you of your joy in the Christian life. It arrests your spiritual growth. It also cripples your usefulness in the Lord's service. Your assurance of salvation is a very important thing to know. Spurgeon is correct to point out that it is our duty to obtain full assurance. "We should not have been commanded to give diligence to make our calling and election sure if it were not right for us to be sure. I am sure it is right for a child of God to know that God is his Father, and never to have a question in his heart as to his sonship."[2]

Compare 1 John 5:13 with John 20:31. Both are purpose statements for writing. John's purpose in his Gospel was evangelistic: "These are written so that you may believe that Jesus is the Christ." Now he writes in his letter with a purpose of assurance of salvation: "that you might know that you have eternal life." John's Gospel was written to help us come to know Christ, and his letter was written to help us know that we have come to know Christ. People differ in many ways around the world with respect to culture, diet, skin color, and many other things. But some things are true about human beings no matter where they live. Every human being breathes, eats, sleeps, and drinks water. The same is true in the spiritual realm. Christians might fly under the banner of a particular denomination, but all genuine believers have some things in common, no matter what. This is a major point John makes in his letter. Every true Christian has had an experience of the saving grace of God and has been born of God.

Having an assurance of your salvation is crucial to your spiritual health and growth. It is possible for a person to be saved and not have assurance of salvation. J. C. Ryle has strikingly said, "Faith is the root, and assurance the flower. Doubtless you can never have the flower without the root; but it is no less certain you may have the root, and not the flower."[3] What are the things John is referring to when he says, "I write these things that you might know . . ." Up to this point three things have continually recurred in the letter to help us know that we are truly believers. Robert Law, in one of the most famous commentaries on the book of 1 John entitled *The Tests of Life*,[4] takes these three themes and uses them to show that John was pointing out that we can test the genuineness of our salvation by means of faith, obedience, and love.

Many times we have heard John talk about the subject of faith in Jesus Christ. That's the initiation of our Christian life. Unless we believe in Jesus we cannot be saved. If we have genuinely believed, we have salvation. Faith is the threshold to the Christian life. Secondly, John says there's another evidence of the true believer, obedience. Jesus said, "If you love me, you will keep my commandments" (John 14:15). If you are a child of God, one of the evidences will be an obedient life. The third test of the Christian life is love. Do you have love for fellow believers? Jesus said, "By this all people will know that you are my disciples, if you have love for one another" (John 13:35). John takes these three things and continually comes back to them throughout the letter to bring us to an assurance of salvation.

Confidence of Answered Prayer (vv. 14, 15)

Assurance of salvation is important because, as John says in verse 14, we cannot have a strong prayer life without it. That's why he states, "And this is the confidence . . ." Verses 13, 14 are tied together. John is trying to point out to us that assurance and confidence in our salvation leads to confidence that God answers prayer. If anyone were to say they had known a person who was trustworthy for thirty years and yet doubted him, it would not be very creditable. When we have known God for a considerable time, does it not reflect on his veracity if we doubt him?[5] When I read about the early Christians in Acts, I am amazed at how they prayed boldly and confidently. The Christians of the early church were men and women who knew how to pray. I fear some of us don't know how to pray with confidence.

Notice that John says in verse 14 that we have confidence "toward him." This confidence is built on our access to God. The Bible says that in prayer we approach God with confidence. It also means we have immediate contact with God. The lines between us and Heaven are never jammed. I remember the old days before cell phones when once on Christmas day I picked up my telephone to call my parents in another state, and a recording came on that said, "I'm sorry but all of our lines are busy at this time." I got that same recording for three hours! That never happens when we pray to God. Wherever we are we can have immediate contact with God by prayer. Though Heaven's lines are never jammed, when we sin and refuse to confess it, we block God's calls and delete his contact number.[6]

There are many things about prayer that we don't know or understand. Some of us are still in the kindergarten or elementary school of prayer. Nobody ever graduates from the University of Prayer. Notice again the word "confidence" in verse 14. We have seen this word before in John's letter. The Greek word literally means "all speech" and hence "boldness." God wants you to have boldness before God. Remember Hebrews 4:16: "Let us then with confidence draw near to the throne of grace, that we may receive mercy and find grace to help in time of need." When it comes to prayer, we should have confidence that if we pray and ask for something in God's will, he hears us. Here are some questions to think about. Did Jesus help hurting people during his earthly ministry? Yes, he did. Did he heal people who were sick? Yes, he did. Did he correct people who were wrong in their thinking? Yes, he did. Do you think that all of that and much more that Jesus did in his earthy life he desires to do today? Do you believe that he desires to help you in your time of need? Does he desire to guide you when you need direction? Does he want to help you when you are hurting? Of course he does. Unlike his earthly ministry, Jesus is not physically with us now, so how does he go about doing these things? He does so through the wonderful blessing of answered prayer. This is God's promise to us. Prayer is the God-ordained way we get what we need. Prayer is not positive thinking, spiritual self-hypnosis, or any such thing. Prayer is a spiritually real and vibrant activity by which we bring real needs to a real God who has real love for us and real answers to give us.

John says in verse 14, "if we ask anything . . ." I suppose if I were to ask you to define prayer, you might say, "Prayer is asking God for something." That would be true. Of course we know that prayer is many things (thanksgiving, praise, petition on behalf of others), but prayer is also asking God for specific things. You're not going to receive if you do not ask. It is here that some of us are confused about prayer. Some view prayer as trying to get God to give us something that we want. Prayer for some is like coercing or wrangling God to get him to do what we want him to do. "Maybe if I can pray with fancy words God will give me what I want." But prayer is not like that at all. Prayer is not trying to get what *you* want, but what *God* wants for us. There is a world of difference between those two. True prayer is when we come to God and ask what he wants for our lives. C. H. Dodd said, "Prayer rightly considered is not a device of imploring the sources of God to fulfill our desires, but a means by which our desires may be redirected according to the mind of God and made into the channels for his will."[7]

Not only do we have confidence in prayer, but John says there is a condition of prayer. Don't miss those four crucial words in verse 14: "according to his will." God is not going to give you a blank check for your prayers any more than you would give your children a blank check for all of the requests they have for you. If you are a parent, would you give your children everything they asked for at Christmastime? There are many things I would like to have. I've always wanted to drive a Ferrari. But God has not seen fit to give me one, and I suspect that if I were to ask for one in prayer, the Lord would probably chuckle at that prayer request. Though I would like to own a Ferrari, I need one about as much as I need a hole in my head. God is not going to answer all our wants and greeds, but he does promise he will answer all of our needs, according to his will. Learning the importance of praying in the will of God may be the single most important principle of prayer. Jesus taught us to pray "Your will be done," not "your will be changed."[8]

Of course, this raises the six million dollar question: how do we know what the will of God is? Before we answer that question, we need to consider an even more fundamental question: do we *desire* his will to be lived out in our lives today? Stop and think about that before you answer. Jesus prayed to the Father, "not my will but yours be done." He taught the disciples in Matthew 6 to pray, "your kingdom come, your will be done." Many people think not "your will be done" but "your will be changed." Jesus prayed, "your will be done." Is that true of our lives today? Are we praying that God's will be done? We can't pray that way until we desire God's will in our lives. We can't desire God's will in our lives until we are willing to do God's will before we know what it is. I have to constantly ask myself, *Lord, is this what you want or what I want?*

To pray in the will of God, we have to *discern* the will of God. It is one thing to be willing to do God's will, but we need to discern God's will in our lives. Many people think discerning the will of God is one of the most difficult things to do. But God gives us two great helps to assist us. First, the place to begin is the Bible, the written Word of God. In the Bible God has given us much of his will for our life. There are things that we can read and know that this is what God wants us to do and not to do. Clear directives, positive and negative, are found in the Bible. We don't have to pray about these or consult anyone. God says "do this" or "don't do that," end of subject. God's will for our lives will never contradict his Word. His will is always in conformity with his Word.

When God gives very clear direction on a host of issues as he does in his Word, that knowledge narrows the scope of our praying. For example, suppose a young Christian lady falls in love with someone who is not a Christian. She wants to get married. But the problem is, Paul says that it is not the will of God for a Christian to be unequally yoked with an unbeliever (2 Corinthians 6:14–18), which in context can legitimately be applied to marriage. Should she pray and ask God if it is his will for her to marry the man? No, because God has already made his will in that situation explicit for every Christian. There are some things you don't need to pray for—God has already made it clear. The first place to go to determine what is and what is not God's will is the Bible. We should immerse ourselves in Scripture, learn what God desires and what he despises, then pray accordingly and confidently, as John says.

Periodically I have had the experience of people coming to my office for counseling. Sometimes within minutes I can tell that they are there not to do God's will but to have my blessings on their actions. They want someone who represents the church to be able to say, "Sure, go right ahead and do that," despite what God's Word says. Sometimes people come for counseling, and their minds are already made up. Rather, we should seek to discern God's will and then be willing to do his will without having our mind made up on what we want.

Second, in addition to having the Bible as a source for knowledge of God's will, we have the Holy Spirit who indwells every believer. Let's face it—God's Word doesn't answer every question we have about what we should do. I don't imagine, when you began praying about marrying your future spouse, that you began looking for a verse in the Bible that said, "You shalt marry so and so." We won't find those kinds of things in the Bible. We can rest assured that God the Holy Spirit will always lead us to pray in God's will. As Paul says in Romans 8, the Holy Spirit guides us in our prayers. Sometimes we don't even know how to pray or for what we should pray. Although I catch myself sometimes thinking I know what God *should* do, the fact of the matter is, we don't know what God's will is in many situations. Romans 8 says when we are in that condition and we can't even formulate the right words, the Holy Spirit intercedes on our behalf. Prayer that gets answered is prayer that originates with God, not with us.

Third, to pray in the will of God we have to be willing to *do* the will of God. We can't just desire it, discern it, but then not do it. We have to put it into practice. If God should reveal his will to us point-blank right this very moment with no question as to what it is and no question that it is from God, would we do it? They key to doing the will of God is being willing to do it before we know what it is.

Not only do we have confidence in prayer if we meet the condition of prayer, but John says something about the *certainty* of this kind of praying. In verse 15 we not only have confidence but a conscious certainty of answered prayer before it comes. Notice the word "have." It is in the perfect tense in Greek. The picture in the verse is this: I have some requests, and I have taken these to the Lord in prayer and put them before him, and God does not ignore them or forget them. Has someone ever asked you something and you had every good intention of responding, but then two months later you realized that you had forgotten to get back to the person and answer the request? Do you think God gets so many prayer requests that they get lost at his feet? Do you think he forgets? John says that is not how it works at all. We know God hears us because "we *have* the requests that we *have* asked of him." When we have prayed in faith in the will of God, John is saying, the check is in the mail. God's answer is coming. Look at the first use of "have" in verse 15. It is in the present tense in Greek. You may not have the answer immediately, but God has already answered, and in his timing he will send it to you. That is confidence! But most of us don't pray that way. Most of us are too timid and afraid. Have you ever thanked God for an answer to prayer before you got it? Thank God in advance for his answer before you see it physically manifested or spiritually accomplished. That is what John is telling us here. If we know he hears us, then we also know that we have already received the requests we have asked and have confidence even though we have not received it from him yet.

Twice in verse 15 John uses the word "know." John said, "if we know that he hears us . . . we know we have the requests that we have asked of him." The word "if" here actually conveys the notion of "since." John is not questioning whether or not God hears us. God does. A twofold assurance is given in this verse. First, there is an assurance that God hears our prayers. Second, there is the assurance that God answers our prayers. How does God answer prayer?

In one of four ways. Either he will answer with a direct yes or a direct no, or he may delay the answer, or he may answer your prayer differently than you asked. The early church in Acts prayed for Peter's release from prison, and God answered with a miraculous deliverance. Paul prayed to enter Asia on his missionary journeys, but God said no and redirected him. Mary and Martha prayed for Jesus to come and heal their brother Lazarus, and the Lord delayed his coming for two days. Lazarus died, and Mary and Martha did not understand why the Lord tarried. Jesus answered their prayer by raising Lazarus from the dead, but it was after a delay. Paul prayed that his thorn in the flesh be removed, but God did not answer his prayer for removal. Instead he answered Paul's prayer by adding something to the thorn: his sufficient grace. God declined to answer Paul's prayer with what Paul asked in order to give him what he really needed.

Martin Luther had a good friend named Frederick Myconius who was a great helper to him during the days of the Reformation. In 1540 Myconius became so ill that he was on his deathbed, and the doctors said he was going to die. Lying there he wrote a last letter with trembling hand to Luther telling him how much he appreciated him and that he was about to die. Immediately Luther dispatched a reply to his friend. "I command you in the name of God to live because I still have need of you in the work of reforming the Church. . . . The Lord will never let me hear while I live that you are dead, but will permit you to survive me. For this I am praying, this is my will, and may my will be done, because I seek only to glorify the name of God." Those words are shocking to many of us today. When Myconius received Luther's reply, he was so far gone that he had lost his ability to speak, but remarkably in a few days he completely recovered. He lived six more years to assist in the Reformation and outlived Luther by two months.[9] God answered the believing prayer of Martin Luther for his friend Myconius. Though I would not recommend using such language with God in our prayers, Luther was clearly willing to state in his letter to his friend, "this is my will, and may my will be done." Of course, Luther believed he was praying in the will of God, as his last statement indicates. As Christians we need to know that God answers prayers! Sometimes we pray with tentativeness when we should have confidence in the will of God.

The Sin That Leads to Death (vv. 16, 17)

In verses 16, 17 John issues a call to intercessory prayer. There are many kinds of prayer. Prayer sometimes is focused on praising God. Sometimes prayer is thanksgiving. Sometimes prayer is petition. This is what we normally think of when we pray. Prayer is asking God for something. But there is another type of prayer that the Bible often talks about called intercession. This is prayer for other people. If we are not careful, we can get caught up in self-centered praying in which we constantly ask for our own needs but never come to God on behalf of others. There is certainly a time to pray for our needs, but the Bible has much to say about prayer as intercession for others. John singles out a specific example of how we can pray for others: we should pray for Christians who get involved in sin. John has already affirmed in his letter that Christians can and do sin. He has already addressed the issue for the sinning believer in 1 John 1:8–10. Now he is addressing the issue of our praying for fellow Christians who have sinned.

First John 5:16, 17 has engendered much discussion about what John means by "sin that leads to death." This is one of those passages for which we have lost the key. When you lose a key to your car or your house, you can't get in. Apparently John's readers knew what he was talking about, but we are left somewhat in the dark about it. John does not explain what he means by the phrase "sin that leads to death." It is therefore best to consider all the various possible interpretations.[10] There are four major views as to what John means. The first view is that this is some heinous sin such as murder. Yet there are many murderers whom God has forgiven. Paul comes immediately to mind. This interpretation is unlikely. The second view is that this means apostasy. Here is a person who was truly saved and then rejected Jesus, thus committing apostasy. The problem with this view is that genuine believers do not apostatize. This interpretation is held by many but is only possible if John is referring to someone in the church who is not a genuine believer. The third view is that John is talking about blasphemy against the Holy Spirit, otherwise known as the unpardonable sin. When I was a pastor, people periodically came into my office worried sick whether they had committed the unpardonable sin. The only people who can commit the unpardonable sin are unsaved people. If you are worried you may have committed the unpardonable sin, you haven't committed it. The unpardonable sin is ultimate rejection of Jesus Christ. That's the only sin you can commit in this life that God cannot and will not forgive. I think it is unlikely John is here talking about the unpardonable sin.[11]

The fourth view understands "sin that leads to death" to be a reference to some sin committed by a Christian that leads to physical death as a result of God's discipline. In the Bible death can be either physical or eternal. John calls the one who commits "sin leading to death" a "brother." In almost every usage of the word "brother" in 1 John, John refers to believers. Apparently John is talking about the possibility that a Christian can sin in such a way that

God may choose to take that Christian out of this world prematurely by physical death. Are there any examples of this in the New Testament? Yes, in Acts 5, we read the account of Ananias and Sapphira, who sold a piece of property and pretended to give all of the proceeds to the church when in reality they kept back part of the money for themselves. They pretended what they gave to the church was all. They lied to God and to the church, and God struck each of them dead on the spot. The early church was so pure that a lie could not live in its midst. Though some interpreters suggest Ananias and Sapphira were not genuine believers, there is no evidence in the text of Acts that such was the case. Another example is found in 1 Corinthians 11:28–30. Some of the Corinthian believers were partaking of the Lord's Table in an unworthy manner. As a result, some of them were "weak and ill," and some had died prematurely as a result of God's discipline. You might say that John's "sin that leads to death" in the life of a believer is something like a dishonorable discharge. It has nothing to do with eternal salvation. But John does not tell us what the "sin that leads to death" is.

John says that God will give "life" to those who have not sinned a "sin that leads to death." There are two possible ways to interpret "life" here. It could be a reference to eternal life. It could also be a reference to physical life. Since the sin is one that leads to "death," it is likely that the word "life" means the opposite of "death." If the death referred to is spiritual, then so is the life. If the death referred to is physical, then so is the life.

Most likely John is not talking about a specific sin but has to do with ongoing, willful sin that remains unconfessed to the point that God takes drastic action. John's desire is that we not focus on the specifics of the "sin that leads to death," but rather focus on the notion of "sin not leading to death." That is what we are to pray about. God desires to forgive sins, and he desires intercessors to pray for Christians when they sin. Remember what Samuel said to the people of Israel: "Far be it from me that I should sin against the Lᴿᴳ by ceasing to pray for you" (1 Samuel 12:23). In the church we need to be praying for one another. Peter, in Luke 22:33, in essence told Jesus at the Last Supper, "All these other disciples will forsake you, but I never will. I will stand with you even if I have to die for you, Jesus." Jesus said to him, "The rooster will not crow this day, until you deny me three times that you know me." When Jesus was arrested, Peter was lurking around the place where Jesus was being tried, and what did Peter do? Not once but three times he denied with cursing that he ever knew Jesus. Then the rooster crowed. Do you remember what else Jesus told Peter? In essence he said, "Satan has desired to have you, that he may sift you like wheat. But, Peter, I have prayed for you.

So when you repent of your sin of denying me, and I know you will because I have prayed for you, then you will help other people through their failures too." Peter did repent, and Jesus restored him. He went out and lived a life of spiritual victory, preaching the gospel, writing two books of the Bible, and dying as a martyr—all because Jesus prayed for him.

When we sin, we need some intercessors who will pray for us. Christians need people in the church who will love them enough to pray them through their spiritual downtimes. Christians in such a condition need to be prayed back to the point of spiritual health and vitality. So don't just stand around, pray for somebody!

John is not saying that some sin is worse than others. All sin is sin. That's why he says in verse 17, "All wrongdoing is sin." Notice also that John says, "if anyone *sees* his brother," not if anyone *hears*. Rumors don't count. The sin must be evident and confirmed. There are three things you can do every time you become aware of sin in a fellow believer's life. First, make sure you are confessing sin in your own life. The moment you become aware of sin in your life, you should confess it and forsake it, no matter how small it may appear to be. Second, determine before God that you are going to pray for other Christians when you see sin in their lives. Don't criticize or condemn, but rather pray. Some Christians have a tendency to be critical of sin in other peoples' lives but to ignore the sin in their own life. They develop an attitude of condemnation. Third, ask God to use you to help them overcome the sin in their lives and to be involved in the ministry of restoration. The forgotten ministry of the church is restoring one another when we've sinned. We need to be reminded of what Paul says in Galatians 6:1 concerning a brother who sins: "Brothers, if anyone is caught in any transgression, you who are spiritual should restore him in a spirit of gentleness. Keep watch on yourself, lest you too be tempted."

Our Threefold Knowledge (vv. 18–20)

In 5:18–21 John reverts to a familiar theme of certainty and assurance. With the exception of verse 21, these closing verses all begin with the little phrase, "we know." We know the certainty of God's power to overcome sin in our daily life (v. 18). As John stated previously in the letter, he again reemphasizes the fact that a truly born-again believer does not practice sin. ". . . he who was born of God protects him." Here it is vital to understand the antecedents of "he" and "him." Who is the one who has been born of God? At first it may appear John is speaking of a believer. After all, he has already made the point that Christians have been born of God. But it seems better to understand

John's reference to the one born of God as Jesus. John speaks of Jesus else-where as "the only Son." It is a term used to describe the deity of our Lord. So it is probable that John is here not talking about our guarding ourselves, although that is something we should do in our Christian life, but rather that Jesus himself guards us.[12] The referent of "him" is a believer. It is Jesus him-self who makes available to us the power to gain victory over sin. Notice that last statement in verse 18: "the evil one does not touch him." The word for "touch" in Greek indicates something more than a superficial touch; it rather means "to lay hold of." It was used in papyri for setting fire to something. Satan cannot "set you on fire"; that is, he cannot harm you eternally or other-wise, because Jesus has made sure your wood is wet! Satan cannot undo your salvation. You are eternally secure in Christ. If Satan cannot drag you to Hell, the next thing he wants to do to you is to mar your Christian testimony. I like what Paul says in Romans 16:20: "The God of peace will soon crush Satan under your feet." Notice that it is God who defeats Satan. John is talking about a certainty of Christian power, the ability to live a successful Christian life and overcome the sin problem day by day as you walk with Jesus and serve him.

Not only is there a certainty of God's power, but there is a certainty of our position (v. 19). Again this is nothing new. John is revisiting what he has already written. He has already told us in 1 John 3:10 that everyone lives in one of two spiritual families: Christ or Satan. Take marriage as an example. You are either married or you are not. You are not married until you both say "I do" and the preacher says "You did!" Until that takes place, you're not married. In the same way you are either in the family of God or you are not. Notice the contrast in verse 19 between "we" and "the whole world." We have our spiritual origin in God. The rest of the world lies in the power of Satan. The language John uses here is interesting. The implication is that those who live under the power of Satan are lulled to sleep in that condition. They are spiritually apathetic, asleep, blind, and dead.

It is important to notice how John makes use of the word "world" in verse 19. Here John contrasts believers ("we") with all living unbelievers ("the whole world.") John indicates that his readers who were once unbeliev-ers were a part of "the world," but no longer is that the case. First John 5:19 makes the point that "the whole world," all living unbelievers, is under the sway of the devil.

The third certainty concerns our perception (v. 20). Saved people have a spiritual understanding and discernment that unsaved people do not have. That's why Paul said the unsaved man cannot understand the things of God because there are things that can only be spiritually known and discerned

(1 Corinthians 2:14). Our understanding is twofold. First, "we . . . know him that is true," that is, Jesus. Here is sure footing. We don't have to say "we think" or "we believe," but "we know." This is a tone of certainty, quite different from what many who, "influenced by currents of present opinions, feel as if what was rock to our fathers had become quagmire to us!"[13]

Second, "we are in him who is true." The one "who is true" is God's Son, Jesus Christ. In the fourth century of Christian history, a huge doctrinal controversy arose in the church. The key question was the nature of Jesus. Was he fully God or was he merely "like God"? Those who took the latter position were followers of Arius. The Arians conceded that Christ is God but not the true God. Although they sometimes called Christ "true," their denial that he is consubstantial with the Father made it clear they acknowledged neither the Father nor the Son.[14]

Just as there is a certainty of Christian perception, there is also a certainty of spiritual illusion. Some time ago I was fascinated to visit a holography shop. Three-dimensional holography is amazing to observe. Light and mirrors create 3D images in amazing detail. But it is all unreal, an illusion. Some of the slickest, most creative commercials on television are beer commercials. I have noticed several things about them. First, no one over thirty drinks beer! Rarely do you see someone who is over thirty in a beer commercial. The advertiser is appealing to the younger generation. Second, if there is a car in a beer commercial, it is always brand spanking new. Third, you will never see a Volkswagen, Kia, Hundai, or your ordinary Ford or Chevy. They always use something like a Corvette or a Porsche. Fourth, did you ever notice the women in beer commercials? All of them look like they just walked out of a fashion catalog. They are all tall, thin, gorgeous. Most of the men are tall, thin, and handsome. You never see a guy with a beer belly. They all look like Ben Affleck or Tom Cruise. Fourth, there is usually a party setting with hip music. Everyone is having a great time, projecting the image that you too can have a great time if you will drink this brand of beer. But it is all an illusion. I have always thought that alcohol advertisements should be required to show the flip side of the coin: the seventeen and a half million alcoholics, the eighty thousand alcohol-related deaths annually, the hundreds of thousands injured or impaired because of alcohol-related accidents, or the six thousand teens who die every year because of alcohol.[15] Our spiritual perception is based on the understanding that Christ himself has given us. We discern truth because "we . . . know him who is true."

In verse 20 John uses a word three times that speaks of reality. It is the word "true." In this context the word's primary meaning is that which is real, not illusory. It has substance, permanence, and reality. In a world full of people longing for the real thing but grasping at illusions, John offers the truth: Jesus Christ and his gospel. It is as if John is saying, "This God of whom I have been affirming that Jesus Christ is his sole Revealer, and of whom I have been declaring that through him we may know God and dwell abidingly in him, this—and no one else—is the true God."[16] "We . . . know him who is true [real]." "We are in him who is true." This is eternal life. John began this letter in 1:2, 3 talking about eternal life, and now he concludes where he began. What is eternal life? It is knowing him who is true and being in him who is true. That is eternal life: knowing God and being in Christ. And John says we better know that we know! "I have no confidence in my confidence. I place no reliance upon my own assurance. My assurance lies in the fact that 'Christ Jesus came into the world to save sinners,' and that 'Whosoever believeth in Him hath everlasting life.' I do believe in Him, and therefore I know I have eternal life."[17]

In 1994 Northwest Airlines offered some unusual round-trip tickets. Fifty-nine dollars bought a Mystery Fare ticket that provided a one-day trip to an undisclosed American city. Buyers didn't find out where they were heading until they arrived at the airport the day of the flight. Still, the airline had plenty of takers. In Indianapolis fifteen hundred people crowded the airline counter to buy the Mystery Fare tickets that were sold on a first-come, first-serve basis.

Not surprisingly, when buyers learned their destination, not all were thrilled. One buyer who was hoping for New Orleans but found he had a ticket for Minneapolis walked through the airport terminal yelling, "I have one ticket to the Mall of America. I'll trade it for anything!" Mystery Fare tickets may be a fun surprise for a weekend vacation, but normally the last thing you want is a ticket to a mystery destination. And one time you never want a mystery ticket is on the day of your death. You don't want to face eternity uncertain about whether you will go to Heaven or Hell.[18] Be sure you are really sure.[19]

Little children, keep yourselves from idols.

1 JOHN 5:21

20

Accept No Substitutes!

THE TELEVISION COMMERCIAL interrupts your favorite show. The announcer has a deal for you that you can't refuse! His product can slice, dice, and chop better than anything out else on the market. And not only that, "if you will act now, you will receive a second product absolutely free! This brand item is not sold in stores, so act now, while supplies last! Do not be fooled by imitations that are inferior. Accept no substitutes!" he warns us with a raised voice. Though I have never purchased any item so advertised, I can attest to what happens when, as a husband, I am sent to the store to buy a can of this or a carton of that and I return home with an off-brand, just to save a little money. After enduring my wife's lecture for my stupidity, I discover that, sure enough, an off- brand of cream of mushroom soup is just not as good as the name brand. I should have accepted no substitutes.

It may seem a bit strange to our twenty-first-century ears that John would end his letter with this short, terse, puzzling command: "keep yourselves from idols." Surely no one in any civilized country would worship an idol! After all, an idol is made of stone or wood or metal. Surely only a primitive group of people somewhere in the backwoods of the world would need such a warning. We don't have any idols in American culture, do we? Our idols may not look exactly like a wood or stone carving worshipped by some people group two thousand years ago, but we certainly do have our idols. Back in 2002 America was swept by a hot new television show, *American Idol*. The first-season winner, Kelly Clarkson, was catapulted into immediate stardom. Her debut single, "A Moment Like This," became the fastest music chart-climber in history, reaching number one in less than a week. Second season winner Clay Aiken's debut single, "This Is the Night," reached number one on the Billboard Hot 100 Chart in its first week (only the twelfth song in history to do so!).[1] Of course, not all who are fans of these pop stars are idol worshippers. But some of them are.

Sometimes our idols can be a conglomeration of metal and plastic, circuits and rubber, upholstery and glass, otherwise known as a car. Sometimes our idols can be flesh and blood, as in a spouse, child, grandchild, or parent. Sometimes our idols are less tangible things such as fame, position, or popularity. Ezekiel got it right when he said concerning some of the leaders of his day, "These men have taken their idols into their hearts" (Ezekiel 14:3). All these things and many more can be anyone's idol. Maybe the existentialist philosopher Nietzsche was right when he said, "There are more idols in the world than there are realities."[2] When you think about it, John's warning is actually not that far off the mark, is it? The fact of the matter is, every culture throughout history has always had its own idols. The human heart is an "idol factory."[3] We are prone to make idols of almost anything. We have little difficulty identifying idolatry in other cultures but are often blind to the idolatry rampant in our own backyard.

Idolatry in Ephesus

There was plenty of idolatry in John's backyard. John lived in Ephesus, one of the centers of idolatry in the Roman world. The great goddess Diana was thought to reside in the famous Temple of Diana in Ephesus. The temple took two hundred years to complete and was 420 feet long and 220 feet wide and was one of the Seven Wonders of the Ancient World. Majestic Ionic pillars soared sixty feet into the air. In the center of the temple stood the goddess Diana, robed in a veil of Persian silk. Small replicas of the temple and images of the goddess were for sale. Worship of Diana was at a fever pitch in Ephesus. In Acts 19 Paul tangled with the silversmiths who made little icons of the Temple of Diana and of the goddess Diana.

It might help us to remember just what John has been saying to us in this letter. At the top of the list is the priority and preeminence of Jesus as the Son of God and the necessity to be rightly related to him for the forgiveness of our sins. This is foundational for everything else in this life and the next. For John, Jesus is the real thing, and anything and everything else, if substituted for Jesus, is an idol. The Biblical concept of idolatry consists in that which is not only cultural but intellectual, social, and spiritual. People in Scripture are said to do three things with their idols: they love them, trust them, and obey them.[4] God has three words for idols: tear them down.

Idolatry in the Old Testament

The people of Israel in the Old Testament constantly had problems with idolatry. From the very beginning, over and over again, they fell into idolatry. In Exodus, while Moses is on the mountain receiving God's Ten Commandments, the people grow tired of waiting for Moses to return and coerce Aaron into making an idol—a golden calf. Nothing could be more ironic and tragic! The first two of those Ten Commandments speak about idolatry:

> You shall have no other gods before me. You shall not make for yourself a carved image, or any likeness of anything that is in heaven above, or that is in the earth beneath, or that is in the water under the earth. You shall not bow down to them or serve them, for I the LORD your God am a jealous God, visiting the iniquity of the fathers on the children to the third and the fourth generation of those who hate me, but showing steadfast love to thousands of those who love me and keep my commandments. (Exodus 20:3–6)

When Israel finally entered the promised land, they failed to rid the land of all the pagans who were there. Consequently, over time the people of Israel compromised with pagan cultures and intermarried with pagans. When they did, they often adopted the cultural idols to worship, despite God's prohibition in the First Commandment that they should never have or worship any gods except Yahweh himself. Read the book of Judges and see the chaos that idol worship brought to Israel in the land. Ultimately Canaanite idolatry brought the Northern Kingdom of Israel to destruction by God himself through the hands of the Assyrians. Failing to learn from their northern brother, the Southern Kingdom, Judah, continued to tolerate and practice idolatry. The prophets Isaiah, Jeremiah, Ezekiel, and many others warned the people against idolatry, but to no avail. Psalm 115:4–8 reminds us that we always conform to what we worship. Speaking of idols, verse 8 says "Those who make them become like them." Idolaters resemble the idols they worship. God made us in his image to reflect him. If we do not commit ourselves to him, we will reflect something other than God in his creation. Isaiah 57:3–13 has some potent words about idols. Idolatry destroys morality. Idolatry mocks God. Idolatry disobeys God's word. Idolatry prostitutes God's worship. Listen to the indictment God brings against his people Judah through Jeremiah: "As a thief is shamed when caught, so the house of Israel shall be shamed: they, their kings, their officials, their priests, and their prophets, who say to a tree, 'You are my father,' and to a stone, 'You gave me birth.' For they have turned their back to me, and not their face" (Jeremiah 2:26, 27). Finally God scattered them in his judgment when they were carried away into captivity by the Babylonian Empire. It was only after this debacle some seventy years later when the people returned to the land of Israel that they were cured of their idolatry.

There are some interesting Hebrew words for idolatry in the Old Testament. One word in its noun form can mean "pellets of dung" or "shapeless, loggy things." There is probably some double entendre going on here. An idol is a detestable thing.⁵ Another word used for idols is *hebel* meaning "emptiness, vanity." Still another word for idol in Hebrew is *mipleṣet* meaning "a thing of horror or shuddering."

Idolatry in the New Testament

We often associate idolatry with the Old Testament, since there are so many references to it there. However, you might be surprised that such warnings occur in the New Testament as well. For example, in Acts 7:40 Stephen spoke about the continuation of idolatry begun in Egypt with the golden calf incident. According to Acts 15, the Jerusalem Council addressed the issue of idols (v. 20). Paul says in 1 Corinthians 8:4, "We know that an idol has no real existence." Paul devotes a significant amount of discussion to idols in 1 Corinthians. Ephesians 5:5 says, "For you may be sure of this, that everyone who is sexually immoral or impure, or who is covetous (that is, an idolater), has no inheritance in the kingdom of Christ and God." Colossians 3:5 instructs us to put aside "evil desire, and covetousness, which is idolatry." Here it is obvious that an idol can be something nonmaterial.

John chooses to close this letter with that final statement in verse 21: "Little children, keep yourselves from idols." The word "idol" comes from a Greek word meaning "that which is seen." Ironically, though an idol is "seen," it is unreal and is actually an illusion. An idol is something that has no substance. This statement in verse 21 is in direct contrast to the reality of Jesus that John emphasized in verse 20. John is saying Jesus is the real thing. It's a relationship with Christ that brings about reality and substance. Jesus is the true and real God as opposed to the false gods and idols that are out there. The worship of idols leads to eternal death. The worship of Jesus leads to eternal life. There were probably many in John's audience who were former idol worshippers.

John's warning in verse 21 may be related to Zechariah 13:2: "'On that day, declares the L R D of hosts, I will cut off the names of the idols from the land, so that they shall be remembered no more. And also I will remove from the land the prophets and the spirit of uncleanness.'"⁶

Modern-Day Idols

What is an idol? Whatever you cling to for ultimate reality and security is your idol. Whatever you give your heart to other than God is an idol. John Wesley pictured God as forever saying to us, "My son, give me thy heart! And to give our heart to any other is plain idolatry. Accordingly, whatever takes our heart from him, or shares it with him, is an idol."[7] In the Bible, an idol refers first to a tangible object of worship made of wood, stone, or metal, usually representing the deities of pagan society. But this Biblical definition and usage is expanded to intangibles as well. An idol is anything in your life that you worship or put in place of or above God. Anything that fits that definition is an idol in your life. At the 2007 Emmy Awards, comedian Kathy Griffin won an Emmy for the show she produced and starred in called *My Life on the D-List*. Griffin walked to the stage, accepted the award, blasphemed the name of Jesus, and then concluded her little speech by holding up her Emmy statuette and saying, "This award is my god now."

There are many idols that people can worship today. Money can quickly become an idol. A job can become an idol in your life. Your clothes, car, home, family can all become idols. There are also intangible idols: your talents, gifts, and abilities can become idols. We live in a world that is enamored by beauty. The desire to be beautiful can become an idol. The desire to be young can become an idol. If ever we live in a country that seems obsessed with looking young, it is America. Everything from the fashion industry, the cosmetic industry, the advertisement industry, television entertainment, and a host of other venues makes it clear we are all about looking young and being young. Today in many cases and places youth is revered and age is disdained.

Preachers and Their Idols

Some preachers today are in captivity to the idolatry of self with their self-help, psychologizing preaching. Other preachers, enamored with the constant use of visual imagery in preaching, are in danger of devaluing the text of Scripture and allowing it to be supplanted by image. The false prophets in Jeremiah's day offered people visual imagery over the word of the Lord. An idol is visible, but it is not real. If you watch sports on television, you may have noticed all of the billboard advertisements on the field. What you probably did not notice is that these advertisement logos on the field that you see are sometimes digitally superimposed to cover up what is actually on those billboards. The networks sell advertising and then superimpose the company name of the advertiser over the *real* advertisement on the field. The networks restructure your reality for their own profit. Some of today's preaching offers people virtual reality but not reality. Such preaching is an attempt to restructure spiritual reality for the preacher's own profit. We superimpose our images over that of the Word of God.

This is exactly what happened in Jeremiah's day! Good King Josiah came to the throne after fifty-seven years of his father's and grandfather's evil reigns. They had led the nation into idolatry. Idolatry is the quintessence of virtual reality, image-based worship. The first case of idolatry in Israel occurred when Moses returned with the Ten Commandments and found the people worshipping the golden calf. Think of the difference: a golden calf (image), the Ten Commandments, (God's Word). The second of those commandments prohibits the making of any "image."

Josiah started a spiritual reformation that was a return to the Word of God. He began to tear down the idols. The revival that occurred in Josiah's day was Word-based! It was a rediscovery of God's Word that brought revival and the destruction of idols. He destroyed the virtual reality, the idols, in order to give people back the true reality, God and his Word! Every preacher should read and heed Arthur Hunt's warning that the current devaluation of "text" and its "hostile supplanting by the image" is nothing less than "a direct assault upon 'the religion of the Book.'"[8] Hunt cogently reminds us that the Renaissance was image-based, attempting a revival of pagan Rome; while the Reformation was Word-based. The Renaissance was a return to pagan Rome with its images. The Reformation was a return to first-century Christianity with the preaching of the Word. The money quote in the entire book is: "Pagan idolatry is biblicism's chief competitor because one thrives in the absence of the written word and the other cannot exist without it."[9] Today's culture is primarily image-based. A culture enamored with image is an idolatrous culture. The idea of a man standing to preach the Word to listening people is considered by some to be outdated. Drama, props, video clips, and clever gimmicks replace the simple exposition of the Word. When preaching crowds out the verbal Word of the living God for image, it becomes idolatrous preaching!

Some churches today are in captivity to the idolatry of self. "We are trying to hold at bay the gnats of small sins while swallowing the camel of self."[10] The modern-day cult of the self is alive and well with such phrases as self-help, self-image, and self-esteem. While a good self-image is important, it must be defined Biblically or we will soon degenerate into burning incense to ourselves. The balloon of ego can only hold so much air before it bursts. Some may remember how several years ago movie star Shirley MacLaine championed the cult of the self by saying, "Each soul is its own god. You must never worship anyone or anything other than self. For *you* are God. To love self is to love God."[11]

Guard Your Heart

The list of possible idols seems endless. John says, "Keep yourselves from idols." I don't think John was worried about their bowing down in front of a graven image. He knew there were things besides false religions that they could worship; there was the possibility of worshipping tangible and intangible things that could usurp God in their lives. The word "keep" means "to guard against." Idolatry is something we must guard against in our lives on a daily basis. The world, the flesh, and the devil, our three great enemies, constantly play their siren music in an effort to cause Christians to bow down to whatever is idolatrous in their lives. To fulfill this command, "keep yourselves from idols," will take constant daily vigilance in our thought life. We will have to guard how and where we spend our time, to what we give our money and other resources, and how we think about the world system. To keep ourselves from idols means self-accountability.

When you think about it, John's puzzling final imperative actually is a fitting conclusion to the entire letter. From start to finish John has been at pains to say that the ultimate reality is God through Jesus Christ. Only Jesus is "the true God and eternal life" (5:20). Failure to put him first is to fall prey to idolatry. Luther was right when he said that the first of the Ten Commandments begins with idolatry because the fundamental motivation behind breaking God's laws is idolatry.[12]

The Docetic Gnostics whom John opposed were actually promoting idolatry in their false teaching. To claim that Jesus is not fully human or is not truly God is idolatry. The secessionists who left the orthodox doctrine of Christ and thus left the church (1 John 2:19) were committing idolatry. The false prophets whose teaching originated with the spirit of antichrist were engaged in idolatry. The failure to love others indicates we are making self an idol. The failure to live righteous lives is motivated by many things, but the heart of it all is idolatry. Everything John addresses in this letter is in one way or another related to idolatry.

The early Italian Reformer Savonarola is well known for his desire to cleanse Florence of materialism and immorality by having people cast away their material possessions that tempted them to have an immoral lifestyle in the "bonfire of vanity." Savonarola once saw an elderly woman worshipping at a statue of the Virgin Mary. He observed her daily trek to pay homage to the statue and was impressed with her devotion and virtue. A fellow priest, however, warned Savonarola that things are not always as they appear. Savonarola learned that this woman in her youth had been the model for the artist's sculpture of Mary. She had worshiped at the statue ever since. In the Christian church today we need a "bonfire of vanities" in our heart. All idolatry begins in the heart and must be exterminated there first.[13]

Last words stick. "Keep yourselves from idols." This practical injunction will save us from many a heartache. In our weakness we can never afford to neglect to keep ourselves from all false worship. These golden words in their simplicity, in their depth, in their certainty, in their comprehensiveness are worthy to be the last words of John's letter. They stand through the ages as the solid foundation and the shining apex of Christianity.[14] To the twenty-first century believer, John warns, "Keep yourselves from idols." Another famous John, with the last name of Wesley, also spoke about idols in a one-sentence prayer we all should pray: "And as the shadows flee before the sun, so let all my idols vanish at thy presence!"[15] Don't get high on anything but God.[16] Accept no substitutes!

2 JOHN

The elder to the elect lady and her children, whom I love in truth, and not only I, but also all who know the truth, because of the truth that abides in us and will be with us forever: Grace, mercy, and peace will be with us, from God the Father and from Jesus Christ the Father's Son, in truth and love. I rejoiced greatly to find some of your children walking in the truth, just as we were commanded by the Father. And now I ask you, dear lady— not as though I were writing you a new commandment, but the one we have had from the beginning—that we love one another. And this is love, that we walk according to his commandments; this is the commandment, just as you have heard from the beginning, so that you should walk in it. For many deceivers have gone out into the world, those who do not confess the coming of Jesus Christ in the flesh. Such a one is the deceiver and the antichrist. Watch yourselves, so that you may not lose what we have worked for, but may win a full reward. Everyone who goes on ahead and does not abide in the teaching of Christ, does not have God. Whoever abides in the teaching has both the Father and the Son. If anyone comes to you and does not bring this teaching, do not receive him into your house or give him any greeting, for whoever greets him takes part in his wicked works. Though I have much to write to you, I would rather not use paper and ink. Instead I hope to come to you and talk face to face, so that our joy may be complete. The children of your elect sister greet you.

2 JOHN

21

Deniers and Deceivers

THE OBTRUSIVE KNOCK on my front door came on a Saturday mid-morning. I was lazily enjoying my day and half-resented the interruption. When I opened the door, there stood two young men in white dress shirts—clean-cut, all-American guys with smiles on their faces and bicycles parked on the sidewalk in front of my house. "Good morning! We are out visiting for the Church of Jesus Christ of Latter-day Saints. May we talk to you?" Kindly but firmly I responded in the negative. I further told them that Mormonism was a cult and that they were teaching false doctrine concerning the person and work of Jesus Christ. I urged them to repent of their false doctrine and turn to Jesus Christ, the Son of God, who alone paid the price for their sins on the cross and who alone was the way, the truth, and the life. It became immediately apparent they weren't accustomed to this kind of rejoinder. They made one final attempt to weaken my resolve, but to no avail. They returned to their bicycles and pedaled down the street, probably shaking their heads at the poor deluded soul they had just encountered. Some people might consider my response to these two Mormon missionaries as less than hospitable. They would be correct! In fact, I was merely practicing what John teaches all Christians to do in this letter of 2 John. False doctrine is serious business because eternal souls are at stake. In John's day false teachers sought to infiltrate the church and peddle their false doctrine. John resisted them sternly and teaches us today to do the same.

Greeting (vv. 1–3)

John began his first letter in a rather unusual way and without a formal salutation as was customary at the time. He begins this second letter with something of a more formal opening (vv. 1–3), but still in a very unusual way. John calls himself "the elder,"[1] and the church to whom he writes he calls "the elect lady and her children." So strange is this opening that some have suggested John was actually writing to a woman, a matron, and her children. But it is better to interpret "elect lady" as a reference to a particular local church, probably somewhere in Asia Minor. In his first letter John often spoke of his readers as "children." Such symbolic usage is probably his strategy here. If the word translated "lady" refers to an individual, then it would be stretching credibility to suppose that she had a sister by the same name who is mentioned in verse 13 as well: "The children of your elect sister greet you." It is highly unlikely that this is a reference to literal children of a literal sister. Personification is John's way of writing about the church and her members.

John speaks of his love for the Christians to whom he writes. He loves them intently as evidenced by his choice to use the emphatic first-person pronoun in Greek. His use of the phrase "in truth" (v. 1) can be taken in two ways. He may mean something like "whom I love genuinely or truly."[2] Or he could be speaking of the truth of the gospel. He includes all believers with him when he says, "and not only I, but also all who know the truth." When John uses the word "know," he intends to convey an experiential aspect to it as well. They not only "know" the truth, but they have believed the truth as well. His readers had come to the point where they had committed themselves to the validity of the gospel as "truth." The truth here is ultimately the truth of the gospel, which means the truth about Jesus and all it entails. The essential content of Christianity is conveyed in this notion of "truth." John says the truth "abides" in us and "will be with us forever." Here John is personifying the truth to refer to Jesus or perhaps the Holy Spirit who indwells every Christian and who will be with us eternally. Christians who truly possess the truth, which is eternal life through Christ who is the truth, are eternally secure based on Christ's abiding presence in his children forever. Furthermore, Christians who possess God's truth are equipped to fend off all false doctrines, as John will make clear in this letter.[3]

John continues his introduction in verse 3 by invoking that great Christian triumvirate of "grace, mercy, and peace." "Grace" describes all that God has done for us in Christ that we did not deserve. "Mercy" is God not giving us all we do deserve! "Peace" is the resulting state we have with God and with others that results from the application of God's grace and mercy to our lives. These three Christian graces from God "will be with us." John associates himself with the group he is addressing. The source of these wonderful gifts is God himself, who is the Father, and his Son, Jesus Christ. Here John firmly identifies and locates Jesus in the Godhead as "Son" to God the Father. Notice the human name "Jesus" and the divine title "Christ," meaning "Messiah."

These Christian blessings have come to us "in truth and love."[4] "Truth" is an attribute of God's character expressed in his Word and his gospel, and "love" is the divine motivation for all God does for those who are his children. John is referring to true belief in Jesus, the incarnate Son of God, and the spirit of genuine love that belief generates.[5]

Love One Another (vv. 4–6)

After his introduction (vv. 1–3), John's letter is composed of three paragraphs (4–6, 7–11, 12–13). Basically what John is saying to us in this letter is: know the truth, walk in the truth, and abide in the truth. In verse 4 John expresses his joy over the fact that "some" of the believers ("your children") are faithfully living out the Christian life, which is what "walking in the truth" means. Apparently, prior to writing, John had encountered some of the members of this congregation, perhaps in their travels. When John says "some," we might infer that some of the members of this congregation were not remaining faithful. But more than likely John means to refer to "some" of the congregation whom he had encountered. Actually it is John's next statement that lets us in on why John is so happy about things. These believers were behaving Christianly: "just as we were commanded by the Father." For John, nothing can take the place of obedience ("walking in the truth") in the Christian life.

Love and obedience always go together in the Christian life. Hence John asks his readers to "love one another" (v. 5). He reminds them that this is "not . . . a new commandment" but one that has been around "from the beginning" of the gospel. John's definition of love is certainly different from most of our modern definitions, which celebrate feelings and sentimentality. Love is more than mere feelings; it is an act of the will. That is why John teaches us to live our lives according to God's commands as revealed in his Word. The word "commandments" (v. 6) is an active proposition entailing that we must do something, namely, obey the commands. The metaphor of "walking" is a good way to describe living the Christian life. The phrase "according to" paints the picture of the old balance scale. John's point is that our behavior should balance out with what God says our behavior should be. Once again John appeals to the fact that this command to love one another finds its source in Jesus himself who taught it to his disciples.[6] Since this command is "from the beginning," John considers it foundational for our Christian conduct.

Correct belief and correct behavior always go together. The Biblical teaching is that right behavior should always follow right belief. Only when we know what we believe and why we believe it will we be in a position to behave it! Ephesians 4:1 is the hinge verse connecting the doctrinal section of Paul's letter (chapters 1–3) with the application section (chapters 4–6): "I, therefore, a prisoner in the Lord, urge you to walk in a manner worthy of the calling to which you have been called." In Philippians 1:27 Paul writes, "Only let your manner of life be worthy of the gospel of Christ." Notice Paul's use of the word "worthy" in both places. The meaning is, "Let your behavior balance out with what the gospel says your behavior should be." Paul and John use the same concept of balance to express how our conduct should be commensurate with the gospel.

Watch for Impostors (vv. 7–11)

With verse 7 John shifts to another topic: false teachers and their false doctrine. False teachers and false doctrine is serious business. A lie can travel halfway around the world while the truth is still putting on its shoes.[7] John calls them "deceivers," a descriptive term that identifies their activity. These deceivers are deniers! They deny the incarnation of Jesus. They have gone out into the world carrying their false doctrine with them. Christian ethics called for Christians to show hospitality to traveling teachers and missionaries when they came to town. But what if the traveling missionary or teacher was a false teacher? John's second letter shows this had become a problem in the early church.[8] Their threat to John's readers was serious, and so John could not wait for a proposed visit but must address the situation with urgency, as implied in verse 12. We are to be on our guard against false teachers and their teaching, and we are not to help or encourage false teachers in any way.

Second John could be an emergency application of the teaching the apostle had already given in 1 John. Denial of the incarnation of Jesus constituted the essence of the false doctrine John combated in both letters. The specter of an incipient form of Gnosticism[9] troubled some of the churches. One of the key false doctrines that Gnosticism propounded was a dualism between matter and spirit. Hence Jesus, in his pre-incarnate state, could not become a man according to this false teaching. This cuts straight to the heart of Christianity, and John wastes no time exposing it as false doctrine. John marks each one of these false teachers as a "deceiver" and "antichrist."[10] The word "antichrist" means "against Christ" or "in the place of Christ." John does not mean that any one of these false teachers is the personal Antichrist spoken of in Revelation as the final world ruler who opposes Christ just before his second coming. Rather, any and all false teachers partake of the character of the final antichrist. The spirit of Antichrist is already at work in the world preparing for the final unveiling of the Antichrist during the time of the Great Tribulation spoken of in Revelation. The rise of religious liberalism since the

Enlightenment, the humanization of God, the deification of man, the growing acceptance of universalism all seem to be paving the way for a coming world dictator. The Bible's inerrancy and authority is routinely denied among many, especially in the mainline denominations. The amazing thing about it is that all of this is done under the guise of a larger conception of God! From the perspective of liberal Christianity, it is conservative, orthodox Christianity that has an anemic, restricted view of God and religion. This is the spirit of antichrist.

Verses 8–11 constitute a paragraph with three main propositions. Verse 8 commands us to self-watch so that we may not lose something but rather "win a full reward." The use of the command "watch yourselves" is the translation of a Greek word used often by Jesus in the Gospels to warn the disciples of deceivers, as well as by Paul and the author of Hebrews. The present imperative stresses the need for us to be on constant guard. Complacency may lead us to a false sense of security, thinking we are beyond the seductive nature of false teachers and their teaching. There is a textual question in verse 8 that may impact how we interpret this verse. In each of the three verbs, there is a question whether the first-person plural (we) or second-person plural (you) should be used. The specific question is whether the verse should read "what you have worked for" or "what we have worked for." The evidence is about equally split, and so neither reading can claim priority.

Three possible interpretations exist for verse 8. First, some see John teaching that it is possible for a genuine believer to lose his or her salvation. Second, others think John is teaching, based on the context of verse 9, that those who don't continue in sound doctrine give evidence they were never genuinely converted in the first place. Third, it is possible that John is referring to loss of rewards for genuine believers. John Stott captures the essence of this approach: "The thought is not of their winning or losing their salvation (which is a free gift), but their reward for faithful service. The metaphor seems to be taken from the payment of labour, since *reward* (*misthos*) is a workman's wage (as in Mt. xx:8; Jn. iv:36; Jas. v.4)."[11] Since the larger context of the New Testament, including John's writings, indicate that those who are genuinely converted cannot lose their salvation, option one is incorrect. Options two and three are both possible. If the term "full reward" refers to final salvation, then option two may be correct, especially in the light of what is said in verse 9. However, the full New Testament teaching concerning rewards indicates that there are rewards for believers that extend beyond the reward of eternal salvation, which is the heritage of all believers. This is borne out by a study of the usage of the Greek word translated as "reward" throughout the Greek

New Testament. For an example, notice what Paul says in 1 Corinthians 3:14. Sometimes the reference is to eternal salvation, and sometimes the reference is to rewards believers will receive in Heaven for their earthly service. This latter option may be John's meaning in verse 8.[12]

Verse 9 informs us that those who depart from the fellowship and do not abide in sound Christian doctrine give evidence by their actions that they were never truly converted. Conversely, those who do abide in sound doctrine have true salvation. The one who "goes on ahead" and "does not abide in the teaching of [about] Christ" does not possess a relationship with God; hence he is unsaved. The phrase "goes on ahead" refers to advancing beyond the clear teaching of the gospel into the territory of false doctrine. The false teachers John is referring to considered themselves progressives, advanced thinkers. Progress in the Christian life is commendable. Growth in spiritual maturity is the order of the day. However, progressive thinking beyond gospel truth leads to untruth and is condemned for the error that it is.[13] This appears to be John's way of saying that they were never saved in the first place (compare 2:19), not that they were genuinely saved and then lost their salvation because they did not remain in orthodox doctrine. Those who abide in sound doctrine give evidence of a genuine salvation experience.

Once again John connects the Father and Jesus the Son in such a way as to teach that one cannot know God without knowing his Son, Jesus. As John records Jesus saying in his Gospel (14:6), Jesus is the only way to God, and "No one comes to the Father except through me." The exclusivity of Jesus as the only true way of salvation is taught clearly by John here in this letter as well as in his Gospel. There is no place here or anywhere in the New Testament for universalism[14] (all will be saved) or inclusivism (an implicit faith response to general revelation apart from knowledge of Jesus can bring about salvation).[15] All of us know someone, whether at school, work, or another venue, who believes that in the end everyone is going to Heaven. Likewise, all of us know someone who believes that people can experience salvation without knowledge of Jesus Christ. Such beliefs are part and parcel of the current cultural atmosphere. The problem is, such beliefs are directly contradicted by Scripture. If universalism is true, why go out of your way to tell others about Jesus, whether they live across the street or halfway around the world? If inclusivism is true, why not tell people that all that matters is that they respond in some generic way to God based on his revelation of himself in nature? These false doctrines are very popular today, sadly even among some Christians.

In verses 10, 11 John instructs us on how we should respond when false teachers come to our home attempting to persuade us of their errant ways. First, we are not to receive them into our house. Second, we are not even to give them "any greeting," for in doing so we are at that point "taking part in [their] wicked works." Notice, it is bad enough to *believe* false doctrine, but those who do also engage in "wicked works" in disseminating such false doctrine. Some may think that to refuse to invite visiting false teachers into your home ranges from, at the very least, inhospitable to, at the most, downright rude. But if you will think about it for a moment, you can see the unwisdom of inviting them into your home. If you do so, when the false teacher knocks on your neighbor's door down the street, he can say, "Well, your neighbor, Dr. Allen, just a few doors down, let me in, and we had a wonderful talk!" My disobedience could lead to someone else's spiritual destruction.[16]

According to the Barna Research Group, current statistics on the question of absolute truth are alarming, even shocking. From a random pool of just over one thousand adults in the United States, one-third of all adults (34 percent) believe that moral truth is absolute and unaffected by the circumstances. Slightly less than half of the born-again adults (46 percent) believe in absolute moral truth.[17] No doubt a similar if not higher percentage would say they do not believe in absolute doctrinal truth.

Yours Sincerely, John (vv. 12, 13)

Verse 11 concludes the body of the letter. Basically John has made three primary appeals to his readers: 1) continue to love fellow Christians, 2) guard against false teaching, and 3) reject false teachers. These three commands flow directly from John's emphasis on "love" and "truth" in verses 1–3. "Love" and "truth" should ever be our watchwords! Love will always be the result of those who obey the truth.

John draws the short letter to a close in verses 12, 13. He has much to write but declines to do so because he would rather communicate with them face-to-face (literally in Greek, "mouth to mouth") rather than in writing. Written communication is sometimes prone to being misunderstood. In face-to-face conversation the hearer has an opportunity to question the speaker to make sure there is no misunderstanding. John's stated reason for his desire to speak face-to-face is "so that our joy may be complete." John not only wants to teach the truth, he wants to personally fellowship with those to whom he is currently writing, as such close fellowship and face-to-face communication would complete his joy and the joy of those who accompany him. Distance sometimes makes written communication necessary. But no amount of smiley faces attached to a sentence in an email can take the place of the warm smile of a human face. Ink cannot put an arm around someone's shoulder and console, encourage, or rebuke. There is no substitute for personal Christian fellowship. We all need each other in the local church!

In verse 13 John signs off his letter much the same way as he began it by sending greetings to them from "children" of a sister church whom he refers to as "your elect sister." As in verse 1, notice that John's use of the word "elect" does not refer to individual election, but to corporate election as he views the local congregation as a whole to be an elect body.

False teachers along with their teaching should never be accepted, encouraged, or endorsed by Christians. We should never engage in fellowship with false teachers, no matter how affable or sincere they may be. As John says, their works are "wicked" (v. 11). Our priorities should be "truth and love" (v. 3). Our response to problems with false teachers and false teaching should be resistance. Truth and love, like the right and left ventricle of the heart, function as the circulatory system of the church. When the two are functioning freely, the body of Christ is healthy.

3 JOHN

The elder to the beloved Gaius, whom I love in truth. Beloved, I pray that all may go well with you and that you may be in good health, as it goes well with your soul. For I rejoiced greatly when the brothers came and testified to your truth, as indeed you are walking in the truth. I have no greater joy than to hear that my children are walking in the truth. Beloved, it is a faithful thing you do in all your efforts for these brothers, strangers as they are, who testified to your love before the church. You will do well to send them on their journey in a manner worthy of God. For they have gone out for the sake of the name, accepting nothing from the Gentiles. Therefore we ought to support people like these, that we may be fellow workers for the truth. I have written something to the church, but Diotrephes, who likes to put himself first, does not acknowledge our authority. So if I come, I will bring up what he is doing, talking wicked nonsense against us. And not content with that, he refuses to welcome the brothers, and also stops those who want to and puts them out of the church. Beloved, do not imitate evil but imitate good. Whoever does good is from God; whoever does evil has not seen God. Demetrius has received a good testimony from everyone, and from the truth itself. We also add our testimony, and you know that our testimony is true. I had much to write to you, but I would rather not write with pen and ink. I hope to see you soon, and we will talk face to face. Peace be to you. The friends greet you. Greet the friends, each by name.

3 JOHN

22

Down with Diotrephes;
Long Live Demetrius!

THIRD JOHN DIFFERS FROM 2 John in many ways.[1] One key difference is that 2 John is written to a group of people, while 3 John is written to a single individual, Gaius. As in the previous letter, John calls himself "the elder." In addition to the recipient, Gaius, two other individuals appear in this letter: Diotrephes and Demetrius. We cannot identify any of these names with anyone bearing these names in the New Testament since there is not enough information given by John to do so. The name Gaius, a common name in the first century, occurs four times in the New Testament (Acts 19:29; 20:4; 1 Corinthians 1:14; Romans 16:23). The "brothers" whom John mentions in verse 3 and again in verses 5–8 can be identified as itinerant teachers. Whereas 2 John is negative in tone with respect to itinerant false prophets, 3 John is positive about those who teach the truth. Unlike 2 John, where itinerant teachers who were false prophets are denounced, these teachers are highly recommended to Gaius by John. Stott is correct in suggesting that 2 and 3 John "must be read together if we are to gain a balanced understanding."[2] In 3 John the problem addressed is one of authority in church leadership and its abuse. Diotrephes is singled out by John for his pride, stubbornness, and desire for personal aggrandizement. John becomes a perfect example to all pastors and church leaders today in that in both of these short letters, his authority as an apostle is balanced with his love for the church. John is an "elder" in age but also as a church leader. He teaches us how to speak the truth in love with respect to difficult church problems.

John loved Gaius and trusted him to do the right thing in the problem situation in the church. Four times in this short letter John addresses Gaius as

269

"beloved" (vv. 1, 2, 5, 11). The emphatic use of the personal pronoun "I" in verse 1 emphasizes John's love for this man.

It is not possible to determine from the letter alone whether Gaius and Diotrephes were members of the same church. They may have belonged to neighboring congregations. Whatever the case, John felt concern that Gaius might be overly influenced by Diotrephes.

The itinerant teachers were probably somewhat under the direction of John. Their ministry to the local churches was vital at a time when all of the apostles but John had passed from the scene. Pastors can identify with Gaius' predicament if he were caught between loyalty to John and some of the local leaders such as Diotrephes. It is not clear from the letter whether doctrine was involved in this problem and whether perhaps Diotrephes may have been in cahoots with the false teachers. This is probably not the case. The problem is a practical one relating to personalities and personal agendas.

Pastors and other church leaders are not immune from the temptations of pride and personal aggrandizement. In fact, just the opposite is the case! Pastors are probably more prone to these temptations and must guard against them at all costs.

The structure of this letter is simple and clear. Verses 1–4 comprise the opening of the letter and contain three parts: a somewhat standard opening address identifying the writer and recipient, a blessing, followed by a statement of encouragement that John's readers are living out the truth of the gospel. Verses 5–12 constitute the body of the letter, with verses 13–15 functioning as the closing. The purpose of the letter can be discerned from its contents. Diotrephes had on some unspecified earlier occasion rejected John and the itinerant teachers whom John calls "brothers." John desired Gaius and the church or churches he represents to support and show hospitality to them and to mark out Diotrephes for the troublemaker he is. The three exhortations found in verses 6, 8, and 11 are key in the letter. Of these four, the most important is verse 11: "Beloved, do not imitate evil but imitate good."

Greeting (vv. 1–4)

Following the opening introduction of verse 1, verses 2, 3 introduce John's prayer for Gaius. John desires for Gaius to experience good physical health in the same way that his spiritual life ("soul") is healthy. External health is important, but not nearly as important as our spiritual health. Spiritual health should come first. Yet many people today are far more concerned about their physical health than their spiritual health. George Whitfield has a fascinating sermon on this verse that is worthy of our consideration. He asks and answers the question of how we can know that our soul prospers. He talks about the sad condition of many people who are more concerned about a pimple on their face than the rottenness in their heart.[3]

Witness the burgeoning health spa industry. Witness also the growing influence of the so-called Word of Faith movement today. One of its chief theological errors is the notion that if you are sick, it is due to sin and/or your lack of faith. Much of the preaching in the Word of Faith movement focuses on physical health and wealth rather than on spiritual health and wealth.[4] As I write these words, my own precious wife begins chemotherapy treatment this week for colon cancer. Though her physical health is currently diminished, she has never been in better spiritual health! The Great Physician not only cares about our physical health but, even more importantly, has brought to us the remedy for our sin in Christ's death on the cross on our behalf. For those who know Christ, the cancer of the soul has been dealt a death blow.

In verses 3, 4 John "rejoiced greatly"[5] that his dear friend Gaius was faithful to the truth and living out the truth. John's faithful ministry had given birth to many spiritual children. Some of these no doubt came to faith in Christ through John's direct ministry. Since John was an apostle, all were in some way under his spiritual leadership. Like an old professor who learns that his former students have now distinguished themselves in their respective disciplines, nothing provides John any greater joy than to hear reports that "my children are walking in the truth." I have had the privilege of serving the Lord and his church as a youth pastor for five years from 1977–1981, as a pastor for over twenty-one years (1982–2004), and as a professor of preaching and New Testament (adjunctively and full-time) since 1985. One of my greatest joys is to receive emails from former members of my youth group and churches or my former students telling me what my preaching and teaching has meant to them. When I hear they are "walking in the truth," living a life consistent with the gospel, my joy cup is full! May God help us all to be like Gaius in our own Christian conduct, daily reflecting Christ in all we say and do.

Notice all of the emotive terms in these first four verses: John loves Gaius; he is concerned for his physical and spiritual welfare; he rejoices in his spiritual progress. John's own warm heart of love for the Lord and for fellow Christians oozes from these verses.

Support for Itinerant Teachers (vv. 5–8)

In the body of the letter (vv. 5–12), John addresses three problems: 1) his request that support be shown to the itinerant teachers that John himself had sent to the church had been denied by Diotrephes and others; 2) John was concerned that Gaius might be influenced by the behavior of Diotrephes; and 3) he needed to secure Gaius's help for the itinerant teachers. In verses 5–8 John praises Gaius for his hospitality toward the itinerant teachers. "It is a faithful thing you do for all your efforts for these brothers, strangers as they are, who testified to your love before the church." Gaius acted toward the traveling teachers consistently with what he believed. They were "strangers" to him, people whom he had never met before. In the culture of the first century, a stranger was viewed as a potential threat to the community. The modern-day concept of hotels and motels did not exist. Strangers had no standing by custom or law. They needed a patron to vouch for them. Letters of recommendation were important in such a culture. Refusal to accept the recommended stranger was tantamount to refusing and dishonoring the one who commended him.[6] These "strangers" were Christian brothers who deserved to be treated in a Christian manner. Gaius showed them hospitality, and these "brother strangers" gave public testimony to the church about how Gaius had helped them. What Gaius did for these traveling teachers was valuable not only for themselves but also for the Christian community. He provided the necessary material means for their travel and ministry. Gaius did this "in a manner worthy of God"; that is, since the teachers are emissaries of Christ, they should be treated as one would treat God himself or in the same way as God would treat them.

Gaius was right to do what he did because these traveling teachers had gone out in the name of Jesus and for his sake to fulfill his purpose. One purpose of their travel was evangelistic. Furthermore, these teachers had not taken or received any support from unbelievers in the process. When John uses the word "Gentiles" here, he is using it in the sense of those who do not know Christ. Non-Christians are under no obligation to support Christian missions, but we Christians are! That's why John says in verse 8 that "we *ought* to support people like these" traveling teachers. The verb is in the present tense and expresses our continual obligation to support them. Because of their work, and because they do not receive support from nonbelievers, John solicits for them not only hospitality but financial support. When we render this kind of aid, we become "fellow workers for the truth." We may not be able to travel to foreign lands to carry the gospel, but when we support those who do with our prayers, our finances, and our encouragement we become fellow laborers with them in the gospel. Gaius opened his heart, his home, and his hand to fellow Christian teachers, and we should do the same.

Rebuke of Diotrephes (vv. 9–11)

Now John turns his attention to address the problem that motivated his writing to Gaius in the first place. A man named Diotrephes spurned John's authority, slandered John with "wicked nonsense," refused to provide the necessary hospitality to the traveling teachers, prohibited those within the church who desired to show hospitality to those teachers, and even worked to expel them from the fellowship (vv. 9, 10)! Obviously Diotrephes carried significant authority in the church. In verse 9 John mentions a letter he had written to the church. This letter cannot be the current letter or 1 or 2 John. What letter is he referring to? There is no way to know. John had written to commend the traveling teachers, but Diotrephes rejected John's instructions. Not only that, but he then proceeded to defame the character and authority of John verbally by "talking wicked nonsense" against John. The Greek phrase literally reads "gossiping evil words against us." Diotrephes was bad-mouthing John with his unjustified charges, but his gossip was nothing more than verbal nonsense.

John doesn't mince words in his condemnation of Diotrephes' unchristian actions. In fact, he is so miffed about it that he hopes to come and confront Diotrephes personally to rectify the situation.[7] Public exposure is John's plan when he arrives. This is John's meaning when he writes, "I will bring up what he is doing." This old "Son of Thunder" can still live up to his nickname!

Diotrephes' action was causing a serious division within the church that had to be addressed. John gives us an insight into the motivation for Diotrephes' actions. He was a man who "likes to put himself first." This is a fascinating word that occurs only here in the entire New Testament.[8] The word connotes the idea that Diotrephes loved to be the leader and to exercise authority in the church. He wanted to control others, like some people in the church today. This is ambition for leadership, and it is especially problematic with someone who is unqualified to lead! I have seen this problem many times in churches, and it is not limited just to laypeople either! Sometimes pastors or church staff members are afflicted with the "I want to be first" syndrome. This was the problem with some of history's great leaders. George Armstrong Custer, for example, finished last in his class at West Point. Just two years later, at the age of twenty-three, because of his exploits during the Civil War he had been named a brigadier general. Like Diotrephes, he was an "impulsive blabbermouth" with an ego the size of the eastern Montana Territory, where he ingloriously lost the Battle of Little Bighorn along with his life in 1876.[9] There is only one who is preeminent in the church, and his name is Jesus Christ (Colossians 1:18). When Peter addressed fellow pastors in 1 Peter 5:1–4, he reminded them that they must shepherd God's flock, "not domineering over those in your charge, but being examples to the flock." A pastor is a shepherd, not a swaggering dictator. I have seen some pastors who are so full of themselves they can strut sitting down! Diotrephes is still among us, unfortunately.

Following this sad and sordid description of Diotrephes in verses 9, 10 John inserts a direct command in verse 11, the first and only imperative in the letter: "do not imitate evil but imitate good." The present tense indicates that the prohibited action has not yet taken place. John desires Gaius not to begin to imitate Diotrephes in his evil actions. Rather Gaius is to imitate good. John's mitigated appeal in verse 8 ("we ought to support people like these") is now followed by a direct command. In context, the "good" here has already been stated in verse 8: support the traveling teachers. A general maxim appears at the end of verse 11: "Whoever does good is from God; whoever does evil has not seen God." John's point is that your character and behavior evidences your relationship with God, or lack of it. The description "has not seen God" means "has not come to know God." John is speaking of seeing with the mind rather than the eyes. Consistent evil behavior is evidence that one is unregenerate.

Praise for Demetrius (v. 12)

In verse 12 John applies his hospitality point of the letter to a specific person, Demetrius. Gaius and the church are to receive Demetrius and show him hospitality. John provides a threefold testimony to the character of Demetrius. First, he "has received a good testimony from everyone." Second, by way of personification, he has received a good testimony "from the truth itself." This means Demetrius lives in a manner consistent with the truth. Third, John adds his own personal testimony concerning Demetrius with an added motivation to Gaius: "you know that our testimony is true." With such testimony it would be impossible for anyone to refuse to show hospitality to Demetrius.

Yours Sincerely, John (vv. 13–15)

The letter closes with John's personal statement of his hope and desire to see Gaius and the church soon to talk face-to-face in verses 13, 14. This is followed by a final greeting in verse 15 that, on more careful scrutiny, says much about John, Christian love, and fellowship. "Peace be to you" is an appropriate benediction given the situation John is addressing. "Peace" is nothing more than the experience of "God's covenant blessing, protection, and provision in all its fullness."[10] John's fellow believers who are with him when he writes also send greetings to Gaius. The fact that John calls them "friends" may hark back to John 15:14, 15 where Jesus told his disciples that he lays down his life for his "friends." Finally, John asks Gaius to greet those who are in the church "each by name." This says a great deal, doesn't it? John thought of each one of the congregation and included each in his greeting. Can you imagine if you had been there in church the Sunday after Gaius received the letter from John? I can envision Gaius going around and greeting each brother or sister on John's behalf. "Bill, John told me to give you his greeting!" "Sarah, John sends you his personal greeting!" "Jim, John asked me to give you his greetings personally!" "Mary, John asked me to greet you by name!" How special it must have made all those Christians feel that John would not only send greetings but send greetings to each of them by name! After all, Dale Carnegie was right when he said that if we want to win friends and influence people, we should remember that a person's name is the sweetest and most important sound in any language to him or her. When you remember someone's name, you pay him or her a subtle compliment. In Christian fellowship when you remember someone's name, you show him or her that he or she is special to you and to God's kingdom work.

Third John may be a short letter, but it is powerfully important for us today. There are many lessons here, both direct and indirect, for Christian living. In closing, are you a Diotrephes or a Demetrius? When people think of you, do they think of someone who is selfless, seeking to give himself on behalf of others in Christian service, or do they think of someone who is selfish, always seeking to be first and in charge? You may think to yourself, *I'm not a pastor or church staff member, a deacon, or in any position of leadership in the church. I don't have any influence. I doubt anyone notices my attitude.* You may not be a leader or in a position of leadership, but it would behoove all of us to remember that every Christian is the best Christian that somebody knows. The church and the world are always watching . . . not to mention God.

If you are in a leadership position in someone's church, and especially if you are a pastor, let me offer a salient word of warning: don't become a Diotrephes who loves to be first. We all know preachers who are too big for their britches. You know the type. He exudes arrogance, either in the pulpit, outside the pulpit, or both. Joseph Parker, a contemporary of Spurgeon, painted the picture of the prideful person in unforgettable prose: "Here is a little contemptible person who stuffs the unworthy sack, which he calls himself, with the shavings and sawdust of his own self-interest."[11]

Probably for most preachers their pride is not that extreme, but it is pride nonetheless. Scripture has much to say about pride. Pride caused Satan to be cast out of Heaven. Pride caused Adam and Eve to sin and be cast out of the garden. It brought down prophets, priests, and kings in Old Testament times. It kept many a Pharisee and Sadducee out of Heaven in Jesus' day. It caused Pilate to wash his hands concerning Jesus of Nazareth. Pride goes before a fall, Scripture says. Of the seven things God says he hates, first on the list is pride (Proverbs 6:16–19). There are few sins as destructive as pride. The Latin word for pride is "*superbia*," which means "aspiring to be on top." More than one preacher has been brought low by pride. Only God is on top.

Like John, from the early church through today preachers have warned their fellow preachers about pride. John Chrysostom ("the golden mouthed") called pride the chief sin of preachers. He concluded his rhetorically powerful list of sins with the memorable line, ". . . all these and many other kinds of beasts dwell upon that rock of pride." You will not read more convicting pages about pride than Charles Bridges's chapter "The Influence of Spiritual Pride" in his justly famous nineteenth-century work *The Christian Ministry*.[12] Note especially his reference to Cotton Mather's comments about his own pride when he was a young preacher. And don't miss Spurgeon's chapters "The Minister's Self-Watch" and "The Minister's Fainting Fits" in his *Lectures to My Students*. In the latter Spurgeon pungently states, "Be content to be nothing, for that is what you are."[13] Andrew Blackwood, the great homiletician, once stated that among preachers, "pride still remains Soul Enemy Number One."

C. S. Lewis said concerning pride, "There is no fault which makes a man more unpopular, and no fault which we are more unconscious of in ourselves. And the more we have it ourselves the more we dislike it in others."[14] When we are genuinely humble, we should beware lest Satan smuggle the thought of our own humility into our mind. The experienced demon Screwtape reminded his demonic understudy Wormwood that he must conceal from his patient God's true end of humility in his life.[15] Preachers especially must guard against vainglory and false modesty, which is just another form of pride. Beware when pride shows up in the guise of humility. Leave it to Mark Twain to cleverly drive this point home: "If I ever achieve humility, I'll sure be proud of it."

Pride gets around. As Benjamin Franklin said in *Poor Richard's Almanac, 1732–1757*, "Pride breakfasted with Plenty, dined with Poverty, and supped with Infamy."[16]

The worm of pride is ever threatening to eat into the fruit of the Spirit in your life. The poison of pride ever sits inconspicuously on life's shelf.

Sometimes it takes very little to puff up these proud preacher hearts of ours. A little success, a little prosperity, and we are ready to burn incense to our own accomplishments. Let the world bestow on us a few of its flatteries and we are ready to throw in our lot with it. Pride is ever beside you in the crowded highway and the lonely street. It follows you to the office, to the pulpit, and back home again. It dogs your footsteps when you go to church, kneels beside you when you pray, and whispers in your ear while you preach. It assaults your every relationship, your every sacrifice, and your every sermon. It is your constant companion, arriving early and staying late. It never leaves you night and day 'til death do you part. Pride is the hound of Hell that can only be defeated by the hound of Heaven.

The fact is, most of us just don't like to humble ourselves. It's not in our nature. But the Lord knows how to balance our lives. He will allow almost anything to prevent spiritual pride and to quash it when it rears its ugly head in our lives. James reminds us, "Humble yourselves before the Lord, and he will exalt you" (James 4:10). If you're not willing to preach in the basement, you have no business preaching in the bay window. The trick is improving your preaching talent and skills without simultaneously attempting to carve out your own niche in the Preaching Hall of Fame.

Instead of an unwelcome intruder, seek to make humility the spouse of your soul to whom you have wedded yourself forever. To reflect God's light, don't seek the limelight. Sometimes we get confused as to who is the light of the world! Even the donkey that brought Jesus into Jerusalem knew the applause was not for him. If you get too big for your britches, don't be surprised if God gets you a smaller pair of britches. Be very careful that your ambition and your ability do not carry you beyond where your character can sustain you. Let the Diotrephes in us be crucified. Long live Demetrius!

Soli Deo gloria!

Notes

Author's Preface

1. For an analysis of how I go about my own sermon preparation for expositional preaching that uses 1 John 2:15–17 as an example, see my "Preparing a Text-Driven Sermon," *Text-Driven Preaching: God's Word at the Heart of Every Sermon* (Nashville: B&H, 2010), pp. 101–134.

2. C. S. Lewis, *God in the Dock* (Grand Rapids: Eerdmans, 1970), pp. 201, 202.

Chapter One: Meet Jesus: God in Human Flesh!

1. Johannine authorship has often been questioned, but there is no reason to abandon the traditional view that the Apostle John is the author. For an accessible summary of this question and all other background issues, helpful especially to pastors, see, among others, Barry Joslin, "Getting Up to Speed: An Essential Introduction to 1 John," *Southern Baptist Journal of Theology* 10.3 (2006), pp. 4–27; Stephen Smalley, *1, 2, 3 John*, Word Biblical Commentary, vol. 51 (Waco, TX: Word, 1984), p. xxxii; Daniel Akin, *1, 2, 3 John*, New American Commentary, vol. 38 (Nashville: B&H, 2001), pp. 22–27; and more recently Robert Yarbrough, *1–3 John*, Baker Exegetical Commentary on the New Testament (Grand Rapids: Baker, 2008), pp. 5–15. See also Donald Guthrie, *New Testament Introduction*, 4th rev. ed. (Leicester: Apollos/Downers Grove, IL: InterVarsity, 1990), pp. 858–886; and Andreas Köstenberger, L. Scott Kellum, and Charles Quarles, *The Cradle, the Cross, and the Crown: An Introduction to the New Testament* (Nashville: B&H, 2009), pp. 781–808. On the question of Johannine authorship of the Gospel of John and corresponding discussion on the epistles, I recommend the following three works: Craig L. Blomberg, *The Historical Reliability of John's Gospel: Issues and Commentary* (Downers Grove, IL: InterVarsity Press, 2001), pp. 22–40; D. A. Carson, *The Gospel According to John* (Leicester, UK: Inter-Varsity; Grand Rapids, Eerdmans, 1991), pp. 68–81; and C. S. Keener, *The Gospel of John*, 2 vols. (Peabody, MA: Hendrickson, 2003).

2. A helpful work for pastors on the Johannine epistles summarizing issues of form, style, content, authorship, theology, etc., is Ruth Edwards, *The Johannine Epistles*, New Testament Guides Series (Sheffield, UK: Sheffield Academic Press, 2001 reprint). A helpful work for those working with the Greek text in sermon preparation, in addition to exegetical commentaries, is Martin Culy, *I, II, III John: A Handbook on the Greek Text* (Waco, TX: Baylor University Press, 2004). The introduction (pp. xi-xxiv) offers significant help from linguistics and discourse analysis in analyzing the syntactical and semantic structure of the letter, in a non-technical, pastor-friendly format.

3. Martin Luther, *The Catholic Epistles*, in *Luther's Works*, vol. 30, ed. Jaroslav Pelikan (St. Louis: Concordia Publishing House, 1967), p. 221.

4. The editors of the UBS Greek New Testament, 4th edition, and Nestle-Aland Greek New Testament, 27th edition, place a dash at the end of verse 1 and 2 to signify the parenthesis.

5. Grace Sherman and John Tuggy, *A Semantic and Structural Analysis of the Johannine Epistles* (Dallas: Summer Institute of Linguistics, 1994), pp. 15–17. This work is an often overlooked resource on the Johannine letters that is informed by contemporary linguistic principles (primarily the Beekman/Callow model of discourse analysis) used by the Wycliffe Bible Translators. It contains much material that is useful to the preacher who is committed to text-driven (genuine expository) preaching.

6. There are five occurrences of the neuter relative pronoun in Greek in this passage (four in verse 1 and one in verse 3). All of them have as their antecedent the phrase "word of life." John is using this phrase with a double meaning, referring to the message about Jesus and to Jesus himself, who is the "Word" (cf. John 1:1).

7. Joseph Parker, *Ephesians–Revelation*, in *The People's Bible*, vol. 27 (Grand Rapids: Baker, 1959), p. 348.

8. Colloquially expressed by Rob Lacey, *The Word on the Street* (Grand Rapids: Zondervan, 2004), p. 460.

9. Scholars differ concerning the nature of the false teachers whom John opposes in 1 John. This question relates closely with the question of the purpose for the epistle as well. The prevalent view concerning the opponents in 1 John is that they were peddling an incipient form of Gnosticism. I recommend one or more of the following articles on Gnosticism for pastors: Nicholas Perrin, "Gnosticism," *Dictionary for Theological Interpretation of the Bible*, gen. ed., Kevin Vanhoozer (Grand Rapids: Baker, 2005), pp. 256–259; Kurt Rudolph, "Gnosticism," *Anchor Bible Dictionary*, vol. 2, editor-in-chief, David Noel Freedman (New York: Doubleday, 1992), 1033–1040; D. M. Scholer, "Gnosis, Gnosticism," *Dictionary of the Later New Testament and Its Developments*, eds. Ralph Martin and Peter Davids (Downers Grove, IL: InterVarsity, 1997), pp. 400–412; E. M. Yamauchi, "Gnosticism," *Dictionary of New Testament Background*, eds. Craig Evans and Stanley Porter (Downers Grove, IL: InterVarsity, 2000), pp. 414–418. Recently the Gnostic view has been challenged by Daniel Streett, *They Went out from Us: The Identity of the Opponents in First John*, in *Beihefte zur Zeitschrift für die neutestamentliche Wissenschaft und die Kunde der älteren Kirche*, vol. 177, ed. James D. G. Dunn et al. (Berlin/New York: de Gruyter, 2011). Streett makes a good, though not airtight, case that the opponents John is combating are not false teachers promoting proto-Gnosticism, but rather were Jewish believers who separated themselves from the church (1 John 2:19) "because they reneged upon their initial confession of Jesus as the Messiah, probably in order to return to the relative security of the Jewish synagogue" (p. 2). Streett provides the most comprehensive survey and critique of the various options. Whatever decision is made concerning the opponents John is addressing will obviously impact how one preaches the passages that make specific reference to the opponents in the letter.

10. So argued by J. P. Louw and E. Nida, eds., *Greek-English Lexicon of the New Testament Based on Semantic Domains*, vol. 1 (New York: United Bible Societies, 1988), p. 279. See also Yarbrough, *1–3 John*, p. 37. Ralph Laurin, *1 John: Life at Its Best* (Grand Rapids: Kregel, 1987), p. 25 says it well: "When John tells us in

one instance that Jesus Christ has been 'seen with our eyes' and in another instant that he has 'looked upon' Him, he is not wasting words. It is amplification rather than duplication. When he says 'which we have looked upon' he refers to something more than an optical perception. This is spiritual apperception."

11. The same Greek word for "touch" in 1 John 1:1 is used by Luke in this scene.

12. This denial of the incarnation will also be addressed by John in 2 John 7: "For many deceivers have gone out into the world, those who do not confess the coming of Jesus Christ in the flesh."

13. The "of" in the genitive construction in Greek may be a "genitive of product" with the meaning "the word that produces life." See Daniel B. Wallace, *Greek Grammar Beyond the Basics* (Grand Rapids: Zondervan, 1996), p. 106.

14. Luther, *The Catholic Epistles*, p. 223.

15. Also called "Modalistic Monarchianism." On modalism, see James Leo Garrett, *Systematic Theology: Biblical, Historical, and Evangelical*, vol. 1 (Grand Rapids: Eerdmans, 1990), pp. 277–279; or Wayne Grudem, *Systematic Theology: An Introduction to Biblical Doctrine* (Grand Rapids: Zondervan, 1994), p. 242.

16. As noted by Charles Simeon, *James–Jude*, Expository Outlines on the Whole Bible, vol. 20 (Grand Rapids: Zondervan, 1955), p. 358. Simeon was the great professor of homiletics at Cambridge University in the nineteenth century. He was committed to genuine Biblical exposition and is often called the father of evangelical homiletics.

17. The word is *koinonia* in Greek, from the root word *koinē*, which means "common." Rudolf Schnackenburg, *The Johannine Epistles*, trans. Reginald and Ilse Fuller (New York: Crossroad, 1992), pp. 63–69 has an excellent discussion of "fellowship" in an excursus.

18. G. Campbell Morgan, *Westminster Pulpit*, vol. 5 (Westwood, NJ: Revell, 1954), p. 61.

19. Ibid., p. 62.

20. Ibid., pp. 66–68.

21. Augustine, *Confessions*, Book I, I, (1) (Oxford, UK: Oxford University Press, 1998), p. 3.

22. Bruce Metzger, *Textual Commentary on the Greek New Testament*, 2nd ed. (New York: United Bible Societies, 1994), p. 639, gives *hēmeis* a "B" ranking because of the quality of its manuscript support and because of the likelihood that copyists would alter *hēmeis* to *humin* rather than vice versa.

23. So I. H. Marshall, *The Epistles of John* (Grand Rapids: Eerdmans, 1978), pp. 106, 107.

24. So Smalley, *1, 2, 3 John*, p. 14.

25. A gloss of the final line from the poem "Casey at the Bat" by Earnest Lawrence Thayer, ca. 1888. Mudville's hometown hero, Casey, strides to the plate in the final inning with two outs, two men on base, and his team down by a score of 4–2. "Ten thousand eyes were on him and five thousand tongues applauded" as he stepped to the plate. The count went 0 and 2. At the next pitch, Casey swung with all of his might, and the final stanza of the poem brilliantly concludes:

Oh! somewhere in this favored land the sun is shining bright;
The band is playing somewhere, and somewhere hearts are light.

And somewhere men are laughing, and somewhere children shout;
But there is no joy in Mudville—mighty Casey has struck out.

From contemporary culture, another illustration for "full joy" that could be used with certain audiences comes from the Star Trek movie *Generations*, where Whoopi Goldberg's character, Guinan, explains to Captain Picard that being in the Nexus (an extra-dimensional energy ribbon where one's thoughts and desires shape reality, though unreal, and one can supposedly find ultimate peace and fulfillment) is like "being inside joy." This level of joy can only begin to be approximated in this life by those who know Christ and will become eternal reality in Heaven.

26. Paraphrase of the quotation, "Joy is the flag which is flown from the castle of the heart when the King is in residence there." Robert Rainey.

Chapter Two: When Sin Meets Forgiveness

1. See http://www.baylor.edu/content/services/document.php?id=42307.

2. J. B. Phillips, *Plain Christianity* (New York: Macmillan, 1954), p. 49.

3. Augustine, in his sermon on 1 John 1:1—2:6 (Homily I of his sermons on 1 John), speaks with reference to 1:6 of not "making light" of these sins that we sometimes call "light," an example of his occasional rhetorical play on words in his preaching. Augustine, *Homilies on the First Epistle of John*, I.6, in *Nicene and Post-Nicene Fathers*, vol. 7, ed. Phillip Schaff (Edinburgh: T & T Clark/Grand Rapids: Eerdmans, 1956), p. 464.

4. My gloss on a line by George W. Truett, famed pastor of First Baptist Church in Dallas, Texas for forty-seven years (1897–1944), in his sermon on 1 John 1:5–10, in *A Quest for Souls* (Dallas: Baptist & Standard Publishing, n. d.), p. 241.

5. F. J. A. Hort, *Cambridge and Other Sermons* (London/New York: MacMillan, 1898), p. 107.

6. The debate about whether 1 John is better described as a letter about tests of salvation (whether one's faith is genuine or spurious) or tests of fellowship (whether a genuine believer is in fellowship with God or not) is somewhat misplaced. The fact is, it is both! Sometimes John's focus is testing whether one's faith is genuine or not; at other times his focus is on the issue of whether fellowship with God and other believers is interrupted or maintained by those who are genuine believers. This will be reflected throughout the sermons in this volume.

7. Perfect tense in Greek. "Him" refers to Jesus for two reasons: 1) Jesus is implied by the reference to hearing, and 2) God is the subject of the message.

8. The former word, *apangellomen*, stresses the source of the message, based on the prefixed preposition *apo*. The latter word, *anangellomen*, stresses the receptor to whom those who announce pass the message, based on the prefixed preposition *ana*, "back." J. P. Louw and E. Nida, eds., *Greek-English Lexicon of the New Testament Based on Semantic Domains*, vol. 1 (New York: United Bible Societies, 1988), p. 411 point out that this word in verse 5 implies detailed report.

9. Joseph Parker, *Ephesians–Revelation*, The People's Bible, vol. 27 (Grand Rapids: Baker, 1959), p. 350. Parker was pastor of the People's Temple in London and a contemporary (and sometimes rival!) of Spurgeon.

10. Paraphrased from the excellent sermon on 1 John 1:5 by R. W. Church, *Village Sermons*, first series (New York: Macmillan & Co., 1899), 299–302.

11. The use of "we" in these verses may be used by John to include himself and those to whom he is writing or may be a literary device conveying the sense "whoever might say this . . ."

12. The three "if we say" statements may refer to what the false teachers say and what John's readers would say if they followed the false teachers.

13. C. H. Spurgeon, *The Treasury of the New Testament*, vol. 4 (Grand Rapids: Zondervan, 1950), p. 480.

14. See F. W. Danker, ed., *A Greek-English Lexicon of the New Testament and Other Early Christian Literature*, 3rd ed. (Chicago: University of Chicago Press, 2000), pp. 42, 43.

15. Word pictures used by R. Yarbrough, *1–3 John*, Baker Exegetical Commentary on the New Testament (Grand Rapids: Baker, 2008), p. 55.

16. As Thompson pointed out, "The phrase put the truth into practice . . . is found in the Old Testament (Neh 9:33) but is paralleled more closely in Jewish texts from 200 B.C. to A.D. 200, such as Qumran Scrolls, the Testaments of the Twelve Patriarchs, and the apocryphal book of Tobit, where it has the meaning of living in accord with the truth." Marianne Thompson, *1–3 John*, InterVarsity Press New Testament Commentary (Downers Grove, IL: InterVarsity Press, 1992), p. 41.

17. See R. Candlish, *The First Epistle of John Expounded in a Series of Lectures* (Edinburgh: Adam and Charles Black, 1866), pp. 32–34.

18. Ibid., p. 33. Four of these items in my list and the idea to express it in this fashion come from Candlish's description of what it means to "walk in darkness."

19. Henry Beard and Christopher Cerf, *The Official Politically Correct Dictionary and Handbook* (New York: Villard, 1992), pp. 82, 87.

20. I. H. Marshall, *The Epistles of John*, New International Commentary (Grand Rapids: Eerdmans, 1978), p. 111 thinks there is no semantic distinction. Others, such as Stephen Smalley, *1, 2, 3 John*, World Biblical Commentary, vol. 51 (Waco, TX: Word, 1984), p. 20 see a distinction between nature and deeds flowing from nature.

21. Spurgeon, *Treasury of the New Testament*, p. 486.

22. So argued by Marshall, *Epistles of John*, pp. 23, 24 and Smalley, *1, 2, 3 John*, p. 24 respectively.

23. See the discussion of "fellowship" in the previous sermon on 1 John 1:1–4.

24. On the subject of hamartiology, and in preparation for preaching 1 John, I would recommend that pastors read the following: John Owen, *Overcoming Sin and Temptation*, eds. Kelly Kapic and Justin Taylor (Wheaton: Crossway, 2006); Bernard Ramm, *Offense to Reason: The Theology of Sin* (San Francisco: Harper & Row, 1985); Cornelius Plantinga, *Not the Way It's Supposed to Be: A Breviary of Sin* (Grand Rapids: Eerdmans, 1995). Good theological analysis, not to mention sermon illustrations, abound!

25. An example of the rhetorical flourish of R. G. Lee's preaching. R. G. Lee, *Heart to Heart* (Nashville: Broadman, 1977), p. 132. Lee was known for studying the dictionary every day and developed a vocabulary unparalleled by most preachers. He was not known as an expositor but was famous for his word pictures and especially for his sermon on Ahab and Jezebel entitled "Payday Someday," which he preached more than 2,000 times before his death.

26. Adapted from Gaston Foote, *How God Helps* (Nashville: Abingdon, 1966), pp. 95, 96.

27. Grace Sherman and John Tuggy, *Semantic and Structural Analysis* (Dallas: Summer Institute of Linguistics, 1994), p. 27. See Louw and Nida, *Greek-English Lexicon*, 88.310.

28. Calvin noted how this verse contradicts Roman Catholic practices such as indulgences and confession to a priest. John Calvin, *The Gospel According to St. John 11–21 & the First Epistle of John*, in *Calvin's New Testament Commentaries*, eds. David Torrance and Thomas Torrance, trans., T. H. L. Parker (Grand Rapids: Eerdmans, 1959), pp. 239, 240.

29. See Spurgeon, *Treasure of the New Testament*, p. 489.

30. See Sherman and Tuggy, *Semantic and Structural Analysis*, p. 27.

31. Interestingly, Jesus uses similar terminology ("not to have sin") four times in John's Gospel: 9:41; 15:22, 24; 19:11.

32. George Morrison, *Morning Sermons* (Grand Rapids, MI: Baker, 1971), p. 125. Morrison (1866–1928) was a Scottish Presbyterian preacher whose sermons are worth your study for insights on effective communication and painting word pictures.

33. Plantinga, *Not the Way It's Supposed to Be*, p. 21.

34. Martin Luther, *The Catholic Epistles*, in *Luther's Works*, vol. 30, ed., Jaroslav Pelikan (St. Louis: Concordia, 1967), p. 236.

35. Gregory the Great wrote the most significant and influential book on pastoral care in the era of the Church Fathers, entitled *The Book of Pastoral Care*. He offered advice to pastors on how to counsel a variety of problems, including the dangers of insincerity and self-deception.

> The insincere are to be admonished to realize how burdensome is the business of duplicity that they guiltily bear. For in the fear of discovery, they ever try to defend themselves even dishonourably, and are ever agitated with fear and apprehension. Now, nothing is more safely defended than sincerity, nothing easier to speak than the truth. But when a man is forced to defend his deceit, his heart is wearied with the toilsome labour of doing so. . . . For commonly, though they are discovered in their fault, they shrink from being known for what they are, and they screen themselves under a vale of deceit. . . . (Gregory I, *The Book of Pastoral Care*, 3.11.)

See also Schaff and Wace, *ANPF*, 12:33.

36. Angel Martinez, *The Fountain of Youth and Other Revival Sermons* (Grand Rapids: Zondervan, 1957), p. 119.

37. Craig Brian Larson, ed., *Contemporary Illustrations for Preachers, Teachers, and Writers* (Grand Rapids: Baker, 1997), p. 98.

38. Wise words from Charles Simeon, *James–Jude*, Expository Outlines on the Whole Bible, vol. 20 (Grand Rapids: Zondervan, 1955), p. 372.

39. "Experience shows that if we think lightly of our past misdoings, they retain their full power to cramp and deprave our later life. Yet assuredly they were not meant to haunt us as ghastly spectres of memory. There is no way out of the contradiction but through a firm belief in God's forgiveness—not His indifference, but His forgiveness, which has power to change the substance of our darkest recollections

by a heavenly chemistry of its own, so that we are sent forth upon our way sorrowful yet always rejoicing." Hort, *Cambridge and Other Sermons*, p. 108.

40. How does the claim of verse 8 differ from verse 10? There are three views: 1) sin nature vs. acts of sin; 2) both are identical claims to have never sinned; 3) the claim in verse 8 denies a person is guilty for committing sin, while in verse 10 the claim is that no sin has been committed since conversion.

41. Looking at the Greek verbal tense from an aspect point of view rather than purely a tense point of view, the perfect tense verb in verse 10 may call special attention to the stative aspect of the verbal action expressed as "we have not sinned." In other words, the perfect tense verb here serves as a way of "grammaticalizing the speaker's conception of the verbal process as a state or condition" (Stanley Porter, *Verbal Aspect in the Greek of the New Testament with Reference to Tense and Mood*, in Studies in Biblical Greek 1 [New York: Peter Lang, 1989], p. 257). Porter is offering the preacher a big boost in interpretation and even in sermonic expression of this concept if one does not get too dizzy from standing on the top rung of his linguistic ladder!

42. Sherman and Tuggy, *Semantic and Structural Analysis*, p. 28.

43. Andrew Persson, *Translator's Notes on 1, 2, 3, John* (Dallas: Summer Institute of Linguistics, 1997), pp. 13–17.

Chapter Three: Jesus Our Advocate at Heaven's Court

1. A great illustration used by A. W. Tozer in his sermon on this text. A. W. Tozer, *Twelve Sermons Relating to the Life and Ministry of the Christian Church*, The Tozer Pulpit, ed. Gerald Smith, vol. 2 (Camp Hill, PA: Christian Publications, 1994), p. 47.

2. So noted by the Anglican Puritan Nathanael Hardy (1618–1670) in a sermon on 1 John 2:2 in *The First General Epistle of St. John the Apostle, Unfolded and Applied* (Edinburgh: James Nichol, 1865), p. 136.

3. F. W. Farrar, *Truths to Live By* (New York: Thomas Whittaker & Bible House, 1903), p. 97.

4. Augustine and Luther took *parakletos* in John 14–16 more in the sense of "comforter" rather than "advocate," but it seems clear that John intends the sense of "advocate" here.

5. William Barclay, *The Letters and the Revelation*, in The New Testament: A New Translation, vol. 2 (London: Collins, 1969), p. 227.

6. A marvelous point made by James Montgomery Boice, *The Epistles of John* (Grand Rapids: Zondervan, 1979), p. 47. Boice was pastor of the Tenth Presbyterian Church in Philadelphia until his death in 2000. He was a gifted preacher and writer. His work on the Johannine letters reads like a combination commentary/sermon and is a valuable resource for preaching John's epistles.

7. The Greek preposition *pros* in the phrase "with the Father" signifies relationship. William Alexander aptly calls this "*pros pictorial*" because it paints the picture of Jesus our Advocate being "face to face" with the Father. (*The Epistles of St. John*, The Expositor's Bible [New York: A. C. Armstrong & Son, 1903], p. 103).

8. Robert Murray McCheyne, *Memoirs and Remains of the Rev. Robert Murray Mc'Cheyne* (Edinburgh: Morrison and Gibbs, 1883), p. 156.

9. Martin Luther, *The Catholic Epistles*, in *Luther's Works*, vol. 30, ed. Jaroslav Pelikan (St. Louis: Concordia, 1967), pp. 235, 236.

10. I have written on this subject elsewhere in "The Extent of the Atonement: Limited or Universal?" in *Whosoever Will: a Biblical-Theological Critique of Five-Point Calvinism*, eds. David L. Allen and Steve Lemke (Nashville: B&H Academic, 2010), pp. 61–107 and in "Preaching for a Great Commission Resurgence," in *Toward a Great Commission Resurgence: Fulfilling God's Mandate in our Time*, eds. Adam Greenway and Chuck Lawless (Nashville: B&H, 2010), pp. 281–298.

11. Otherwise called "particular redemption." This view is held by all five-point Calvinists and all Hyper-Calvinists.

12. A position held by all Moderate Calvinists (four-point Calvinists who reject limited atonement in the sense that Jesus suffered *only* for the sins of the elect), all non-Calvinists, and all Arminians. Not all non-Calvinists are Arminians.

13. When it comes to the question of the *intent* of the atonement, there are two views. Here the question is why God provided atonement in the first place. The first view says that God's *intent* for the atonement was that Jesus should die *equally* for the sins of all people so that everyone is placed in a condition whereby they can be saved from their sin if they believe in Christ. This is the view of most non-Calvinists and all Arminians. The second view says that Jesus died for the sins of all people, but with *unequal* intent. This is the view of Moderate Calvinists. Moderate Calvinists are generally defined as those who adhere to four of the five points of Calvinism with respect to soteriology, the doctrine of salvation. Moderate Calvinists do not agree with their High-Calvinist counterparts that the atonement is limited in its *extent*. They believe that Jesus substituted for the sins of all people. In this they agree with their non-Calvinist counterparts. However, they do believe the atonement is limited in its *intent*.

14. So noted by D. A. Carson, *The Difficult Doctrine of the Love of God* (Wheaton: Crossway, 2000), p. 17. Noted Calvinist R. L. Dabney said:

> In 1 John 2:2, it is at least doubtful whether the express phrase, 'whole world,' can be restrained to the world of the elect as including other than Jews. For it is indisputable, that the Apostle extends the propitiation of Christ beyond those whom he speaks of as 'we,' in verse first. The interpretation described obviously proceeds on the assumption that these are only Jewish believers. Can this be substantiated? Is this catholic epistle addressed only to Jews? This is more than doubtful. It would seem then, that the Apostle's scope is to console and encourage sinning believers with the thought that since Christ made expiation for every man, there is no danger that He will not be found a propitiation for them who, having already believed, now sincerely turn to him from recent sins." R. L. Dabney, *Lectures in Systematic Theology* (Carlisle, PA: Banner of Truth, 2002), p. 525.

Notice in Dabney's statement that he clearly affirms that Christ died for the sins of all people. Simon Kistemaker is correct when he notes that the impression one gets from reading John's letter is that the original readers were mostly Gentile (Kistemaker, *James, Epistles of John, Peter and Jude*, New Testament Commentary [Grand Rapids: Baker, 1995], p. 207). The evidence seems to support at the very least a mix of Jews and Gentiles. This makes it virtually impossible to interpret "our sins" in 1 John 2:2 to refer to Jewish believers alone. Albert Barnes, a moderate Calvinist, wrote, "If he had died only for a part of the race, this language *could not* have been used (*Hebrews–Jude*, Notes on the New Testament, vol. 13 [Grand Rapids: Baker, n.d./reprint of 1884–85 ed.], p. 291).

15. See Martin Culy, *I, II, III John: A Handbook on the Greek Text* (Waco, TX: Baylor University Press, 2004), p. 24.

16. Charles Hodge, one of the foremost thinkers in Reformed theology, rightly said:

> This is what is meant when it is said, or implied in Scripture, that Christ gave Himself as a propitiation, not for our sins only, but for the sins of the whole world. He was a propitiation effectually for the sins of his people, and sufficiently for the sins of the whole world. Augustinians have no need to wrest the Scriptures. They are under no necessity of departing from their fundamental principle that it is the duty of the theologian to subordinate his theories to the Bible, and teach not what seems to him to be true or reasonable, but simply what the Bible teaches." Charles Hodge, *Systematic Theology*, vol. 2 (Grand Rapids: Eerdmans, 1993), pp. 558, 559.

In a sermon from this text preached on December 4, 1859, Charles Hodge noted: "So that no man has a right to say there is no ground for his acquittal, though there may be ground for the acquittal of others. Christ's righteousness is not only of infinite value, but is equally available or suitable for all mankind." (Hodge, *Princeton Sermons* [London: Thomas Nelson & Sons, 1879), p. 51).

Hodge believed that Christ suffered for the sins of all people.

Some may think that Calvin and others taught that Christ *only* suffered for the sins of the elect because they interpret "world" in 1 John 2:2 as limited to the church, following Augustine. However, Jerome Zanchi and Jacob Kimedoncius, first-generation reformers like Calvin, interpret the passage the same way, and yet Richard Muller acknowledges that these two men held to a form of universal redemption, just like Heinrich Bullinger who himself took an unlimited reading of 1 John 2:2. It is therefore important to note that while there may be agreement *in principle* among moderate Calvinists on universal redemption, there may be *practical* differences in terms of their exegesis of specific passages. See p. 82 of my "The Atonement: Limited or Universal?" along with footnote 19 on p. 68 of the same chapter.

17. E. Polhill, "The Divine Will Considered in Its Eternal Decrees," in *The Works of Edward Polhill* (Morgan, PA: Soli Deo Gloria, 1998 reprint), pp. 163, 164.

18. Historically, as well as theologically, "bold proclamation" has been understood to entail the opportunity to tell any and every soul anywhere anytime that Christ died for his or her sins according to the Scriptures.

19. The preacher will need to decide how much of the theological debate over the extent of the atonement to explain to the people in a sermon. I would not recommend more detail on the subject than I have given here. Some will no doubt think I have given too much. On the other hand, people need to know something about the subject of the extent of the atonement. The main thing is that we should be as fair as possible to both views when we deal with a passage on the extent of the atonement in our preaching. At the very least, whatever our own interpretation is, we need to make our hearers aware of the other view.

20. J. C. Ryle, *Expository Thoughts on the Gospel*, vol. 3 (Grand Rapids: Baker, 1979), p. 186.

21. J. Stuart Holden, *Chapter by Chapter Through the Bible: Expository and Devotional Comments*, vol. 4 (London: Marshall Brothers, n.d.), p. 272.

22. James Denney, *The Way Everlasting* (London: Hodder and Stoughton), p. 296.

23. Ibid., p. 298.

24. Ibid., p. 305.

25. Luther, *The Catholic Epistles*, p. 237.

Chapter Four: The "Know So" Test

1. Adrian Rogers, *What Every Christian Ought to Know* (Nashville: B&H, 2005), p. 29.

2. Robert Yarbrough, *1–3 John*, Baker Exegetical Commentary on the New Testament (Grand Rapids: Baker, 2008), p. 84. On the significance of the perfect tense, Zerwick said that the perfect tense "is not a past tense but a present one, indicating not the past action as such but the present 'state of affairs' resulting from the past action." Maximilian Zerwick, *Biblical Greek: Illustrated by Examples* (Rome: Scripta Pontificii Instituti Biblici, 1963), p. 96.

3. Louis Albert Banks, *John and His Friends: A Series of Revival Sermons* (New York: Funk & Wagnalls, 1899), p. 66.

4. F. W. Danker, ed., *A Greek-English Lexicon of the New Testament and Other Early Christian Literature*, 3rd ed. (Chicago: University of Chicago Press, 2000), p. 1002. The verb is not the ordinary verb, *phulassein*, "to keep," but *tēreō*, "to keep watch over; guard."

5. F. W. Farrar, *Truths to Live By* (New York: Thomas Whittaker & Bible House, 1903), pp. 118, 119.

6. B. H. Carroll, *An Interpretation of the English Bible*, vol. 16 (Nashville: Broadman Press, 1913), p. 315. Carroll was the founder and first president of Southwestern Baptist Theological Seminary in Fort Worth, Texas. A crack shot with a firearm, he was a member of the Texas Rangers, the famous law enforcement outfit founded prior to Texas's statehood.

7. Charles Sylvester Horne, "A Letter to Children," in *The Kensington Congregational Pulpit*, vol. 2, no. 5 (South Kensington, London: Callard, Stewart & Watt, 1901), p. 56.

8. Interestingly, John will use this same logic in 2:15–17 when he says it is impossible to love God and the world at the same time.

9. Rob Lacey, *The Word on the Street* (Grand Rapids: Zondervan, 2004), p. 461.

10. As in the title of Dale Carnegie's famous book *How to Win Friends and Influence People*.

11. Farrar, *Truths to Live By*, pp. 119, 120.

12. For a thorough study of John's use of "love" in his epistles, see Ceslaus Spicq, *Agape in the Gospel, Epistles, and Apocalypse of John*, in *Agape in the New Testament*, 3 vols., vol. 1 (St. Louis and London: B. Herder Book Co., 1966), 3–56. See also Leon Morris, *Testaments of Love: A Study of Love in the Bible* (Grand Rapids: Eerdmans, 1981) for a helpful study of "love" in the New Testament. It is well

indexed by topic, author, and Scripture references. Another very helpful work is Peter Kreeft, *Knowing the Truth of God's Love* (Ann Arbor, MI: Servant Books, 1988).

13. F. W. Danker, ed., "teleiow," *A Greek-English Lexicon*, pp. 996, 997.

14. Leon Morris, *Testaments of Love*, p. 161.

15. Paraphrased from Farrar, *Truths to Live By*, pp. 128, 130–133.

16. John Flavel, "Of the Imitation of Christ in Holiness of Life, and the Necessity of It in Believers," *The Method of Grace in the Gospel of Redemption*, The Works of John Flavel, vol. 2 (Edinburgh: The Banner of Truth Trust, 1997 reprint), p. 399. This is Flavel's sermon on 1 John 2:6.

17. Ibid.

18. Charles M. Sheldon, *In His Steps* (Chicago: Advance Publishing Co., 1899). See also Charles Sheldon, *In His Steps* (Grand Rapids: Zondervan, 1967 reprint). Sheldon's novel was subtitled "What Would Jesus Do?" Though published a hundred years earlier, this novel helped spawn the WWJD (What Would Jesus Do?) frenzy back in the 1990s, which also included a 2010 movie by the same title. Janie Tinklenberg designed the first WWJD bracelet in 1989. Ten years later, the bracelet was selling at a rate one million per month.

Chapter Five: All You Need Is Love

1. F. W. Danker, ed., "αγαπɔ," *A Greek-English Lexicon of the New Testament and Other Early Christian Literature*, 3rd ed. (Chicago: University of Chicago Press, 2000), pp. 5–7; Colin Brown, "Love," *Dictionary of New Testament Theology*, vol. 2, ed. Colin Brown (Grand Rapids: Zondervan, 1976), pp. 538–551.

2. See the excellent book by D. A. Carson, *Love in Hard Places* (Wheaton: Crossway, 2002), pp. 16, 17.

3. The word is *neos* in Greek. See Danker, *Greek-English Lexicon*, p. 669.

4. The word is *kairos* in Greek. See ibid., pp. 497, 498.

5. A less likely but possible meaning is Calvin's suggestion: "He says *new* because God as it were daily renews it by suggesting it, so that believers may exercise themselves in it throughout their whole lives." John Calvin, *The Gospel According to St. John 11–21 & The First Epistle of John*, in *Calvin's New Testament Commentaries*, eds. David Torrance and Thomas Torrance, trans. T. H. L. Parker (Grand Rapids: Eerdmans, 1959), p. 248.

6. Ibid., p. 249.

7. See Martin Culy, *I, II, III John: A Handbook on the Greek Text* (Waco, TX: Baylor University Press, 2004), p. 32.

8. The tense of the verb in Greek is imperfect and may connote repeated action in the past.

9. Carson, *Love in Hard Places*, p. 60.

10. Ibid., p. 61.

11. Jerry Vines, *Exploring 1, 2, 3 John* (Neptune, NJ: Loizeaux, 1989), p. 56.

12. F. W. Boreham, *A Tuft of Comet's Hair* (London: Epworth, 1927), p. 12. Boreham was an Australian Baptist pastor who wrote fifty-five books and was a household name in the first half of the twentieth century. He was known for his masterful word crafting and his marvelous illustrations. He was once introduced to a gathering of preachers in Edinburgh, Scotland as "the man whose name is on all our lips, whose books are on all our shelves, and whose illustrations are in all our sermons."

13. William Barclay, *The Letters of John and Jude*, rev. ed. (Philadelphia: Westminster, 1976), pp. 47, 48.

14. Charles Spurgeon used this pungent metaphor in one of his sermons on 1 John. Spurgeon, *The Treasury of the New Testament*, vol. 4 (Grand Rapids: Zondervan, 1950), p. 581.

15. Clarence Macartney, *You Can Conquer* (Nashville: Abingdon, 1954), p. 31.

16. Craig Brian Larson, *Contemporary Illustrations for Preachers, Teachers, and Writers* (Grand Rapids: Baker, 1996), p. 240. Some have questioned the accuracy of this story and similar accounts. See http://pascalfroissart.online.fr/3-cache/1994-leventhal.pdf.

17. Macartney, *You Can Conquer*, p. 22.

Chapter Six: Family Secrets

1. So Calvin, *The Gospel According to John 11–21 and The First Epistle of John*, trans. by T. H. L. Parker (Grand Rapids: Eerdmans, 1959), p. 251.

2. So taken by James M. Boice, *The Epistles of John* (Grand Rapids: Zondervan, 1979), pp. 72, 73.

3. See David Black, *Using New Testament Greek* (Grand Rapids: Baker, 1993), pp. 80, 81; and Duane Watson, "1 John 2:12–14 as *Distributio, Conduplutio,* and *Expolitio*: A Rhetorical Understanding," *Journal for the Study of the New Testament* 35 (1989), pp. 97–110.

4. See Robert Yarbrough, *1–3 John*, Baker Exegetical Commentary on the New Testament (Grand Rapids: Baker, 2008), p. 115. Yarbrough's explanation for the shift makes good sense: "The first-person present form of *graphō* . . . is used to convey a relatively higher degree of feelings and urgency. . . . My translation 'The reason I am writing' attempts to express in English the gist of John's direct, personal, and emphatic tone" p. 121.

5. John uses the Greek conjunction *hoti* six times in these three verses. The key question is whether he intends to be declarative ("I write that . . . ") or causal ("I write because . . . "). The latter is the intended meaning and actually includes the former sense. See ibid., pp. 120, 121.

6. The Greek word for forgiveness, *aphiēmi*, means "to release from legal or moral obligation or consequence, *cancel, remit, pardon*" (F. W. Danker, ed., "afihmi," *A Greek-English Lexicon of the New Testament and Other Early Christian Literature*, 3rd ed. [Chicago: University of Chicago Press, 2000], p. 156). When God forgives our sins, it is a release from our legal and moral obligation to pay for our sins as well as a release from the consequences of our sin, which are spiritual death and eternal punishment.

7. Don't miss the wonderful sermon preached in 1854 on this text by Henry Melvill, "God's Glory in the Forgiveness of Sin for His Name's Sake," *One Hundred Sermons by Rev. Henry Melvill, with Thirty-Seven Sermons by Other Ministers,* three volumes in one (London: The Pulpit Office, Glasshouse Yard, Blackfriars, n. d.), pp. 185–192.

8. Gerald Mann, *When One Day at a Time Is Too Long* (Austin, TX: Riverbend Press, 1994), p. 268.

9. Charles Sylvester Horne, "A Letter to Children," in *The Kensington Congregational Pulpit*, vol. 2, no. 5 (South Kensington, London: Callard, Stewart & Watt,

1901), pp. 56, 57. The illustration occurs in Horne's sermon to children based on this text.

10. Three things are in order here. First, we must resist the efforts of those who would attempt to foist an agenda-driven gender inclusivism on a text of Scripture where such is not warranted by the text itself. Second, we must remember that the Greek masculine participle semantically encodes gender inclusivity when used generically and when the context clearly supports such. Third, preachers need to make clear to their hearers that here in 1 John 2:12–14, women are not excluded from what John is saying. This is further made clear by the fact that all of John's readers, regardless of gender, are included under his first rubric "little children."

11. See F. W. Danker, ed., "paidion," *Greek-English Lexicon*, p. 749: "One who is treasured in a way a parent treasures a child. . . . as a form of familiar address on the part of a respected person, who feels himself on terms of fatherly intimacy with those whom he addresses."

12. For an example of a topical sermon appended to this text that in no way offers exposition of the text itself or is connected to the text in any way (in fact, the sermon never references the text beyond its listing under the sermon title), see Henry Ward Beecher, "A Sermon to Young Men," *Forty-Eight Sermons*, vol. 1 (London: R. D. Dickinson, 1871), pp. 39–53. This sermon is also reprinted in *Newman to Robertson*, in A *Treasury of Great Preaching*, vol. 4, eds. Clyde Fant and William Pinson (Dallas: Word, 1971, 1995), pp. 304–316, though I know not why.

13. I have an in-depth discussion of these matters in my *Hebrews*, New American Commentary, vol. 35 (Nashville: B&H, 2010), pp. 96–115.

Chapter Seven: Don't Decorate Your Cell

1. Warren Wiersbe, *Be Real* (Wheaton: Victor Books, 1985), p. 65.

2. Present imperative with the negative particle *mē* indicates a command to stop an action already in progress.

3. Charles Simeon, *James–Jude*, Expository Outlines on the Whole Bible, vol. 20 (Grand Rapids: Zondervan, 1955), p. 399.

4. F. W. Danker, ed., "κοσμος," *A Greek-English Lexicon of the New Testament and Early Christian Literature* (Chicago: University of Chicago Press, 2000), pp. 561–563.

5. Ibid., "αγαπə," pp. 6, 7.

6. Eloquently stated by the blind bard of Scotland, the gifted preacher George Matheson, *Thoughts For Life's Journey* (New York: Hodder & Stoughton, 1907), pp. 213, 214.

7. These examples represent my slight variation of those given by David Tappan, *Sermons on Important Subjects* (Boston: W. Hilliard and Lincoln & Edmands, 1807), pp. 152–156. This is a sermon on 1 John 2:15–17 worth reading today from one of the most prolific writers in America in the eighteenth century. Tappan was a pastor for eighteen years in Newbury and then Harvard Professor of Divinity until his death.

8. The genitive phrase is objective. There is an understood subject, "our," the word "love" is an event noun, and the object of our love is "the Father."

9. Augustine, *Homilies on First John*, II.11, in *Nicene and Post-Nicene Fathers*, vol. 7, ed. Phillip Schaff (Edinburgh: T&T Clark/Grand Rapids: Eerdmans, 1956),

p. 473. Also in F. W. Farrar, *Truths to Live By: A Companion to Everyday Christian Life* (New York: Thomas Whittaker Bible House, 1903), p. 156.

10. The genitive phrase in Greek is subjective: the flesh is doing the lusting. This phrase is an example of metonymy, a figure of speech that in this case substitutes the desire for the object of the desire. See E. W. Bullinger, *Figures of Speech Used in the Bible: Explained and Illustrated* (Grand Rapids: Baker, 1968 reprint), p. 601.

11. The word is *epithumia* in Greek, a compound word composed of the preposition *epi* ("upon") and *thumos* ("heat"). The word connotes "heat upon heat" and suggests the notion of being "hot after something."

12. William Barclay, *The Letters of John and Jude*, rev. ed. (Philadelphia: Westminster, 1976), p. 57.

13. John Calvin, *The Gospel According to St. John 11–21 & the First Epistle of John*, in *Calvin's New Testament Commentaries*, eds. David Torrance and Thomas Torrance, trans. T. H. L. Parker (Grand Rapids: Eerdmans, 1959), p. 254.

14. Richard Sibbes, "The Pattern of Purity," in *Miscellaneous Sermons and Indices*, Works of Richard Sibbes, vol. 7, ed. Alexander Grosart (Edinburgh: The Banner of Truth Trust, 1982 reprint), p. 514.

15. The genitive phrase is subjective; it is the eyes doing the lusting.

16. C. S. Lewis, *The Four Loves* (New York: Harcourt Brace Jovanovich, 1960), pp. 38, 39.

17. The genitive phrase is objective; it is our boastful desire for life's status.

18. William Barclay, *New Testament Words* (Philadelphia: Westminster, 1964), p. 47. Barclay's treatment of this word is the best I've seen. Don't miss it!

19. Farrar, *Truths to Live By*, pp. 157, 158.

20. Warren Wiersbe, ed., *Treasury of the World's Greatest Sermons* (Grand Rapids: Kregel, 1977), p. 81.

21. W. J. Dawson, *The Threshold of Manhood* (New York: Fleming H. Revell, 1909), p. 89.

22. Illustration used by Alexander Maclaren in a sermon on this text in *The God of the Amen* (New York: Funk and Wagnalls, 1891), p. 253.

23. Jerry Vines, *Exploring 1, 2, 3 John* (Neptune, NJ: Loizeaux, 1989), p. 72.

24. D. L. Moody, *Anecdotes, Incidents and Illustrations* (Chicago: The Bible Institute Colportage Association, 1898), pp. 26, 27.

25. Calvin, *First Epistle of John*, p. 255.

26. Phraseology taken from a sermon on this text by Alexander Maclaren, *The God of the Amen*, p. 250.

27. "You may narrow your life down till you become contented with it in its narrowness, just as the prisoner, long imprisoned, forgets the green, bright world outside and the singing of the lark, and at last is content with his cell, and even comforts himself that his cell is better than another next to him; and so because there is a lower depth still opening which he has not yet reached, he is happy in his narrow world, and congratulates himself on his imprisonment." Dawson, *The Threshold of Manhood*, p. 101.

28. "Choose, therefore, the will of God as the supreme law of your life, and devotion to the supreme, will deliver you from the cramping influences of the merely secondary, into the large liberty of that Kingdom whose subjects 'abide forever.'"

J. Stuart Holden, *Redeeming Vision* (London: Robert Scott), p. 208. (From Holden's sermon on 1 John 2:15–17.)

29. John Bunyan, *Pilgrim's Progress* (Grand Rapids: Baker, 1984 reprint), pp. 108–121.

30. Dawson, *The Threshold of Manhood*, p. 84.

31. The Hebrew phrase is *hebel habelim*, where the doubling of the word is the Hebrew way of expressing the superlative. "Super-vanity" with an exclamation point is Solomon's point. Everything individually and all things together that constitute "the world" are classed as "vanity," and the Hebrew word connotes a vapor, a wisp of smoke, emptiness, nothingness, zero, zilch, *nada*, what's left after you pop a soap bubble, etc.

32. Essentially paraphrased from Thomas Chalmers's famous sermon on 1 John 2:15–17, "The Expulsive Power of a New Affection," in *The Works of Thomas Chalmers: Complete in One Volume* (Philadelphia: J. Towar, and D. M. Hogan, 1830), pp. 381–388; as well as "The Expulsive Power of a New Affection," *Wesley to Finney 1703–1875*, in *A Treasury of Great Preaching*, eds. William Pinson and Clyde Fant, vol. 3 (Dallas: Word, 1971), pp. 300–307.

33. See Alexander Maclaren, *After the Resurrection* (London: Hodder and Stoughton, 1902), pp. 148–152 for this rhetorical flourish on unfulfilled desires in his sermon on this text, which I have adapted somewhat.

34. Craig Larson, ed., *Contemporary Illustrations for Preachers, Teachers, and Writers* (Grand Rapids: Baker, 1996), p. 283.

35. Lewis, *The Four Loves*, p. 190.

Chapter Eight: Liar! Liar!

1. Martin Luther, *The Catholic Epistles*, in *Luther's Works*, vol. 30, ed. Jaroslav Pelikan (St. Louis, Concordia, 1967), pp. 252, 253.

2. Zane Hodges argued that to interpret "us" in the statement "they went out from us" as simply "us Christians" distorts the text. The antichrists had not left the churches; that is why there was a problem in the first place. Hodges noted the parallel of this phrase in verse 19 with the exact same phrase in Greek in Acts 15:24. Here the legalists (Judaizers) are said to be some who "went out from us." Thus Hodges thinks it is better to understand verse 19 as indicating a schism that had already occurred between the antichrists (false teachers) and the apostolic circle.

3. Robert Yarbrough, *1–3 John*, Baker Exegetical Commentary on the New Testament (Grand Rapids: Baker, 2008), p. 145.

4. See Andreas Köstenberger and Michael J. Kruger, *The Heresy of Orthodoxy* (Wheaton: Crossway, 2010), p. 97: "In sum, the secessionists seem to have rejected the apostolic witness, including that borne by John's Gospel (1 John 1:1–5); denied that Jesus was the Messiah (1 John 2:22–23); and most likely also denied the atonement rendered by Christ (1 John 5:6). It is unclear whether they were Gnostics, whether followers of Cerinthus or Docetists or some other variety or early gnosis, or simply people (Jews) who denied that Jesus was the Messiah."

5. J. B. Cranfill, ed., *Sermons and Life Sketch of B. H. Carroll* (Philadelphia: American Baptist Publication Society, 1893), pp. 13–23.

6. James M. Boice, *The Epistles of John* (Grand Rapids: Zondervan, 1979), p. 87.

7. On the subject of anointing in Scripture, consult Leland Ryken, James Wilhoit, and Tremper Longman III, eds., *Dictionary of Biblical Imagery* (Downers Grove, IL: InterVarsity Press, 1998), pp. 33, 34. For a good summary of the Biblical teaching on anointing, see Jerry Vines, *Spirit Works: Charismatic Practices and the Bible* (Nashville, B&H, 1999), pp. 100–106 and F. E. Marsh, *Emblems of the Holy Spirit* (Grand Rapids: Kregel, 1957), pp. 70–91. For John's specific use of the term "anointing" in 1 John 2:20 and again in verse 27, see Gary Burge, *The Anointed Community: The Holy Spirit in the Johannine Tradition* (Grand Rapids: Eerdmans, 1987), pp. 174, 175.

8. So rightly interpreted by Augustine in his sermon on this passage, but then wrongly equated by him with the Eucharist. Augustine, *Homilies on the First Epistle of John*, 3.5, *Nicene and Post-Nicene Fathers*, vol. 7, ed. Phillip Schaff (Edinburgh: T&T Clark/Grand Rapids: Eerdmans, 1956), p. 480.

9. See David Black, "An Overlooked Stylistic Argument in Favor of *panta* in 1 John 2:20," *Filologia Neotestamentaria* 5 (1992), pp. 205–208.

10. Adapted from F. E. Marsh, *Emblems of the Holy Spirit*, pp. 75–77. See the helpful chart on John's use of "know" (*oida*) in 1 John in Robert Yarbrough, *1–3 John*, p. 151.

11. Wisely noted by Boice, *Epistles of John*, p. 83.

12. Jerry Vines, *Exploring 1, 2, 3 John* (Neptune, NJ: Loizeaux, 1989), pp. 88, 89.

13. F. W. Farrar, *Truths to Live By: A Companion to "Everyday Christian Life"* (New York: Thomas Whittaker, 1903), pp. 170.

14. Ibid., p. 179.

15. For example, see the New American Standard Bible.

Chapter Nine: The Unction Function

1. For a presentation on the openness of God by those who advocate it, consult Clark Pinnock, Richard Rice, John Sanders, William Hasker, and David Basinger, *The Openness of God: A Biblical Challenge to the Traditional Understanding of God* (Downers Grove, IL: InterVarsity Press, 1994) and John Sanders, *The God Who Risks: A Theology of Divine Providence*, rev. ed. (Downers Grove, IL: InterVarsity Press, 2007). For a rebuttal of this position, see the excellent work by Bruce Ware, *God's Lesser Glory* (Wheaton: Crossway, 2000) and also John Frame, *No Other God: A Response to Open Theism* (Phillipsburg, NJ: P&R Publishing, 2001).

2. Steve Chalke and Alan Mann, *The Lost Message of Jesus* (Grand Rapids: Zondervan, 2003), p. 182. Brian MacLaren made the same accusation in *The Story We Find Ourselves In: Further Adventures of a New Kind of Christian* (San Francisco: Jossey-Bass, 2003), p. 102ff. This critique of the Biblical doctrine of penal substitution is well answered in a number of places, one of the best of which is Steve Jeffery, Michael Ovey, and Andrew Sach, *Pierced for Our Transgressions: Rediscovering the Glory of Penal Substitution* (Wheaton: Crossway, 2007), especially pp. 228–233.

3. See, for example, Earnest Campbell, "A Lover's Quarrel with Preaching," in *What's the Matter with Preaching Today?*, ed. Mike Graves (Louisville: Westminster/John Knox, 2004), p. 52, where Campbell (former Professor of Preaching at Garrett Evangelical Theological Seminary) writes: "I believe that while Jesus is the

only way for us, he is not necessarily the only way for others. The Great Commission needs to be revisited in a pluralistic age. True, Jesus said, 'No one comes to the Father except through me' (John 14:6), but he did not say that the Father comes to no one save through the Son. God is not a prisoner of the incarnation. . . . It is preposterous and indefensible to deny the possibility of salvation to the billions who share this planet with us but do not share our faith."

4. The Greek grammar itself probably indicates this. See Daniel B. Wallace, *Greek Grammar Beyond the Basics: An Exegetical Syntax of the New Testament* (Grand Rapids: Zondervan, 1996), p. 372. Robert Yarbrough takes it this way in *1–3 John*, Baker Exegetical Commentary on the New Testament (Grand Rapids: Baker, 2008), p 166.

5. See F. E. Marsh, *Emblems of the Holy Spirit* (Grand Rapids: Kregel, 1971), pp. 69–91. In this chapter Marsh identifies fourteen things specifically stated in Scripture that someone is anointed to: honor, sanctification, minister, see, know, do good, stand, rule, receive, save physical life, healing, preach, victory, and die. Of the more than fifty books authored by W. A. Criswell, pastor for more than fifty years of First Baptist Church in Dallas, Texas, *The Holy Spirit in Today's World* is the fruit of a series of sermons he preached on the subject back in the late 1960s. Well-balanced and Biblically solid, though out of print, this book is a helpful resource to pastors on the subject of the Holy Spirit. Two other excellent works include Sinclair Ferguson, *The Holy Spirit*, Contours of Christian Theology (Downers Grove, IL: InterVarsity Press, 1996) and James Hamilton, *God's Indwelling Presence: The Holy Spirit in the Old and New Testaments*, NAC Studies in Bible and Theology, ed. Ray Clendenen (Nashville, B&H Academic, 2006).

6. Luther made this point well in his lectures on 1 John. Martin Luther, *The Catholic Epistles*, Luther's Works, vol. 30, ed. Jaroslav Pelikan (St. Louis: Concordia, 1967), pp. 262, 263.

7. J. B. Phillips, *Plain Christianity* (New York: Macmillan, 1954), p. 70.

8. This report draws information from four nationwide telephone interviews conducted by The Barna Group, each including between 1,002 to 1,005 adults randomly selected, during the years 1995, 2000, 2005, and 2008. The range of sampling error associated with a survey of 1,000 people is ±1.5 to ±3.5 percentage points at the 95 percent confidence level. Each of the surveys utilized minimal statistical weighting to calibrate the aggregate sample to known population percentages in relation to several key demographic variables. All interviews were conducted among a sampling of adults in the forty-eight continental states (http://www.barna.org/barna-update/article/21-transformation/252-barna-survey-examines-changes-in-world-view-among-christians-over-the-past-13-years). Doug Groothuis, *Truth Decay: Defending Christianity Against the Challenges of Postmodernism* (Downers Grove, IL: InterVarsity Press, 2000) is one of my favorite books dealing with this subject. A very helpful book for pastors.

9. I recommend John MacArthur's *Charismatic Chaos* (Grand Rapids: Zondervan, 1992) as an excellent resource that evaluates charismatic excesses in light of Scripture. See especially pp. 47–65 on the question of whether God gives direct revelation today. On 1 John 2:27, see p. 96.

10. On the illuminating work of the Holy Spirit, see Millard Erickson, *Christian Doctrine*, 2nd ed. (Grand Rapids: Baker, 1998), pp. 889, 890 and Wayne Gru-

dem, *Systematic Theology: An Introduction to Biblical Doctrine* (Grand Rapids: Zondervan, 1994), pp. 644, 645. The Puritan John Owen has written extensively on this subject as well: John Owen, *A Discourse Concerning the Holy Spirit*, vols. 3, 4, The Works of John Owen, ed. William Goold (Edinburgh: Banner of Truth, 1967 reprint).

11. Jerry Vines, *Spirit Works* (Nashville: B&H, 1999), p. 43. Every pastor should read Vines's chapter "The Unction Function" in that book, pp. 96–106, which deals Biblically with the subject of anointing.

12. James Beverly, *Holy Laughter and the Toronto Blessing* (Grand Rapids: Zondervan, 1995), p. 193.

13. Vines, *Spirit Works*, p. 70. These five tests are found at the end of each chapter in Vines's *Spirit Works*, an excellent book that examines the modern-day charismatic movement in Christianity. In addition to MacArthur's *Charismatic Chaos* listed above in footnote 9, see also Hank Hanegraff, *Counterfeit Revival* (Nashville: Thomas Nelson, 2001).

14. Yarbrough, *1–3 John*, p. 168.

Chapter Ten: Ready or Not, Here I Come!

1. That verse 28 is the beginning of a new paragraph is confirmed by Grace Sherman and John Tuggy, *A Semantic and Structural Analysis of the Johannine Epistles* (Dallas: Summer Institute of Linguistics, 1994), pp. 53, 54 and Martin Culy, *I, II, III John: A Handbook on the Greek Text* (Waco, TX: Baylor University Press, 2004), p. 61. Hence I have chosen to present two sermons rather than one on the short paragraphs 2:26, 27 and 2:28, 29.

2. J. P. Louw and E. Nida, eds., *Greek-English Lexicon of the New Testament Based on Semantic Domains*, vol. 1 (New York: United Bible Societies, 1988), p. 307 define the word as "a state of boldness and confidence, sometimes implying intimidating circumstances."

3. Yarbrough is correct that the repetition of the imperative "to abide" likely suggests that we are at the "rhetorical center" of this section. *1–3 John*, Baker Exegetical Commentary on the New Testament (Grand Rapids: Baker, 2008), p. 169.

4. Daniel Akin, *1, 2, 3 John*, New American Commentary, vol. 38 (Nashville: B&H, 2001), p. 128.

5. For an excellent overview of this subject, consult Lamar Cooper, "The Second Coming of the Messiah in the Old Testament," *The Return of Christ: A Premillennial Perspective*, eds. David L. Allen and Steve Lemke (Nashville: B&H Academic, 2011), pp. 160–205.

6. Roy B. Zuck, *A Biblical Theology of the New Testament*, electronic edition (Chicago: Moody Press, 1994), 237.

7. *The NET Bible* has a helpful footnote on John's meaning here. "The verb γεννάω (*gennaō*) presents a translation problem: (1) should the passive be translated archaically 'be begotten' (the action of the male parent; see BDAG 193 s.v. 1.a) or (2) should it be translated 'be born' (as from a female parent; see BDAG 194 s.v. 2)? A number of modern translations (RSV, NASB, NIV) have opted for the latter, but (3) the imagery expressed in 1 John 3:9 clearly refers to the action of the male parent in procreating a child, as does 5:1 ('everyone who loves the father loves the child fathered by him'), and so a word reflecting the action of the male parent is called for

here. The contemporary expression 'fathered by' captures this idea." *The NET Bible* (Richardson, TX: Biblical Studies Press, 2001), p. 2281.

8. From the distinction between *oida* and *ginōskō*. See A.T. Robertson, *The General Epistles and the Revelation of John*, Word Pictures in the New Testament, vol. 6 (Nashville: Broadman, 1933), p. 219. "If you know by intuitive or absolute knowledge that Christ (because of verse 28) is righteous, then 'ye know,' or 'know ye' (*ginōskete* either indicative or imperative) by experimental knowledge (so *ginōskō* means in contrast with *oida*)."

9. A picturesque metaphor by Louis Albert Banks, *John and His Friends: A Series of Revival Sermons* (New York: Funk & Wagnalls, 1899), p. 100.

Chapter Eleven: Who's Your Daddy?

1. Charles Spurgeon, *Treasury of the New Testament*, vol. 4 (Grand Rapids: Zondervan, 1950), p. 520.

2. Gaston Foote, *How God Helps* (Nashville: Abingdon, 1966), p. 121.

3. Adapted from Alexander Maclaren, *Ephesians, Epistles of Peter, Epistles of John*, in *Expositions of Holy Scriptures*, vol. 16 (Grand Rapids: Eerdmans, 1944), pp. 291, 292. Maclaren was a contemporary of Spurgeon who pastored a Baptist church in Manchester, England and whose sermons are always worth reading for their expositional content. His multi-volume *Expositions of Holy Scripture* should be on every pastor's bookshelf.

4. The verb is in the perfect tense.

5. F. W. Farrar, *Truths to Live By* (New York: Thomas Whittaker, 1903), p. 188.

6. C. S. Lewis, *The Screwtape Letters & Screwtape Proposes a Toast* (New York: Macmillan, 1962), p. 17.

7. Spurgeon, *Treasury of the New Testament*, p. 523.

8. Maclaren, *Epistles of John*, p. 301.

9. Ibid., p. 307.

10. Adapted from a sermon preached in 1853 by Henry Melvill, *One Hundred Sermons by the Rev. Henry Melvill* (London: The Pulpit Office, Glasshouse Yard, Blackfriars, n.d.), p. 178.

11. From the hymn "It Belongs Not to My Care," with lyrics by the Puritan Richard Baxter, written in 1681.

12. E. V. Hill, *A Savior Worth Having* (Chicago: Moody Press, 2002), pp. 128–130.

13. Thomas Brooks, *The Complete Works of Thomas Brooks*, ed. Alexander Grosart, vol. 2 (Edinburgh: James Nichol/New York: AMS Press, 1978 reprint of 1866–1867 edition), p. 510. "In quality, though not in equality, *as* is not a note of parility or equality, but of resemblance and similitude: as there is a similitude betwixt the face itself and the image of the face in the glass, but no equality."

14. Rob Lacey, *The Word on the Street* (Grand Rapids: Zondervan, 2004), p. 462.

15. Samuel Davies, "The Nature and Blessedness of Sonship With God," *Sermons of the Rev. Samuel Davies*, vol. 2 (Morgan, PA: Soli Deo Gloria, 1993 reprint), p. 182.

16. Craig Larsen, ed., *Contemporary Illustrations for Preachers, Teachers and Writers* (Grand Rapids: Zondervan, 1996), p. 254.

17. Ibid., p. 208.

18. See James Morrison, *Morrison on James Through Revelation*, The Glasgow Pulpit Series, rev. and ed. Joan Zodhiates (Chattanooga: AMG Publishers, 1984), p. 59.

19. In the *New York Times* bestseller *Heaven Is for Real,* Colton Burpo, four years old at the time of his near-death experience, describes "sitting beside the Holy Spirit" when his paternal great-grandfather, "Pop," walked up to him. While in Heaven, Colton supposedly saw John the Baptist, many different animals, and thousands of colors not known on earth. Colton described all of the people (himself included) as having wings. He claims that he sat in Jesus' lap and that Jesus helped him with his homework. Todd Burpo, *Heaven Is For Real: A Little Boy's Astounding Story of His Trip to Heaven and Back* (Nashville: Thomas Nelson, 2010). Two other works that bring Biblical truth to bear on this subject worth your perusal are Doug Groothuis, *Deceived by the Light* (Eugene, OR: Harvest House, 1995) and William Alnor, *Heaven Can't Wait: A Survey of Alleged Trips to the Other Side* (Grand Rapids: Baker, 1996).

20. Philip Yancey, "John Donne: As He Lay Dying," *Reality and the Vision*, ed. Philip Yancey (Dallas: Word, 1990), pp. 185, 186. See also the recent biography by John Stubbs, *John Donne: The Reformed Soul* (New York: W. W. Norton, 2006), pp. 445-474.

21. A great point expressed in a memorable turn of phrase by James M. Boice, *The Epistles of John* (Grand Rapids: Zondervan, 1979), p. 101.

22. A good point made by Farrar, *Truths to Live By*, p. 199.

23. John Calvin, *The Gospel According to St. John 11–21 & the First Epistle of John*, in *Calvin's New Testament Commentaries*, eds. David Torrance and Thomas Torrance, trans. T. H. L. Parker (Grand Rapids: Eerdmans, 1959), p. 268.

24. As stressed by Charles Simeon, *James–Jude*, Expository Outlines on the Whole Bible, vol. 20 (Grand Rapids: Zondervan, 1955), p. 426.

25. Hill, *A Savior Worth Having*, pp. 127, 128, developed this analogy using a Reggie Jackson home run as an illustration.

26. See the helpful studies by K. Inman, "Distinctive Johannine Vocabulary and the Interpretation of 1 John 3:9," *Westminster Theological Journal* 40 (1977–78), pp. 136–144 and S. M. Baugh, *A First John Reader: Intermediate Greek Reading Notes and Grammar* (Phillipsburg, NJ: P&R, 1999), pp. 50–52. D. Wallace may be correct in his assertions that the present tense verbs in this section of the letter are gnomic, expressing timeless truths (D. Wallace, *Greek Grammar Beyond the Basics* [Grand Rapids: Zondervan, 1996], p. 525). James M. Boice succinctly summarizes seven views on this thorny passage, coming down on the view I have advocated above (Boice, *Epistles of John*, pp. 107–109). Zane Hodges's critique of the view I have taken in this sermon is trenchant and should be given serious consideration, but his own proposal scarcely can be accepted: our "inward self" cannot sin because it has been regenerated. Zane Hodges, *The Epistles of John* (Denton, TX: Grace Evangelical Society, 1999), pp. 140–144.

27. An excellent illustration by Evan Hopkins, *The Law of Liberty in the Spiritual Life* (London: Marshall, Morgan and Scott, 1952), pp. 25, 26.

28. William Barclay, *The Letter of John and Jude*, rev. ed. (Philadelphia: Westminster, 1976), pp. 77, 78.

29. For a different approach to the meaning of 3:4–9, consult Colin Kruse, "Sin and Perfection in 1 John," *Australian Biblical Review* 51 (2003): pp. 60–70. Kruse suggests that the key to the problem is found in the meaning of the Greek word *anomia* ("lawlessness") in verse 4. Sin is viewed here not as a violation of the Mosaic law (notice the absence of *nomos*, the normal word in reference to the Mosaic law), but rather as rebellion against God that is similar to Satan's rebellion against God; hence the references to Satan in this passage. In other words, children of God do sometimes commit sins, as John has previously pointed out, but they cannot commit the sin of rebellion (*anomia*), which is the sin of the devil. If they do, such is evidence they are not children of God but children of the devil. One problem with this approach lies in how one defines *rebellion*. What criteria could be used to measure whether sin rises to the level of rebellion against God? In one sense, all sin is rebellion against God.

30. Farrar, *Truths to Live By*, pp. 62, 63.

31. Spurgeon, *The Treasury of the New Testament*, p. 526.

32. Note the aorist infinitive "to take away."

33. This gets into the theological debate over the peccability and impeccability of Christ. Was Jesus able to sin or was he not able to sin when he was tempted? Actually both positions are legitimately within the boundaries of Christian orthodoxy. The bottom line is this: whether he could have sinned or could not have sinned, he did not sin! See David L. Allen, *Hebrews*, New American Commentary, vol. 35 (Nashville: B&H, 2010), pp. 306–313 for a discussion of this theological issue based on Hebrews 4:15 that presents both sides of the argument. I opt for the impeccability position.

34. Both verbs are in the perfect tense. The verbs are ingressive indicating a coming to see Christ and know him in a personal way, the latter knowledge (personal) being endemic to the meaning of the verb itself.

35. Farrar, *Truths to Live By*, p. 188.

36. Illustration used by Jerry Vines, *1, 2, 3 John* (Neptune, NJ: Loizeaux, 1989), p. 116.

37. The phrase "from the beginning" leaves ambiguous the specific temporal reference intended by John. It can be interpreted in four ways: as a reference to 1) the beginning of all creation; 2) the beginning of the world; 3) the beginning of sin; or 4) the beginning of the devil's rebellion. The latter option is the best.

38. From a sermon by A. B. Van Arsdale, quoted in Gerald Martin, *Great Southern Baptist Preaching* (Grand Rapids: Zondervan, 1969), p. 61.

39. John Wesley, *First Series of Sermons (1–39)*, vol. 1, The Works of John Wesley, 3rd ed., Vol. 5 (Grand Rapids: Baker, 1986 reprint), pp. 232, 233.

40. Rob Lacey, *The Word on the Street* (Grand Rapids: Zondervan, 2004), p. 462.

Chapter Twelve: Love: The Church's Circulatory System

1. Warren Wiersbe, *Be Real* (Wheaton: Victor Books, 1985), p. 120.

2. "The beginning" could possibly refer to the beginning of the preaching of the gospel or the beginning of history. But it seems best to take it to refer to the first time the readers heard the gospel. This is a general temporal reference left undefined by John.

3. The episode of Cain and Abel was well-known in the Christian community as is evidenced by how often it is mentioned in the New Testament: Matthew 23:35; Luke 11:51; Hebrews 11:4; 12:24; and Jude 11.

4. Note the tense of the command, which indicates stopping an action already in progress.

5. Martin Niemöller, "Brotherly Love Versus Hatred of the World," *Luccock to Niebuhr 1885–1984*, A Treasury of Great Preaching, vol. 10, eds. Clyde Fant and William Pinson (Dallas: Word Publishing, 1995), p. 235. Niemöller's preaching is worthy of your study. See especially his *The Gestapo Defied: Being the Last Twenty-Eight Sermons*, 2nd ed. (London: William Hodge and Company, 1942) and *Dachau Sermons*, trans. Robert Pfeiffer (London: Latimer House, 1947).

6. R. G. Lee, *Heart to Heart* (Nashville: Broadman, 1977), p. 129.

7. David A. MacLennan, *Preaching Values in Today's English Version* (Nashville: Abingdon, 1971), p.182.

8. David Read, *Virginia Woolf Meets Charlie Brown* (Grand Rapids: Eerdmans, 1968), p. 78.

9. Arthur A. Cowan, *Bright Is the Shaken Torch* (New York: Charles Scribner's Sons, 1950), p. 93.

10. O. Hallesby, *Why I Am a Christian* (Minneapolis: Augsburg, 1930), p. 123. Hallesby also wrote one of the best books on prayer I've ever read (O. Hallesby, *Prayer*, trans. Clarence Carlsen [Minneapolis: Augsburg, 1931]).

11. A. E. Brooke, *A Critical and Exegetical Commentary on the Johannine Epistles*, International Critical Commentary (Edinburgh: T. & T. Clarke, 1912), p. 94.

12. Leon Morris, *Testaments of Love* (Grand Rapids: Eerdmans, 1981), pp. 220, 221.

13. Note the use of the preposition *huper* in verse 16, which signifies substitution.

14. J. Stuart Holden, *Chapter by Chapter Through the Bible: Expository and Devotional Comments*, vol. 4 (London: Marshall Brothers, n.d.), p. 273.

15. Charles H. Spurgeon, "The Death of Christ," *Classic Sermons on the Cross of Christ*, ed. Warren W. Wiersbe (Grand Rapids: Kregel), p. 62. Spurgeon described God's love for him in this sermon in a picturesque way: "I beheld God's loving kindness to me. I saw how He had dandled me upon the knee of Providence" (p. 60).

16. Lee, *Heart to Heart*, p. 240.

17. John Claypool, *The Light Within You* (Waco: Word Books, 1983), p. 216.

18. Note the emphatic use of the pronoun in Greek.

19. Charles Colson, *Loving God* (Grand Rapids: Zondervan, 1983), pp. 27–34.

20. Gary Burge, *The Letters of John*, NIV Application Commentary (Grand Rapids: Zondervan, 1996), p. 169.

21. Martyn Lloyd-Jones has an excellent sermon on this passage, "Love in Action," in which he develops the difference between liking and loving someone. I am indebted to his insights. Martyn Lloyd-Jones, *Children of God*, vol. 3, Life in Christ: Studies in 1 John (Wheaton: Crossway, 1993), pp. 107–118.

22. B. F. Westcott, *The Epistles of John* (Grand Rapids: Eerdmans, 1966), p. 115 noted that this Greek word, *theōrē*, from which we get our word *theatre*, connotes beholding "as a spectacle on which he allows his eyes to rest." The word is used in John 2:23 concerning those who believed in Jesus when they "saw" the

miracles he did. The word connotes attention, wonder, reflection. B. F. Westcott, *The Gospel According to John* (Grand Rapids: Eerdmans, 1958), p. 45.

23. See A. T. Robertson, *The General Epistles and the Revelation of John*, Word Pictures in the New Testament, vol. 6 (Nashville: Broadman Press, 1933), p. 226.

24. Victor Paul Furnish, *The Love Command in the New Testament* (Nashville: Abingdon, 1972), p. 153.

25. Morris, *Testaments of Love*, p. 224.

26. George Whitfield, *Sermons*, vol. 1 (New Ipswich, NH: Pietan Publications, 1991), p. 241.

27. Another option is to take the phrase as meaning "deeds that are produced by the truth."

28. MacLennan, *Preaching Values in Today's English Version*, p. 183.

29. William Sloane Coffin, "The Call," in *Sermons to Intellectuals*, ed. Franklin Littell (New York: Macmillan, 1963), p. 10.

30. Ibid., pp. 9, 10.

31. Larry Moyer, *Show Me How to Illustrate Evangelistic Sermons* (Grand Rapids, MI: Kregel, 2012), p. 60.

32. Coffin, "The Call," pp. 16, 17.

Chapter Thirteen: How to Send Your Guilt Trip Packing

1. John Wesley, "On Conscience," *Sermons, Volume III*, in *The Works of John Wesley*, 3rd ed., vol. 7 (Grand Rapids: Baker, 1979 reprint), p. 188.

2. See J. P. Louw and E. Nida, *Greek English-Lexicon of the New Testament Based on Semantic Domains*, vol. 1 (New York: United Bible Societies, 1989), p. 307.

3. Martin Luther, *The Catholic Epistles*, in *Luther's Works*, vol. 30, ed. Jaroslav Pelikan (Saint Louis: Concordia, 1967), p. 280.

4. Jerry Vines, *Exploring 1, 2, 3 John* (Neptune, NJ: Loizeaux, 1989), p. 144.

5. Some interpreters take this phrase to mean something along the lines of "since God is greater than our accusing conscience, we had better behave according to his desires." For example, this is the approach taken by John Calvin: ". . . the only security for an evil conscience lies in concealment. But the apostle is here speaking of consciences which God drags out into the light, forces to his judgment seat and disturbs with an awareness of his judgment." *The Gospel According to St. John 11–21 & the First Epistle of John*, Calvin's New Testament Commentaries, eds. David Torrance and Thomas Torrance, trans. T. H. L. Parker (Grand Rapids: Eerdmans, 1959), p. 279.

Martyn Lloyd-Jones pointed out that when we pray, our conscience begins to speak to us and we recall certain things we have said, done, or left undone. Lloyd-Jones, *Children of God*, in *Life in Christ: Studies in First John*, vol. 3 (Wheaton: Crossway, 1993), p. 124. Although this is grammatically possible, contextually it is less likely. James M. Boice, *The Epistles of John* (Grand Rapids: Zondervan, 1979), p. 125 takes the view I advocate. Here one might choose to present both options in preaching on this text.

6. Notice that this concept of confidence was also mentioned in 2:28.

7. Luther, *Catholic Epistles*, p. 280.

8. A point well made by Spurgeon in his treatment of this passage. Charles Spurgeon, *The Treasury of the New Testament*, vol. 4 (Grand Rapids: Zondervan, 1950), pp. 552–556.

9. Luther, *Catholic Epistles*, pp. 281, 282.

10. John Calvin, *First Epistle of John*, p. 280.

11. Adrian Rogers, *Adrianisms: The Wit and Wisdom of Adrian Rogers* (Memphis: Love Worth Finding, 2006), p. 43.

12. Ibid., p. 281.

13. There are many good works on the person and work of the Holy Spirit. Pastors will find especially helpful the following: W. A. Criswell, *The Holy Spirit in Today's World* (Grand Rapids: Zondervan, 1966); Sinclair Ferguson, *The Holy Spirit*, in Contours of Christian Theology, ed. Gerald Bray (Downers Grove, IL: InterVarsity Press, 1996); Jim Hamilton, *God's Indwelling Presence: The Holy Spirit in the Old and New Testaments*, NAC Studies in Bible and Theology (Nashville: B&H Academic, 2006); and H. B. Swete, *The Holy Spirit in the New Testament* (Grand Rapids: Baker, 1964 reprint). Swete deals with the Johannine teaching about the Holy Spirit on pages 147–168. Swete's work is dated (originally published in 1910) but remains a classic.

14. John Flavel, *The Method of Grace in the Gospel Redemption*, The Works of John Flavel, vol. 2 (Edinburgh: The Banner of Truth Trust, 1968 reprint), p. 330: "If therefore we find in ourselves the bond of union, we may warrantably conclude, that we have union with Jesus Christ" (p. 331).

15. John Wesley, "The Witness of the Spirit," *Sermons, Volume 1*, in *The Works of John Wesley*, 3rd ed., vol. 5 (Grand Rapids: Baker, 1979 reprint), pp. 124, 125.

16. Ibid., p. 122.

17. John Wesley, "A Plain Account of Christian Perfection," *The Works of John Wesley*, 3rd ed., vol. 11 (Grand Rapids: Baker, 1978 reprint), p. 480. Though Wesley errs in his notion of entire sanctification, nevertheless he has much to teach us about the subject of sanctification. The best summary of Wesley's view of entire sanctification (Christian perfection), taken directly from the original sources with bibliographic citations, is found in Dale Bruner, *A Theology of the Holy Spirit: The Pentecostal Experience and the New Testament Witness* (Grand Rapids: Eerdmans, 1970), pp. 323–332. Bruner's work on the theology of the Holy Spirit is a must for all pastors. It is Biblically solid and well-balanced.

18. See Edwin Palmer, *The Person and Ministry of the Holy Spirit: The Traditional Calvinist Perspective* (Grand Rapids: Baker, 1958), p. 99.

19. David Jackman, *The Message of John's Letters* (Downers Grove, IL: InterVarsity Press, 1988), p. 105.

20. Warren Wiersbe, *Be Real* (Wheaton: Victor, 1985), p. 133.

21. J. B. Phillips, *Plain Christianity* (New York: Macmillan, 1954), p. 67.

22. Jackman, *The Message of John's Letters*, p. 104.

Chapter Fourteen: Discerning Truth and Error

1. As noted by E. W. Bullinger, *Figures of Speech Used in the Bible* (Grand Rapids: Baker, 1968), p. 543. See also Grace Sherman and John Tuggy, *A Semantic and Structural Analysis of the Johannine Epistles* (Dallas: Summer Institute of Linguistics, 1994), p. 76.

2. Elizabeth Hillstrom, *Testing the Spirits* (Downers Grove, IL: InterVarsity Press, 1995) is a good work to peruse in preaching on this passage.

3. Calvin rightly takes "spirit" metonymically as signifying one who claims to be endowed with the gift of the Spirit to perform a prophet's office. John Calvin, *The Gospel According to St. John 11–21 & the First Epistle of John*, Calvin's New Testament Commentaries, eds. David Torrance and Thomas Torrance, trans. T. H. L. Parker (Grand Rapids: Eerdmans, 1959), p. 284.

4. Martin Luther, *The Catholic Epistles*, in *Luther's Works*, vol. 30, ed. Jaroslav Pelikan (St. Louis: Concordia, 1967), p. 284.

5. A statement wrongly attributed to circus magnate P. T. Barnum.

6. Jonathan Edwards, *The Distinguishing Marks of a Work of the Spirit of God*, in *The Works of Jonathan Edwards*, rev. and ed. Edward Hickman, vol. 2 (Edinburgh: The Banner of Truth Trust, 1974 reprint), p. 265. This sermon also appears in William Barker and Samuel Logan, eds., *Sermons That Shaped America: Reformed Preaching from 1630 to 2001* (Phillipsburg, NJ: P&R, 2003), pp. 62–119.

7. The phrase "you know" in Greek can be imperative or indicative. The majority take it as indicative.

8. Martyn Lloyd-Jones, *The Love of God*, in Life in God: Studies in First John, vol. 5 (Wheaton, IL: Crossway, 1994), p. 31.

9. See Walter Martin, *The Kingdom of the Cults*, ed. Ravi Zacharias (Grand Rapids: Bethany House, 2003), pp.193–260.

10. James Bjornstad, *Counterfeits at Your Door* (Ventura, CA: Regal Books, 1979), pp. 110–112.

11. Timothy George, *Is the Father of Jesus the God of Mohammad?* (Grand Rapids: Zondervan, 2002), p. 75.

12. Bilquis Sheikh, *I Dared to Call Him Father* (Grand Rapids: Chosen Books [Baker], 2003).

13. The term "flesh" here is another metonymy for "human being," a reference to the incarnation of Jesus.

14. Lloyd-Jones, *The Love of God*, p. 34.

15. Jerry Vines, *Spirit Works* (Nashville: B&H, 1999), p. 144.

16. Robert Yarbrough, *1–3 John*, Baker Exegetical Commentary on the New Testament (Grand Rapids: Baker, 2008), p. 227.

17. Calvin, *First Epistle of John*, p. 285.

18. Edwards, *Distinguishing Marks*, p. 267.

19. Though not mentioned here, another test to apply is the materialism test: Are they interested in material wealth? This test derives from 2 Peter 2:2, 3. Sadly, it is not only the false teachers who sometimes get the dollar sign before the cross.

20. John makes use of chiastic structure twice in these verses. This is difficult, if not impossible, to convey in any English translation of the Greek text, and it is difficult to point out in preaching. See Sherman and Tuggy, *Semantic and Structural Analysis*, pp. 77, 78.

A "by this you know" (4:2a)
 B first test (4:2b, 3)
  C the trust (4:4)
 B' second test (4:5, 6a)

A' "by this we know" (4:6b)

A You belong to God (4:4)

   B They belong to the world (4:5)

A We belong to God (4:6)

21. Luther, *Catholic Epistles*, p. 290.

22. Of course, it is true that Roman Catholics believe in the resurrection of Jesus. However, Catholic iconography often pictures Jesus as on the cross or as dead while focusing on the living Mary.

Chapter Fifteen: Want to Play Catch?

1. Peter Kreeft, *Knowing the Truth of God's Love* (Ann Arbor, MI: Servant Books, 1988), p. 16.

2. Geddes MacGregor, *He Who Lets Us Be: A Theology of Love* (New York: Seabury Press, 1975), p. 12.

3. Ibid., p. 52.

4. Martyn Lloyd-Jones, *Life in Christ*, in Life in God: Studies in First John, vol. 5 (Wheaton: Crossway, 1995), p. 47.

5. Rob Lacey, *The Word on the Street* (Grand Rapids: Zondervan, 2004), p. 463.

6. John Stott commented that the statement "God is love" is "the most comprehensive and sublime of all Biblical affirmations about God's being." John Stott, *The Letters of John*, Tyndale New Testament Commentaries (Downers Grove, IL: InterVarsity Press, 2009), p. 160. Concerning this statement Geddes MacGregor wrote, "Either it is nonsense, to say nothing of maudlin humbug, or else it is by far the most exciting statement about God to be found in either the Bible or any other literature in the world" (*He Who Lets Us Be*, p. x).

7. The noun *agapē*, when used here without the article in Greek, indicates a non-symmetrical relationship that is not reversible. Stephen Smalley, *1, 2, 3 John*, Word Biblical Commentary, vol. 51 (Waco, TX: Word, 1984), pp. 239, 240. Note Augustine's error here in his homily on this passage where he interchanges the two propositions, an error he made because he worked from the Latin and not the Greek text. Augustine, *Homilies on the First Epistle of John*, V.4–6, in *Nicene and Post-Nicene Fathers*, ed. Phillip Schaff, vol. 7 (Edinburgh: T&T Clark/Grand Rapids: Eerdmans, 1956), pp. 456, 503.

8. Kreeft, *Knowing the Truth of God's Love*, p. 53.

9. Ibid., p. 59.

10. C. H. Dodd, *The Johannine Epistles*, Moffatt New Testament Commentary (London, 1961), p. 110.

11. C. S. Lewis, *The Four Loves* (New York: Harcourt Brace Jovanovich, 1960), p. 177.

12. Charles Spurgeon, *The Treasury of the New Testament*, vol. 4 (Grand Rapids: Zondervan, 1950), p. 557.

13. See B. F. Westcott, *The Epistles of St. John* (Grand Rapids: Eerdmans, 1966), p. 149.

14. Michael Catt, *I May Be Wrong . . . But I Doubt it!* (Columbus, GA: Brentwood Christian Press, 2000), pp. 22–24. The two best biographies of Cobb are prob-

ably Charles Alexander, *Ty Cobb* (Oxford: Oxford University Press, 1985) and Al Stump, *Cobb: A Biography* (Chapel Hill, NC: Algonquin Books, 1996).

15. Adrian Rogers, *Adrianisms: The Wit and Wisdom of Adrian Rogers* (Memphis: Love Worth Finding, 2006), p. 111.

16. Frederick Danker, ed., "οὕτως," *A Greek-English Lexicon of the New Testament and Other Early Christian Literature*, 3rd rev. ed. (Chicago: University of Chicago Press, 2000), pp. 741, 742.

17. Leon Morris, *Testaments of Love* (Grand Rapids: Eerdmans, 1981), p. 219.

18. Perceptively noted by Lloyd-Jones, *Life in Christ*, p. 66.

19. Lloyd-Jones, ibid., pp. 68–70 develops this well in his sermon on this passage.

20. Ibid.

21. Lewis, *The Four Loves*, p. 183.

22. Kreeft, *Knowing the Truth of God's Love*, p. 53.

23. Ibid., 20.

24. Ibid., 55.

25. Spurgeon, *Treasury of the New Testament*, p. 559.

Chapter Sixteen: "Be My Valentine"—God

1. Edgar Guest, "Sermons We See," *Collected Verse of Edgar Guest* (New York: Buccaneer Books, 1976), p. 599.

2. The genitive (*hē agapē autou*) might be subjective where the meaning would be that God's love reaches its intended target when those he loves love others. If it is objective, the meaning will be that men's love for God is complete only when they love other people. See Leon Morris, *Testaments of Love* (Grand Rapids: Eerdmans, 1981), p. 161.

3. Martyn Lloyd-Jones, *Life in Christ*, in Life in God, Studies in First John, vol. 5 (Wheaton: Crossway, 1995), p. 119.

4. Ibid., p. 121.

5. John Stott, *The Epistles of John* (Grand Rapids: Eerdmans, 1964), pp. 166, 167.

6. Charles Spurgeon, *The Treasury of the New Testament,* vol. 4 (Grand Rapids: Zondervan, 1950), p. 563.

7. John Calvin, *The Gospel According to St. John 11–21 & the First Epistle of John*, in *Calvin's New Testament Commentaries*, eds. David Torrance and Thomas Torrance, trans. T. H. L. Parker (Grand Rapids: Eerdmans, 1959), p. 294.

8. This illustration is adapted and modernized from an illustration that Spurgeon used describing his visit to the art gallery in Versailles. Here is Spurgeon's version:

> If you have visited the picture galleries at Versailles . . . Upstairs in the same palace there is a vast collection of portraits. I have traversed those galleries of portraits without much interest, only here and there pausing to notice a remarkable countenance. Very few persons linger there, everybody seems to walk on as quickly as the polished floors allow. Now, why is it that you are interested by the portraits downstairs and not by those upstairs? They are the same people, very many of them in the same dress; why do you not gaze upon them with interest? The reason

lies here: the portrait in still life, as a rule, can never have the attraction which surrounds a scene of stirring action. There you see the warrior dealing a terrible blow with his battleaxe, or the senator delivering himself of an oration in the assembly, and you think more of them than of the same bodies and faces in repose. Life is impressive; action awakens thought. It is just so with the text. Look at it as a matter of doctrinal statement; 'We love Him, because He first loved us,' and if you are a thoughtful person you will consider it well; but feel the fact itself, feel the love of God, know it within our own souls, and manifest it in our lives, and how engrossing it becomes. (Spurgeon, *Treasury of the New Testament*, p. 570.)

9. Jonathan Edwards, "The Spirit of the True Saints Is a Spirit of Divine Love," in *The Glory and Honor of God*, ed. Michael McMullen, vol. 2, in *Previously Unpublished Sermons of Jonathan Edwards* (Nashville: B&H, 2004), pp. 297–344. This sermon was a previously unpublished sermon by Edwards transcribed by McMullen and published along with nineteen other unpublished sermons. In its original manuscript this sermon runs to eighty-four pages. The sermon was written in the middle to late 1730s and is a detailed topical treatment of what divine love is in the lives of Christians.

10. Ibid., p. 312.

11. Ibid., p. 320.

12. Ibid., pp. 320–326.

13. Ibid., p. 335.

14. Morris, *Testaments of Love*, p. 221.

15. For a good discussion of the Judgment Seat of Christ and matters of eschatology, consult Leon Wood, *The Bible and Future Events: An Introductory Survey of Last-Day Events* (Grand Rapids: Zondervan, 1973). From a premillennial perspective, John Walvoord's *The Millennial Kingdom* (Grand Rapids: Zondervan, 1959) will prove helpful. From an amillennial perspective, see Kim Riddelbarger, *A Case for Amillennialism: Understanding the End Times* (Grand Rapids: Baker, 2003).

16. Edwards, "The Spirit of the True Saints," p. 332.

17. Martin Luther, *The Catholic Epistles*, in *Luther's Works*, vol. 30, ed. Jaroslav Pelikan (Concordia: Saint Louis, 1967), p. 301.

18. Ted Peters, *Sin: Radical Evil in Soul and Society* (Grand Rapids: Eerdmans, 1994), p. 81.

19. Spurgeon, *Treasury*, p. 569.

20. F. W. Boreham, *A Temple of Topaz* (London: The Epworth Press, 1928), pp. 262–272. See also Peter Gunther, ed. *A Frank Boreham Treasury* (Chicago: Moody Press, 1984), pp. 17–23. Preachers would do well to rediscover Boreham today. His more than fifty books are masterpieces of storytelling and wordsmithing. Boreham was the favorite author of John Phillips, the prolific commentator famous for his Exploring series. Boreham is also Ravi Zacharias's favorite author. In fact, Ravi Zacharias Ministries publishes a digital devotional entitled *A Slice of Infinity*, which is a title taken from one of Boreham's essays. He died in 1959.

21. Don't miss D. A. Carson's *Love in Hard Places* (Wheaton: Crossway, 2002) on this entire subject of what it means to love all people, including our enemies.

22. Edwards, "The Spirit of the True Saints," p. 342.

23. From a radio sermon by Max Lucado.

Chapter Seventeen: Faith Is the Victory!

1. Corrie Ten Boom, *Tramp for the Lord* (Fort Washington, PA: CLC Publications, 1974 [2010]), p. 116.

2. Louis Albert Banks, *John and His Friends* (London: Funk & Wagnalls, 1899), p. 158.

3. Rob Lacey, *The Word on the Street* (Grand Rapids: Zondervan, 2004), p. 464.

4. Martin Luther, *The Catholic Epistles*, in *Luther's Works*, vol. 30, ed Jaroslav Pelikan (Concordia: Saint Louis, 1967), p. 309.

5. Charles Swindoll, *Swindoll's Ultimate Book of Illustrations & Quotations* (Nashville: Thomas Nelson, 1998), p. 414.

6. James M. Boice, *The Epistles of John* (Grand Rapids: Zondervan, 1979), p. 156.

7. Ron Dunn, *Victory* (Wheaton: Tyndale House, 1984), p. 25.

8. Ralph Turnbull, ed., "The Christian's Warfare," *The Best of D. L. Moody* (Grand Rapids: Baker, 1971), p. 36.

9. Martyn Lloyd-Jones, *Life in Christ*, Life in God: Studies in First John, vol. 5 (Wheaton: Crossway, 1995), p. 42.

10. Ibid., p. 51.

11. Nelson Price, R. Earl Allen, and Joel Gregory, "Overcomers," in *Southern Baptist Preaching Today*, eds. R. Earl Allen & Joel Gregory (Nashville: Broadman, 1987), p. 307.

12. G. Campbell Morgan, *26 Sermons by G. Campbell Morgan*, vol. 1 (Joplin, MO: College Press, 1969), p. 31.

13. Ibid., p. 35.

14. John Dickson, *Humilitas: A Lost Key to Life, Love, and Leadership* (Grand Rapids: Zondervan, 2011), p. 26.

15. D. Edmund Hiebert, "An Exposition of 1 John 5:1–12," *Bibliotheca Sacra* (April-June 1990), p. 222.

16. Helmut Thielicke, *Faith: The Great Adventure* (Philadelphia: Fortress Press, 1985), p. 28.

17. Adrian Rogers, *Adrianisms: The Wit and Wisdom of Adrian Rogers* (Memphis: Love Worth Finding, 2006), p. 71.

18. Cited in Thielicke, *Faith*, p. 34.

Chapter Eighteen: A Tale of Three Witnesses

1. One of the distinctive features of John's writings is his emphasis on witness. The verbal and nominal form occur forty-seven times in John's Gospel and eight times in 1 John. Six of these are clustered right here in this paragraph.

2. I am approaching this sermon differently from the others in this volume. This sermon is a narrative exposition set up like a courtroom drama. The emphasis on "witness" and "testimony" throughout the passage lends itself to this. For those who choose to preach this following a more traditional expository outline, the structure of the passage is fairly straightforward. Martyn Lloyd-Jones captures it well in his sermon on this passage:

... he divides this up into three main divisions. First of all, you have in verses 6, 7 and 8 what I am describing as the testimony of Jesus Christ and His person. In verses 9 and 10 you have reasons given as to why we should accept the testimony. And in verses 11 and 12 we have the consequences of accepting the testimony—what happens to me as a result of so doing. (Martyn Lloyd-Jones, *Life in Christ*, in Life in God: Studies in First John, vol. 5 [Wheaton: Crossway, 1995], p. 68.)

There is also a significant textual problem in verse 7. The NKJV (as well as later translations) inserts a verse that does not occur in any Greek manuscript prior to the fifteenth century. It is the unanimous opinion of modern textual critics that this verse found in the NKJV is not part of the original text. The preacher must decide how to address this problem if he preaches from a NKJV Bible or if the audience uses a NKJV Bible. I like the way Lloyd-Jones handled it and commend him to you as an example of how to go about this kind of thing in preaching when necessary. (*Life in Christ*, pp. 69–72). Don't miss the sermon on the disputed verse 7 in the NKJV by John Wesley, who, following Bengel, accepts the text as original. It is a good sermon on the Trinity. John Wesley, *First Series of Sermons (40–53); Second Series Begun (54–86)*, vol. 2, The Works of John Wesley, 3rd ed., vol. 6 (Grand Rapids: Baker, 1979 reprint), pp. 199–206.

3. There are four main views on the meaning of "water" and "blood" in this verse. 1) Baptism and the Lord's Supper, 2) a reference to Jesus' side when it was pierced by the Roman soldier and out flowed water and blood, 3) a symbolic reference to the atoning and cleansing work of Christ (blood atones, and water cleanses). The fourth view is the most likely: these first two witnesses, the water and the blood, symbolize the baptism and the death of Jesus. The baptism of Jesus symbolized the inauguration of his ministry and salvation mission. The death of Jesus symbolized the consummation of his ministry and mission. He came for the purpose of dying for the sins of the world. These two great historical events bear witness that Jesus is the Son of God.

4. On the Holy Spirit in 1 John, see Charles Carter, *The Person and Ministry of the Holy Spirit: A Wesleyan Perspective* (Grand Rapids: Baker, 1974) and the companion volume, Edwin Palmer, *The Person and Ministry of the Holy Spirit: The Traditional Calvinist Perspective* (Grand Rapids: Baker, 1958).

5. Jesus is more than a temporary human-divine representative, as some proto-Gnostics claimed. Thus John emphasizes the truth of the incarnation in verse 6a. The Holy Spirit bears witness to this in verses 6b, 7. There is a threefold witness of the Spirit: 1) he bore witness to the incarnation; 2) he bore witness to Jesus' divine Sonship at his baptism; 3) he bears witness in the hearts of believers. Verse 8 is a summary statement of verses 6, 7. "In John the Word is called the Spirit by metonymy, because the Word is from the Holy Spirit, as in John 6:63," says Martin Luther, *The Catholic Epistles*, in Luther's Works, vol. 30, ed. Jaroslav Pelikan (St. Louis: Concordia, 1967), p. 315.

6. Charles Spurgeon, *The Treasury of the New Testament* (Grand Rapids: Zondervan, 1950), p. 606.

7. See J. Stuart Holden, *Chapter by Chapter Through the Bible: Expository and Devotional Comments*, vol. 4 (London: Marshall Brothers, n. d.), p. 275.

8. Adrian Rogers, *What Every Christian Ought to Know* (Nashville: B&H, 2005), p. 27.

9. A. B. Van Arsdale, *Great Southern Baptist Preaching*, ed. Gerald Mann (Grand Rapids: Zondervan, 1969), pp. 74, 75.

Chapter Nineteen: The Haves and the Have-Nots

1. A phrase used years ago by the Southern Baptist evangelist Angel Martinez, *The Fountain of Youth* (Grand Rapids: Zondervan, 1957), p. 105.

2. Charles Spurgeon, *The Treasury of the New Testament,* vol. 4 (Grand Rapids: Zondervan, 1950), p. 612.

3. D. L. Moody, *The Way to God* (Chicago: Moody Press, 1884), p. 101.

4. Robert Law, *The Tests of Life* (Grand Rapids: Baker, 1979 reprint).

5. See Moody, *The Way to God*, p. 67.

6. Rob Lacey, *The Word on the Street* (Grand Rapids: Zondervan, 2004), p. 465.

7. Cited in William Barclay, *The Letters of John and Jude*, The Daily Study Bible Series, rev. ed. (Philadelphia: Westminster, 1976), p. 115.

8. Ibid.

9. James Hewett, ed., *Illustrations Unlimited* (Wheaton, IL: Tyndale House, 1988), p. 425.

10. Robert Yarbrough, *1–3 John*, Baker Exegetical Commentary on the New Testament (Grand Rapids: Baker, 2008), pp. 306–314 has a good discussion on this passage. In my opinion, from a preaching perspective, problem passages like this are best treated by giving all the major views and then presenting the one the preacher considers the most likely interpretation. Another option, though less satisfying homiletically, is to present all the views and leave it to the audience to make their own choice.

11. Yarbrough proposes a variation of this view: ". . . the sin unto death will amount to specific manifestations of unregenerate conduct for which 'blasphemy against the Spirit' serves as an umbrella rubric." Yarbrough, *1–3 John*, p. 308.

12. See the helpful discussion of the five major textual variants on 1 John 5:18 and the possible interpretations in Christopher Bass, *That You May Know: Assurance of Salvation in 1 John*, in NAC Studies in Bible & Theology, ed. Ray Clendenen (Nashville: B&H Academic, 2008), pp. 195–202.

13. Alexander Maclaren, *Epistles of John, Jude, Revelation*, Expositions of Holy Scripture, vol. 17 (Grand Rapids: Eerdmans, 1944), pp. 79, 80.

14. For an accessible summary of the Arian controversy and the Council of Nicaea, see Henry Chadwick, *The Early Church*, The Pelican History of the Church, vol. 1 (Middlesex, UK: Penguin Books, 1967), pp. 133–145 or Louis Berkhof, *The History of Christian Doctrines* (Grand Rapids: Baker, 1975), pp. 83–93. For a more detailed look, consult Albert Newman, *A Manual of Church History*, vol. 1, rev. ed. (Chicago: American Baptist Publication Society, 1931–1933), pp. 320–392 and William Cunningham, *Historical Theology* (London: Banner of Truth Trust, 1969), pp. 267–306. Lots of good sermon illustrations can be found from this event in church history!

15. From statistics listed by the Centers for Disease Control and Prevention (COC) (www.cdc.gov/mmwr/preview) and Mothers Against Drunk Driving (MADD) (www.madd.org/statistics).

16. Maclaren, *The Epistles of John*, p. 40.

17. Spurgeon, *Treasury*, p. 614.

18. Craig Larsen, *Contemporary Illustrations for Preachers, Teachers, and Writers* (Grand Rapids: Baker, 1996), p. 216.

19. Chapter title of his study on 1 John by Fritz Ridenour, *How to Be a Christian Without Being Perfect* (Ventura, CA: Regal, 1986), p. 189. Ridenour's book is a very practical treatment of 1 John that majors on illustration and application and is a helpful resource for pastors when preaching on 1 John.

Chapter Twenty: Accept No Substitutes!

1. Bob Hostetler, *American Idols: The Worship of the American Dream* (Nashville: B&H, 2006), p. 4.

2. Friedrich Nietzsche, *Twilight of the Idols* (Oxford: Oxford University Press, 1998), p. 3.

3. A picturesque phrase (chapter title) in Richard Keyes, "The Idol Factory," *No God but God: Breaking with the Idols of Our Age*, eds. Os Guinness and John Seel (Chicago: Moody Press, 1992), pp. 29–48. Calvin spoke in similar fashion: ". . . man's nature, so to speak, is a perpetual factory of idols." John Calvin, *Institutes of the Christian Religion*, Library of Christian Classics, vol. 20, ed. John T. McNeill; trans. Ford L. Battles (Philadelphia: Westminster, 1960), I.XI.8 (p. 108). For an excellent book on idolatry that would be of great help to the preacher, see Tim Keller, *Counterfeit Gods: The Empty Promises of Money, Sex, and Power, and the Only Hope That Matters* (New York: Dutton, 2009). Don't miss Keller's succinct list of the key categories of idols in our lives followed by brief definitions on pp. 203, 204. Footnote 5 (pp. 178, 179) contains a helpful bibliography of significant works on the subject of idolatry over the past twenty years. Before preaching on this passage or any passage dealing with idolatry, a good read would be Greg Beale's *We Become What We Worship: A Biblical Theology of Idolatry* (Downers Grove, IL: IVP Academic, 2008), especially his conclusion on pp. 284–311. Terry Griffith, *Keep Yourselves from Idols: A New Look at 1 John*, Journal for the Study of the New Testament Supplement Series 233, ed. Stanley Porter (New York: Sheffield Academic Press, 2002), pp. 208–212 argued that 1 John 5:21 "is inspired by the idol polemic of the *LXX* , and that the form of the ending itself has parallels in the Hellenistic Jewish literature of the period. . . . " ". . . the term *eidolon* is almost exclusively used in Jewish contexts to denote pagan images, and is itself a polemical term, being the main semantic vehicle in Greek for conveying Jewish polemic against idolatry" (p. 208). Whether John has in mind pagan images *alone* cannot be known for certain, but this is doubtful in light of the context and the entire New Testament.

4. See Brian Rosner, *Greed as Idolatry: The Origin and Meaning of a Pauline Metaphor* (Grand Rapids: Eerdmans, 2007), pp. 43–46.

5. Ludwig Koehler and Walter Baumgartner, *The Hebrew and Aramaic Lexicon of the Old Testament*, 3rd ed. (Leiden: Brill, 2001), pp. 192–194. Koehler and Baumgartner utilize the most up-to-date linguistic data in their lexicon. I would recommend that pastors use it rather than Brown, Driver, and Briggs.

6. Yarbrough suggests four reasons for connecting John's warning with Zechariah 13:2. First, John considers his readers to be in the eschatological day of which

Zechariah speaks. Second, John cites Zechariah 12 in his Gospel (John 19:37). Third, Zechariah says that the appearance of the Messiah will bring about "a removal of false prophets and the spirit of impurity from the land." John addressed false prophets and the evil spirits that motivated them in 1 John 4:1–6. Fourth, John, like Zechariah, is moved by a vision "of God's faithfulness and radiant purity." The fourth reason is too general, but the first three are reasonable. Robert Yarbrough, *1–3 John*, Baker Exegetical Commentary on the New Testament (Grand Rapids: Baker, 2008), p. 324.

7. John Wesley, *First Series of Sermons (40–53); Second Series Begun (54–86)*, vol. 2, The Works of John Wesley, 3rd ed., vol. 6 (Grand Rapids: Baker, 1979 reprint), p. 436.

8. Arthur Hunt, *The Vanishing Word: The Veneration of Visual Imagery in the Postmodern World* (Wheaton: IL: Crossway, 2003), p. 25.

9. Ibid., p. 71.

10. David Wells, *Losing Our Virtue* (Grand Rapids: Eerdmans, 1998), p. 204.

11. Paul Vitz, *Psychology as Religion* (Grand Rapids: Eerdmans, 1977), p. 125.

12. Martin Luther, *Treatise On Good Works* (1520), in *The Christian in Society I*, Luther's Works, vol. 44, trans. W. A. Lambert (Philadelphia: Fortress, 1966), pp. 30–32.

13. The "bonfire of the vanities" occurred in Florence, Italy, on February 7, 1497, when supporters of the Dominican priest Girolamo Savonarola collected and publicly burned thousands of objects, including mirrors, cosmetics, art, expensive dresses, playing cards, musical instruments, secular song manuscripts, sculpture, and books. These objects were viewed as possible temptations to sin. Novelist Tom Wolfe used Savonarola's bonfire ritual as the title for his 1987 novel *The Bonfire of the Vanities* and its film adaptation.

14. Alexander Maclaren, *Epistles of John, Jude, Revelation*, in Expositions of Holy Scripture, vol. 17 (Grand Rapids: Eerdmans, 1944), p. 47.

15. Wesley, *First Series of Sermons*, p. 444. This is from Wesley's sermon on 1 John 5:21 on the subject of idolatry.

16. Rob Lacey, *The Word on the Street* (Grand Rapids: Zondervan, 2004), p. 465.

Chapter Twenty-one: Deniers and Deceivers

1. Any detailed discussion of the question of authorship of the Johannine epistles and the identity of "the elder" in 2 and 3 John is not advisable in a sermon. Most evangelical scholarship accepts that the author of the Gospel, the three letters, and Revelation is John, the Son of Zebedee and one of the twelve disciples of Jesus. However, pastors need to be at least acquainted with the various views on this subject. While commentary introductions and/or New Testament introductions can be helpful here, they can sometimes be overly detailed. An accessible summary of the data that would be helpful to pastors can be found in James Boice, *The Epistles of John* (Grand Rapids: Zondervan, 1979), pp. 187–193.

2. F. W. Danker, ed., "ἀλ∋θεια," *A Greek-English Lexicon of the New Testament and Other Early Christian Literature*, 3rd ed. (Chicago: University of Chicago Press, 2000), p. 36.

3. I. H. Marshall, *Epistles of John* (Grand Rapids: Eerdmans, 1978), p. 62 says that for John "'truth' signifies what is ultimately real, namely God himself. Hence it can refer to the expression of God in his incarnate Son and in the Christian message. In 2 John 2 it becomes evidence that the truth is tantamount to the spirit of truth who can enter into the believer. The truth stands in contrast to the ultimately unreal and deceptive lies which stem from the devil."

4. Several interpretations are possible for the phrase "in truth and love." Truth and love could be the *reason* for the blessing, the *condition* on which the blessing depends, the *result* expected to come from the blessing, the *means* for conveying the blessing, or an *accompaniment* of the blessing. See Grace Sherman and John Tuggy, *A Semantic and Structural Analysis of the Johannine Epistles* (Dallas: Summer Institute of Linguistics, 1994), p. 107.

5. See James Moffatt, *Grace in the New Testament* (London: Hodder and Stoughton, 1931), p. 300.

6. Notice the lexical chiasm in verses 5, 6 with a) command (v.5), b) love (v.5), b' love (v.6), a' command (v.6).

7. Quotation generally attributed to Mark Twain.

8. The pastoral manual of church order from the early second century known as the *Didache*, or *The Teaching of the Lord to the Gentiles through the Twelve Apostles*, sheds light on this as well. The following passage indicates the intended pattern Christians should follow when it comes to showing hospitality to an itinerant teacher:

> Let everyone that cometh in the name of the Lord be received, and then, when you have proved him, you shall know, for you shall have understanding (to distinguish) between the right and the left. If he that cometh is a passer-by, succor him as far as you can, but he shall not abide with you longer than two or three days unless there be necessity. If the teacher himself is perverse and teaches another doctrine to destroy these things [apostolic teaching], hear him not. (J. Stevenson, ed., *A New Eusebius* [London: SPCK, 1957], p. 128)

9. See the sermon and notes on 1 John 1:1–4.

10. Shifting from the plural "deceivers" in the first part of the verse to the singular "deceiver" in the latter part, along with the article before "deceiver" and "antichrist," is John's way of expressing that they belong to a group characterized by these actions. A. T. Robertson pointed out how the use of the article here sharply brings out each separate phrase. A. T. Robertson, *The General Epistles and the Apocalypse*, Word Pictures of the Greek New Testament, vol. 6 (New York: Harper, 1933), p. 253.

11. John Stott, *The Epistles of John*, Tyndale New Testament Commentaries (Grand Rapids: Eerdmans, 1964), p. 210.

12. See the charts in Robert Yarbrough, *1–3 John*, Baker Exegetical Commentary on the New Testament (Grand Rapids: Baker, 2008), pp. 345, 346.

13. William Barclay, *The Letters of John and Jude*, rev. ed. (Philadelphia: Westminster, 1976), p. 143.

14. Universalism affirms that all people will be released from sin's penalty and restored to God. It denies the Biblical doctrine of eternal punishment. See, for exam-

ple, D. B. Eller, "Universalism," *The Concise Evangelical Dictionary of Theology*, ed. Walter Elwell (Grand Rapids: Baker, 1991), p. 531.

15. See the excellent article on inclusivism by Ken Keathley, "None Dare Call it Treason: Is an Inclusivist a Paul Revere or a Benedict Arnold?" in *Journal for Baptist Theology and Ministry* 1.2 (Fall 2003), pp. 101–114. His definition on p. 114 is helpful:

> Exclusivism holds that an explicit response of repentance and faith to the preaching of the Gospel is necessary for salvation. . . . Pluralism looks upon the non-Christian religions as alternative and valid venues for the salvific work of God. Unlike the classic liberal of times past, the pluralist does not see the various religions as expressions of the same religious impulse, but as unique systems in their own right, believing there should be no attempt to reconcile or judge between the competing truth claims. Offered by its proponents as a mediating position, inclusivism posits that even though the work of Christ is the only means of salvation, it does not follow that explicit knowledge of Christ is necessary in order for one to be saved. In contrast to pluralism, inclusivism agrees with exclusivism in affirming the particularity of salvation in Jesus Christ. But unlike exclusivism, inclusivism holds that an implicit faith response to general revelation can be salvific. God expects from man a response proportional to the light given. Saving faith is not characterized so much by its cognitive content as it is by its reverent quality.

Consult also Ramesh Richard, *The Population of Heaven* (Chicago: Moody, 1994), which should be read by every pastor, and D. A. Carson, *The Gagging of God: Christianity Confronts Pluralism* (Grand Rapids: Zondervan, 1996), pp. 278–300.

16. See Warren Wiersbe, *Be Alert: Second Peter, 2 & 3 John, & Jude* (Wheaton: Victor Books, 1984), p. 114.

17. This report draws information from four nationwide telephone interviews conducted by The Barna Group, each including between 1,002 to 1,005 adults randomly selected, during the years 1995, 2000, 2005, and 2008. The range of sampling error associated with a survey of a thousand people is ±1.5 to ±3.5 percentage points at the 95 percent confidence level. Each of the surveys utilized minimal statistical weighting to calibrate the aggregate sample to known population percentages in relation to several key demographic variables. All interviews were conducted among a sampling of adults in the forty-eight continental states (http://www.barna.org/barna-update/article/21-transformation/252-barna-survey-examines-changes-in-world-view-among-christians-over-the-past-13-years).

Chapter Twenty-two: Down with Diotrephes; Long Live Demetrius!

1. See the charts in Daniel Akin, *1, 2, 3 John*, The New American Commentary, vol. 38 (Nashville: B&H, 2001), pp. 235–237.

2. John Stott, *The Epistles of John*, Tyndale New Testament Commentaries (Grand Rapids: Eerdmans, 1964), pp. 212.

3. George Whitfield, *Sermons*, vol. 1 (New Ipswich, NH: Pietan Publications, 1991), p. 243.

4. On the Word of Faith movement, see the following: Bruce Barron, *The Health and Wealth Gospel* (Downers Grove, IL: InterVarsity Press, 1987); Hank Hanegraff, *Christianity in Crisis* (Eugene, OR: Harvest House, 1993); and John MacArthur, *Charismatic Chaos* (Grand Rapids: Zondervan, 1992), pp. 264–290.

5. John employs the aorist tense translated "rejoiced greatly" followed by two present participles. Since his joy is not a single event, it is best rendered with the English perfect tense, which better implies the point that John remains joyful. So noted by Grace Sherman and John Tuggy, *A Semantic and Structural Analysis of the Johannine Epistles* (Dallas: Summer Institute of Linguistics, 1994), p. 126.

6. For an excellent description of hospitality in the Mediterranean world of the first century and the light it sheds on 3 John, see B. J. Malina, "The Received View and What It Cannot Do: III John and Hospitality," *Semitica* 35 (1986): pp. 171–194. Colin Kruse offers a helpful summary of this article in *The Letters of John*, Pillar New Testament Commentary, ed. D. A. Carson (Grand Rapids: Eerdmans, 2000), pp. 215, 216. Another helpful resource for the pastor would be the article by John Koenig on "Hospitality" in the *Anchor Bible Dictionary*, vol. 3, ed. David Noel Freedman (New York: Doubleday, 1992), pp. 299–301.

7. The "if" in verse 10 is a condition that is not necessarily in doubt.

8. The word is a compound word composed of the Greek word for "love" and "first." It is defined as "to have a special interest in being in the leading position," with a "focus on controlling others." F. W. Danker, ed., "φιλοπροτευω," *A Greek-English Lexicon of the New Testament and Other Early Christian Literature*, 3rd ed. (Chicago: Chicago University Press, 2000), p. 1058.

9. Nathanial Philbrick, *The Last Stand: Custer, Sitting Bull, and the Battle of the Little Bighorn* (New York: Viking, 2010.

10. Robert Yarbrough, *1–3 John*, Baker Exegetical Commentary on the New Testament (Grand Rapids: Baker, 2008), p. 385.

11. Joseph Parker, *Ephesians–Revelation*, in Preaching Through the Bible, vol. 27 (Grand Rapids: Baker, 1959), p. 347.

12. Charles Bridges, *The Christian Ministry* (London: The Banner of Truth Trust, 1967), pp. 151–154.

13. Charles Spurgeon, *Lectures to My Students* (Grand Rapids: Zondervan, 1972 reprint), p. 164. Paige Patterson once told me when I was a freshman in college back in 1975 that every preacher should read this book "at least once every two or three years for the rest of their ministry." That might not be often enough.

14. C. S. Lewis, *Mere Christianity: A Revised and Amplified Edition, with a New Introduction, of the Three Books, Broadcast Talks, Christian Behavior, and Beyond Personality* (New York: HarperCollins, 2001), p. 121.

15. C. S. Lewis, *The Screwtape Letters & Screwtape Proposes a Toast* (New York: Macmillan, 1962), p. 63.

16. *The Autobiography of Benjamin Franklin, Including Poor Richard's Almanac, and Familiar Letters* (New York: Cosimo, 2005), p. 231.

Scripture Index

1 Peter

1:8	141
2:2	86
3:7	171
5:1–4	274
5:8	91

2 Peter

2:1	177
3:8	110
3:9	55

1 John

1:1	280
1:1–4	34, 111, 227, 312
1:1–5	293
1:2	128
1:2, 3	246
1:3	127
1:5	187
1:5–10	49, 148, 171
1:8–10	146, 241
1:9	65, 87, 170
2	127, 185
2:1	34, 146
2:2	191, 286, 287
2:3	114
2:3–6	73, 74, 79
2:5	187
2:7	63
2:7–11	27, 63
2:15–17	92
2:19	176, 255, 264, 280
2:20	121
2:20, 21	27
2:20, 27	113
2:22, 23	293
2:27	114
2:28	301
2:29	135
2:29–4:19	128
3	181, 185
3:1	90
3:2	114, 128
3:5, 8, 11	128
3:9	296
3:10	152, 244
3:14	114
3:19	114
3:21	127
3:21, 22	127, 129
3:24	114

4	185
4:1–6	311
4:2	24, 303
4:4	303, 304
4:5	304
4:5, 6	303
4:6	304
4:7, 8	33
4:8	74
4:8, 16	201
4:12	192
4:12, 17	187
4:1 4	192
4:16	187
4:17	127, 129
5:1	296
5:5	224
5:6	293
5:13	42
5:14	127
5:15	114
5:18	114
5:18–21	233, 243
5:19	54
5:20	252, 255
5:21	243

2 John

1	260
1–3	259, 261, 265
3	260, 266
4	261
4–6, 7–11, 12–13	261
5	261
6	261
7	262, 281
8	263
8–11	263
9	264
10, 11	264
11	265, 266
12	28, 262
12, 13	265
13	266

3 John

1	270
1, 2, 5, 11	270
1–4	270
2, 3	270
3	269
3, 4	271

General Index

Index of Sermon Illustrations

Emptiness of Life without Christ
Per his instructions before his death, a
man's ashes are spread across the
sky in a fireworks display—for four
seconds, and if we don't know Christ
our life will be a short time of glory
but that is all, 142
George Armstrong Custer finished last in
his class at West Point but because of
Civil War exploits become a brigadier
general at only 23, but because of
pride loses his life and the battle at
Little Bighorn, 273

Eternal Life
Natalie Cole served as church secretary
for $2 an hour though she would come
into an abundant trust from her father
Nat King Cole later, and as Christians
we will have a great inheritance in
Heaven someday but must serve faithfully now, 139

False Prophets
No one counterfeits $3 bills because there
is no such thing, and false prophets
only proclaim false versions of the true
gospel, 111

Fear
In *A Charlie Brown Christmas* Lucy tells
Charlie Brown he has pantaphobia—
the fear of everything, but all who do
not know Christ should have at least
one fear—the fear of judgment, 204

Following Jesus
In the Charles Sheldon novel *In His Steps*
a congregation begins asking about
every situation, "What would Jesus
do?" 70–71
Natalie Cole served as E. V. Hill's
secretary for $2 an hour though she
would come into an abundant trust
from her father Nat King Cole later,
and as Christians we will have a great

inheritance in Heaven someday but
must serve faithfully now, 139
Teen girl, asked by mocking friends why
she won't take part in wrong actions
they are about to do, answers that she
doesn't want to hurt her father, and we
should say no to temptation because
we love our Father, 145
When a candle is removed from an otherwise dark room, that room becomes
dark again, and we need to allow
Jesus' light to continue to shine in our
hearts, 146

Forgiveness
Woody Allen, when asked what he would
like to hear God say: "You are forgiven," 31
During a Barbara Walters TV interview,
the wife of baseball great Wade
Boggs says she has forgiven him for
an earlier extramarital affair, to the
interviewer's amazement, 88

Guilt
An ostrich hiding its head in the sand,
imagining itself to be safe from predators, is as foolish as humans who think
they can hide their sins from God, 42
Alice Metzinger (actually Katherine
Power), unable to stand the guilt any
longer, turns herself in to the authorities after being underground for many
years, 45

Healing
Luther sends a message to his ill friend
Myconius who believes he is near
death: "I command you in the name of
God to live because I still have need
of you in the work," and in answer to
Luther's prayers Myconius recovered,
240

Idols
Some *American Idol* fans treat the win-
ners like gods, 249–50

Kathy Griffin, after winning an Emmy: "This award is my god now," 253

Savonarola sees a woman worshiping daily at a statue of Mary but learns she was the model for that statue and is really worshipping herself, 255–56

Jesus Our Advocate
On the TV series Perry Mason never lost a case, and neither will Jesus, 51

Jesus' Death for Us
Asked to donate to a charity, a man agrees but says he must give all he can, just as his father would have done, a picture of Jesus' giving all for us, 89

Judgment
In *A Charlie Brown Christmas* Lucy tells Charlie Brown he has pantaphobia—the fear of everything, and all who do not know Christ should have at least one fear—the fear of judgment, 204

Light
When a candle is removed from an otherwise dark room, that room becomes dark again, and we need to allow Jesus' light to continue to shine in our hearts, 146

Love of God and Jesus for Us
In the novel *Screwtape Letters* a demon is warned that guiding humans into Hell is difficult because God loves making "these disgusting little human vermin into sons," 137

Asked to state the core of his beliefs, theologian Karl Barth answers, "Jesus loves me, this I know, for the Bible tells me so," 155

In the climactic scene in the film *Field of Dreams* a son asks his father, from whom he had been estranged, "Wanna play catch?" but in the gospel the Father asks us, "Wanna play catch?" 194–95

Loving God
Children touring a hospital ask why the doctors and nurses wash their hands so much and are told, "They love health and hate germs," and we should love God but hate the world, 95

Loving Others
If our body's circulatory system shuts down, we die; if the church's circulatory system (love) shuts down, the church will have a spiritual coronary, 73

Just as a musical composition we've heard many times seems fresh and new because of a skilled conductor or a familiar food prepared by a culinary wizard tastes like a new dish, so the love Christ commanded is new in its quality and authority, 75

A young boy, asked why he goes way across Chicago to attend Moody's church instead of closer ones, says, "They just have a way of loving a fellow over there," 81

Allegedly William Booth, founder of The Salvation Army, sent a one-word telegram to Army workers to encourage them: "Others!" and some of them did just that even on the sinking ship *Empress of Ireland*, 159–60

Shy, ignored little boy rejoices because he gave a valentine to each of his classmates and didn't miss a one, and Jesus didn't forget even one of us when he died on the cross, 208

Dale Carnegie: to influence others, remember what is sweetest to them—their name, 275

Obedience
Astronaut Charles Duke shares the importance of complete obedience to NASA when he and others walked on the moon—they had only sixty seconds' of fuel left for takeoff, and we need to be fully obedient to God, 215

Prayer

Dorothy and her friends approached the Wizard of Oz in trembling and fear, but we can approach God with confidence because of the shed blood of Jesus, 167

Luther sends a message to his ill friend Myconius who believes he is near death: "I command you in the name of God to live because I still have need of you in the work," and in answer to Luther's prayers Myconius recovered, 240

Pride

George Armstrong Custer finished last in his class at West Point but because of Civil War exploits became a brigadier general at only 23, but because of pride lost his life and the battle at Little Bighorn, 273

Mark Twain: "If I ever achieve humility, I'll sure be proud of it," 276

Purpose of Life

Augustine: "Our heart is restless until it rests in you," 27

A man chases his wind-blown hat onto a busy highway and is killed, and people in this world often chase after trivial things and it costs them their life, 106

Per his instructions before his death, a man's ashes are spread across the sky in a fireworks display—for four seconds, and if we don't know Christ our life will be a short time of glory but that is all, 142

Return of Jesus Christ in the Future

When President Eisenhower arrives at a private residence to visit a six-year-old boy who has cancer, the father answers the door in jeans and a T-shirt—will we be ready to meet Jesus when he returns?, 131

Revival

Author, when teenaged preacher, part of group (Real Life) that led youth revivals in various churches, 25

Salvation

Trying to live the Christian life without assurance of salvation is like driving a car with the brakes on, 61

In the novel *Screwtape Letters* a demon is warned that guiding humans into Hell is difficult because God loves making "these disgusting little human vermin into sons," 137

Satan

A boy in Bogotá, Colombia loses his eyes to "organ nappers," and Satan blinds sinners to the truth of the gospel, 81–82

Serving God

Natalie Cole served as E. V. Hill's secretary for $2 an hour though she would come into an abundant trust from her father Nat King Cole later, and as Christians we will have a great inheritance in Heaven someday but must serve faithfully now, 139

A baseball player who hits a home run still has to run the bases, and though our salvation in Christ is sure, we still have to serve Him daily now, 145

Astronaut Charles Duke shares the importance of complete obedience to NASA when he and others walked on the moon—they had only sixty seconds' of fuel left for takeoff, and we need to be fully obedient to God, 215

Spiritual War

When Pinkerton, a Union spy, inflates the number of Confederate forces, General McClellan decides not to attack, and we too sometimes overestimate the power of the enemy and don't engage the battle, 181

When the Civil War began, Secretary of State Seward thought the war would last only ninety days; we must not underestimate the power of our enemy, 217

When General Wolfe won the Battle of Quebec, Canada was conquered, though the fighting went on for many more years, and we have victory over Satan as soon as we come to Christ but must keep fighting as long as we are on earth, 217

General Eisenhower accompanies a terrified soldier to the riverside to help him have courage for the battle, 218

Truth

This world is much like Vanity Fair in Bunyan's *Pilgrim's Progress*, where truth cannot be found, 105

Barna: one-third of adults in the U.S. do not believe there is such a thing as absolute truth, 121–22, 265

Universality of Sin

One child grabbing a toy from another child and the ensuing battle between them reveals the sinfulness of human nature, 41

An ostrich hiding its head in the sand, imagining itself to be safe from predators, is as foolish as humans who think they can hide their sins from God, 42

A dog is not a dog because it barks but barks because it's a dog: a sinner is not a sinner because he sins but sins because he is a sinner, 42

During a Barbara Walters TV interview, baseball great Wade Boggs says he had been involved in an earlier extramarital affair for one reason—he is a sinner, to the interviewer's amazement, 88

Victory over Sin

Our knowing God's Word well limits Satan's ability to devour us, making

him like a fangless snake or a toothless lion, 91

Ignoring our enemies (the world, the flesh, and the Devil) would be like ignoring slipperiness and gravity while climbing the Alps, 102

General Eisenhower accompanies a terrified soldier to the riverside on to help him have courage for the battle, 218

Three young men on a bus try to goad a black man into a fight, but he refuses, then gives them a business card revealing that he is Joe Louis, who would become world champion and perhaps the greatest boxer ever, and we serve Jesus, who gives us victory, 220

Witness for Christ

A patient in a Russian prison hears about Christ from a converted Jew who is beaten to death that very evening, and that patient later receives Christ and writes a best-selling book about the gulags; his name is Alexander Solzhenitsyn, 156

The World

Children touring a hospital ask why the doctors and nurses wash their hands so much and are told, "They love health and hate germs," and we should love God but hate the world, 95

Charles Dutton, asked how he transitioned from prison life to a successful acting career, says he never decorated his cell because he wanted to be reminded every day that place was only temporary, and we should remember continually that this world is not our home, 104

This world is much like Vanity Fair in Bunyan's *Pilgrim's Progress*, where truth cannot be found, 105

A man chases his wind-blown hat onto a busy highway and is killed, and people in this world often chase after trivial things and it costs them their life, 106

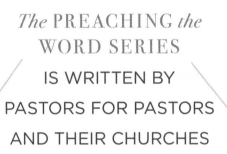

The PREACHING *the*
WORD SERIES
IS WRITTEN BY
PASTORS FOR PASTORS
AND THEIR CHURCHES

crossway.org/preachingtheword